United States Edition RNAB

2010 Year C

Workbook for Lectors, Gospel Readers, and Proclaimers of the Word

Graziano Marcheschi, MA DMin

with Nancy Seitz Marcheschi

LTP
LITURGY
TRAINING
PUBLICATIONS

WORKBOOK FOR LECTORS, GOSPEL READERS, AND PROCLAIMERS OF THE WORD 2010, UNITED STATES EDITION © 2009 Archdiocese of Chicago. All rights reserved.

Liturgy Training Publications, 3949 South Racine Avenue, Chicago IL 60609, 1-800-933-1800, fax 1-800-933-7094, orders@ltp.org, www.LTP.org.

Editor: Lorie Simmons
Production Editor: Kris Fankhouser
Typesetter: Jim Mellody-Pizzato
Original book design: Jill Smith
Revised design: Anna Manhart and Jim Mellody-Pizzato
Cover art: Barbara Simcoe
Interior art: Anna Manhart

LTP now prints the text of *Workbook for Lectors, Gospel Readers, and Proclaimers of the Word* with ink that contains renewable linseed oil on paper that is 100% recycled and contains a minimum of 40% postconsumer waste. The paper for this product was de-inked by a process that uses PCF (Processed Chlorine Free) technologies, unlike many de-inking processes that use toxic bleach. ♲

The printing process used to manufacture this book uses a non-heatset process that significantly reduces emission of volatile organic compounds (VOCs) into the atmosphere.

LTP continues to work toward responsible stewardship of the environment. For more information on our efforts, please go to www.LTP.org/environment.

Printed in the United States of America.
ISBN 978-1-56854-734-3
WL10

CONTENTS

The Author

Graziano Marcheschi is an author, actor, storyteller, and lecturer, and directs Lay Ecclesial Ministry Formation for the Archdiocese of Chicago. He holds a master's degree in drama from the University of Minnesota, a Master of Divinity from Loyola University Chicago, and a Doctor of Ministry from the University of St. Mary of the Lake/Mundelein Seminary. Graziano serves on the faculty of the Institute of Pastoral Studies, Loyola University Chicago. Among his publications are *Workbook for Lectors, Gospel Readers, and Proclaimers of the Word; Scripture at Weddings* (Liturgy Training Publications); contributions to *The Catholic Bible, Personal Study Edition* (Oxford University Press), and *The Word Well Spoken: Skills for the Lector* (Audiotapes, St. Anthony Messenger Press).

Nancy Marcheschi, choreographer and Co-director of the Anawim Players, is a teacher of music, performing arts, and religion at Pope John XXIII School in Evanston, Illinois.

Dedication

To Francis Cardinal George, OMI, who has been a great mentor and support in the work of empowering the laity for service in the Church.

In accordance with c. 827, permission to publish was granted in Chicago, Illinois, on February 10, 2009, by the Very Reverend John F. Canary, Vicar General of the Archdiocese of Chicago. Permission to publish indicates that there is nothing contained in the work contrary to Catholic teaching. No legal responsibility is assumed by this permission.

INTRODUCTION

As readers of the word, we are part of a very important process in the life of the Church. "In Sacred Scripture, the Church constantly finds her nourishment and her strength, for she welcomes it not as a human word, 'but as what it really is, the word of God' (1 Thessalonians 2:13; cf. *Dei Verbum* 24). 'In the sacred books, the Father who is in heaven comes lovingly to meet his children, and talks with them' (*Dei Verbum* 21)" (CCC, #104). In fact, "the Church has always venerated the Scriptures as she venerates the Lord's Body. She never ceases to present to the faithful the bread of life, taken from the one table of God's Word and Christ's Body' (cf. *Dei Verbum* 21). We play a role in helping to present the Word to the people during the liturgy.

We learn from the Constitution on the Sacred Liturgy that Christ "is present in his word, since it is he himself who speaks when the holy Scriptures are read in the Church." We proclaim scripture to experience the Christ present now in our midst and to make present the past events of salvation history. Liturgy allows us to participate in those events, to experience their power, and their ability to transform.

Using This Book

Proclaiming the scriptures is a ministry that involves your whole life, not just your communication skills. So make these scriptures a part of your life every week, and especially during the week prior to the liturgy in which you will proclaim.

Read through all three scriptures for your assigned Sunday in this book. Because all three have been chosen for this day, it is important to look at them together. The Gospel can often teach you much about how the first reading should be proclaimed.

Build your prayer for the week around the scripture passage you will proclaim on Sunday. At some point as you are becoming familiar with your passage, read it directly from your Bible, reading also what comes before and after it to get a clear sense of its context.

Always read all three commentaries. There are suggestions in each that can help you with your own passage. As you read the commentaries, refer to the sections of the scripture passage being discussed and make your own margin notations.

Read the scriptures again using your own margin notes and those printed in the text to remind you of the commentary suggestions.

Always read scriptures aloud taking note of stress and pause suggestions. After several readings, alter the stress markings to suit your style and interpretation.

Using Additional Resources

The better you understand the meaning of your passage, the more effectively you will proclaim it and so help the assembly to understand it. Although the commentaries in this book will help you, lectors may wish to dig deeper. Also, lectors need to develop a life-long habit of turning to the scriptures for study and prayer. Additional resources that will help you to do this are listed at the end of this introduction.

In the beginning was the Word, and the Word was with God, and the Word was God.

Transparency and Drama

In this *Workbook for Lectors, Gospel Readers, and Proclaimers of the Word*, you will read about oral interpretation, dramatic pauses, and about creating characters. Good lectors use these techniques from the world of theater, not to draw attention to themselves, but to draw attention to the word. When people experience good proclamation, they forget the lector in front of them and they hear the scripture in a powerful way. That goal is best achieved by skillful use of all the available reading techniques. Of course, lectors who are overly dramatic, who become more focused on how they proclaim than on what they proclaim may find that their listeners stop believing them. Artifice (an imitation of artfulness) can become an obstacle to good proclamation.

Avoiding artifice does not mean settling for mediocrity. Often the failure to use appropriate techniques leads to a kind of mediocre reading that guarantees the scripture will not be heard. Lectors who cannot differentiate one character in a reading from another, who read too fast or too slow, who have too little energy and don't use the colorful words of a passage, who read in a monotone without rising and falling dynamics and pacing—these readers only draw attention to themselves. The assembly cannot see beyond them. But really good proclaimers—who utilize appropriate techniques for the material being read—draw the assembly into the reading.

True Humility

All lectors need a model of true humility as they work toward excellence in their proclamation. We look to Christ who "emptied himself, taking the form of a slave . . . [and] humbled himself, becoming obedient to death, even death on a cross" (Philippians 2:7–8). Jesus, the Word, humbles himself each Sunday by making himself dependent on us who proclaim him in the assembly. He depends on us to communicate him as a living and vital word. Jesus, alive in every line of scripture, is indeed, obedient "unto death."

This Sacred Ministry

God's word is "living and effective" (Hebrews 4:12) and it "goes forth from [God's] mouth . . . achieving the end for which [he] sent it" (Isaiah 55:11), yet we

God so loved the world that he gave his only Son, so that everyone who believes in him might not perish but might have eternal life.

know that doesn't happen automatically. People must receive and embrace the word and allow it to become a transforming influence in their lives. Before they can do that, lectors must help them to hear it.

Reading as Interpretation

Reading is a form of interpretation. The same word spoken by two lectors will not be "heard" in exactly the same way. Pacing, the words stressed, pauses, volume, tone color, and intensity are all elements that interpret the text. Your responsibility is to make sure your interpretation upholds the plain sense of the text, the author's clear intent, and that you enable the text to speak to everyone.

Conveying the Full Content of a Passage

God's word can also lose its power, beauty, and spiritual import if a reader fails to communicate the full content of a passage, which clearly consists of more than the words. In fact, every text contains three kinds of content: intellectual/theological, emotional, and aesthetic.

The author makes certain points or shares specific details, or tells a specific story, behind which is a theological teaching or spiritual insight. That is the intellectual/theological content. Much of what we encounter in scripture also contains emotional content. We usually call this tone, and it is as much a part of the message as is the cognitive component. If Paul is urgent or peremptory in one of his letters but the assembly is unaware of it because the lector has not communicated that part of the content, then the assembly has not heard Paul's message in its entirety. Finally, every passage contains aesthetic dimensions—elements that make it beautiful. Rhythm, suspense, picturesque language, and imagery all add to the pleasure we take in fine literature. As lectors, we must help our assemblies experience the beauty of the fine literature we call scripture.

To acquire the intellectual/theological content, begin by reading the scripture and the commentary. Next, search the text for the emotion the author is expressing—the emotional content. Finally, look for the aesthetic devices the author employs—repetition, simile, metaphor, irony, and so forth—the aesthetic content.

Tools of the Trade

Margin Notes. Notes may introduce new ideas or repeat information in the commentary. They may offer hints about a character's feelings. Often they address you as the reader ("Slowly. Tenderly. Build in intensity.").

Build. "Build" refers to increasing vocal intensity as you speak a certain word or sentence. That could be done by speaking louder, but a quieter voice might produce the same effect. Sometimes "build" is achieved by speaking faster and sometimes by speaking slower. The point is to show more intensity of feeling, greater urgency, or concern. Lack of intensity is one of the great "sins" of proclamation.

Stress (Bold Print). Some words are more important than others. Some are more expressive and carry more emotion. The bolding used within the scripture texts in this book attempts to identify the operative words in a sentence, the ones which convey the meaning.

This is my commandment: love one another as I love you.

Echoes. Some words are "echoes" of words that went before. For example, "You shall be a glorious crown . . . a royal diadem" (Isaiah 62:3) Here "diadem" echoes "crown" so it needs no stress. In such cases, emphasize the new idea: royal.

Words That Sound like What They Mean. "Pop," "fizz," and "gulp" are obvious. Some are more subtle: "smashed," "vast," "in haste," "implore," "gleamed." These words usually require special emphasis. The author (or translator) has chosen them carefully to convey the desired meaning. Let them do their work.

Word Value. "Shock" is always a more interesting word than "bean." "Shock" sounds like what it means and immediately conjures up vivid images. "Bean" won't even make your mouth water. Word value is also determined by context. The words "one, two, three . . ." are neutral by themselves, but put in context they intensify: "Three seconds until lift-off! One . . . two . . . !" If, in reading that sentence, "One, two . . ." sounds the same as when followed by "buckle my shoe" you've got work to do.

Words are your medium, like a painter's brush or a sculptor's chisel. You must understand the words before you can communicate them. Most words have a dictionary meaning (denotative) and an associational meaning (connotative). "House" and "home" both mean "dwelling," yet they communicate different *feelings*. Be alert to subtle differences in connotative meanings and *express them*.

Separating Units of Thought with Pauses. Running too many words together blurs meaning and fails to distinguish ideas. Punctuation does not always indicate clearly what words to group together or where to pause. Identify the units of thought and use your voice to distinguish one from another. The listener depends on you for this organization of ideas. With the letters of Paul, in particular, you must carefully identify individual ideas and share them one at a time.

Scripture in this book is set up in sense lines—one complete idea per line of text. Typically, there will be at least a slight pause at the end of each line. But good reading will require you to look for other needed pauses *within* individual lines. Moving from one thought unit to another within a paragraph requires shifts in *mood* and *pacing*. Don't rush these transitions but honor them with a healthy pause, letting the silence "speak."

Pauses are never "dead" moments. Something is always happening during a pause. Practice will teach you how often and how long to pause. *Too many pauses* make a reading choppy; too few cause ideas to run into one another. *Too long* a pause breaks the flow. If pauses are *too short*, your listeners will be struggling to keep up with you. A substantial pause always follows "A reading from . . ." and both precedes and follows "The word [Gospel] of the Lord."

Ritardando. *Ritardando,* an Italian word, refers to the practice, common in music, of becoming gradually slower as you approach the end of a piece. On the last line of a song you automatically slow down and expand the words. Many readings end this way—with a decreased rate but increased intensity.

Characters. Usually several characters populate the scripture passages you will read. Do your best to distinguish one from another. Be in touch with each character's thoughts, feelings, and motivations, and suggest differences through subtle changes in pitch, pacing, or by subtly expressing each character's emotion. Differentiating between characters is the mark of a fine reader. But don't ever confuse proclamation with stage theatrics. You are suggesting characters, not "becoming" them.

Narrator. The narrator is often the pivotal role of a passage. Timbre, pitch, rate, and energy can make the same words convey very different moods or meaning. Sometimes the narrator is objective: "Jesus took Peter, James and John . . ." (Matthew 17:1; Mark 9:2). But often the narrator has great interest in the events and characters of a story: "And he was transfigured before them and his clothes became *dazzlingly white*" (Mark 9:2–3). Know the narrator's point of view.

Openings and Closings. First, establish eye contact with the assembly and announce, *from memory,* "A reading from . . . ." Then take a pause (three full beats!) before starting the reading. The correct pronunciation is "A [uh] reading from . . ." instead of "A [ay] reading . . . ." Do not vary from the prescribed introductory formula. Names of characters are often the first word of a reading. Highlight names so listeners don't miss who the subject is. Pause again (three beats!) at the end of the reading and establish eye contact before announcing (again, from memory) "The word [Gospel] of the Lord." Always pronounce "the" as *"thuh"* except before words beginning with a vowel as in *"thee* Acts of the Apostles." Your inflection of the last line of the reading should always signal that the reading is about to end. Then, after a pause to establish eye contact with the assembly, add "The word of the Lord." Maintain eye contact while the assembly makes its response.

Follow the custom of your parish, but it is recommended that a substantial period of silence follow each of the readings. Both approach and departure from the ambo should be made with reverence, neither too fast nor too slow.

Magnify the LORD with me; let us exalt his name together.

Blessed are the poor in spirit, for theirs is the kingdom of heaven.

Eye Contact and Eye Expression. Eye contact is your means of connecting with those to whom you minister. You should look at the assembly during the middle *and* at the end of every thought or sentence. That means you look down at the beginning, look up in the middle, look down quickly as you approach the end, and then look up again as you finish the sentence. This "down, up, down, up" pattern must not appear mechanical or choppy. Through meaningful "eye expression" you help the listeners enter the story.

Pace. The larger the church, the larger the assembly, and the more complex the text, the *slower* you must read. It's better to be too slow than too fast. Your listeners have not spent time with this reading as you have. They need time to absorb it—to catch your words and comprehend what they mean.

However, too slow can also be deadly. Besides being boring and making every text sound the same, this method robs the material of its natural cadences and makes it impossible to communicate the energy or passion of the author.

You'll read more naturally if you read ideas rather than words, if you share images rather than sentences. Dialogue, because of its need to imitate real conversation, often moves at a faster pace than the rest of the passage.

Using the Microphone. Know your public address system. If it echoes, speak even more slowly than usual (but without losing a natural cadence or the inherent energy of the text). If you hear "popping," you're probably standing too close to the microphone. If you are the first reader, go to the ambo before the start of Mass to adjust the height of the microphone. If you

are proclaiming the second reading or Gospel, adjust the microphone position when you reach the ambo.

Gestures and Posture. It is hard to imagine a text that requires the use of gestures. They can be distractions and should be used rarely if ever. Whether you like it or not, your body posture speaks. Make sure it says what you want it to. Don't let your face or body contradict the good news you announce. Remember, lectors are allowed to smile!

Pronunciation. Pronunciation aids are provided in the margin notes (see the key at the end of this introduction). Various internet pronunciation guides allow you to hear the word spoken aloud. Doing a simple search like: "Bible pronunciation guide."

Literary Forms

Each literary form demands a different approach.

Stories. Stories must be "told," not "read." You don't have to memorize them, but you do have to tell them. You are the storyteller. Make the story yours, then share it with your listeners.

Know the story and its context—what precedes and follows it. Know the significance of the events for the characters involved. Understand the chronology of the plot. Identify the climax and employ your best energy there. Use the language. Don't throw away any good words.

Settings give the context in which the action unfolds and usually appear at the beginning of a reading. Don't rush the description.

Characters must be believable. Understand their motivation—why they feel, act, and speak as they do. Characters are often identified by their relationship to another character ("the *parents* of the one who had gained his sight," says John 9:18). Give stress to those identifying words. Create the characters as distinct individuals, changing the inflection and tone of your voice for each one.

Dialogue reveals character. What a character says and *how* are nearly infallible clues to personality. Besides subtly distinguishing one character from another with your voice, learn to let the speakers listen to and answer one another as in real conversation.

Bring the dialogue to life and build suspense in the story, revealing one detail at a time.

Epistles. The epistles are simply letters. Know *who wrote* the letter and *who received* it. Many biblical resources explain the circumstances around a particular letter. Whether addressed to an individual or

The LORD's word is true; all his works are trustworthy.

to all the faithful of a particular city, each epistle is also addressed to the faithful gathered in your church.

The tone of each letter may vary, but the delivery is always direct. Letters are like conversations between the writer and the person or community addressed.

The purpose or intent of each letter dictates the tone. Very often Paul is the writer. As teacher and spiritual leader, he is motivated by multiple concerns: to instruct, console, encourage, chastise, warn, settle disputes, and more. When reading from one of his letters, be aware of what he's trying to accomplish. Paul is always direct and earnest; even when he exhorts, he never stops loving his spiritual children.

Go slowly in the epistles. It takes time for the assembly to catch the ideas you toss at them. Paul's theology can be tricky, and the style is often a tangle of complex sentences. Many times his mood and purpose changes within a single passage. Thinking of Paul's role as teacher, disciplinarian, or "companion on the journey" will help keep you from rushing. Love your listeners and desire their good as much as Paul and the other letter writers do.

Prophetic Writing. The intensity of emotion and degree of urgency required in proclaiming the writing of the prophets make some lectors uncomfortable. But the urgency has to be there.

A pervasive theme in the Old Testament is that *we are chosen.* With election comes responsibility. Prophets were to remind the Chosen People about those responsibilities—not a popular task. Though not shown in the text, prophetic words are spoken with vocal exclamation points. One must work up courage to tell people what they don't want to hear.

In addition to troubling the comfortable, prophets comforted the troubled. With equal passion, the great seers spoke *threat* and *consolation, indictment* and *forgiveness.* You must do the same for the chosen people you call "parish."

As with the epistles, use resources to learn the situation in which a prophet ministers. Prophets vary. Be attentive to style as well as content. Beware of fast transitions, the instant climaxes, and the frequent lack of conclusions. Often a prophet abruptly stops.

Willingly or reluctantly the prophets were compelled to speak for God. Don't rob them of their intensity. We still need to hear their words.

Poetry. The Old Testament contains much poetry—a marvelously effective and economical form of communication. Rich with imagery and emotions, poetry makes special demands on the proclaimer.

Take time. Poetry is gourmet food, eaten slowly and savored. Go slowly with readings like this passage from Baruch for the Second Sunday of Advent, Year C (Baruch 5:8–9):

> The forests and every fragrant kind of tree
>   have overshadowed Israel at God's command;
>   for God is leading Israel in joy
>   by the light of his glory,
>   with his mercy and justice for company.

You need to respond to images by letting yourself "smell" and "feel" as well as "see" the "forests" and "fragrant . . . tree." Word choice in poetry affects meaning more than in any other writing because it affects *sound* and *rhythm.*

Sound and meaning go hand-in-hand in poetry. Even in a language that you don't understand, poetry recited well should touch your emotions.

Rhythm is what distinguishes poetry from prose. It's what makes words sound like music. Compare these two verses: "In times past, God spoke in partial and various ways to our ancestors through the prophets" (Hebrews 1:1), and "For Zion's sake I will not be silent, for Jerusalem's sake I will not be quiet" (Isaiah

62:1). The first line is smooth and flat, but the second has a rhythmic beat flowing through it that makes it exciting.

Repetition fills poetry. Yet instead of feeling redundant, repetitions intensify our emotional experience. In Hebrew poetry, *parallelism* is a technique used to repeat, balance, and develop ideas in a poem. For example, this is the first verse of Psalm 19:

> The heavens declare the glory of God;
> the sky proclaims its builder's craft.

Two parallel images express one idea. Since the two thoughts mean the same thing, this is *synonymous* parallelism. *Antithetic* parallelism uses opposing images to express one idea. Proverbs 15:15 says:

> Every day is miserable for the depressed,
> but a lighthearted person has a continual feast.

Contrasting ideas make a similar point. Look for these and other forms of parallelism.

Pronunciation Key

bait = bayt	thin = thin
cat = kat	vision = VIZH*n
sang = sang	ship = ship
father = FAH-<u>ther</u>	sir = ser
care = kair	gloat = gloht
paw = paw	cot = kot
jar = jahr	noise = noyz
easy = EE-zee	poison = POY-z*n
her =her	plow = plow
let = let	although = ahl-<u>THOH</u>
queen = kween	church = cherch
delude = deh-L<u>OO</u>D	fun = fun
when = hwen	fur = fer
ice = īs	flute = f<u>loo</u>t
if = if	foot = foot
finesse = fih-NES	

Recommended Works

Church Documents

Catechism of the Catholic Church. United States Catholic Conference, Inc., 1994.

Dei Verbum (Dogmatic Constitution on Divine Revelation). In *Vatican II: The Conciliar and Post Conciliar Documents*, edited by Austin Flannery, OP, Northport, New York: Costello Publishing Company, Inc., 1992.

"Introduction to the Lectionary." In *Lectionary for Mass: Study Edition*. Chicago, Illinois: Liturgy Training Publications, 1998.

Resources for Proclaiming God's Word

Meagher, Virginia, and Paul Turner. *Guide for Lectors*. Chicago, Illinois: Liturgy Training Publications, 2007.

Meyers, Susan E. *Pronunciation Guide for the Sunday Lectionary*. Chicago, Illinois: Liturgy Training Publications, 1998.

_____. *A Well-Trained Tongue: Formation in the Ministry of the Reader*. Chicago, Illinois: Liturgy Training Publications, 1996.

_____. *A Word That Will Rouse Them: Reflections on the Ministry of Reader*. Chicago, Illinois: Liturgy Training Publications, 1996.

General Reference Works on the Bible

Boadt, Lawrence. *Reading the Old Testament: An Introduction*. New York, New York/Mahwah, New Jersey: Paulist Press, 1984.

Brown, Raymond E. *An Introduction to the New Testament*. The Anchor Bible Reference Library. New York, New York: Doubleday, 1997.

Catholic Study Bible: New American Bible. New York: Oxford University Press USA, 1990.

The New Jerome Biblical Commentary. Raymond E. Brown, Joseph Fitzmyer and Roland E. Murphy, eds. Englewood Cliffs, New Jersey: Prentice Hall, 1990.

Perkins, Pheme. *Reading the New Testament: An Introduction*. New York, New York/Mahwah, New Jersey: Paulist Press, 1988.

Commentaries on the Gospel according to Luke

Johnson, Luke Timothy, Daniel J. Harrington, and Donald P. Senior. *The Gospel of Luke*. Sacra Pagina Series. Collegeville, Minnesota: The Liturgical Press, 2005.

Senior, Donald. *Passion of Jesus in the Gospel of Luke*. Collegeville, Minnesota: The Liturgical Press, 1992.

1ST SUNDAY OF ADVENT

Lectionary #3

READING I   Jeremiah 33:14–16

Remember that meaning is carried as much by the *sound* of your words as by the words themselves.

The entire first reading is spoken in God's voice, in tones of authority and reassurance.

"In those days, in that time": a distinctive feature of biblical literature. Repetition is a literary device used to achieve emphasis. Make this emphasis clear by increasing energy in your voice from the first expression to the second.

Another repetition that requires increasing energy.

Pause, and then read the final line with great dignity.

A reading from the Book of the Prophet Jeremiah

The days are **coming**, says the LORD,
    when I will **fulfill** the promise
    I made to the house of **Israel** and **Judah**.
In **those** days, in that **time**,
    I will **raise** up for David a **just shoot**;
    he shall do what is **right** and **just** in the land.
In those days **Judah** shall be **safe**
    and **Jerusalem** shall dwell **secure**;
    this is what they shall **call** her:
    "The LORD our **justice**."

READING I In today's text a people who have grown tired and dusty waiting for the fulfillment of God's promise are alerted that the anticipated event draws near. Jeremiah assures Israel that God will not abandon them, that God will keep the promise made to King David to secure his throne forever and raise up Israel's Messiah from his descendants. Israel was living in troubled times. Invasion and exile were not far off. But God had made promises, and Israel clung to those promises in good times and in bad. The promise contained in today's reading was

at least partially fulfilled when Israel returned from exile. Christian tradition sees Jesus, the Messiah, the "just shoot" that springs from the stump of David's family tree, as the ultimate fulfillment of the prophecy. He is "The Lord our justice," our hope and salvation.

What lesson is God teaching us through the prophet Jeremiah? To trust in God's promises? To endure in faith even when fulfillment is a long time coming? To see with eyes of faith what human eyes cannot see? All this and more: to long for fulfillment so much that we help bring it

about, not only through prayer but through lives driven by God's generous love.

READING II Today's readings remind us what this season is all about. The Christ of Advent is no helpless child, but the "Lord" of the universe who will return in glory to judge the earth. Christ's coming is a serious event not meant for the feeble of heart. Paul prays for the recently converted Thessalonians that they be strengthened and purified for the great and terrible day of Christ's return.

The word "Lord" appears four times in this text. Paul speaks with great love and tenderness in the opening lines.

Speak words like "strengthen," "blameless," and "holiness" as if they were a prayer for those you address.

Paul urges greater effort in doing what is right—a more exhortative tone here. He's saying: you learned from me *how* to behave—and you *are* behaving that way. Now do it even more.

Let this sentence remind those being exhorted that "easy excuses will not be accepted."

READING II   1 Thessalonians 3:12—4:2

A reading from the first Letter of Saint Paul to the Thessalonians

Brothers and sisters:
May the Lord make you **increase** and abound in **love**
    for one **another** and for **all**,
    just as **we** have for **you**,
    so as to **strengthen** your hearts,
    to be **blameless** in **holiness** before our God and Father
    at the coming of our Lord **Jesus** with all his **holy** ones. Amen.

Finally, brothers and sisters,
    we earnestly ask and **exhort** you in the Lord Jesus that,
    as you **received** from us
    how you should **conduct** yourselves to **please** God
    —and as you **are** conducting yourselves—
    you do so even **more**.
For you **know** what **instructions** we gave you
    through the Lord **Jesus**.

Paul and others expected that this would happen in their lifetime, so he offers advice about how believers ought to be living their lives in anticipation of the second coming.

Of course, Jesus did not come then, nor may he come in our lifetime. As we drew near the new millennium, many were convinced that the end was near. They were wrong. But the advice Paul offers remains important whether Christ's coming is millennia away or before our next birthday. There is no better time to "conduct [our]selves in a way pleasing to God" and no better season to begin to make

changes in our lives than right now. Paul tells the Thessalonians: You have done well . . . but you can do better. His reassurance in the first paragraph is as sincere as the words of a parent to a daughter and her spouse on their wedding day. By calling for greater fidelity to Christ and the Gospel, Paul reminds us that our individual lives can anticipate the great transformation the entire world will experience when Christ truly comes again.

GOSPEL A terrible storm, full of thunder, lightening and blowing wind, rages through the first paragraph. In the second, the sun appears and the sky momentarily brightens. But in the final paragraph, clouds close in again, dark and menacing in the distance. Luke is painting, with vivid colors, a scene of what the last times will bring. He paints with words that should not be muted, but allowed to speak boldly their apocalyptic message full of fear and fury. The challenge for you will be to announce that some

Apocalyptic imagery starts immediately. Don't rush. Give the solemn words the sound they require.

Though avoiding melodrama, make these lines arresting and sobering.

A vocal shift. More solemn and awe-inspiring, with a far-off focus.

Focus is back on the ground. Speak bluntly.

This is direct address; the tone is urgent and forthright. "Carousing," "drunkenness" and "anxieties" = three distinct dangers.

"Like a trap" should sound like what it means.

Let Jesus' strong, arresting words prepare your listeners to "stand before the Son of Man." Slow your pace as you reach the last words: "before . . . Man."

GOSPEL   Luke 21:25–28, 34–36

A reading from the holy Gospel according to Luke

Jesus said to his disciples:
"There will be signs in the **sun**, the **moon**, and the **stars**,
　　and on **earth** nations will be in **dismay**,
　　perplexed by the **roaring** of the sea and the waves.
People will **die** of **fright**
　　in anticipation of what is **coming** upon the world,
　　for the powers of the **heavens** will be **shaken**.
And then they will see the **Son** of **Man**
　　coming in a **cloud** with **power** and great **glory**.
But when these signs **begin** to happen,
　　stand **erect** and **raise** your heads
　　because your **redemption** is at **hand**.

"Beware that your **hearts** do not become drowsy
　　from **carousing** and **drunkenness**
　　and the **anxieties** of daily life,
　　and that day catch you by **surprise** like a **trap**.
For that day will assault **everyone**
　　who lives on the face of the earth.
Be **vigilant** at all times
　　and **pray** that you have the **strength**
　　to **escape** the tribulations that are **imminent**
　　and to **stand** before the **Son** of **Man**."

"will die of fright" with all the attendant horrors without lapsing into cheap theatrics. Luke's strong and striking images are meant to catch us and convince us that the Christ is not just the babe in the manger whom we'll celebrate in a few weeks, but a cosmic Lord whose "glory" fills us with awe.

Some Gospel texts are meant to comfort. This is not one of them. But Luke is not trying to terrify, either. He offers hope, reminding us we don't have to be among

those who panic: we can "stand erect and raise [our] heads," knowing our "redemption," not destruction, "is at hand." The sense of urgency continues into the final paragraph because Christ will come—at Christmas, at the end of time, and at the time of our own deaths. Therefore, vigilance is an everyday necessity. And as we wait patiently, we must also observe the exhortation to avoid indulgence, drunkenness, and caring too much about the things of the world. Each year, Advent helps to remind us that meaningful living means looking beyond the cares of everyday life. This text,

with its stark and riveting imagery (including the final sentence!), can be a great gift to your community if it reminds them that each day of earthly life could become the portal that leads to eternal life.

2ND SUNDAY OF ADVENT

Lectionary #6

READING I   Baruch 5:1–9

Imperatives, spoken with joy, not harshness. Imagine speaking the name of your city when you say "Jerusalem." Contrast "take off" and "put on."

A reading from the Book of the Prophet Baruch

Jerusalem, **take off** your robe of **mourning** and **misery**;
    put on the splendor of **glory** from God forever:
Wrapped in the cloak of **justice** from God,
    bear on your head the **mitre**
    that displays the **glory** of the **eternal name**.
For God will show all the **earth** your splendor:
    you will be **named** by God forever
    the **peace** of **justice**, the **glory** of God's **worship**.

With confidence in what God can and will do.

Up, Jerusalem! **stand** upon the **heights**;
    look to the east and see your **children**
gathered from the **east** and the **west**
    at the **word** of the Holy One,
    rejoicing that they are **remembered** by God.

Lost children reunited to grieving parents: tenderness and joy.

Led away on **foot** by their **enemies** they **left** you:
    but **God** will bring them **back** to you
    borne **aloft** in **glory** as on royal **thrones**.

A memory of the pain which is now ending.

For God has **commanded**
    that every **lofty** mountain be made **low**,
and that the age-old **depths** and **gorges**
    be filled to **level** ground,
    that Israel may advance **secure** in the glory of God.

Speak with conviction and joy!

READING I A people in exile hears words of comfort and promises of restoration; a broken people is roused with images of wholeness. The prophets often spoke of divine displeasure or retribution, but this message is full of hope. Notice that Baruch uses clothing images to suggest the dramatic change the people will undergo: "Take off . . . put on . . . ."

"Jerusalem" personifies all God's people. And Baruch's message, though addressed to exiled Jews, speaks also to

us who sometimes understand "mourning and misery" better than the salvation he announces. Baruch's words stir us to a radical hope and to the possibility of return from our own exile of discouragement or spiritual alienation. This is the encouragement of one who sees with God's eyes the hope that is nearing fulfillment.

Balance and variety are part of every good reading. Opportunities to vary your intensity lie in images that require tenderness, for example: "see your children gathered from the east and the west." And for anxious people at a hectic time of year,

what thought could be more arresting than that of being "remembered by God." It's a profound image that needs time to do its work of healing.

"Led away on foot by their enemies" is the only reference to the exile in Babylon from which God is delivering the people, but your awareness of that painful exile will enable you to herald its end with convincing joy. In the Gospel we'll hear again of filling "depths" and leveling "lofty mountains"; take your time here, so that when Luke quotes Isaiah 40:3–5 (which

Don't rush this poetic image.

Slowly, as if seeing the impossible happening before your eyes.

The **forests** and every **fragrant** kind of tree
    have **overshadowed** Israel at God's **command**;
for God is **leading** Israel in **joy**
    by the **light** of his **glory**,
        with his **mercy** and **justice** for company.

READING II   Philippians 1:4–6, 8–11

A reading from the Letter of Saint Paul to the Philippians

Review the section on letters in the introduction.
Take time to scan the assembly before and as you read. Make it a prayer.

Brothers and sisters:
I pray always with **joy** in my every **prayer** for **all** of you,
    because of your **partnership** for the **gospel**
    from the **first** day until **now**.
I am **confident** of this,

Renewed energy here!

    that the one who **began** a **good** work in you
    will continue to **complete** it
    until the day of **Christ Jesus**.
God is my **witness**,
    how I **long** for all of you with the **affection** of Christ **Jesus**.
And this is my **prayer**:

"The day of Christ Jesus" is the day of Christ's return.

Again, a sincere prayer for your own assembly's growth in holiness.

Note, and don't rush, all the separate "intentions" in this prayer.

    that your **love** may increase ever **more** and **more**
    in **knowledge** and every kind of **perception**,
    to discern what is of **value**,
    so that you may be **pure** and **blameless** for the day of **Christ**,
    filled with the fruit of **righteousness**
    that comes through **Jesus Christ**

A smile would not be inappropriate.

    for the **glory** and **praise** of **God**.

---

inspired this passage), the assembly will recognize these familiar images. The impossible is happening; God is at the front of the march leading Israel in joy.

READING II Philippians is Paul's "letter of joy" written, ironically, from a prison somewhere (perhaps Rome or Ephesus). Paul writes to a community for whom he holds much love and gratitude. They have been generous with him and they have been faithful to the teaching

he first shared with them. Scan the assembly before you start and let your simple delivery convey Paul's sincere love for those he addresses. He states confidently his assurance that God will continue to do good in and through this community of believers.

Paul is addressing the entire Christian community of Philippi, not individual members, so the expressions "I pray . . . for all of you" and "how I long for all of you" become especially important. Of course, Paul's words are also addressed to us today who must understand that God's call

to greater holiness comes to us as a community, as Church, not as single members.

Paul applauds as well as challenges his readers: the best way to praise God, he says, is to do even more of what you've been doing. The Advent season embodies the tension inherent in the kingdom— which has arrived, but is yet to come in fullness. Paul points to this same truth when he reminds the Philippians that the good work "begun" in them must now be made "complete." Appreciate "what is of value," he says, and you will continue to

GOSPEL   LUKE 3:1–6

Don't rush through the list.

Caesar = SEE-zer
Judea = joo-DEE-uh
Ituraea = ih-too-REE-ah
Trachonitis = trak-uh-NĪ-tis
Lysanias = li-SAY-nee-uhs
Annas = AN-uhs
Caiaphas = KĪ-uh-fuhs
Zechariah = zek-uh-RĪ-uh

Pause after "Caiphas," and then resume slowly, with the announcement of John's ministry.

"Proclaiming a baptism . . . the prophet Isaiah": an "indirect quote" that can be spoken in the "voice" of John.

Speak slowly but energetically with solemn authority.

Speak with a slightly faster tempo here.

Slow gradually toward: "the salvation of God."

A reading from the holy Gospel according to Luke

In the fifteenth year of the reign of **Tiberius Caesar**,
    when **Pontius Pilate** was **governor** of Judea,
    and **Herod** was tetrarch of **Galilee**,
    and his brother **Philip** tetrarch of the region
        of **Ituraea** and **Trachonitis**,
    and **Lysanias** was tetrarch of **Abilene**,
    during the high **priesthood** of **Annas** and **Caiaphas**,
    the **word** of **God** came to **John** the son of **Zechariah**
        in the **desert**.
John went throughout the **whole** region of the **Jordan**,
    proclaiming a **baptism** of **repentance** for the **forgiveness**
        of **sins**,
    as it is **written** in the book of the words of the prophet **Isaiah**:
        *A **voice** of one **crying out** in the **desert**:*
        *"**Prepare** the way of the **Lord**,*
            *make **straight** his **paths**.*
        *Every **valley** shall be **filled***
            *and every **mountain** and **hill** shall be made **low**.*
        *The **winding** roads shall be made **straight**,*
            *and the **rough** ways made **smooth**,*
        *and all **flesh** shall see the **salvation** of **God**."*

yield a rich harvest of justice. What is of value during Advent is Jesus, the incarnate word of God. Say that to your listeners who, during this often distracting season, may need a reminder about what is truly of value.

GOSPEL Luke takes his readers down the halls of royalty, along the corridors of power, both civil and religious, only to lead us, finally, into the desert where a lonely wild man claims to hear the word of God. By the time he

reaches the main point of the first paragraph: "the word of God came to John" Luke has already established the historical and geographic context for the coming of the kingdom of God. By reading Luke's impressive list with measured deliberateness, and then focusing not on any of the imperial personages, but on John, the desert prophet, your delivery reinforces Luke's point that God's logic and rules transcend ours. God's will is accomplished not through the wise and mighty, but through lowly instruments like Mary, John, and maybe even us.

The beautiful, but almost too-familiar poetry from Isaiah promises that the desert will be transformed. These powerful images speak of more than the landscape; they announce the straightening of the human spirit, the filling of empty hearts, the smoothing of the way that leads to healing and reconciliation. The poetry also assures us that nothing will stop God's plan of bringing salvation to all. Since some "rough ways" still remain, however, the task is to convince listeners that God is at work even in our day.

IMMACULATE CONCEPTION

Lectionary #689

READING I   Genesis 3:9–15, 20

A reading from the Book of Genesis

Don't let the familiarity of this "classic" story rob your reading of nuance or reduce it to caricature.

The narrator's tone suggests the wrongness of Adam's deed even as you begin.

God is unaware of any transgression, so God's first question is objective.

Caught "in the act" and needing to cover up, Adam responds. Is he panicked, coolly controlled, or remorseful? Adam's reference to his "nakedness" alerts God to his misdeed, so emphasize it.

Contrast the defensive responses of the man and the woman. Who is more assertive, more defensive? Does one exhibit remorse or shame? Is one of them more afraid?

God's rebuke of the serpent contrasts in tone with the comments to Adam and Eve. God is not parental here— a judgment is handed down, uncompromising and severe.

After the man, **Adam**, had eaten of the **tree**,
 the LORD God **called** to the man and **asked** him,
  "Where **are** you?"
He answered, "I **heard** you in the garden;
 but I was **afraid**, because I was **naked**,
  so I **hid** myself."
Then he asked, "Who **told** you that you were naked?
You have **eaten**, then,
 from the **tree** of which I had **forbidden** you to eat!"
The man replied, "The **woman** whom you **put** here with me—
 she **gave** me fruit from the tree, and so I **ate** it."
The LORD God then asked the **woman**,
 "Why did you **do** such a thing?"
The woman answered, "The **serpent tricked** me into it,
 so I **ate** it."

Then the LORD God said to the **serpent**:
 "Because you have **done** this, you shall be **banned**
  from all the **animals**
  and from all the wild **creatures**;
 on your **belly** shall you crawl,
  and **dirt** shall you eat
  all the **days** of your **life**.

READING I Why *this* text for a Marian solemnity in the middle of Advent? It's because Mary is the new Eve who, in contrast to the first Eve, surrenders completely to the divine will. Her assent to God's will makes possible the Incarnation and the undoing of the damage wrought in the garden. Adam and Eve's efforts to evade responsibility for their actions contrast with Mary's heroic willingness to accept the responsibility God offers her. This passage and its finger-pointing episode are therefore very important, both theologically and pastorally. Does not our

own Advent journey seek to be a pilgrimage from the rebellion of Adam and Eve to the obedience of Mary? As you read, don't exaggerate these "First Parents" beyond our ability to recognize ourselves in them.

This important story presents the Judeo-Christian understanding of the origin of sin: it came from prideful and disobedient humanity and continues because so often we continue to substitute our will for God's. An immediate consequence of sin is alienation and mistrust: the man blames the woman and the woman blames the serpent. Adam and Eve's dialogue with

God should not sound like children hiding fault from a stern parent. These are adults who have chosen quite deliberately and have brought dire penalties upon themselves and all humanity, although in this passage the penalties are leveled primarily at the serpent.

Verse 15 ("I will put enmity . . .") is often referred to as the protevangelium, the first Gospel, the Bible's earliest assurance that God will ultimately deliver humanity from sin and its consequences. The early Church Fathers gave us this concept, pointing out the relationship between

These lines are central to today's solemnity.

Contrast the snake's futile strikes at "his heel" and the offspring's damaging blows to the serpent's head.
Pause, and then read slowly the reminder that Eve is mother of us all.

> I will put **enmity** between **you** and the **woman,**
>   and between **your** offspring and **hers;**
> **he** will strike at your **head,**
>   while **you** strike at his **heel.**"
>
> The man called his wife **Eve,**
>   because she became the **mother** of all the **living.**

READING II   Ephesians 1:3–6, 11–12

A reading from the Letter of Saint Paul to the Ephesians

Brothers and sisters:

Don't just talk about praising God. Do it!

> **Blessed** be the **God** and **Father** of our **Lord** Jesus **Christ,**
>   who has **blessed** us in Christ
>   with every spiritual **blessing** in the **heavens,**

Help the listeners understand what it is they are to be *grateful* for.

>   as he **chose** us in him, before the foundation of the **world,**
>   to be **holy** and without **blemish** before him.

Pause after the phrase "in love . . ." so that your listeners understand what God's motivation is.

> In **love** he **destined** us for **adoption** to himself
>   through Jesus **Christ,**
>   in accord with the **favor** of his **will,**
> for the **praise** of the glory of his **grace**
>   that he **granted** us in the **beloved.**

"In him" means in Christ.
"One" refers to God the Father.

> In **him** we were also **chosen,**
>   **destined** in accord with the **purpose** of the One
> who accomplishes **all** things according to the **intention**
>   of his **will,**
> so that we might **exist** for the praise of his **glory,**
> we who **first** hoped in **Christ.**

Use *ritardando* (gradually slowing to the end) with the phrase "We who first hoped . . . ."

Eve and Mary. On this solemnity, we identify Mary with "the woman" and Christ with her "offspring." So at the end of this reading, Eve is a sign of hope, not loss, for she becomes "mother of all the living," as Mary is the mother of all who live in Christ.

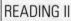 **READING II** In a world of random violence where earthquakes and hurricanes come out of nowhere, where children disappear every hour, and wars rage round the world, a voice dares sing a hymn of praise to God's bountiful

goodness. It is the voice of Paul, the voice of the Church, proclaimed by you, the lector. For two millennia, the voice has insisted that God has created a good and purposeful world, that a benign will governs that world, and that, in fact, the ruler of the world has *chosen* us to become "holy and without blemish." Such good news must be proclaimed in joy and with great energy. Instead of original sin, Paul focuses us on the original blessing, God's loving initiative on our behalf.

God's plan has been accomplished in us who believe and have accepted "adoption" through Jesus Christ. What's more, we have received an inheritance—the opportunity to live our lives as a song of praise to the God who made us, chose us, and continues to call us.

On this solemnity of Mary, who was chosen from all time to be the immaculate vehicle of God's will, words and phrases like "chose," "destined," "before the foundation of the world," "holy and without blemish" are especially significant and

GOSPEL Luke 1:26–38

A reading from the holy Gospel according to Luke

The angel **Gabriel** was sent from **God**
  to a town of **Galilee** called **Nazareth**,
  to a **virgin** betrothed to a man named **Joseph**,
  of the house of **David**,
  and the virgin's **name** was **Mary**.
And coming to her, he said,
  "**Hail**, full of **grace**! The **Lord** is with you."
But she was greatly **troubled** at what was said
  and **pondered** what sort of **greeting** this might be.
Then the angel **said** to her,
  "Do not be **afraid**, Mary,
  for you have found **favor** with **God**.
Behold, you will **conceive** in your womb and bear a **son**,
  and you shall name him **Jesus**.
He will be **great** and will be called **Son** of the Most **High**,
  and the Lord **God** will give him the **throne** of **David** his **father**,
  and he will **rule** over the house of **Jacob forever**,
  and of his **Kingdom** there will be no **end**."
But **Mary** said to the angel,
  "How can this **be**,
  since I have no **relations** with a **man**?"

A divine messenger comes to a nowhere town to find a virgin marrying into the royal house. That is a lot to say in one sentence, and all of it is important! Pay careful attention to your pacing, and pauses are essential.

After naming Gabriel, Nazareth, Joseph, and David, speak of Mary in a way that keeps her name from getting lost among the others.

Mary's deep distress should color the narration that speaks of it.

"Do not be afraid" is a formula that often precedes an announcement of divine intervention.

"Throne," "rule," "house of Jacob," and "kingdom" all reinforce the angel's initial assertion of the greatness of Mary's child.

Mary is asking "how," not "if" it will happen.

require extra emphasis. The repeated references to Christ, which need repeated stress, remind us that in the beginning when things went wrong, there also existed the One who would make them right again.

The final paragraph reiterates what went before. Read slowly and joyfully and with the awareness that each of your listeners is among those "chosen," as was Mary—the first to hope in Christ and, as a consequence, called blessed forever.

GOSPEL The reading of this Gospel on the solemnity of the Immaculate Conception is likely responsible, at least in part, for the all too common yet erroneous assumption that the solemnity refers to Mary's conception of Jesus without having "relations with a man" when, in fact, it refers to her own unique conception. By the time of the story that unfolds in today's Gospel, Mary has already led an exemplary life of openness to the will of God that makes her the uniquely fertile ground in which divinity can root and grow.

It is the angel's greeting that's most redolent of the themes of this day. "Hail, full of grace," the angel calls out, "you have found favor with God." Shocking, confusing words even in the ears of one so attuned to God's ways and will. But then God has never acted this way before. There is no precedent for what is about to unfold in the life of this young virgin, if she but gives her consent. The drama is staggering—the rest of human history hinges on the response made in this humble place by an even humbler young woman. A divine messenger

This is a solemn yet joyful proclamation.

Speak of Elizabeth's pregnancy in a joyous tone meant to reassure.

Even if spoken softly, these words convey strength and conviction.

And the angel said to her in **reply**,
    "The Holy **Spirit** will come **upon** you,
    and the **power** of the Most **High** will **overshadow** you.
Therefore the **child** to be **born**
    will be called **holy**, the Son of **God**.
And behold, **Elizabeth**, your **relative**,
    has **also** conceived a son in her **old age**,
    and this is the sixth **month** for her who was called **barren**;
    for **nothing** will be **impossible** for God."
Mary said, "**Behold**, I am the **handmaid** of the **Lord**.
May it be **done** to me according to your **word**."
Then the angel **departed** from her.

announces, explains, and reassures. The angel speaks of a son who will be "great . . . called Son of the Most High . . ." and will be given "the throne of David."

   If Mary had doubted like Zachariah (see Luke 1:5–25), she too might have been struck dumb. But her question seems to ask, not "if" but "how" what the angel has announced will be achieved. The angel is quick to respond asserting God's, not Mary's, role in the conception and alluding to Elizabeth's conception as a guarantee that God will act as promised. No human voice can fully capture the unique

moment here narrated. But surely you will give this your most careful and solemn, yet tender reading.

   Mary's "fiat" ("May it be done . . ."), whether whispered or strongly confident, is central to this solemnity and season, for in surrendering to God's will she makes possible the Incarnation. Invite Mary to speak through you those words filled with unique strength and amazing boldness.

3RD SUNDAY OF ADVENT

Lectionary #9

READING I   Zephaniah 3:14–18a

Zephaniah = zef-uh-NĪ-uh

Build in intensity from the first to second line.

Joyfully announce this reversal of fortune!

The cause for rejoicing that dispels fear.

"Fear not" is a constant theme through scripture. Don't waste the words.

This is a God who loves and cares, rather than lords over. These words should comfort.

A reading from the Book of the Prophet Zephaniah

Shout for joy, O daughter **Zion**!
  Sing **joyfully**, O **Israel**!
Be **glad** and **exult** with all your **heart**,
  O daughter **Jerusalem**!
The LORD has removed the **judgment** against you,
  he has turned **away** your **enemies**;
the King of **Israel**, the LORD, is in your **midst**,
  you have no further **misfortune** to fear.
On **that** day, it shall be said to **Jerusalem**:
  Fear not, O Zion, be not **discouraged**!
The LORD, your **God**, is in your midst,
  a mighty **savior**;
he will **rejoice** over you with **gladness**,
  and **renew** you in his **love**,
he will sing **joyfully** because of you,
  as one sings at **festivals**.

READING I   In the midst of this meditative, preparatory season of Advent, this Sunday's readings emphasize exuberant joy at the anticipated coming of the Lord. The prophet Zephaniah makes one of only two appearances in the Sunday cycle of readings with a passage that greatly diverges from the somber tone of the rest of his prophetic book. But his poetry commanding Israel to "exult" fittingly expresses the spirit of Gaudete (Rejoice!) Sunday. Zephaniah mostly predicted judgment, a theme characteristic of the final Sundays of each liturgical year.

But here his words are full of hope and joy. Israel is to "sing" and "be glad" because God comes not to judge, but to save and "renew." Whether joyful or full of dread, God's proclaimed word is always meant to rouse the listener. Your listeners will indeed be moved if you convey the surging energy of the opening lines that communicate the same message three times: "Shout for Joy . . . Sing joyfully . . . Be glad . . . !" You don't need to increase volume, but your intensity must surely build as you command rejoicing and then

announce the reasons why. Be full of the joy you announce and make eye contact as you encourage the assembly to "fear not . . . ." That will slow your delivery and ensure that rather than simply mouthing words, you are sharing your conviction that God truly saves and renews! Again, persuade listeners that God loves them this much.

READING II   This text is often used in scripture proclamation workshops to illustrate the dichotomy that

READING II   Philippians 4:4–7

A reading from the Letter of Saint Paul to the Philippians

Brothers and sisters:
Rejoice in the Lord **always**.
I shall say it **again**: rejoice!
Your **kindness** should be known to **all**.
The Lord is **near**.
Have no **anxiety** at all, but in **everything**,
    by **prayer** and **petition**, with **thanksgiving**,
    make your requests **known** to God.
Then the **peace** of God that surpasses all **understanding**
    will **guard** your **hearts** and **minds** in Christ **Jesus**.

"Rejoice" must sound like rejoicing. Build in intensity from the first to second "rejoice."

This is the heart of the message.

Despite the short phrases, avoid a choppy delivery.

Pause and make eye contact, then speak of a peace that surpasses understanding.

GOSPEL   Luke 3:10–18

A reading from the holy Gospel according to Luke

The **crowds** asked John the **Baptist**,
    "What should we **do**?"
He said to them in **reply**,
    "Whoever has **two** cloaks
    should **share** with the person who has **none**.
And whoever has **food** should do **likewise**."
Even **tax** collectors came to be baptized and **they** said to him,
    "**Teacher**, what should **we** do?"

The narrator is a biased observer who is on John's side.

Short pause to shift from narrator to character voice.

Questions are sincere: answers are direct and challenging.

too often exists between what words mean and how they sound when a lector speaks them. Will you be one of those lectors who says, "Rejoice . . . I shall say it again: rejoice!" in a flat monotone that contradicts the meaning of Paul's words? Capturing the spirit of Paul's words does not mean grinning like a Cheshire cat or bouncing like a clown. Joy can be an inner, deep-felt emotion. But even when subdued, it must not be mistaken for anger, sullenness, or sadness. Eye contact can, again,

be the key to helping you sound like you mean what you say. Try this experiment as you prepare your reading. Look at someone in the face and say "rejoice" without emotion. You and the other will immediately detect the inauthentic tone.

It's from this text that Gaudete Sunday takes its name. Paul writes to a community he held in great esteem, encouraging them (and us!) with one key idea: "The Lord is near." Whether anticipating the coming of Christ at the end of time, or at Christmas, or in the Eucharist, our attitude should be the same: profound joy characterized by

"peace" and the absence of "anxiety." Let your tone convey that deep joy, speaking slowly and with great sincerity as you exhort the assembly to "make [their] requests known." The final line calls for conviction that God will give peace to those who seek Christ.

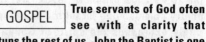 **GOSPEL** **True servants of God often see with a clarity that stuns the rest of us. John the Baptist is one of these and he wastes no words nor does**

He answered them,
"Stop collecting **more** than what is **prescribed**."
Soldiers also asked him,
"And what is it that **we** should do?"
He told them,
"Do not practice **extortion**,
do not **falsely** accuse anyone,
and be **satisfied** with your **wages**."

Now the **people** were filled with **expectation**,
and all were asking in their **hearts**
whether **John** might be the **Christ**.
John **answered** them all, saying,
"**I** am baptizing you with **water**,
but one **mightier** than I is coming.
I am not **worthy** to loosen the **thongs** of his **sandals**.
He will baptize you with the Holy **Spirit** and **fire**.
His **winnowing** fan is in his hand to clear his **threshing** floor
and to gather the **wheat** into his barn,
but the **chaff** he will **burn** with unquenchable **fire**."
Exhorting them in many other ways,
he preached good **news** to the people.

Shift eye contact for each part of the response.

A shift in tone. The crowd wants it to be true!

John's tone is strong and unequivocal.

Make eye contact here.

Pause before last sentence. Then remind them that they've heard "good news."

he stand on ceremony: ". . . share with the person who has none . . . . Stop collecting more than is prescribed . . . . Do not falsely accuse . . . ." Such clarity, and the bluntness that often accompanies it, comes from seeing as God sees, and from knowing that, in God, the future can be quite different from the past. John offers a vision of a new way of being to those classes of people who inquire of him "What should we do?" Don't overdramatize the dialogue. Blunt and unadorned will better capture the spirit of the Baptist. John has filled the people with "expectation." They sense in him the newness, the possibilities, that will be ushered in by the Kingdom of God. So they ask if he is "the Christ." Speak that question with the expectancy and eagerness of the crowd. John's response is unequivocal: "one mightier than I is coming." He speaks with strength, not weakness, about being "unworthy to loosen . . . his sandals." We sense that John, too, is longing for the Christ. Let that longing characterize his description of what the "mightier" one will do when he comes. But the final line says it all: while John's tone is "exhorting," it never stops sounding like "good news!"

4TH SUNDAY OF ADVENT

Lectionary #12

READING I   Micah 5:1–4a

A reading from the Book of the Prophet Micah

Thus says the LORD:
You, Bethlehem-Ephrathah
   too **small** to be among the clans of **Judah**,
from **you** shall come **forth** for me
   one who is to be **ruler** in Israel;
whose **origin** is from of **old**,
   from **ancient** times.
Therefore the Lord will give them **up**, until the time
   when **she** who is to give birth has **borne**,
and the rest of his kindred shall **return**
   to the children of Israel.
He shall stand **firm** and **shepherd** his flock
   by the **strength** of the LORD,
   in the majestic **name** of the LORD, his **God**;
and they shall **remain**, for now his **greatness**
   shall reach to the **ends** of the **earth**;
   he shall be **peace**.

Note that the entire first paragraph is spoken in God's voice.

Imagine helping an insecure youngster, in whom you recognize great potential, to believe what you believe about him/her.

Bethlehem-Ephrathah = BETH-luh-hem-EPH-ruh-thuh

Reverence the memory of David.

The tone is more somber here. Speak with a faster pace until the words "has borne," and then slower until the end of the sentence.

Note the contrasts: he stands "firm," but he also "shepherds"; he "shepherds," but with "strength"; yet the strength is not his own but from "the Lord."

Pause before and after the powerful final line. Speak one word at a time.

READING I   This is the prophet Micah's only appearance in the Sunday Lectionary. During his life, he experienced the military invasion of both parts of the then-divided kingdom established by King David. Despite impending disaster, Micah offers hope of deliverance, and it is Bethlehem, David's birthplace, that is the sign of hope. This small village was overshadowed by the capital city of Jerusalem. But in today's text, God's voice announces to insignificant Bethlehem that out of her will come the ideal king of Israel, her Messiah. The pronoun "you" is twice repeated as if God were saying, "You, yes *you*, Bethlehem!" Then God announces the role that Bethlehem will play in the life of the nation. "From of old, from ancient times" alludes to David and the beginnings of his dynasty from which the anticipated messiah will come, so speak those words with reverence.

"Therefore the Lord will give them up . . . children of Israel" differs in tone and content from what goes before and after. The promise of the messiah is made, but the time of waiting for its fulfillment will not be easy. The Lord will allow Israel and Judah to fall into the hands of other nations until a woman (the mother of the messiah) gives birth to this great ruler. Because these lines focus on those awaiting deliverance and on promises of restoration, they are an important part of this Advent reading.

The description of the coming monarch fuses power and gentleness into one ideal leader. This king will personify peace, not simply bring it. This reading not only reassures us that an ancient promise

READING II   Hebrews 10:5–10

A reading from the Letter to the Hebrews

Brothers and sisters:
When **Christ** came into the **world**, he said:
"**Sacrifice** and **offering** you did not **desire**,
but a **body** you prepared for me;
in **holocausts** and **sin** offerings you took no **delight**.
Then I said, 'As is **written** of me in the **scroll**,
behold, I come to do your **will**, O God.'"

First he says, "**Sacrifices** and **offerings**,
holocausts and **sin** offerings,
you neither **desired** nor **delighted** in."
These are offered according to the **law**.
Then he says, "**Behold**, I come to do your **will**."
He takes away the **first** to establish the **second**.
By this "**will**," we have been **consecrated**
through the offering of the **body** of Jesus **Christ once** for **all**.

Many times your chief task is to lead your listeners "by the hand" to keep them from getting lost in a passage that feels like a maze. This is one of those times.

Your attitude is that of a teacher who presents evidence, then explains what was presented. The tone is that of a classroom lecture, not a first person testimony.

Use a higher pitch to signal you are quoting. Contrast the words "Sacrifice and offering" with "body."

A review of what we've heard so far: "First he says . . . then he says . . . ."

This is a parenthetical aside saying that the old rituals were under the "law" from which Christ's death freed us. Balance the "first (covenant)" with "the second (covenant)."

The "teacher" yields to the "believer." Make an emotional investment: it's more than a summary, it is the author's (and your) declaration of faith.

---

was fulfilled in Jesus; it also fuels our hope that the fullness we await, Christ's glorious manifestation at the second coming, will not disappoint.

READING II In the Bethlehem manger, we perceive the wood of the cross; in the shadow of the cross, we remember the mother placing her naked child in the manger. This reading reminds us that the reason God became human was to save us from our sins. In the last sentence we are told that Christ's willing self-sacrifice is the cause of our salvation.

What precedes are all those aspects of the old law which are presented as not leading to sanctification. The author places words from Psalm 40 in the mouth of Jesus. "Sacrifice and offering . . . holocausts and sin offerings" are probable references to the four chief types of Old Testament sacrifices which the author says are no longer efficacious. From the Psalm we learn that God values obedience over sacrifice; rituals matter, but obedience matters more!

So the theology of this difficult text says: because God no longer delights in the burnt "offerings" and "sacrifices" of the old law, Christ became human (took on the body "prepared for me"), so that through that body he could offer a "sacrifice" of perfect obedience to God's will.

GOSPEL Twice Mary is called "blessed" in this text. The reasons why echo the themes of Advent: Mary bore the Christ child and, in humble obedience, she "believed" (trusted) that God's words to her "would be fulfilled." We don't read this text simply to remember what God did so long ago, but also to recall

GOSPEL   Luke 1:39–45

A reading from the holy Gospel according to Luke

Mary set out
and traveled to the **hill** country in **haste**
to a town of **Judah**,
where she entered the house of **Zechariah**
and greeted **Elizabeth**.
When Elizabeth **heard** Mary's greeting,
the infant **leaped** in her womb,
and Elizabeth, **filled** with the Holy **Spirit**,
cried out in a **loud** voice and said,
*"**Blessed** are you among **women**,
and blessed is the **fruit** of your **womb**.*
And how does this **happen** to **me**,
that the mother of my **Lord** should **come** to me?
For at the moment the sound of your **greeting** reached my **ears**,
the **infant** in my **womb** leaped for **joy**.
Blessed are you who **believed**
that what was **spoken** to you by the Lord
would be **fulfilled**."

Reflect on the dynamic that draws these women together, causing one to rush and the other to react in astonished joy. Suggest the sense of urgency, but don't rush. Take time naming Mary's relatives: Zechariah and Elizabeth.

Narrate with joy and stress "filled with the Holy Spirit."

"Blessed" can be stressed both times it occurs, but the second time with even more intensity.

The joy expressed by the child in her womb is on Elizabeth lips as she speaks.

This is the climax. Does Elizabeth's blessing perhaps include the countless others (your assembly!) who also have trusted in God's word?

that we, too, must continually birth the Christ in our midst and live with sure faith that God's promises to *us* will be fulfilled.

With breathless energy, this reading, full of the images, rhythms, and moods of Advent, speaks of expectant waiting and of joy over the growing promise kicking in a womb; of hope rushing toward fulfillment which though near, is not yet at hand.

Why does Mary hasten to Elizabeth's side? Because she has received an angelic promise and the sign given her as divine assurance is Elizabeth's own pregnancy.

The expectant mothers rejoice not only in each other's presence, but in the divine favor each has received, that each now recognizes in the other.

Elizabeth experiences her child's movement at Mary's appearance as especially significant. This "leaping" establishes from the beginning an intimate connection between Jesus and his precursor, John. Note that it is the prompting of the Holy Spirit that impels Elizabeth to address Mary and her child as "blessed."

Elizabeth's first words to Mary are especially significant. Aware of her own good fortune, Elizabeth recognizes one more blessed than herself. Her earnest question to Mary reveals not only the keenness of her Spirit-filled insight, but also her sincere humility. What sound echoes in her words—an explosion of delight as arms reach out to embrace a cousin, or a slow and muted expression of God's mysterious interaction with human lives?

NATIVITY OF THE LORD: VIGIL

Lectionary #13

READING I   Isaiah 62:1–5

A reading from the Book of the Prophet Isaiah

For **Zion's** sake I will not be **silent**,
    for **Jerusalem's** sake I will not be **quiet**,
until her **vindication** shines forth like the **dawn**
    and her **victory** like a burning **torch**.

Nations shall **behold** your vindication,
    and all the **kings** your **glory**;
you shall be called by a **new** name
    pronounced by the mouth of the LORD.
You shall be a glorious **crown** in the hand of the LORD,
    a **royal** diadem held by your **God**.
No **more** shall people call you "**Forsaken**,"
    or your land "**Desolate**,"
but you shall be called "**My Delight**,"
    and your land "**Espoused**."
For the LORD **delights** in you
    and makes your land his **spouse**.
As a young **man** marries a **virgin**,
    your **Builder** shall marry **you**;
and as a **bridegroom** rejoices in his **bride**
    so shall your **God** rejoice in **you**.

Long-awaited news can be announced loudly, with great energy or softly with real but muted zeal.

Often an idea stated in the first line of a pair of lines is immediately repeated, in different words, in the second line, for example, "not be silent" / "not be quiet"; "vindication . . . like the dawn" / "victory like a burning torch"; "Nations shall behold your vindication" / "kings your glory"; "glorious crown" / "royal diadem." This literary device creates emphasis if you build your intensity from the first to the second expression.

Stress the language that speaks of fulfillment and newness: "vindication," "dawn," "victory," "glory."

Note the intimacy between God and his people: they are held in God's own hands.

The great reversal of fortune God promises is spotlighted by the brief recollection of former "forsaken" and "desolate" times which God says will be "no more!"

Note spousal imagery of the last four couplets. In each pair of lines, second line receives greater stress. Passionate/tender marriage language suggests God's enduring covenant with the chosen people whose repeated infidelities are transformed into the innocence of a "virgin" bride.

READING I | During these weeks of Advent preparation, we have pondered the centuries-long wait of Israel for the messiah. But for those who wait, the time of fulfillment comes. Isaiah paints a vibrant picture of what the day of fulfillment will bring as he offers to people who are weary with waiting a reason to rejoice. Centuries would pass before that fulfillment would actually arrive, yet joyful hope practically explodes from the page. Despite decades of destruction and exile at the hands of foreign invaders, Isaiah insists that the people dream of the glorious events that will accompany the messianic era. He creates a sense of joyous anticipation which you must express in your reading. His images are timely and timeless: a joyous wedding feast, a grand coronation.

The good news flows from the start. "For Jerusalem's sake," Isaiah tells us, God cannot, will not be silent! To a people long deprived of hope, Isaiah announces that hope is justified and fulfillment near! And he does it speaking not for God, but in God's own voice. The exile and all it represented — punishment for infidelity and disobedience — will end and restoration will follow. The metaphors Isaiah employs to express the healing and reconciling work God will accomplish are a name change ("no more shall men call you 'Forsaken' ") and a wedding feast. A name expresses one's identity, so changing names means changing identity. Israel's new name, "My Delight" will be known among the nations! God's intimate love for Israel is further expressed through tender spousal imagery that presents God as the young lover and Israel as the bride.

READING II Acts 13:16–17, 22–25

A reading from the Acts of the Apostles

When **Paul** reached **Antioch** in **Pisidia** and entered
   the **synagogue**,
  he **stood** up, **motioned** with his hand, and said,
   "Fellow **Israelites** and you **others** who are God-fearing, **listen**.
The **God** of this people Israel **chose** our ancestors
  and **exalted** the people during their sojourn
   in the land of **Egypt**.
With uplifted **arm** he **led** them out of it.
Then he removed **Saul** and raised up **David** as **king**;
  of him he **testified**,
   'I have found **David**, son of Jesse, a man after my own **heart**;
  he will carry out my every **wish**.'
From this man's **descendants** God, according to his **promise**,
  has brought to Israel a **savior**, Jesus.
John **heralded** his coming by proclaiming a **baptism** of **repentance**
  to all the people of **Israel**;
  and as John was **completing** his course, he would say,
  'What do you suppose that I **am**? I am not **he**.
Behold, one is coming **after** me;
  I am not **worthy** to unfasten the **sandals** of his **feet**.'"

... synagogue, a setting ... unlike yours.

"Motioned with his hand . . ." is an indication that he's asking them for silence.

Recount the history, keeping in mind where you're headed—Jesus! It's not history for its own sake.

Speak of David with affection and pride, but remember that he's not the main focus of the passage.

This is the climax of the text. Speak with greater energy. Take a pause before "Jesus."

Imagine John trying to convince his followers he is not what they "suppose." Then, as if watching Jesus standing on the opposite shore, speak the last line simply and sincerely.

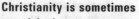

READING II Christianity is sometimes surprisingly concrete, particular, and historical. God makes *choices*—one nation from among others, one king over another; God *works in history*—through human events and through the lives of individual human beings. Playing favorites and getting very involved in human events may not fit a modern notion of appropriate divine behavior, but it is an integral part of the divine portrait presented by the Judeo-Christian scriptures.

Paul was keenly aware of this reality and in today's text he stands in the synagogue responding to an invitation from the officials that anyone with an exhortation for the people should speak. He addresses both Israelites and "God-fearing" non-Israelites with a review of salvation history that serves as an introduction to the more impassioned comments that will follow. Unfortunately, we don't hear Paul's exhortation today, for this pericope (excerpt) ends where the exhortation begins.

Paul's tone may be a bit more reserved than in other passages, but he speaks with authority for the benefit of Israelites who may have heard it all before and for those who are hearing it for the very first time. Your assembly likely includes some for whom this is a review and others who have never heard it before. But like Paul's audience, all can benefit from Paul's review of salvation history.

By alluding to King David, Paul reminds his listeners that the human, political institution of kingship was one of the means God used to protect, sustain, and nourish

GOSPEL Matthew 1:1–25

A reading from the holy Gospel according to Matthew

The book of the **genealogy** of **Jesus Christ**,
  the son of **David**, the son of **Abraham**.

Abraham became the father of **Isaac**,
  Isaac the father of **Jacob**,
  Jacob the father of **Judah** and his brothers.
Judah became the father of **Perez** and **Zerah**,
  whose **mother** was **Tamar**.
Perez became the father of **Hezron**,
  Hezron the father of **Ram**,
  Ram the father of **Amminadab**.
Amminadab became the father of **Nahshon**,
  Nahshon the father of **Salmon**,
  Salmon the father of **Boaz**,
  whose **mother** was **Rahab**.
Boaz became the father of **Obed**,
  whose **mother** was **Ruth**.
Obed became the father of **Jesse**,
  Jesse the father of **David** the **king**.

David became the father of **Solomon**,
  whose **mother** had been the wife of **Uriah**.
Solomon became the father of **Rehoboam**,
  Rehoboam the father of **Abijah**,
  Abijah the father of **Asaph**.
Asaph became the father of **Jehoshaphat**,
  Jehoshaphat the father of **Joram**,
  Joram the father of **Uzziah**.

Don't rush the "litany" of names. Rehearse pronunciations.

Renew your energy every few lines.

Perez = PAYR-ez
Zerah = ZEE-ruh
Tamar = TAY-mahr
Hezron = HEZ-ruhn
Ram = ram
Amminadab = uh-MIN-uh-dab
Nahshon = NAH-shun
Salmon = SAL-muhn
Boaz = BOH-az
Rahab = RAY-hab
Obed = OH-bed
Ruth was the great-grandmother of King David.

Uriah = yoo-RĪ-uh
Rehoboam = ree-huh-BOH-uhm
Abijah = uh-BĪ-juh
Asaph = AY-saf
Jehoshaphat =jeh-HOH-shuh-fat
Joram = JOHR-uhm
Uzziah = yuh-ZĪ-uh
Uzziah was struck with leprosy for usurping the role of priests. See 2 Chronicles 26:16–20.

---

the people throughout their history. We begin to realize that Paul is presenting much more than a history lesson. He is expounding profound theology that sees God woven into the fabric of all of life.

Paul's lesson climaxes in Jesus and John the Baptist. Once again, we hear of the concrete actions of God, taking on human flesh in a particular person and at a particular time and place in history. John, the herald who prepared the way, was one of the great personages of the Advent season just ended, and it is appropriate that we should hear of him again tonight.

Paul quotes John's famous words that perfectly set the stage for the events that we celebrate in this liturgy. John's words also set an agenda both for this Christmas season and for every day of the year: seeing ourselves for who we are and Christ for who he is.

GOSPEL | If the second reading from Paul didn't drive home the point that God works through the "scandal" of particularity, then surely this Gospel passage will. God *chose* not only a

people from whom to draw the messiah, but a particular *family* as well, and that family lineage is unashamedly presented here. Its inclusion accomplishes several theological objectives. First, it makes clear that Jesus is all that Israel is—descended from Abraham, descended from David, descended from saints and sinners, people who have borne the burden of their "election" for many centuries and generations.

Second, it shows that God can use anyone to accomplish the divine plan—Jew and Gentile, insider and outsider, men and women. That last point is obvious to

Jotham = JOH-thuhm

Ahaz = AY-haz

Hezekiah = hez-eh-KĪ-uh

Manasseh = muh-NAS-uh

Mannasseh was Israel's worst king.

Josiah = joh-SĪ-uh

Josiah was one of Israel's best kings, a reformer.

Jechoniah = jek-oh-NĪ-uh

The exile was the nation's greatest trial.

Shealtiel = shee-AL-tee-uhl

Zerubbabel = zuh-ROOB-uh-b*l

Abiud = uh-BĪ-uhd

Eliakim = ee-LĪ-uh-kim

Azor = AY-zohr

Zadok = ZAD-uhk

Achim = AH-kim

Eliud = ee-LĪ-uhd

Eleazar = el-ee-AY-zer

Matthan = MATH-uhn

"Fourteen" is a deliberate redundancy. Stress each recurrence.

Uzziah became the father of **Jotham**,
   Jotham the father of **Ahaz**,
   Ahaz the father of **Hezekiah**.
Hezekiah became the father of **Manasseh**,
   Manasseh the father of **Amos**,
   Amos the father of **Josiah**.
Josiah became the father of **Jechoniah** and his brothers
   at the time of the **Babylonian exile**.

After the Babylonian exile,
   Jechoniah became the father of **Shealtiel**,
   Shealtiel the father of **Zerubbabel**,
   Zerubbabel the father of **Abiud**.
Abiud became the father of **Eliakim**,
   Eliakim the father of **Azor**,
   Azor the father of **Zadok**.
Zadok became the father of **Achim**,
   Achim the father of **Eliud**,
   Eliud the father of **Eleazar**.
Eleazar became the father of **Matthan**,
   Matthan the father of **Jacob**,
   Jacob the father of **Joseph**, the husband of **Mary**.
Of **her** was born **Jesus** who is called the **Christ**.

Thus the total number of **generations**
   from **Abraham** to **David**
   is **fourteen** generations;
   from **David** to the Babylonian **exile**,
   fourteen generations;
   from the Babylonian **exile** to the **Christ**,
   fourteen generations.

us, but it wasn't then. There are five women in the list of Jesus' ancestors, all of them Gentiles (except Mary), and one is a harlot! Unusual circumstances surround each one's marriage and all exhibit amazing initiative, playing significant roles in the unfolding of God's plan.

From the vantage point of proclamation, this genealogy presents one of the great challenges in the Lectionary, tempting some to omit it from the reading. But consider what is lost by excluding it. The genealogy begins Matthew's Gospel

because, like Paul in the reading from Acts, Matthew wants to conjure up the whole of salvation history, implying that to know Jesus one must know the story and characters of the Old Testament. The genealogy is also significant liturgically, for it reinforces the lengthy, protracted, often painful waiting that proceeded the time of fulfillment.

While the genealogy presents Jesus' lineage, it is not simply the history of one nuclear family, but of all people of faith who descend from Abraham, the "father of all believers." Your reading should convey

that awareness. Any family tree will include names that provoke a smile of recognition while others leave one unmoved. But in reading this list, you needn't try to make each name stand out distinct and unique. In fact, the opposite is better. Read with confidence and authority allowing the rhythm of the repetitions to create a chant-like litany, though the familiar names should make you slow down, as images from that character's life color the way you speak the name.

Matthew stresses details of Jesus' conception and the role of Joseph.

Deliver the words "before they lived together" with care about the "delicacy" of the situation.

Stress the words "righteous man." Insert a brief pause before the word "quietly."

The angelic encounter asserts Jesus' divine origin and his messianic destiny.

Take time with the translation of the name "Emmanuel," which is the climax of the reading.

Make a subtle vocal shift for the quotation.

Sustain eye contact after speaking "Jesus."

Now this is how the **birth** of Jesus **Christ** came about.
When his mother **Mary** was betrothed to **Joseph**,
but **before** they lived together,
she was found with **child** through the Holy **Spirit**.
Joseph her **husband**, since he was a **righteous** man,
yet unwilling to **expose** her to **shame**,
decided to divorce her **quietly**.
Such was his **intention** when, **behold**,
the **angel** of the **Lord** appeared to him in a **dream** and said,
"**Joseph**, son of **David**,
do not be **afraid** to take Mary your **wife** into your **home**.
For it is through the Holy **Spirit**
that this child has been **conceived** in her.
She will bear a **son** and you are to name him **Jesus**,
because he will **save** his people from their **sins**."
All this took place to **fulfill**
what the Lord had said through the **prophet**:
Behold, the **virgin** *shall* **conceive** *and bear a* **son**,
and they shall name him **Emmanuel**,
which means "**God** is **with** us."
When Joseph **awoke**,
he **did** as the angel of the Lord had **commanded** him
and took his **wife** into his **home**.
He had no **relations** with her until she bore a **son**,
and he **named** him Jesus.

[Shorter: Matthew 1:18–25]

The birth narrative contrasts with what went before. Here is a story (that should sound like one!) of divine activity: Mary conceives "through the Holy Spirit" and Joseph is counseled by an "angel." Through his careful attention to the details of the conception ("when betrothed . . . but before they lived together"), Matthew is addressing disputes over Jesus' legitimacy.

While Luke highlights Mary's role in the birth of Jesus, Matthew spends more time on Joseph through whom Jesus derives his Davidic lineage—another reason for proclaiming the genealogy. Joseph is "righteous" from the start, but it's the angelic intervention that enables him to embrace God's plan, even if he doesn't completely understand it. It is to Joseph, not Mary, that the angel addresses the "do not be afraid" formula that very often precedes announcements of God's saving intervention. Much more than reassurance to a shaken fiancé, the angel's words to Joseph reassert Jesus' divine origins and his messianic destiny, in which Joseph is now given a central role.

A quote from the prophet Micah announces the coming of "Emmanuel," a name that means "God is with us." This Gospel text reminds us that, in Jesus, God came among us in a unique and unimaginable way, but that miracle was made possible by generations of believers who never lost faith and never abandoned hope.

NATIVITY OF THE LORD: MIDNIGHT

Lectionary #14

READING I   Isaiah 9:1–6

A reading from the Book of the Prophet Isaiah

"Light" is the operative word. Contrast it with "darkness" and "gloom" as the energy and pacing of your reading slowly grow.

The people who walked in **darkness**
   have seen a **great light**;
upon those who dwelt in the land of **gloom**
   a **light** has shone.

Imagine the line without the first as.

You have brought them **abundant** joy
   and great **rejoicing**,
as they **rejoice** before you as at the **harvest**,
   as people make **merry** when dividing **spoils**.

Build energy on each successive phrase (yoke, pole, rod): all three lead to the word "smashed."

For the **yoke** that **burdened** them,
   the **pole** on their **shoulder**,
and the **rod** of their **taskmaster**
   you have **smashed**, as on the day of **Midian**.

"Smashed," "tramped," and "burned" sound like what they mean.

For every **boot** that tramped in **battle**,
   every **cloak** rolled in **blood**,
   will be **burned** as fuel for **flames**.

Speak tenderly and with growing dignity.

For a **child** is born to us, a **son** is given us;
   upon **his** shoulder **dominion** rests.

The titles can be spoken with a bold or quiet energy.

They name him **Wonder-Counselor**, God-**Hero**,
   Father-Forever, **Prince** of **Peace**.

The sense of this sentence is: his dominion, which he exercises from David's throne and over David's kingdom and which he confirms and sustains by judgment and justice both now and forever, is vast and forever peaceful.

His dominion is **vast**
   and forever **peaceful**,

READING I The original meaning of this classic text differs from what our Christian faith and tonight's liturgy allow us to find in it now. This hymn-like text was intended for the coronation ritual that would usher in the reign of a new king, who, it was hoped, would be *the* king, the messiah, who would banish "darkness" by the "light" of his reign. The new King would reign over this land that had known the darkness of conquest and the shame of exile at the hands of the Assyrians. To this afflicted land Isaiah announces an awe-inspiring reversal of fortune personified by "a child . . . a son" who will bear the royal titles — Wonder Counselor, Prince of Peace — always bestowed on kings at the time of coronation.

But in the context of this Christmas liturgy, we hear in Isaiah's words a prophecy fulfilled, a promise kept in the person and ministry of Jesus. We too have "walked in darkness" and on us also a light "has shone." Sin is the darkness that claimed us; Christ, the light that banished the night.

Isaiah likens the joy of the new era to that of harvest festivals and battlefield victory. Neither image may be within your experience, so find your own analogy — some communal experience which spreads excitement even to those not directly involved in the events. The joy of deliverance is often proportionate to the distress that preceded it. Isaiah's brief but powerful allusions (yoke, pole, and rod) recall an odious oppression, which is now mercifully "smashed."

from **David's** throne, and over his **kingdom**,
　　which he **confirms** and **sustains**
by **judgment** and **justice**,
　　both **now** and **forever**.
The **zeal** of the LORD of **hosts** will **do** this!

READING II Titus 2:11–14

The word "Beloved" sets the tone.

This is a birth announcement.

A reading from the Letter of Saint Paul to Titus

Beloved:
The grace of **God** has **appeared**, saving **all**
　　and training us to **reject** godless ways and worldly **desires**

Keep the tone joyful, not scolding.

　　and to live **temperately**, **justly**, and **devoutly** in this age,
as we **await** the blessed **hope**,

Stress the word "appearance" again to parallel the opening line.

　　the **appearance** of the **glory** of our great **God**
and **savior** Jesus **Christ**,
　　who **gave** himself for us to **deliver** us from all **lawlessness**

The word "cleanse" is a baptismal reference.
The word "eager" characterizes the tone of the reading.

and to **cleanse** for himself a people as his **own**,
eager to do what is **good**.

GOSPEL Luke 2:1–14

This is one of the best cadenced texts in the four Gospel accounts.

"In those days" is an elegant and momentous beginning.

A reading from the holy Gospel according to Luke

In those days a **decree** went out from **Caesar Augustus**
　　that the whole **world** should be **enrolled**.
This was the **first** enrollment,
　　when **Quirinius** was governor of **Syria**.

Quirinius = kwih-RIN-ee-uhs

READING II　The entire Christian mystery is present in every feast and the solemnity of the Nativity of the Lord is no different. This brief reading alludes to Christ's birth at Bethlehem ("the grace of God has appeared"), his saving self-sacrifice at Calvary ("who gave himself for us"), and his future coming in glory ("we await the . . . appearance of the glory of our great God"). The reading begins like a birth announcement—great news, especially because the child born at Christmas is born in each of us who are

made in his image and likeness. This line calls for the same joy heard in Isaiah's jubilant declaration of the arrival of light!

God's coming has consequences for those who believe. The appearance of grace not only saves, but also "trains" us to reject those things that are born of darkness. Paul tells us what we can do as we await the glorious return of Christ.

The entire reading is one 75-word sentence. Because of its length, read slowly, pausing and maintaining a joyful tone. As we celebrate the "first coming," we are reminded of the second. "The

appearance of the glory" echoes Paul's opening line and draws a connection between the two comings. Help your listeners hear the parallel. The words "gave himself" in the final lines refers to Christ's self-sacrifice and thus points to the destiny of this manger-child, a reminder of death even as we celebrate birth. The word "eager" in the last line suggests the tone of the entire reading, telling us not only how to read, but how to respond to the appearance of grace.

Jesus' royal lineage comes through his adoptive father, Joseph. Don't rush the city names.

So **all** went to be enrolled, **each** to his own **town**.
And Joseph **too** went up from Galilee from the town of **Nazareth**
   to **Judea**, to the city of **David** that is called **Bethlehem**,
   because he was of the **house** and **family** of David,
   to be enrolled with **Mary**, his **betrothed**, who was with **child**.
While they were **there**,
   the **time** came for her to have her **child**,
   and she gave **birth** to her firstborn **son**.

Speak slowly and simply. Let the words do their work.

She wrapped him in **swaddling** clothes and laid him in a **manger**,
   because there was no **room** for them in the **inn**.

Now there were **shepherds** in that region living in the **fields**
   and keeping the **night** watch over their **flock**.

Use a bit faster pacing to suggest the sudden appearance and the fearful reaction.

The **angel** of the **Lord** appeared to them
   and the **glory** of the Lord **shone** around them,
   and they were struck with **great fear**.
The **angel** said to them,

The angel calms fear by announcing "good news of great joy." What does that suggest about your tone and energy?

   "Do not be **afraid**;
   for **behold**, I proclaim to you **good** news of great **joy**
   that will be for **all** the people.
For **today** in the city of **David**

Stress the words "savior," "Christ," and "Lord."

   a **savior** has been born for you who is **Christ** and **Lord**.
And this will be a **sign** for you:

Don't rush. You don't want to waste a single word!

   you will find an **infant** wrapped in **swaddling** clothes
   and lying in a **manger**."
And **suddenly** there was a **multitude** of the heavenly host
    with the angel,
   praising **God** and saying:
    "**Glory** to God in the **highest**
      and on earth **peace** to those on whom his **favor** rests."

GOSPEL In Luke's Gospel, grace appears despite political forces that would impede it and world leaders who might find it threatening. Luke's formal and poetically cadenced introduction sets a grand tone worthy of the Isaiah prophecy that precedes it. To bring new life to this familiar story, take notice of the details and contrasts that over-familiarity with the story may have caused us to overlook. This "child of the house of David," who did not even merit a

room in the inn, was instead "laid in a manger." Although angels announce his birth, the only humans told of it are lowly shepherds who, like Mary, react with fear when the angel appears. "Do not be afraid" is the angel's immediate exhortation, an oft-used sacred formula that invariably signals the announcement of God's saving intervention. Notice also the royal personages (Caesar, Quirinius) the census that sets the world in motion ("all went to be enrolled"), and the obscure village of Nazareth contrasted with Judea and Bethlehem, the

birthplace of the Davidic dynasty. The contrasts are striking, and taking time to note the details as you read should both slow and color the story.

No human speaks in this passage, only the angel and the heavenly host. But Luke's narrative voice is heard throughout—the voice of a faith-filled believer.

NATIVITY OF THE LORD: DAWN

Lectionary #15

READING I   Isaiah 62:11–12

A short reading requires a slower pace.

Proclaim the first word "See" as if it were "Behold!"

Stress the words "reward" and "recompense," not the prepositions.

Build energy from "holy people" to "redeemed . . . ."

"Frequented" is unusual and unexpected. Stress it with a joyful inflection, then *ritardando* (gradual slowing to the end).

A reading from the Book of the Prophet Isaiah

See, the LORD proclaims
    to the **ends** of the **earth**:
say to daughter **Zion**,
    your **savior** comes!
Here is his **reward** with him,
    his **recompense** before him.
They shall be called the **holy** people,
    the **redeemed** of the LORD,
and **you** shall be called "**Frequented**,"
    a **city** that is not **forsaken**.

READING I   Echoing the joy of exiles returning to their homeland, and proclaiming the euphoria of pilgrims visiting the rebuilt temple at Jerusalem, this short passage bubbles with images of restoration and renewal. The reproach of former days is gone. It is God who announces this, for it is God who has so radically reversed the people's fortune. No longer abandoned, the holy city will now be "Frequented." It shall know the sound of laughter and rejoicing for the holy people of God are returning accompanied by their savior. Though originally celebrating Israel's deliverance from Babylonian captivity, in the setting of this dawn Christmas liturgy, we apply those themes of revitalization and salvation to the birth of Jesus.

This brief text is a song, a poem that requires your slowest pacing. Like music, poetry stretches and fills more time than prose speech. You have few words, so use all of them ("daughter," "savior," "recompense," "redeemed," "frequented") and give them the intensity and rhythm of poetic recitation, allowing the images extra time to do their work.

READING II   It's Christmas Day, but we celebrate more than the birth of a baby. Paul makes clear what was born for us on Christmas Day: salvation, which came about not through any work of our own, but through God's "mercy." This act of God makes possible our own rebirth

READING II Titus 3:4–7

A reading from the Letter of Saint Paul to Titus

Announce salvation, then the reason why.

Beloved:
When the **kindness** and generous **love**
   of God our savior **appeared**,
not because of any righteous **deeds** we had done
   but because of his **mercy**,
he **saved** us through the bath of **rebirth**
   and **renewal** by the Holy **Spirit**,
whom he **richly** poured out on us
   through **Jesus Christ** our savior,
so that we might be **justified** by his grace
   and become **heirs** in hope of eternal **life**.

Use *ritardando* (gradual slowing to the end) with the words ". . . of his mercy."

Vocally connect the first clause ("When the kindness . . . appeared") with the third clause ("he saved us through . . . Holy Spirit"). The parenthetical clause in-between, however, is also important, so don't rush.

Pause after the word "Spirit" above and vocally build from one clause to the other, slowing on the words "hope of eternal life."

through the "bath" of baptism and the outpouring of the Holy Spirit. At any moment of the liturgical year, we contemplate not only the feast at hand, but the entirety of the Christian mystery. And so on this solemnity of the Nativity of the Lord we can speak of the Holy Spirit, poured out anew and fully through Jesus Christ our Savior. Paul carefully reiterates why these things occurred—that we might be "justified" and made "heirs of eternal life." Yes, it's Christmas, and our thoughts turn to

manger and magi, but what we celebrate is the fullness of what was inaugurated on this solemnity by the kind and generous love of God: "grace," "hope," and "eternal life." You are proclaiming Christ's birth in this text just as surely as if you were reading today's Gospel from Luke. But you are also announcing that the Christian mystery is happening within us. Announce that good news with joy and profound gratitude.

GOSPEL This Gospel story begins and ends with shepherds who hear and respond, witness, and announce. Like Mary, they believe that the word spoken to them will be fulfilled. After witnessing its fulfillment in the person of an infant occupying a manger, they go forth in confidence and faith, "glorifying and praising God." Besides the angels, it is shepherds who first "amaze" others with the Good News of the birth of the savior. Once again, Christ's coming changes all of

GOSPEL   Luke 2:15–20

A reading from the holy Gospel according to Luke

When the **angels** went away from them to **heaven**,
  the **shepherds** said to one another,
  "Let us **go**, then, to **Bethlehem**
  to **see** this thing that has taken place,
  which the **Lord** has made **known** to us."
So they went in **haste** and found **Mary** and **Joseph**,
  and the **infant** lying in the **manger**.
When they **saw** this,
  they made known the **message**
  that had been **told** them about this child.
All who **heard** it were **amazed**
  by what had been **told** them by the **shepherds**.
And **Mary kept** all these things,
  reflecting on them in her **heart**.
Then the shepherds **returned**,
  glorifying and **praising** God
  for all they had **heard** and **seen**,
  just as it had been **told** to them.

You're not announcing the departure of an airplane. This is miraculous.

Speak the shepherds' words with enthusiastic energy.

Pause after "Mary and Joseph," and then speak the words "and the baby!" as if suddenly seeing the child. (It's only the "infant" who's lying in the manger!)

Don't rush. Speak as if the words were sinking in and astonishing you.

An earlier translation rendered "kept" as "treasured." Give "kept" that nuance. Pause between "these things" and "reflecting."

The shepherd's mood is joyous. Differentiate "heard" (expectation) and "seen" (fulfillment).

life and reverses expectations. These lowly (some would say *contemptible*) shepherds, prove themselves to be model disciples. Having heard the angelic announcement, they don't tarry, but proceed "in haste" to the manger. Faith propels them and faith opens their eyes to the infant lying in a bed of hay. They not only see, they *understand* the angelic announcement that this is the Christ. The awe and amazement with which the shepherds first reacted to the angels' appearance is now shared by "all"! It's a day of miracles in which we ponder one of the greatest mysteries—God among us! And we see the array of responses: the amazement of "all" who heard the message, Mary's quiet reflecting on these things "in her heart," and the shepherds' "glorifying and praising" of God for "all they had heard and seen."

NATIVITY OF THE LORD: DAY

Lectionary #16

READING I   Isaiah 52:7–10

A reading from the Book of the Prophet Isaiah

Proclaim slowly, with growing energy. "Feet" represent the whole person.

Proclaim slowly: each phrase is a separate thought. Distinguish them by visualizing a different image for each.

Pause before the word "Hark." Don't overstress the word.

The words "directly" and "before their eyes" are an intentional redundancy. Stress *both* expressions.

The chorus of joy widens. Stress the words "ruins" and "redeems" instead of "Jerusalem."

The last four lines are a summary and a promise, reminding us of what God has done and what God will do.

How **beautiful** upon the **mountains**
　　are the **feet** of him who brings **glad tidings**,
announcing **peace**, bearing good **news**,
　　announcing **salvation**, and saying to **Zion**,
"Your **God** is **King**!"

Hark! Your sentinels raise a cry,
　　together they **shout** for **joy**,
for they see **directly**, before their **eyes**,
　　the LORD **restoring** Zion.
Break out together in **song**,
　　O **ruins** of Jerusalem!
For the LORD **comforts** his people,
　　he **redeems** Jerusalem.
The LORD has **bared** his holy arm
　　in the sight of all the **nations**;
all the ends of the **earth** will **behold**
　　the **salvation** of our **God**.

READING I   This triumphant hymn celebrates the end of exile and God's restoration of Israel. The prophet exults at the sight of the Lord leading a jubilant people back to a ruined Jerusalem, which now will be restored to its former glory. This proclamation of good news can be compared to the angelic declaration to the shepherds at Bethlehem. In this liturgy, that angelic message is clearly linked to Isaiah's poetry. Salvation has come; God's eternal reign has dawned. Whether spoken from the mountains or hovering over a humble stable, that kind of announcement generates enthusiastic energy and great hope.

Isaiah's swift and nimble messenger bounds the hills, leaving in his wake only footprints and words of peace. The tidings are so wonderful that even the herald is made beautiful by them, and the joy of the herald is picked up by the "sentinels" who recognize that God is indeed restoring Zion (Jerusalem). Then, even the scattered stones of ruined Jerusalem are urged to join the jubilation, which eventually extends even to "the ends of the earth."

Isaiah's prophecy announces both a spiritual and a concrete reality, and both warrant great excitement. Perhaps it is saints and poets who best perceive the spiritual dimensions of God's salvation, but who couldn't rejoice over the presumed-dead victims of an earthquake suddenly emerging from the rubble. That's the kind of miracle being celebrated here—and more! God is not only delivering people from exile and rebuilding their city, but he returns with them to establish a home among them forever. Isaiah's words invite

READING II   Hebrews 1:1–6

A reading from the Letter to the Hebrews

"Partial" means "incomplete." Distinguish "partial" from "various."

Contrast "in these last days" with "In times past."

Brothers and sisters:
In times **past**, God spoke in **partial** and **various** ways
   to our **ancestors** through the **prophets**;
   in these **last** days, he has spoken to us through the **Son**,
   whom he made **heir** of all **things**
   and **through** whom he created the **universe**,
      who is the **refulgence** of his **glory**,
      the very **imprint** of his **being**,
      and who **sustains** all things by his mighty **word**.

Probably based on a liturgical hymn of praise. Continue building intensity to the end of the paragraph.

When he had accomplished **purification** from **sins**,
      he took his **seat** at the right **hand** of the **Majesty** on **high**,
      as far **superior** to the **angels**
      as the **name** he has inherited is more **excellent** than theirs.

"Accomplished purification" means our salvation.

Assert the superiority of Christ over the angels.

For to **which** of the angels did God ever say:
   *You are my **son**; this day I have **begotten** you?*
Or again:

Jesus' "inherited" name is "son." Assert the uniqueness of that relationship to God.

   *I will be a **father** to him, and he shall be a **son** to me?*
And **again**, when he leads the **firstborn** into the world, he says:
   *Let all the **angels** of God **worship** him.*

Speak with love. Don't let the ending be anticlimactic.

---

us into the unimaginable wonder of God's presence among us.

READING II The second reading and Gospel exhibit a decidedly theological character. Given the narrative aspects of the solemnity, that might seem a bit odd, but for Christmas Day the Lectionary provides readings that focus on the divine and preexistent nature of Christ, a wonderful complement to the colorful birth narratives of the other Nativity liturgies.

The letter to the Hebrews is less a letter than a written homily. Its author calls it a "message of encouragement" (13:22) directed at Christians who are in danger of losing their faith in hopes of rekindling their faded zeal. That's the historical situation; the liturgical context is the great solemnity of the Lord's nativity, a most fitting time to dwell on the preeminence of Christ who is superior to every angelic being and God's greatest gift to the world.

The author contrasts God's past dialogue with people, which was "partial"

with God's full and climactic communication through the living Word, Jesus "the Son." The word "Son" leaps from the page and becomes the key to the entire text. It will require stress each time it recurs. The litany of the Son's attributes that follows ("made heir . . . through whom he created . . . refulgence of his glory . . . the very imprint . . . who sustains all things") describe his irreplaceable role in God's plan of salvation.

Make your proclamation a joyous acknowledgement of these truths rather than a lawyer's or preacher's attempt at

GOSPEL John 1:1–18

A reading from the holy Gospel according to John

There is a preexistence theme in this Gospel reading that echoes Genesis. Proclaim it slowly.

> In the **beginning** was the **Word**,
>> and the **Word** was with **God**,
>> and the Word **was** God.
> He was in the **beginning** with God.
> **All** things came to be **through** him,
>> and without him **nothing** came to be.

This is one time where prepositions need stress.

"Life" indicates *all* of life, including yours.

> What came to be through him was **life**,
>> and this life was the **light** of the human **race**;
>> the light **shines** in the darkness,
>> and the darkness has not **overcome** it.

Shift your tone to signal a new subject.

> A man named **John** was sent from **God**.
> He came for **testimony**, to testify to the **light**,
>> so that **all** might **believe** through him.
> **He** was not the light,
>> but came to **testify** to the light.
> The **true** light, which enlightens **everyone**,
>> was **coming** into the world.

Again, stress the prepositions.

> He was **in** the world,
>> and the world came to **be** through him,
>> but the world did not **know** him.
> He came to what was his **own**,
>> but his own **people** did not **accept** him.

Speak without judgment. Stress with awe what Christ made possible: becoming children of God.

---

persuasion, which was the author's original purpose in writing. Apparently there was some question regarding the preexistent Christ's superiority over the angels which the author seeks to put to rest. After all, the author asks, which of the angels did God ever call "my son"? Speak the closing lines as a father speaking with love, warmth, and pride of his new and firstborn son.

GOSPEL | This Gospel contemplates the great mystery of God's

self disclosure which began with creation, continued in the history of Israel, and culminates in the life and ministry of Jesus, the Christ. John's prologue was probably an early Christian hymn, perhaps to Wisdom. But though the hymn expounds profound theology, it rings with praise. Even the asides about John the Baptist, which were perhaps later insertions into the poetic text, assert Christ's supremacy.

Utilizing a literary form called staircase parallelism, (where the last word of one phrase becomes the first word of the

next) this beautifully balanced prologue introduces the dominant themes of the Gospel according to John: Christ's preexistence, life, light and darkness, the world, and witness. Stress those topics, for they are the themes that will dominate the life and ministry of the Word made flesh.

The opening line, of course, is an intentional echo of Genesis, reminding us that God's self-communication is nothing new. Active from the beginning and the source of all life, the word is also light for all. Though shining in a darkened world, darkness has not overcome the light.

There should be a growing intensity on the "not," "nor," and "but" phrases.

But to those who **did** accept him
    he gave **power** to become **children** of **God**,
    to those who believe in his **name**,
    who were born not by **natural** generation
    nor by **human** choice nor by a **man's** decision
    but of **God**.

Speak as if you were witnessing the birth.

And the **Word** became **flesh**
    and made his **dwelling** among us,
    and we saw his **glory**,
    the glory as of the **Father's** only **Son**,
    full of **grace** and **truth**.

This is another aside. Speak with conviction and slowly.

John **testified** to him and **cried** out, saying,
    "This was he of whom I said,
    'The one who is coming **after** me ranks **ahead** of me
    because he existed **before** me.'"

Recall the "fullness" of which you and your parish have partaken.

From his **fullness** we have all received,
    grace in place of **grace**,

Contrast "law" with "grace," and "Moses" with "Jesus."

    because while the **law** was given through **Moses**,
    grace and **truth** came through Jesus **Christ**.
No one has ever **seen** God.
The only **Son**, **God**, who is at the Father's **side**,

The closing speaks of the deep relationship between Father and Son.

    has **revealed** him.

[Shorter: John 1:1–5, 9–14]

Struggle between the light and the darkness into which he was born persists to the point that his own people did not know or accept him. He does not force himself on those who reject him, but those who accept him he makes "children of God."

This reading clearly highlights the Baptist's role as a witness to Christ, an apt reminder that our calling and John's are one: that through us others might believe. The second mention of John reinforces the importance of witness and testimony.

The evangelist speaks of the Word becoming flesh as if he were watching the birth of a child. These classic lines deserve your best reading. Perhaps the feeling is the joy-mixed-with-fear emotion we call awe, or maybe what's called for is assertive testimony about God's willingness to live "among us" where we experience "his glory." Whether you choose joy, pride, or gratitude, let the same emotion characterize the Baptist's assertion that "the one . . . coming after me ranks ahead of me."

In the last paragraph, "law" and "Moses" contrast with "grace" and "Jesus."

Avoid sounding didactic here; instead, stress how fortunate we are to have received the revelation of God in Jesus.

Great poetry invites us back into its chambers over and over again. The poetry of this prologue loses nothing from being familiar; only our lack of confidence in its power could diminish its ability to move and inspire.

HOLY FAMILY OF JESUS, MARY, AND JOSEPH

Lectionary #17

READING I   1 Samuel 1:20–22, 24–28

A reading from the first Book of Samuel

In those days **Hannah conceived**, and at the end of her **term**
> bore a **son**
>> whom she called **Samuel**, since she had **asked** the LORD
>> for him.

The next time her husband **Elkanah** was going up
> with the rest of his **household**
>> to offer the customary **sacrifice** to the LORD and to fulfill
>> his **vows**,
> Hannah did **not** go, **explaining** to her husband,
> "Once the child is **weaned**,
> I will **take** him to **appear** before the **LORD**
> and to **remain** there **forever**;
> I will offer him as a perpetual **nazirite**."

Once Samuel was **weaned**, Hannah brought him up with her,
> along with a three-year-old **bull**,
> an **ephah** of flour, and a skin of **wine**,
> and **presented** him at the temple of the LORD in **Shiloh**.

After the boy's **father** had sacrificed the young **bull**,
> Hannah, his mother, approached **Eli** and said:
> "**Pardon**, my lord!
As you **live**, my lord,
> I am the woman who stood **near** you here, **praying** to the LORD.

"In those days . . ." culminates a long period of waiting. "At the end . . . term" suggests the period of her entire pregnancy.

Pause, renew energy, and continue.
Elkanah = el-KAY-nah

She's anticipating the time when she will have to give up her son, but mercifully the time is not yet!

nazarite = NAZ-uh-right

Again, a long period of time has elapsed. These are sacrificial offerings, not a shopping list
Ephah = EE-fah
Shiloh = SHĪ-loh

She addresses the very priest who had prophesied her pregnancy, speaking with courage and resolve. Imagine leaving a child in these circumstances and you'll understand the poignancy of this final line.

There is a choice of readings today. Speak with the liturgy coordinator or homilist to find out which readings will be used.

READING I   Instituted by Pope Leo XIII, this feast focuses on the family of Nazareth as a model for our own Christian families. These readings do more than teach right behavior in families. They make present within the worshipping assembly the healing power of God and they provide visions of family life lived in accord with God's perfect will.

1 SAMUEL. Desperate because of her sterility, Hannah had gone to the sanctuary at Shiloh and there begged God's mercy. She vowed that if God gave her a son, she would "give him to the Lord for as long as he lives." Today's reading begins with the joyous announcement of God's answer to that prayer. Hannah's gratitude is in every line, for by blessing her with a child, God has also removed the reproach and humiliation of sterility. Hannah forgoes a pilgrimage to Shiloh, planning instead to go when the child is older. There she will dedicate him to the Lord and leave him there forever as a Nazirite—one who is consecrated to God and who lives a strict ascetic lifestyle.

You can sense Hannah's desire to mother this special child for as long as possible. But eventually she keeps her promise and brings him to Eli, where, with exemplary trust, she leaves him in the care of others to be trained in the ways of the Lord. There is clear kinship between Hannah and Mary, the mother of Jesus, especially in their trust in God and the

"I prayed for this **child**, and the LORD **granted** my request.
Now I, in turn, **give** him to the LORD;
    as long as he **lives**, he shall be **dedicated** to the LORD."
Hannah **left** Samuel **there**.

Or:

READING I   Sirach 3:2–6, 12–14

A reading from the Book of Sirach

God sets a **father** in honor over his **children**;
    a **mother's** authority he confirms over her **sons**.
Whoever **honors** his father **atones** for sins,
    and **preserves** himself from them.
When he prays, he is **heard**;
    he stores up riches who **reveres** his mother.
Whoever **honors** his father is **gladdened** by children,
    and, when he prays, is **heard**.
Whoever reveres his father will live a **long life**;
    he who obeys his father brings **comfort** to his mother.

My son, take care of your father when he is **old**;
    grieve him not as long as he **lives**.
Even if his mind fail, be **considerate** of him;
    revile him **not** all the days of his life;
kindness to a father will not be **forgotten**,
    firmly planted against the **debt** of your sins
    —a house raised in **justice** to you.

Sirach = SEER-ak

This is a collection of proverbs commanding respect of *both* **parents. Each proverb stands on its own.**

This is the first chiasmus, perhaps addressed to adolescents in the assembly.

This is the second chiasmus. Address the young-adult children in the assembly.

This is the third chiasmus.

Address the adult children of aging parents. Your tone conveys the care and solicitude owed the elderly.

The last two lines refer back to "kindness to a father." They make more sense if you imagine the words "it will be" before each line.

---

great love they lavish on their sons. Much of the text is spoken in Hannah's voice, which is redolent of her faith and sacrifice. Her words as she offers her child to the Lord are brave and emblematic. Are not all parents asked to see their children as gifts from God who, first and foremost, belong to God?

SIRACH. The Book of Sirach belongs to the body of biblical writing known as Wisdom literature, and although it does not appear in the Hebrew Scriptures or in Bibles of non-Catholic Christians, it has always held a special place in Catholic teaching and liturgy. Sirach presents here a commentary on the fourth commandment, making its injunction to "honor" father and mother the hallmark of the right relationship of children to parents. The verb "honor" and its close synonym "revere" appear five times in the text. Note that Sirach uses the word to suggest "showing respect for," "being a credit to," and "accept responsibility for," rather than "complying with the demands of." Since the Holy Family is our model today, we should understand "honor" in the way we'd expect Jesus to give it and Joseph and Mary to receive it. The multiple repetitions of the word present a challenge to the lector, so take advantage of the common biblical literary device called chiasmus found here. Chiasmus is a cross parallel that reverses the word order of two balanced ideas. Ordinary parallels look like this: the Lord (a) sets a father (b) over his children; (c) God (a) confirms a mother's authority (b) over her sons (c). A chiasmus reverses our expectation of a, b, c, a, b, c, sequence and gives us a, b, c, b, a, c instead, sending the focus to the

READING II 1 John 3:1–2, 21–24

A reading from the first Letter of Saint John

"Beloved" sets the tone.

Beloved:
See what **love** the Father has **bestowed** on us
　　that we may be called the **children** of **God**.
And so we **are**.

Speak in an awed, joyful, and grateful tone here.

The reason the **world** does not **know** us
　　is that it did not know **him**.

Read as an explanation contrasting "us" and "him," and then pause before the word "Beloved."

Beloved, we are God's **children now**;
　　what we **shall** be has not yet been **revealed**.

Again, speak with grateful wonder.

We **do** know that when it **is** revealed we shall be **like** him,
　　for we shall **see** him as he **is**.

This much we do know: we will be *like* him; we will *see* him!

Beloved, if our **hearts** do not **condemn** us,
　　we have **confidence** in God and **receive** from him
　　　　whatever we ask,
　　because we keep his **commandments** and do what **pleases** him.

There is a shift in tone here. Speak with confident energy. This is an "if/then" clause, even though the "then" is missing.

And his commandment is **this**:
　　we should **believe** in the **name** of his **Son**, Jesus **Christ**,
　　and **love** one another just as he **commanded** us.

There are two commandments named: belief and love.

Those who **keep** his commandments **remain** in him, and **he** in **them**,

The consequences of keeping commandments: we remain in him; he remains in us.

　　and the way we **know** that he remains in us
　　is from the **Spirit** he **gave** us.

Conclude with another joyful and confident announcement.

Or:

---

phrase that's out of sequence. Notice how in all three instances, the chiasmus shifts the focus to the relationship of children and their mothers, making an otherwise more father-oriented text more balanced.

　　Remember you are teaching the children of all ages in your assembly, reminding them of both their responsibilities and the rewards that accrue to those who honor parents. The first couplet might be addressed to youngsters and adolescents still under the direct authority of their parents; the next six lines might be aimed at young adults leaving the nest or already

parents themselves; the last three couplets speak to adult children of their duties to aging parents. In a society where growing numbers of elderly are alone or forgotten, these lines might be the most important. But throughout, you must challenge and persuade.

READING II **1 JOHN.** John describes God's love for us as the love of a Father for his children. Understanding the healthy and loving relationships of children and parents gives us a glimpse of

God's unconditional and transforming love for us. And, as wonderful as that may be, it is only a shadow of what we'll experience when we see God face to face. Though the specifics of that new life are not yet revealed, we know this much: we will become like God and we will understand God, not like now as through a veil, but fully.

　　Our relationship with God can be viewed as a circle of love that provides the motivation for the kind of behavior that characterizes right relationship with God, our Father. First, God loved us and made us

READING II   Colossians 3:12–21

A reading from the Letter of Saint Paul to the Colossians

Speak out of your recognition that God has first loved you.

Brothers and sisters:
Put on, as God's chosen ones, **holy** and **beloved**,
  heartfelt compassion, kindness, humility, gentleness,
    and patience,

Don't drone on in shopping list fashion. The sentences speak of healing and peace, important themes for families. Address each virtue to a different face in the assembly. These are instructions about how to live out peace in family and all relationships. Speak with authority and concern.

  bearing with one another and **forgiving** one another,
  if one has a **grievance** against another;
  as the Lord has **forgiven** you, so must **you** also do.

Here is the most important virtue!

And over all these put on **love**,
  that is, the bond of **perfection**.

Don't throw away this important exhortation.

And let the **peace** of Christ control your hearts,
  the **peace** into which you were also called in **one** body.

The pace should quicken a bit here.

And be thankful.
Let the word of Christ dwell in you **richly**,
  as in all wisdom you **teach** and **admonish** one another,
  singing **psalms**, **hymns**, and spiritual **songs**
  with **gratitude** in your hearts to God.

Proclaim more slowly here, with great sincerity and maintaining eye contact.

And whatever you do, in **word** or in **deed**,
  do **everything** in the name of the Lord **Jesus**,
  giving **thanks** to God the Father **through** him.

Give even and equal emphasis to each instruction, picturing those whom your words are meant to help.

Wives, be subordinate to your husbands,
  as is **proper** in the Lord.
Husbands, **love** your wives,
  and avoid **any** bitterness toward them.

"children." In response, we keep God's commandments, believing in Christ, the Son, and loving one another. The result is that we have confidence to ask of God whatever we need.

John describes how we become the human family on earth that we are meant to be: we trust in God's Holy Spirit, we believe in our own goodness as God's children, we believe in God's Son, Jesus, who came to save us, and we respond in love by loving one another, including the outcast, the stranger, and the enemy, who all are part of God's family. But just as the world

failed to recognize Jesus as God's Son, so it will fail to recognize us as God's children. The more we imitate Jesus, the more we anticipate the fullness of life promised us in Christ, and the brighter the light of our witness.

COLOSSIANS. The hardest place to live out the exhortations Paul offers here is in the family. It's easier to express "kindness, humility, gentleness and patience" when the world is looking; in the privacy of the home, there's often another side of us that prevails. But Paul is asking only

that we give what has first been given us. After all, he says, we are "God's chosen . . . holy and beloved." Awareness of that grace is what must fuel our commitment to live holy lives—"bearing with one another and [hardest of all!] forgiving one another." Again, knowledge that God has first forgiven us is what calls and compels us to forgive others. Paul then commands us to put a layer of "love" over all the other virtues because in any relationship kindness, humility, patience, and the rest will surely fail at times. But if love remains, it will remind us who we are, call us back to

Children, obey your parents in **everything**,
    for this is **pleasing** to the Lord.
Fathers, do **not** provoke your children,
    so they may not become **discouraged**.

[Shorter: Colossians 3:12–17]

GOSPEL   Luke 2:41–52

A reading from the holy Gospel according to Luke

Accent the family's observance of annual ritual.	Each **year** Jesus' **parents** went to **Jerusalem** for the feast of **Passover**,

Each **year** Jesus' **parents** went to **Jerusalem** for the feast
    of **Passover**,
    and when he was **twelve** years old,
    they went **up** according to festival **custom**.
After they had **completed** its days, as they were **returning**,
    the boy Jesus remained **behind** in Jerusalem,
    but his **parents** did not **know** it.
Thinking that he was in the **caravan**,
    they journeyed for a **day**
    and **looked** for him among their **relatives** and **acquaintances**,
    but not **finding** him,
    they **returned** to Jerusalem to **look** for him.
After **three days** they **found** him in the **temple**,
    sitting in the midst of the **teachers**,
    listening to them and asking them **questions**,
    and all who **heard** him were **astounded**
    at his **understanding** and his **answers**.

Margin notes (left column):

His age is an important point.

Enjoy the storytelling and the suspense that's created.

"Thinking" is an important word here.

Their anxiety starts to build now.

Stretch the words "after three days."

---

our true natures, revive the virtues, and enable us to go the extra mile.

Paul says we are to "put on" the virtues, an allusion to the robing of the catechumens as they emerge from the baptismal waters. When speaking those words, you are asking your listeners to put on those virtues that will transform them into the image of Christ. Both first and second paragraphs end with an admonition to be thankful, for gratitude should always characterize the Christian life. Each paragraph offers a formula for living in gratitude.

The final, controversial paragraph stresses family members' responsibilities, not their superiority over one another. Submission, obedience, and love are to be done "in the Lord," which means the first two (submission, obedience) are not slavish or void of respect, and the last (love) is not free of duties or its own brand of submission. The household code articulated in these lines is derived from Stoic teaching and reflects a Greek view of spousal/family relationships, which does not play well

in our culture. The Christian element of this passage is expressed not in calls for submission, but by the exhortation to forgive "as the Lord has forgiven you," by the phrase "in the Lord," and in the injunction to "love."

GOSPEL   On this "family" Sunday, the Gospel tells us that Jesus grew up in a home marked by pious observance of Jewish law. It shows us family interaction characterized by love,

The parents, too, are amazed.

What is the tone of Mary's voice: disappointment, anger, relief?

Jesus doesn't acknowledge her anxiety.

Remember that there are three things to narrate: Jesus obeys; Mary treasures; Jesus advances. Proclaim with affection.

When his parents **saw** him,
   they were **astonished**,
   and his **mother** said to him,
   "**Son**, why have you **done** this to us?
Your father and I have been **looking** for you with great **anxiety**."
And **he** said to them,
   "**Why** were you looking for me?
Did you not **know** that I must be in my **Father's house**?"
But they did not **understand** what he said to them.
He went **down** with them and came to **Nazareth**,
   and was **obedient** to them;
   and his **mother** kept all these things in her **heart**.
And Jesus advanced in **wisdom** and **age** and **favor**
   before **God** and **man**.

patience, parental respect, and filial submission—in fact, all of the virtues enumerated in the Colossians text. Mary and Joseph must even forgive the worry Jesus caused them and live with a wonder they cannot fully understand, a wonder every family sometimes encounters in the mysterious interactions of domestic life.

Before anything else, this is a story. For you, as a storyteller, the Christology embedded here is secondary to the details of the narrative. In this day when images of missing children adorn milk cartons and buses, a lost boy story elicits added poignancy. But Luke begins with reserve. The search among the relatives suggests a growing anxiety that hasn't yet reached the point of posting pictures.

Jesus is found amazing his listeners in the temple. Mary and Joseph, too, are astonished at the sight of him, but for different reasons. Mary asks why he has done this, clearly implying intentionality on his part. Jesus' demeanor is ingenuous, and he responds with two questions of his own. What might his attitude and questions evoke from Mary when she finally discovers him? Is her anxiety soothed or fueled by his puzzling questions?

"They did not understand" suggests the pain of any parent who cannot understand a much loved child, and it leads to the muted tones of the last paragraph. Here you must shift focus *slowly* from obedience, to unspoken questions, to Jesus' natural growth to manhood.

MARY, THE MOTHER OF GOD

Lectionary #18

READING I   Numbers 6:22–27

With short readings especially, don't start until the assembly is well settled. Don't rush. God speaks to Moses who is to speak to "Aaron and his sons."

Allow yourself to pray this cherished text. This will keep you from reading too fast or too slowly. Keep in mind that each invocation is distinct.

Slow down as you reach the words "and give you peace."

Stress "name," not "my." Slow down as you reach the words "I will bless them."

A reading from the Book of Numbers

The LORD said to **Moses**:
"Speak to **Aaron** and his **sons** and **tell** them:
    This is how you shall **bless** the Israelites.
Say to them:
    The LORD **bless** you and **keep** you!
    The LORD let his face **shine** upon you,
        and be **gracious** to you!
    The LORD look upon you **kindly**
        and give you **peace**!
So shall they invoke my **name** upon the **Israelites**,
    and I will **bless** them."

READING I This prayer was already ancient when Mary herself heard it spoken in synagogue services. No doubt it often touched Jesus' ears as well, and today it blesses each of us as we begin the new year. The blessing formula thrice invokes God's divine name in unintended but striking anticipation of our Trinitarian invocations. For the ancient Jews, such a blessing would convey great reverence and awe, because for them a name captured and conveyed all that a person was and has done. Speaking God's name in blessing invoked God's presence among those blessed. What an appropriate reading for this most ancient celebration of Mary, whose "yes" made possible God's presence among us in human form.

God tells Moses to teach the blessing to Aaron and his sons from whom all of Israel's priests would be descended. As you speak the blessing, imagine how Mary might have prayed it for her son Jesus, or how you would pray it over a child leaving home. Note the subtle differences in each invocation: the first asks the Lord to shelter and sustain, the second asks that God's face shine its saving light upon us, and the last asks again for God to "look" upon us and to grant a "peace" that only God can give. Avoid a slow monotone or an over-articulated delivery of this classic prayer. The lines that introduce and follow the blessing reinforce the prevailing mood of graciousness and compassion.

READING II Paul tells the Jesus story most succinctly here, but his every detail is important. What was Paul trying to say, and what is the Church teaching us by selecting this reading for

READING II   Galatians 4:4–7

A reading from the Letter of Saint Paul to the Galatians

"Fullness of time" means God's timing.
Pause after "Son" and mentally insert
"who was born."
Jesus was human and subject to the law,
all for the sake of *saving* us from the law.

Don't read this as a courtroom argument,
but gently and slowly to surprise us again
with this amazing truth.
Pause between the words "Abba,
Father" and use the same inflection
for both words.

Brothers and sisters:
When the **fullness** of time had come, God sent his **Son**,
    born of a **woman**, born under the **law**,
    to **ransom** those under the law,
    so that we might receive **adoption** as **sons**.
As **proof** that you are sons,
    God sent the **Spirit** of his Son into our **hearts**,
    crying out, "**Abba, Father!**"
So you are no longer a **slave** but a **son**,
    and if a **son** then also an **heir**, through **God**.

today? Two points are immediately apparent: Jesus is "born of a woman" (Mary), becoming one like us and sharing our human frailty. He is also "born under the law" and lived subject to it, as we see by his submission to circumcision in today's Gospel. But neither of these key points—that deserve stress—is the main point of the reading.

That is found in Paul's announcement, probably borrowed from an early creed, that "God sent his Son . . . that we might receive adoption as sons." Therein lies the meaning of this solemnity and of the entire Christmas season. Christ's coming through Mary transformed us from "slaves" to children of God. Now, Paul enthuses, we can even call God "Abba!" (Note the exclamation point, and remember "Daddy" is really a better translation of Abba than "Father.")

Paul's aim is to teach and inspire. The teaching occurs in that somewhat torturous first sentence where five clauses require slow reading with careful attention to commas and pauses. The inspiration follows in the final sentence: where formerly we were "slaves," now each has been made a member of the family, a child and "heir" who receives an equal share of God's bountiful inheritance. Sadly, overexposure has inoculated us to this amazing news. But your enthusiastic tone can make this "news" once again.

GOSPEL (For additional insights on this reading please see the commentary for the Nativity of the Lord, Mass at Dawn.) Shepherds find what was announced by angels. Filled with amazement, they make known to others what was told them about this child, and all who

Review the commentary from Christmas Mass at Dawn.

This text contains three scenes with key words: a) arrival of the shepherds who "saw" and "made known"; b) Mary, who quietly "kept" . . . "reflecting"; and c) the eighth day when the child is given his "name."

Proclaim slowly here. Suggest the depth of her pondering.

Use more energy at the words "Then the shepherds . . ." with a faster pace on middle lines and a slower pace at the end.

Pause. Time has elapsed. The accent should be on the "name" given him.

GOSPEL Luke 2:16–21

A reading from the holy Gospel according to Luke

The shepherds went in **haste** to **Bethlehem**
    and found **Mary** and **Joseph**,
  and the **infant** lying in the **manger**.
When they **saw** this,
  they made known the **message**
  that had been **told** them about this **child**.
All who **heard** it were **amazed**
  by what had been **told** them by the **shepherds**.
And **Mary kept** all these things,
  reflecting on them in her **heart**.
Then the shepherds **returned**,
  glorifying and **praising** God
  for all they had **heard** and **seen**,
  just as it had been **told** to them.

When **eight days** were completed for his **circumcision**,
  he was named **Jesus**, the name given him by the **angel**
  before he was **conceived** in the womb.

hear it are amazed. In the midst of this seeing and announcing and amazement sits Mary, keeping all these things in her heart.

A new year calls us to reflect, sort out, and understand. Today's text from Galatians helps us understand that our lives are fundamentally changed by Christ. Here the shepherds quickly understand that the world is radically changed, and Mary can't help but ponder the drastic changes her son will bring to her life and maybe even her world. If God becoming human were not a world-altering event, would it be

worth the bother? God comes for our sakes, not God's, to change the world forever. That's what all the amazement is about.

Mary sits serenely at the heart of this reading. She is serene, not from a lack of awareness, but despite it. That's why extra time is needed for the short line that tells of her musings. Mary is not oblivious to what has happened in her world and the world beyond. Let the line invite your assembly to realize how much they, too, have to contemplate and treasure.

By introducing the theme of Jesus' name, the last paragraph connects the

Gospel with the first reading. Numbers showed us God's presence shining down upon us like the sun. Jesus' name reminds us God doesn't shine from afar, but from within and among us. To dwell among us and save us: that was God's plan long before Jesus "was conceived in the womb" of the one who was to become the mother of Emmanuel, God among us.

EPIPHANY OF THE LORD

Lectionary #20

READING I   Isaiah 60:1–6

Highlight the references to light and darkness. Notice the synonymous parallelism (see the introduction) used in almost every couplet (paired lines) in which the second line of the couplet repeats, balances, or develops what was stated in the first. Although ideas are repeated, these are not redundancies; each time, build energy from the first to second line.

Don't let the series of couplets lure you into a singsong delivery. Focus on each line's meaning to avoid that trap.

These are tender images. Don't waste them.

Pause here, and then start section with renewed energy. "Riches . . . wealth" require built up intensity for variety.

"Dromedaries" are single-humped camels.

Midian = MID-ee-uhn

Ephah = EE-fah

"Gold and frankincense" tie this text to the Gospel. The reading begins and ends in joyful praise.

A reading from the Book of the Prophet Isaiah

Rise up in **splendor**, Jerusalem! Your **light** has come,
    the glory of the LORD shines upon you.
See, **darkness** covers the earth,
    and thick **clouds** cover the peoples;
but upon **you** the LORD **shines**,
    and over you appears his **glory**.
Nations shall walk by your **light**,
    and **kings** by your shining **radiance**.
Raise your **eyes** and look **about**;
    they all gather and **come** to you:
your **sons** come from **afar**,
    and your **daughters** in the arms of their **nurses**.

Then you shall be **radiant** at what you see,
    your heart shall **throb** and **overflow**,
for the riches of the **sea** shall be **emptied** out before you,
    the **wealth** of nations shall be brought to you.
Caravans of **camels** shall **fill** you,
    dromedaries from **Midian** and **Ephah**;
all from **Sheba** shall come
    bearing **gold** and **frankincense**,
    and proclaiming the **praises** of the LORD.

READING I An epiphany is a moment of revelation that manifests something previously hidden. Today's solemnity celebrates the manifestation of Christ to the nations, and it is only the first of other "epiphanies" that will manifest the divinity of Jesus. The Church also celebrates Jesus' Baptism in the Jordan and his changing of water into wine at Cana as manifestations of the divine made human in Jesus.

In Isaiah's poetic vision, dark and gloom give way to the light and the glory of the Lord. Jerusalem, now shrouded by "darkness" and "thick clouds," will become a source of light that will illumine the way of nations and kings, who will walk by her "shining radiance."

Isaiah's original audience heard in the first part of the reading the promise that the exiles would return to Jerusalem. In the second part they heard the prediction that many Gentile pilgrims would one day come to pay homage to the city. Our ears hear that and more, for now we know that God's glory "appears" among us in the person of Jesus, while the pilgrimage of Gentiles to Jerusalem is fulfilled in the embrace of Jesus by so many peoples of the earth. The Church even hears its own mission described in this beautiful prophecy: as the body of Christ, it is we who now must be light for a world wrapped in darkness.

Proclaim Isaiah's words with joy and intensity (not to be mistaken for "volume"). Note that some of the details we commonly associate with the magi are derived from this text, not Matthew's account, so don't gloss over Isaiah's kings and camels!

Here Paul asserts that he was given a special "revelation." Go slowly because the meaning of this sentence is obscure at best.

Use "namely" to draw focus on what follows.

The "revelation" isn't named yet. Former generations were denied it, but now apostles (such as Paul) have glimpsed it.

These last three lines name the hidden truth that's now revealed. Three distinct images: "coheirs," "same body," and "copartners." Distinguish them carefully.

READING II   Ephesians 3:2–3a,5–6

A reading from the Letter of Saint Paul to the Ephesians

Brothers and sisters:
You have heard of the **stewardship** of God's **grace**
　　that was **given** to me for your **benefit**,
　　namely, that the **mystery** was made **known** to me
　　　by **revelation**.
It was **not** made known to people in **other** generations
　　as it has **now** been revealed
　　to his holy **apostles** and **prophets** by the **Spirit**:
　　that the **Gentiles** are **coheirs**, members of the same **body**,
　　and **copartners** in the promise in Christ **Jesus**
　　　through the **gospel**.

GOSPEL   Matthew 2:1–12

A reading from the holy Gospel according to Matthew

When Jesus was born in **Bethlehem** of **Judea**,
　　in the days of King **Herod**,
　　behold, **magi** from the **east** arrived in **Jerusalem**, saying,
　　"Where is the newborn **king** of the **Jews**?
We saw his **star** at its **rising**
　　and have come to do him **homage**."

Before anything else, this is a story. Proclaim it as such.

"East" suggests the magi's foreign, exotic identity. They are astrologers.

READING II   Saint Paul is unique in the history of Christianity for the depth and importance of his contribution. From prison, he asserts here his distinctive role as apostle to the Gentiles. It wasn't his choice, he says, but a responsibility "given" to him by God. The work of evangelizing the Gentiles might not have been assured without Paul's efforts, so today's solemnity owes much to him. But it is Christ's drum, not his own, that Paul is beating here.

　　Paul has received a "revelation" unknown to former generations. God's own

Spirit has inspired the deep insight Paul now clearly enunciates: Gentiles have become coheirs with the Jews. This was an unsettling thought to many of the early Jewish followers of Christ. Jesus was their messiah, come to save Israel. But Paul explains that in Christ, Gentiles and Jews are members of the same body. Through the preaching of the Gospel, Gentiles receive a share in the promises of Christ. For Jewish Christians, this news was like hearing the reading of a will and

learning the inheritance isn't all yours, but to be shared with others you didn't know were part of the family.

　　Remember that Ephesians was written when the unity of Jew and Gentile was a settled fact, so this passage celebrates rather than argues for that reality. Imagine yourself speaking joyfully not to those whose inheritance must now be shared (the Jews), but to those who've been added to the will (the Gentiles).

　　Take time with phrases like "the stewardship of God's grace," "not made

"Herod" introduces an undercurrent of threat.

When King Herod **heard** this,
    he was greatly **troubled**,
    and all Jerusalem **with** him.
Assembling all the chief **priests** and the **scribes** of the people,
    he inquired of them **where** the Christ was to be **born**.
They said to him, "In **Bethlehem** of **Judea**,
    for **thus** it has been written through the **prophet**:

This comes from Micah 5:1, but is altered by Matthew.

        And *you*, ***Bethlehem***, *land of **Judah**,*
            *are by no means **least** among the rulers of Judah;*
        *since from **you** shall come a **ruler**,*
            *who is to **shepherd** my people **Israel**."*

The note of danger is sounded once again.

Then Herod called the magi **secretly**
    and **ascertained** from them the **time** of the star's **appearance**.
He sent them to **Bethlehem** and said,

King Herod is cunning.

    "**Go** and search **diligently** for the child.
When you have **found** him, bring me **word**,
    that I **too** may go and do him **homage**."
After their audience with the king they **set** out.
And **behold**, the **star** that they had seen at its **rising**
      preceded them,
    until it came and **stopped** over the place where the **child** was.

This is familiar, comforting imagery.

They were **overjoyed** at seeing the star,
    and on entering the **house**
    they saw the **child** with **Mary** his **mother**.

"House" is unexpected. They find him with Mary.

Note that they don't kneel, but rather "prostrate."

They **prostrated** themselves and did him **homage**.
Then they opened their **treasures**
    and offered him gifts of **gold**, **frankincense**, and **myrrh**.
And having been **warned** in a **dream** not to **return** to Herod,
    they **departed** for their country by another **way**.

Both relief and derision are found in this sentence. In the nick of time, the necessary information was kept from King Herod.

known . . . in other generations" to establish the suspense that leads to the unveiling: "the Gentiles are coheirs." The stress on oneness ("coheirs," "same body," "copartners") echoes in all three readings today, for God's self-revelation in Christ is a gift to be shared with all the nations!

GOSPEL Matthew gives the familiar story unique texture by using contrasts and threats that differ strikingly from the angels and shepherds we typically associate with Jesus' birth.

While the shepherds rejoice at the announcement of the savior's birth, Herod "and all of Jerusalem" are "greatly troubled." The magi come to the capital and its palace seeking the newborn king, only to learn that his birth was prophesied to occur in a humble village. Herod lets the foreigners go to seek him, while he plots the demise of this potential rival.

Although many of Matthew's words are expected and comforting in their familiarity ("magi," "Bethlehem," "east," "star," "child," "shepherd," "gold, frankincense and myrrh"), other words are unexpected

("King Herod," "house," "prostrated"). We anticipate kneeling, not prostration, magi entering a stable not a house; Herod is supposed to loom over the end of Jesus' life, not its beginning. It's the presence of Herod, of course, that colors the text with a sense of impending danger. Herod's deceit and covert plotting anticipate the threat that will haunt Jesus all his days and foreshadow his Passion.

BAPTISM OF THE LORD

Lectionary #21

READING I   Isaiah 40:1–5, 9–11

A reading from the Book of the Prophet Isaiah

From the tenderness of the first paragraph, build to a muted intensity in the voice that "cries out . . . prepare the way of the Lord!"

Comfort, give **comfort** to my **people**,
  says your God.
Speak **tenderly** to Jerusalem, and **proclaim** to her
  that her **service** is at an **end**,
  her **guilt** is **expiated**;
indeed, she has **received** from the hand of the LORD
  double for all her **sins**.

Suggest how incredible it is that these events will occur, remembering these are poetic images, not literal prophecies of what will happen to mountains, but of what, even more incredibly, will happen to human hearts.

  A **voice** cries out:
In the **desert** prepare the **way** of the LORD!
  Make **straight** in the wasteland a **highway** for our God!
Every **valley** shall be **filled** in,
  every **mountain** and **hill** shall be made **low**;
the **rugged** land shall be made a **plain**,
  the **rough** country, a broad **valley**.
Then the **glory** of the LORD shall be **revealed**,
  and **all** people shall see it **together**;
  for the **mouth** of the LORD has **spoken**.

Believe it, you say, "for the mouth of the Lord has spoken." Isaiah insists you "cry out" as on a mountaintop. That calls for intensity rather than volume, belief rather than decibels.

Go **up** on to a **high** mountain,
  Zion, **herald** of glad **tidings**;
cry out at the **top** of your voice,
  Jerusalem, **herald** of good **news**!

There is a choice of readings today. Speak with the liturgy coordinator or homilist to find out which readings will be used.

The Christian West more often focused on the historical aspects of the events surrounding the Nativity of the Lord, while the East stressed their theological significance. By placing the feast of Christ's Baptism at the end of the Christmas season, the Church enables us to conclude the season with a theological reflection on the epiphany (manifestation) of God in the incarnate Jesus.

READING I **ISAIAH 40.** It should be no surprise that the lyric poetry of this passage has inspired both classical and contemporary liturgical music. The opening lines give you your agenda ("give comfort to my people . . .") and instruction on how to read ("speak tenderly"). A message of newness and fresh starts dominates the passage: "guilt is expiated," winding ways are made straight, and all people together will see the glory of the Lord! That calls for a tone of confidence and joy. Normally proclaimed during Advent, today this reading helps us conclude the Christmas season with its images of hope and renewal.

Isaiah was announcing the end of Israel's exile in Babylon. He is the one speaking in the wilderness, announcing the fulfillment of all God's promises. But today we visualize John the Baptist as the one whose voice cries from the wilderness, announcing the fulfillment of God's ultimate promise: the coming of Israel's

God's "strong arm" also "gathers the lambs." God's "reward" (and "recompense")—emphasized instead of the prepositions "with" and "before"—is the comfort of "his bosom."

Fear **not** to cry out
  and **say** to the cities of **Judah**:
  Here is your **God**!
Here comes with **power**
  the Lord **GOD**,
  who rules by his **strong** arm;
here is his **reward** with him,
  his **recompense** before him.
Like a **shepherd** he **feeds** his flock;
  in his **arms** he gathers the **lambs**,
carrying them in his **bosom**,
  and **leading** the ewes with **care**.

Or:

READING I   Isaiah 42:1–4, 6–7

These are exalted lines. Give them their due and don't rush. Stress God's initiative and choice.

A reading from the Book of the Prophet Isaiah

Thus says the LORD:
Here is my **servant** whom I **uphold**,
  my chosen one with whom I am **pleased**,
upon whom I have put my **spirit**;
  he shall bring forth **justice** to the nations,
not crying out, **not** shouting,
  not making his voice heard in the street.

This is not wishful thinking, but a prophecy of what God will accomplish through his servant.

A bruised reed he **shall** not break,
  and a smoldering **wick** he shall not **quench**,
until he establishes **justice** on the earth;
  the coastlands will wait for his **teaching**.

"Until he establishes" is in context with the two clauses that precede it. "Coastlands will wait . . ." stands alone as a new thought.

messiah. John is the new herald who stands on Zion's peak and proclaims, "Here is your God." Israel experienced God's saving power in her deliverance from exile. But today's liturgy enables us to hear an even greater truth: the God who "comes with power," who rules with a strong arm and at the same time gathers the lambs will bring salvation to all the world, not just the Chosen People. God's mercy will reach the ends of the earth. Images of strength are interwoven with images of tenderness—reassurance offered to all.

ISAIAH 42. Elements of this first reading are embedded in the Gospel where we hear the same "in whom I am well pleased" addressed to Jesus that God here addresses to the "servant" or "chosen one." Four sections of the Book of Isaiah are known as songs of the "suffering servant," poetic sections that pay tribute to a "chosen one" whose fidelity to God's will results in suffering and shame and whose mission is to bring justice. There is much scholarly speculation regarding the identity of the suffering servant. Is it Isaiah himself, the nation, a future Messiah? But

in today's liturgy the suffering servant is clearly identified with Jesus, and Jesus himself often saw his life as the embodiment of these prophecies. Because the Gospel leans on this "servant song," your reading should ready our ears for the subtle echoes that will follow.

The opening lines read like a job description for God's servant, but of course they are much more. They are a blessing that becomes a self-fulfilling prophecy, as the positive expectations we place on children draw the best out of them. Speak

Pause to make a transition and shift to a more personal tone. Stress the repeated "I" and the verbs ("called," "grasped," formed"), which suggest the fullness with which the servant is infused with God's Spirit. Blend tenderness and strength.

I, the LORD, have called you for the **victory** of justice,
 I have grasped you by the **hand**;
I **formed** you, and **set** you
 as a **covenant** of the people,
 a **light** for the nations,
to **open** the eyes of the **blind**,
 to bring out **prisoners** from **confinement**,
 and from the **dungeon**, those who live in **darkness**.

A reading from the Letter of Saint Paul to Titus

Make eye contact and, with great conviction, deliver the opening announcement ("The grace . . . appeared") from memory.

Beloved:
The **grace** of God has appeared, **saving** all
 and **training** us to **reject** godless **ways**
 and worldly **desires**
 and to live **temperately**, **justly** and **devoutly** in this age,
as we **await** the blessed **hope**,

"The appearance of . . . God" is the "blessed hope" of the previous line.

 the **appearance** of the **glory** of our great **God**
 and savior Jesus **Christ**,

This is not just a reminder of what Christ did for us; it is also a listing of what we must do in response, that is, abandon lawlessness and do what is good.

who **gave** himself for us to **deliver** us from all **lawlessness**
 and to **cleanse** for himself a **people** as his **own**,
 eager to do what is **good**.

Take a deep breath and begin with renewed energy here.

 When the **kindness** and generous **love**
 of God our savior **appeared**,
 not because of any righteous **deeds** we had done
 but because of his **mercy**,

Make this point very deliberately: God saved us "because of his mercy," not because of any merit on our part.

 he **saved** us through the bath of **rebirth**

these lines with the same parental tone you hear in the Gospel's voice from heaven.

 In the second paragraph, God no longer talks *about* the servant but *to* him. "I have called you . . ." says the Lord, to be light, to open eyes, to free prisoners! These lines, similar to words Jesus quotes to describe his own ministry, convey God's encouragement and commissioning of the servant for a ministry of healing and hope. Speak them with a blend of tenderness and strength.

READING II **TITUS. On this day that commemorates Jesus'** Baptism, this text from Titus focuses us on the gift of our Baptism through which Christ cleansed and saved us. The first paragraph announces salvation and immediately lists the kind of behaviors that Baptism requires of us: to abandon godless ways and the desires of the world and to live devout and disciplined lives. Baptism is just the beginning of our life in the Spirit. Christ came once, but he will come again. We live now in a time of anticipation, eagerly awaiting his return and living

according to his teaching and expectations. He "cleansed" us that we might become a people of "his own," but belonging to Christ means that we forsake "lawlessness" and instead eagerly seek "to do what is good."

 We did nothing to deserve God's mercy and love. God sought us out; God "richly poured out," that is, saturated us with the Holy Spirit that we might have the means with which to live the new life into which we were initiated. This new life has

and **renewal** by the Holy **Spirit**,
   whom he richly **poured out** on us
     through Jesus **Christ** our savior,
so that we might be **justified** by his **grace**
     and become **heirs** in **hope** of eternal **life**.

Or:

> There is much good news here—the Holy Spirit, justification, hope, and eternal life! Speak with energy and end on a joyful note.

READING II   Acts 10:34–38

A reading from the Acts of the Apostles

Peter proceeded to speak to those **gathered**
   in the house of **Cornelius**, saying:
"In truth, I see that God shows **no partiality**.
Rather, in every nation **whoever** fears him and acts **uprightly**
   is **acceptable** to him.
You know the word that he sent to the **Israelites**
   as he proclaimed peace through **Jesus Christ**, who is Lord of **all**,
what has happened **all over** Judea,
   beginning in Galilee **after** the baptism
   that **John** preached,
   how God **anointed** Jesus of Nazareth
   with the **Holy Spirit** and **power**.
He went about doing **good**
   and healing all those **oppressed** by the devil,
   for God **was** with him."

> Peter is in the home of a Gentile who, without Baptism, has received the Holy Spirit.

> "In truth, I see" suggests Peter's growing awareness, which comes slowly at first then gradually builds momentum.

> These words tell us that God is working in and through Jesus. Speak them with conviction.

> Let this be your own statement of faith. Slow down as you approach the words "for God was with him."

real consequences: through it we are "justified by grace" and made "heirs . . . of eternal life." The entire text consists of two very long sentences. Don't rush. Instead, share one idea at a time and do it both with joy and urgency. Baptism is a gift that places on each of us important responsibilities. Remind us of that today.

ACTS. Peter briefly alludes to Jesus' Baptism in this short text and presents Christ as the sacrament of God to the world, the manifestation and the implementation of God's will among people. He understands that what Isaiah said would be accomplished through the suffering servant, God has achieved in Christ.

But this same Peter who knew Jesus well and speaks of him so powerfully, continues learning the full meaning of the Jesus event he had been so privileged to experience. Only by reading the entire tenth chapter of Acts, which provides the context, will you appreciate the meaning of the discourse presented here. A God-given vision has brought Peter to the home of the Gentile Cornelius where he discovers that God plays no favorites. Formerly an adamant proponent of "Jesus only for the Jews," Peter suddenly recognizes the error of his ways. He now realizes that Jesus is not Israel's exclusive possession, but the embodiment of God's infinite love sent and meant for all of humanity.

Speaking to a Gentile, who even before Baptism received the gift of the Holy Spirit, humbles Peter and colors his tone. "You know the word that he sent . . ." indicates that he is reviewing the ministry of Jesus less with the didactic tone of a teacher and more with the joy of a fellow believer speaking to new friends about his old friend, Jesus.

You'll better serve Luke's theological purposes by stressing God's initiative rather than John's role.

Try speaking the words "were asking in their hearts" as if they were a question posed directly to John.

Stress John's emphasis on the contrast between his baptism of *water* and the Messiah's of *Spirit* and *fire.*

Pause before the words "and was praying" to give them added emphasis.

There are echoes of the First Reading here. God's voice might best be rendered as encouraging and gentle.

GOSPEL   Luke 3:15–16, 21–22

A reading from the holy Gospel according to Luke

The **people** were filled with **expectation**,
　　and all were **asking** in their hearts
　　　　whether **John** might be the **Christ**.
John **answered** them all, saying,
　　"**I** am baptizing you with **water**,
　　　　but one **mightier** than I is coming.
I am not **worthy** to loosen the **thongs** of his **sandals**.
He will baptize you with the Holy **Spirit** and **fire**."

After all the people had been **baptized**
　　and Jesus **also** had been baptized and was **praying**,
　　heaven was **opened** and the Holy **Spirit**
　　　　descended upon him
　　in bodily form like a **dove**.
And a **voice** came from heaven,
　　"**You** are my beloved **Son**;
　　with **you** I am well **pleased**."

GOSPEL   As in today's other readings, *God's* action dominates in this Gospel. Though this is the Gospel chosen for the feast of the Baptism of the Lord, Luke alludes to Jesus' Baptism only briefly. And although Luke presents John as the object of much speculation among the people, he underplays John's role as Jesus' baptizer. Why? It's because for Luke the Baptist was not the first of the New Testament figures, but rather the last of the Old Testament prophets. Luke resolves the "anticipation" in the people's hearts by having John point to one "might-

ier" than himself. The result is that Luke shifts our focus from the action of Jesus' human companion (John), to the *divine* action manifested in the voice from heaven and the descent of the Spirit.

John understood the limits of his ministry: "I baptize with water." But, even without knowing for certain who it would be, he asserts with confidence that the one who follows him will administer a Baptism of Spirit and fire!

Jesus is praying when the skies open; he is already in deep communion with God. Then the heavenly voice addresses him

directly: "You are my beloved Son. . . ." In Matthew, the voice addresses the crowd, but here it's an intimate moment between Father and Son. It's also a moment of high drama and high Christology, but presented in few and simple words. You needn't overdramatize the divine manifestation; simple and sincere will serve best, as long as your energy conveys the significance of the moment.

Lectionary #66

READING I   Isaiah 62:1–5

The opening lines are pregnant with joyous news begging to be shared.

Good news can be expressed vigorously or softly, but the vehicles of your expression are words like "vindication" and "victory," "dawn," and "torch."

Remember, when an idea is expressed twice ("silent"/"quiet"; "crown"/"diadem") you must *increase* intensity on the second expression to avoid sounding redundant.

Speak like a lover, not a politician. Stress the words expressing transformation. Contrast "Forsaken . . . Desolate," with "My Delight . . . Espoused."

Make eye contact here.

The reading peaks here: don't waste this touching imagery.

A reading from the Book of the Prophet Isaiah

For **Zion's** sake I will not be **silent**,
    for **Jerusalem's** sake I will not be **quiet**,
until her **vindication** shines forth like the **dawn**
    and her **victory** like a burning **torch**.

Nations shall **behold** your vindication,
    and all the **kings** your **glory**;
you shall be called by a **new** name
    pronounced by the mouth of the LORD.
You shall be a glorious **crown** in the hand of the LORD,
    a **royal** diadem held by your **God**.
No **more** shall people call you "**Forsaken**,"
    or your land "**Desolate**,"
but you shall be called "**My Delight**,"
    and your land "**Espoused**."
For the LORD **delights** in you
    and makes your land his **spouse**.
As a young **man** marries a **virgin**,
    your **Builder** shall marry **you**;
and as a **bridegroom** rejoices in his **bride**
    so shall your **God** rejoice in **you**.

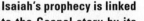 **READING I** Isaiah's prophecy is linked to the Gospel story by its rich marriage imagery. Yet neither passage is about weddings per se; each is about the power of God to transform what was, into what we thought could never be. Each text shows the manifestation of the glory of God and heralds the coming of the messianic age.

Isaiah's prophecy speaks directly and passionately to the whole people of Israel, here represented by Zion and Jerusalem. But the text announces more than restoration and renewal following Israel's exile.

Isaiah gives us a powerful metaphor in which God is a lover in ardent pursuit of his beloved. This bridegroom is ready to rain down favors upon Jerusalem, the bride, who will no longer be "Forsaken" or "Desolate," but henceforth will be "My Delight."

Although intended to comfort Jerusalem at a time of national upheaval, these words have lasting relevance. Isaiah's prophecy teaches that God longs for us, as a people and as individuals, just as a lover longs for his bride.

Isaiah's poetry is unparalleled in its passionate expression of divine love. It's a great privilege to speak these words. Doubtless you will speak them to an assembly who needs the assurance of God's love more than they even realize. In the final couplets, that love is characterized as so personal and transforming that even the drinking of water-changed-to-wine wouldn't be enough to celebrate it.

READING II In this text, Paul addresses the Corinthians, who have

Remember that Paul is teaching *and* peacemaking. Peacemaking is communicated through your tone, your degree of emphasis, and the calming way you enumerate the various gifts. Teach through your emphasis on the Spirit as the sole dispenser of gifts. These lessons could be taught by a frustrated and angry teacher or one that's patient and understanding. Let Paul sound like the latter.

Paul gives us one of his best examples of balance. By slow and careful attention to his comparisons you will help the assembly hear that balance.

Another translation of the phrase "for some benefit" is "for the common good."

Address a different section of the assembly on each "to another . . . ." This listing is challenging. Don't rush. Distinguish one gift from the other. In each line, stress the gift named, *not* "another." Pause slightly after "another" before you name each gift.

Pause before this important summary line. Slow down as you approach the words "as he wishes."

This story contains much symbolic meaning. Let the homily expound those levels. Tell the story by creating believable characters, suspenseful plot, and arresting images. It's a story of human embarrassment and human compassion. Mary's role is significant, the interchange with her son fascinating. Jesus' take-charge attitude and the confusion, even irritation, of the headwaiter give texture to the story.

managed to turn extraordinary gifts of the Holy Spirit, such as prophecy and the ability to speak in foreign tongues, into sources of discord and pride. Paul wants the Corinthians not only to put the gifts into proper perspective, remembering that love supersedes them all, but to realize that they are given for the common good, not for the glory of the one gifted. Rather than ranking the gifts, Paul asserts the value of each. He reminds the Corinthians to keep their focus on the *source* of the gifts and the *reason* each is given, rather than succumbing to pride and competition.

READING II   1 Corinthians 12:4–11

A reading from the first Letter of Saint Paul to the Corinthians

Brothers and sisters:
There are different **kinds** of spiritual **gifts** but the same **Spirit**;
   there are different forms of **service** but the same **Lord**;
   there are different **workings** but the same **God**
   who **produces** all of them in **everyone**.
To each **individual** the **manifestation** of the Spirit
   is given for some **benefit**.
To **one** is given through the Spirit the expression of **wisdom**;
   to **another**, the expression of **knowledge** according
     to the **same** Spirit;
   to **another**, **faith** by the same Spirit;
   to **another**, gifts of **healing** by the one Spirit;
   to **another**, mighty **deeds**;
   to **another**, **prophecy**;
   to **another**, **discernment** of **spirits**;
   to **another**, varieties of **tongues**;
   to **another**, **interpretation** of tongues.
But **one** and the **same** Spirit produces **all** of these,
   distributing them **individually** to each **person** as he **wishes**.

GOSPEL   John 2:1–11

A reading from the holy Gospel according to John

There was a **wedding** at **Cana** in **Galilee**,
   and the mother of **Jesus** was there.
Jesus and his disciples were **also** invited to the wedding.

Paul is teaching an insight that Christians have struggled to learn for 2,000 years: we are all different, yet one in Christ; we manifest unique gifts and distinct ministries, yet it is one and the same God who inspires them in everyone. Paul is a master of balance and contrast as he reveals unity by demonstrating diversity. For him, each unique manifestation of the Spirit is a sign of the *whole;* just as a hand or foot does not exist alone but each recalls and needs the body of which it is a part.

Such is the nature of community—gifted because of its individual members, but truly Church only when joined together as one. Besides instructing the Corinthians on how to discern true gifts, Paul wants to make *peace* among them. And that peace is achieved only when we value and recognize the need for every person's unique contribution.

GOSPEL   The revelation of Christ to the world continues in this Gospel reading. Just as he was disclosed

When the **wine** ran **short**,
   the **mother** of Jesus said to him,
   "They have no **wine**."
And **Jesus** said to her,
   "**Woman**, how does **your** concern affect **me**?
My **hour** has not yet **come**."
His mother said to the **servers**,
   "Do **whatever** he **tells** you."
Now there were six stone **water** jars there for Jewish
   ceremonial **washings**,
   each holding twenty to thirty **gallons**.
Jesus **told** them,
   "**Fill** the jars with **water**."
So they filled them to the **brim**.
Then he told them,
   "Draw some **out** now and take it to the **headwaiter**."
So they **took** it.
And when the headwaiter **tasted** the water that had become **wine**,
   without knowing where it **came** from
   —although the servers who had **drawn** the water **knew**—,
   the headwaiter called the **bridegroom** and said to him,
   "Everyone serves **good** wine **first**,
   and **then** when people have drunk **freely**, an **inferior** one;
   but **you** have kept the **good** wine until **now**."
Jesus did this as the **beginning** of his **signs** at **Cana** in **Galilee**
   and so **revealed** his **glory**,
   and his **disciples** began to **believe** in him.

The exchange between mother and son is playful, not harsh.

Your delivery of "Do whatever he tells you" signals that Mary somehow heard a "yes" in Jesus' voice.

Emphasize the function, number, and size of the jars.

The groom and the headwaiter are likely relatives. The tone of the dialogue should reflect that. The headwaiter is clearly unhappy.

This is the first of seven signs in John's Gospel. The belief that follows the sign is significant. Emphasize it.

---

to the Magi under a shimmering star, and a voice from heaven named him the "beloved" at his Baptism, so today the transformation of water into wine reveals the initiation of Jesus' sacred mission of manifesting the kingdom of God.

This story comes from the Gospel according to John. It is a poignant and engaging narrative, but also full of theological meaning on the symbolic level. Like the rest of John's account, the Cana story is layered with levels of meaning we don't find in the other evangelists. Water for Old

Testament ceremonial washings changes into superabundant wine, symbolizing the dawn of the messianic age, and even prefiguring Christ's Passion. As here water is changed to wine, wine will eventually change to blood, the new means of purification. So in a sense, Calvary starts at Cana. When Jesus tells Mary his "hour" has not yet come, he uses a word that in John always refers to his Passion. The miracle at Cana is the first of the "signs" that manifests Jesus' glory, but it only foreshadows the greatest of the signs that manifest his glory: his death on the cross.

The oral reading of a story can't communicate all those theological layers. Substrata of theology are the stuff of homilies, not readings. As proclaimer, what you *can* do is highlight the words, phrases, and images that point to John's deeper meanings: "My hour has not yet come," "Jewish ceremonial washings," "brim," "revealed his glory," "disciples began to believe in him." In John, washings, abundance, transformation, glory, and the response of faith all point to the *hour* that is yet to come. Now the clock has started ticking.

3RD SUNDAY IN ORDINARY TIME

Lectionary #69

READING I   Nehemiah 8:2–4a, 5–6, 8–10

Nehemiah = nee-uh-MĪ-uh

Clearly identify Ezra. The tone must be solemn and hope-filled.

Don't rush. Present are men, women, and even children!

Take a breath, and then stress the length of time Ezra reads.

Your pace can quicken a bit here, but keep it upbeat to suggest the people like what they hear.

These details add texture to the story. Slow your pace here.

Note the act of reverence for God's word. Don't "shout" the "Amen, amen." Intensity is more important than volume.

Ezra both reads and interprets.

A reading from the Book of Nehemiah

Ezra the **priest** brought the **law** before the **assembly**,
　which consisted of **men**, **women**,
　and those children **old** enough to **understand**.
Standing at one end of the open place that was before
　the **Water** Gate,
　he **read** out of the book from **daybreak** till **midday**,
　in the **presence** of the **men**, the **women**,
　and those **children** old enough to understand;
　and all the people listened **attentively** to the book of the **law**.
Ezra the **scribe** stood on a wooden **platform**
　that had been **made** for the occasion.
He **opened** the scroll
　so that all the people might **see** it
　—for he was standing **higher up** than any of the people—;
　and, as he **opened** it, all the people **rose**.
Ezra blessed the LORD, the great **God**,
　and all the **people**, their hands raised **high**, answered,
　"Amen, amen!"
Then they **bowed** down and **prostrated** themselves
　before the LORD,
　their faces to the **ground**.
Ezra read **plainly** from the book of the law of God,
　interpreting it so that all could **understand** what was read.

READING I   From today's First Reading and Gospel, in which we witness public, liturgical reading of scripture and observe very different but emotional responses from the listening assemblies (although the Gospel narrative ends before describing the hostility of Jesus' listeners), one thing becomes clear: the proclamation of scripture should not leave people unmoved.

Although quite capable of ignoring and forgetting God's law, the Hebrew people had a notion of law that was distinctive. Rather than a burden, they saw law as a means of liberation. The law teaches us the ways of God and frees us to follow God's will, which leads to life, rather than our own will, which leads to destruction.

In today's text, Ezra addresses an assembly that had lost touch with its roots in the law following the Babylonian exile. Ezra convenes the people and, in the solemn service described here, rains the words of God's law upon them. The people's "Amen" indicates their willingness to let the law guide every area of their lives. The period of restoration that saw the rebuilding of the walls of the city of Jerusalem was also a time when the returned survivors of the exile embraced the Torah as their constitution.

Ezra's ceremony marks a new day in the life of the nation, and your retelling should highlight its importance. The length of their listening ("from *daybreak* till *midday*") signals its significance, as does the presence of "the men, women and [even] children." That latter line recurs, almost like a chant, and adds dignity to this solemn occasion. Don't rush past it either time.

There are three identifications here. Distinguish them, but at a good pace.

Then **Nehemiah**, that is, His **Excellency**, and Ezra
    the **priest-scribe**
  and the **Levites** who were **instructing** the people
  said to all the people:
  "Today is **holy** to the LORD your God.
Do not be **sad**, and do not **weep**"—
  for all the people were **weeping** as they heard the words
    of the **law**.

Make eye contact here.

He said further: "**Go**, eat rich **foods** and drink sweet **drinks**,
  and allot **portions** to those who had nothing **prepared**;
  for today is **holy** to our LORD.

End energetically and upbeat.

Do not be **saddened** this day,
  for **rejoicing** in the LORD must be your **strength**!"

READING II 1 Corinthians 12:12–30

A reading from the first Letter of Saint Paul to the Corinthians

Brothers and sisters:
As a body is **one** though it has many **parts**,
  and all the **parts** of the body, though **many**, are **one** body,
    so also **Christ**.
For in one **Spirit** we were all **baptized** into one **body**,
  whether **Jews** or **Greeks**, **slaves** or **free** persons,
  and we were all given to **drink** of one **Spirit**.

Start strong with good eye contact.

Proclaim slowly, respecting Paul's carefully balanced ideas. Pause before the words "so also Christ," speaking them while looking directly at the assembly.

Many sensory words and images fill this text: the people "listened," the scroll is held up for all to see, the people prostrate themselves with faces "to the ground," and they are encouraged to taste "rich foods and sweet drinks." Attention to these sense words will help you and your listeners visualize this scene and more fully experience the events described.

The sequence of action in Ezra's ceremony is proclamation, explanation, worship, and response. Our worship follows the same pattern: we proclaim and explain; we

offer up Christ as an act of worship and then go forth to live out our response in daily life. When Ezra's assembly hears God's word, their response is immediate and profound. They likely experience both the beauty of the law and profound guilt over their failure to interiorize it. All of the details add to the solemnity of the proclamation: Ezra's use of a platform, the opening of the scroll, the people's rising in reverence with arms upraised, and speaking a double "Amen." Don't slight the people's remorseful reaction, but sadness is not the dominant tone. The people are told to celebrate because

the law is received not as a yoke but as an agent of God's restoration.

 Today's reading continues last week's text in which Paul addresses the Corinthian community regarding their disputes over spiritual gifts. He writes to restore peace, impart sound teaching, and correct misunderstandings that have led some astray—and he accomplishes all this with apparent wit and humor.

Enjoy the wit and humor of a talking "foot" and "ear."

Long readings require added attention to pacing. Hold your listeners' attention by varying the tempo. "If the whole body were . . . . Where would the . . . be?" can move more quickly than sections which are more clearly instructional, such as "But as it is God has placed . . . ." Stress the importance of the "weaker" members.

Paul is discussing the "private" parts of our bodies that we clothe more carefully.

Renew your energy here. This is an important line.

Emphasize the word "all," not the preposition "with."

Now the **body** is not a **single** part, but **many**.
If a **foot** should say,
    "Because I am not a **hand** I do not **belong** to the body,"
    it does **not** for this reason belong any **less** to the body.
Or if an **ear** should say,
    "Because I am not an **eye** I do not **belong** to the body,"
    it does **not** for this reason belong any **less** to the body.
If the **whole** body were an **eye**, where would the **hearing** be?
If the whole body were **hearing**, where would the sense
    of **smell** be?
But as it **is**, God placed the **parts**,
    each **one** of them, in the body as he **intended**.
If they were all **one** part, where would the **body** be?
But as it **is**, there are many **parts**, yet **one** body.
The **eye** cannot say to the **hand**, "I do not **need** you,"
    nor again the **head** to the **feet**, "I do not need **you**."
Indeed, the parts of the body that seem to be **weaker**
    are all the more **necessary**,
    and those parts of the body that we consider less **honorable**
    we surround with **greater** honor,
    and our less **presentable** parts are treated with greater **propriety**,
    whereas our **more** presentable parts do not **need** this.
But God has so **constructed** the body
    as to give **greater** honor to a part that is **without** it,
    so that there may be no **division** in the body,
    but that the **parts** may have the same **concern** for one another.
If one part **suffers**, **all** the parts suffer **with** it;
    if one part is **honored**, all the parts **share** its joy.

Whereas earlier he taught about the need for all the *gifts* in the community, here he argues for the necessity of all the *members* of the community. As each gift is unique and necessary, so is each Jew, Greek, slave, and free person. But their *distinctiveness* is only part of the reality; they are also *alike* by virtue of each one's membership in the body.

Read the section on the body as if speaking to nations who think they can go it alone, reminding them no matter how strong they may be, each needs the others

to survive. On the individual level, Paul's teaching is all the more relevant: everyone matters, each has something to contribute, and none should be discounted! Even so serious a message can be delivered with humor. Paul personifies "foot" and "ear" making them exaggerated spokespersons of petulance. Failing to recognize a playful tone in these lines would do Paul a great disservice. Like a wise teacher or parent, Paul knows how to use humor to coax sense into feuding factions.

The climax occurs at the line "Now you are Christ's body"— a powerful statement that equates Christ with his Church. Once we know we are all necessary parts of one body, we can distinguish roles and responsibilities and even designate titles without implying that the functions make the members greater or lesser. Some functions matter more than others. All members matter the same. Paul's list of ministerial functions gives primacy to the first three, which are given personal titles (apostles,

This is the climax of the reading. Help your assembly hear this great truth as if for the first time.

Don't rush through the questions. Pause before announcing "The word of the Lord."

Now **you** are Christ's body, and individually **parts** of it.
Some people God has designated in the church
    to be, **first, apostles; second, prophets; third, teachers;**
    then, mighty **deeds**;
    then gifts of **healing, assistance, administration,**
    and varieties of **tongues**.
Are **all** apostles? Are all **prophets**? Are all **teachers**?
Do **all** work mighty **deeds**? Do all have gifts of **healing**?
Do all speak in **tongues**? Do all **interpret**?

[Shorter: 1 Corinthians 12:12–14, 27]

GOSPEL   Luke 1:1–4, 4:14–21

Use these lines to reassure your own listeners. Note Luke's stress on his method and precision. Take it slowly.

A reading from the holy Gospel according to Luke

Since **many** have undertaken to compile a **narrative** of the events
    that have been **fulfilled** among us,
      just as those who were **eyewitnesses** from the **beginning**
    and **ministers** of the **word** have handed them **down** to us,
    I **too** have decided,
    after investigating everything accurately **anew**,
    to **write** it down in an orderly **sequence** for you,
    most excellent **Theophilus**,
    so that you may realize the **certainty** of the teachings
    you have **received**.

Theophilus = thee-OF-uh-luhs

A significant pause and a breath at the end of the first paragraph will signal introduction of new, unrelated material. Jesus returned full of the Holy Spirit. Luke establishes early on the Spirit's influence on Jesus' ministry.

Jesus returned to **Galilee** in the **power** of the **Spirit**,
    and news of him **spread** throughout the whole **region**.
He taught in their **synagogues** and was **praised** by **all**.

prophets, teachers), while the others constitute a second rank and are listed impersonally as gifts (mighty deeds, gifts of healing, tongues). The roles that matter more carry more responsibility, not more privilege.

    Paul's closing rhetorical questions anticipate a negative response. The world, of course, would be no better off if everyone were a teacher than the body would be if every part were a foot. It is the diversity of the body that enables it to function.

GOSPEL Today's Gospel combines fragments from chapters one and four of Luke, despite no clear connection between them. The fragment from chapter one provides insight into Luke's purpose and methodology. First we learn that "many" have attempted to write about Christ; Luke is not the first. Second, we see that Luke was a meticulous researcher who, after "investigating everything accurately anew" and relying on "eyewitnesses," created a "narrative" (that is, a life of Jesus, rather than a "Gospel," as Mark announces at the start of his work). Luke tells us his writing is more historical than that of the other synoptics whose work is less biography and more proclamation of the Christ event. (By our standards, of course, none of the synoptics writes a strict biography.) Luke uses these glimpses into his method to reinforce the confidence of Theophilus (who can be both an individual and a representative of Luke's wider audience) in the instruction he received.

Highlight this reference to Jesus' hometown.

He came to **Nazareth**, where he had grown **up**,
  and went according to his **custom**
    into the **synagogue** on the **sabbath** day.
He stood up to **read** and was handed a **scroll** of the prophet **Isaiah**.
He **unrolled** the scroll and found the **passage** where it was written:
  *The **Spirit** of the **Lord** is **upon** me,*
    *because he has **anointed** me*
    *to bring **glad** tidings to the **poor**.*
  *He has **sent** me to proclaim **liberty** to **captives***
    *and **recovery** of sight to the **blind**,*
  *to let the **oppressed** go **free**,*
  *and to proclaim a year **acceptable** to the **Lord**.*
Rolling up the scroll, he handed it **back** to the attendant
  and sat **down**,
  and the **eyes** of **all** in the synagogue looked **intently** at him.
He said to them,
  "**Today** this **Scripture** passage is **fulfilled** in your **hearing**."

Concern for the poor is a recurring theme in Luke.

Make us wonder about the Nazareth assembly's response to the proclamation by highlighting how all looked "intently at him."

Pause. Then, making eye contact, convincingly speak Jesus' bold assertion.

Now the Lectionary jumps from the start of the Gospel according to Luke to the beginning of Jesus' Galilean ministry. Throughout his account, Luke delights in chronicling the crowd's enthused response to Jesus. That enthusiasm is here evident in "he was praised by all"—although very soon their praises will turn to venom! The Spirit reference is especially significant for it establishes Luke's contention that Jesus' entire ministry is dominated by the Spirit. Luke's details add color and poignancy to the story: it is the "Sabbath" and

Jesus is in Nazareth, "where he had grown up," going to the synagogue, "according to his custom." Jesus looks for the passage from Isaiah he wishes to proclaim and reads it with great intentionality, immediately applying it to himself, identifying himself as the anointed one who will bring God's world-shaking message of liberation for the oppressed and inclusion for the marginalized. This concern for the poor becomes emblematic of Luke's Gospel account.

The passage from Isaiah looks back to the Old Testament from which it is derived and looks forward to the ministry of Jesus

it so aptly describes. The verses immediately following today's text chronicle the crowd's outrage on hearing the last line. The march toward Calvary has already begun. Jesus knows how Israel deals with her prophets and, thus, what the fulfillment of this prophecy will bring. But today the last line can be delivered innocent of that awareness and with a strong conviction that its fulfillment continues in our day.

4TH SUNDAY IN ORDINARY TIME

Lectionary #72

READING I — Jeremiah 1:4–5, 17–19

A reading from the Book of the Prophet Jeremiah

The **word** of the LORD came to me, saying:
Before I **formed** you in the womb I **knew** you,
    before you were **born** I **dedicated** you,
    a **prophet** to the nations I **appointed** you.

But do you **gird** your **loins**;
    stand up and **tell** them
    all that I **command** you.
Be not **crushed** on their account,
    as though I would **leave** you crushed before them;
for it is **I** this day
    who have made you a **fortified city**,
    a pillar of **iron**, a wall of **brass**,
    against the whole **land**:
    against Judah's **kings** and **princes**,
    against its **priests** and **people**.
They will **fight** against you but not **prevail** over you,
    for I am **with** you to **deliver** you, says the LORD.

This is not common, everyday speech. It is a divine call heard deep in the heart. Give it proper dignity.

His ministry will be to all *the nations, not just Israel.*

"But do you gird your loins" is an order, not a question. It means to bind up your clothing to be ready for action!

*The meaning of "as though I would leave you . . ." is "*lest* I leave you crushed." "It should read more as warning than a reassurance.* Here *we have our reassurance.*

Stress the verbs, not the prepositions, except for the final "with."

READING I | Jeremiah was a reluctant prophet. Called at an early age, he protested that he was too young and didn't know how to speak. But God would not take no for an answer and instead offered encouragement for the difficult task ahead. Today's reading, in fact, sounds more like preparation for battle than for prophecy. The role of the prophet was never sought because it was always perilous, and it was perilous even though prophets were almost always sent to their *own* people, a fact that made the prophetic task no less a burden and no less a danger.

Like Israel's other prophets, Jeremiah is sent to a people in whom God's law has already been planted, but who have allowed the weeds of idolatry to choke that word from their hearts. It is often those who should have known better who are least inclined to listen when someone reminds them they have strayed.

So God fortifies Jeremiah, reassuring him that "it is I who have made you a pillar of iron, a wall of brass." God tells Jeremiah the divine hand was upon him from before he was born, for God "knew him," set him

apart and "appointed" him for the difficult task he would undertake. But while the task of prophecy is burdensome and dangerous, the word God speaks through the prophet does not fail to accomplish that for which it is sent. When God promises Jeremiah his enemies will "not prevail over [him]," God uses the ancient formula first addressed to Moses and then to all the prophets after him: "I am with you." That's the great truth you must emphasize as you read: the prophet never ventures forth alone, for God is always at his side. Trust and fidelity to God's word are the prophet's

READING II 1 Corinthians 12:31—13:13

A reading from the first Letter of Saint Paul to the Corinthians

Brothers and sisters:
Strive **eagerly** for the **greatest** spiritual gifts.
But I shall **show** you a still more **excellent** way.

If I speak in **human** and **angelic** tongues,
    but do not have **love**,
    I am a resounding **gong** or a clashing **cymbal**.
And if I have the gift of **prophecy**,
    and comprehend all **mysteries** and all **knowledge**;
    if I have all **faith** so as to move **mountains**,
    but do not have **love**, I am **nothing**.
If I give away **everything** I **own**,
    and if I hand my **body** over so that I may **boast**,
    but do not have **love**, I **gain nothing**.

Love is **patient**, love is **kind**.
It is not **jealous**, it is not **pompous**,
    it is not **inflated**, it is not **rude**,
    it does not seek its own **interests**,
    it is not **quick-tempered**, it does not **brood** over **injury**,
    it does not **rejoice** over **wrongdoing**
    but rejoices with the **truth**.
It **bears** all things, **believes** all things,
    hopes all things, **endures** all things.
Love never **fails**.
If there are **prophecies**, they will be brought to **nothing**;
    if **tongues**, they will **cease**;
    if **knowledge**, it will be brought to **nothing**.

Use the introduction to signal something important is going to be shared.

Pause, make eye contact, and speak with confidence here. In the three "If . . . but" clauses, the "if" clause should be faster, and the "but" clause should be slower.
The point will be lost if the "if" clauses are not positive and energetic.

Don't stress the word "love," but what love *does* and *doesn't do*.

Contrast what love does with what will happen to everything else. Don't rush.

---

task; it is God who fights the fight and wins the battle. That's a promise that still holds true today.

 READING II This stunning piece of religious rhetoric is a favorite at weddings. Its sublime poetry is a work of genius that names all that our hearts desire and strive for. It paints an ideal we can't help but cherish, no matter how many times we might fail to live it. Weddings are not the only time to contemplate ideals; the

profound wisdom of a text like this makes even Ordinary Time extraordinary.

Continuing his instruction to the Corinthian community that he founded, Paul sets up a contrast between the charismatic gifts the people were arguing over and the gifts that really matter. Go ahead and seek the gifts of prophecy and teaching, he exhorts them, but I will show you greater, more enduring gifts whose value surpasses all the others. He begins by acknowledging that tongues, prophecy, knowledge, faith, and even self-sacrifice

(he ranks them in that order) come to absolutely nothing if they are not expressions of genuine love.

Having named love as the gift that surpasses all the rest, he enumerates all of love's attributes, telling us what love does and doesn't do. This is more than just another of Paul's lists. It is a celebration, not an enumeration, of the qualities of love. Imagining someone to whom, in all charity, you would want to speak these words (a bridal couple, a friend who won't forgive another, a parent and child who've been estranged) will help you find the tone and

For we know **partially** and we **prophesy** partially,
    but when the **perfect** comes, the **partial** will pass **away**.
When I was a **child**, I used to **talk** as a child,
    think as a child, **reason** as a child;
    when I became a **man**, I put **aside** childish things.
At present we see **indistinctly**, as in a **mirror**,
    but **then** face to **face**.
At present I know **partially**;
    then I shall know **fully**, as I am fully **known**.
So **faith**, **hope**, **love** remain, these **three**;
    but the **greatest** of these is **love**.

[Shorter: 1 Corinthians 13:4–13]

Address "faith," "hope," and "love" to three different individuals or sections in the assembly.

GOSPEL Luke 4:21–30

The solemn tone of the opening sentence should help the assembly understand why the crowd responds with high praise.

The rest of the reading will contrast with the positive response reported here.

The reading turns on this line. Can he really be what he seems? Where did he get this wisdom?

Capernaum = kuh-PER-nee-*m

A reading from the holy Gospel according to Luke

Jesus began speaking in the **synagogue**, saying:
    "**Today** this Scripture passage is **fulfilled** in your **hearing**."
And all spoke **highly** of him
    and were **amazed** at the gracious **words** that came
        from his **mouth**.
They also **asked**, "Isn't this the son of **Joseph**?"
He said to them, "**Surely** you will quote me this **proverb**,
    '**Physician**, cure yourself,' and say,
    'Do here in your **native** place
        the things that we heard were done in **Capernaum**.'"

pacing you need to proclaim these eloquent words.

"Love never fails" states the topic of the final paragraph. Prophecies, knowledge, stock portfolios, lawnmowers will cease. Love will not. Other things of value will pass away. Love will not. Paul is on a roll, free-associating more in the manner of an extemporaneous exhortation than a reasoned discourse. He concludes, contrasting the ways of youth and ignorance with those of maturity and insight. As children we act like children. At present we see partially and indistinctly. But one day, when we know fully, we shall fully understand that of all that was, and is, and ever will be, only love endures forever.

GOSPEL If his neighbors had their way, Jesus' ministry might have ended before it began. Foreshadowing the trajectory of his entire ministry, this inaugural episode begins with praise and ends in violence and rejection. What his neighbors do to Jesus here, Israel eventually will do as well. But why does the hometown boy experience rejection that turns ugly and hostile? Jesus gives one reason: no prophet is accepted in his own town. He's too familiar to be taken too seriously, especially if he comes to offer a critique. After all, the Nazarenes knew his whole family. They didn't expect someone so close to them to be able to see what they couldn't see or to possess wisdom and insight they didn't somehow impart to him. And it's just that kind of wisdom Jesus brings to the synagogue—the people don't recognize it and it threatens them.

Here is where Jesus crosses the line by challenging Israel's favored status.

Don't make these words a rebuke, but a "lesson" meant to instruct. Had they listened, they would have been converted.

Zarephath = ZAYR-uh-fath

Sidon = SĪ-duhn

Elisha = ee-LĪ-shuh

Naaman = NAY-uh-muhn

They are filled with righteous anger— often the most threatening kind. Don't exaggerate, but let the hostility be heard.

Suggest Jesus' confident gaze that parted the crowd before him.

And he said, "**Amen**, I say to you,
    no **prophet** is **accepted** in his own native **place**.
Indeed, I tell you,
    there were many **widows** in Israel in the days of **Elijah**
    when the sky was **closed** for three and a half **years**
    and a severe **famine** spread over the entire **land**.
It was to **none** of these that **Elijah** was sent,
    but only to a widow in **Zarephath** in the land of **Sidon**.
Again, there were many **lepers** in Israel
    during the time of **Elisha** the prophet;
    yet not **one** of them was **cleansed**, but only **Naaman**
        the **Syrian**."
When the people in the synagogue **heard** this,
    they were all filled with **fury**.
They **rose** up, **drove** him out of the **town**,
    and led him to the **brow** of the **hill**
    on which their town had been **built**,
    to **hurl** him down **headlong**.
But Jesus **passed** through the **midst** of them and went **away**.

Initially, they are caught up in his gracious words and the clarity of his teaching. But at the same time that they marvel and smile, a darker emotion sets in that is expressed in the words "Isn't this the son of Joseph?" Were it not for that question, it would almost seem Jesus picked the fight with his neighbors by citing proverbs that put them on the defensive and alluding to Elijah and Elisha—prophets who, because they were rejected by their own people, took their ministry to foreigners. Nobody

likes to be told they are like ancestors who failed to recognize God's prophet and were less deserving of divine favor than pagan outsiders. But in fact, the people's hostility emerges even before Jesus insinuates that he, too, will be forced to bring his message to foreigners because his own will reject it. And the hostility seems to flow from the familiarity of his face and the unfamiliarity of his teaching. The neighbors don't want to be stretched and challenged, especially by one of their own. So their humor turns dark. The sins of their ancestors are repeated. Another prophet almost meets with doom.

But the power of God in God's anointed is manifest as Jesus passes confidently through their midst and goes away.

In proclaiming this text, don't soften Jesus' obvious edge and don't dampen the hostility of the crowd. Yes, it's Ordinary Time, but the road that ends at Calvary starts here in Nazareth.

5TH SUNDAY IN ORDINARY TIME

Lectionary #75

READING I Isaiah 6:1–2a, 3–8

A reading from the Book of the Prophet Isaiah

In the year **King Uzziah** died,
    I saw the **Lord** seated on a **high** and lofty **throne**,
    with the **train** of his **garment filling** the temple.
Seraphim were stationed above.

They **cried** one to the other,
    "**Holy**, **holy**, **holy** is the LORD of hosts!
All the earth is **filled** with his **glory**!"
At the **sound** of that cry, the frame of the door **shook**
    and the house was **filled** with **smoke**.

Then I said, "**Woe** is me, I am **doomed**!
For I am a man of **unclean** lips,
    living among a **people** of unclean lips;
    yet my **eyes** have seen the **King**, the LORD of **hosts**!"
Then one of the seraphim **flew** to me,
    holding an **ember** that he had taken with tongs
        from the **altar**.

He touched my **mouth** with it, and said,
    "**See**, now that this has touched your **lips**,
    your wickedness is **removed**, your sin **purged**."

Then I heard the voice of the **Lord** saying,
    "**Whom** shall I send? Who will **go** for us?"
    "Here **I** am," I said; "send **me**!"

Uzziah = yuh-ZĪ-uh

Pause before "I saw" to imagine the powerful vision you will narrate.

Don't waste the triple "holy." Build intensity to create a textured rather than flat delivery of the angels' praise. You can build by increasing or decreasing volume, but sustain intensity.
Shaking and smoke are signs of God's presence.

Isaiah experiences fear and deep unworthiness here.

Speak with Isaiah's awe and gratitude for this merciful initiative from God.

Don't rush here. Recovering from the "terror" of encountering God, Isaiah responds with muted confidence.

READING I The German theologian and philosopher Rudolph Otto characterized people's experience of the holy as a *mysterium tremendum et fascinans*—a terrifying and fascinating mystery, wholly other, yet compassionate and gracious. In each of today's readings we find manifestations of the holy to be terrifying and yet attractive. This results from the human person's awareness of smallness and unworthiness in the presence of God's overwhelming majesty. Yet none of today's readings dwells on the vision of awe-inspiring holiness but on the call that lies at the heart of that vision.

Isaiah experiences the call to his prophetic office within the great temple, God's earthly dwelling, where God, who is "wholly other," sits like a mighty warrior Lord on a "high and lofty throne." All of his images speak of grandeur and might: God's train fills the temple, God is attended by Seraphim (who appear nowhere else in scripture) while smoke and tremors attend the divine apparition. Singing a three-fold "Holy," angels proclaim God's perfect holiness. This is a meeting of the human and divine, and while God remains "wholly other," Isaiah's dialogue with the angel and the Lord reveals a God who is also merciful and attractive (*fascinans*). So, while creating the mystery and majesty of the divine apparition, don't let the more important dialogue that follows be obscured.

Initially, Isaiah is overwhelmed by the chasm between God's greatness and his own unworthiness. He even fears for his life, for seeing God is something no human can endure. But God takes the initiative in calming Isaiah's fear. The "ember" is an

READING II 1 Corinthians 15:1–11

A reading from the first Letter of Saint Paul to the Corinthians

Although they've heard the Gospel, his tone is urgent because they have lost so much.

I am **reminding** you, brothers and sisters,
　　of the **gospel** I preached to you,
　　which you indeed **received** and in which you also **stand**.
Through it you are also being **saved**,
　　if you hold **fast** to the word I **preached** to you,
　　unless you believed in **vain**.

Stress and contrast "if . . ." and "unless . . . ."

Here are the basic tenets of the faith. Build energy as you go.

For I **handed** on to you as of **first** importance what I also **received**:
　　that Christ **died** for our **sins** in accordance with the **Scriptures**;
　　that he was **buried**;
　　that he was **raised** on the third **day**
　　　　in accordance with the **Scriptures**;
　　that he appeared to **Cephas**, then to the **Twelve**.
After that, Christ appeared to more
　　than **five hundred** brothers at **once**,
　　most of whom are still **living**,
　　though some have fallen **asleep**.
After that he appeared to **James**,
　　then to **all** the apostles.

Cephas = SEE-fuhs

He's using these events to bolster faith. You should do the same.

Stress and contrast "James," "all," and "me."

Last of all, as to one born **abnormally**,
　　he appeared to **me**.
For I am the **least** of the apostles,
　　not fit to be **called** an apostle,
　　because I **persecuted** the church of God.
But by the **grace** of God I **am** what I **am**,
　　and his grace to me has **not** been **ineffective**.

Don't overdo the self-deprecation. Speak with confidence, emphasizing God's mercy.

---

instrument of healing and forgiveness, not of punishment, so speak of it in positive, not fearful, tones. God's question is spoken not just to Isaiah, but to every person; communicate that by scanning the assembly. Finally, overcoming the *tremendum* and yielding to the *fascinans*, Isaiah says enthusiastically, "send me!"

READING II | Paul's dual objective here is to review the essentials of the faith he himself had taught the

Corinthians and to reassert the indispensability of faith in bodily resurrection— Christ's and ours! Yet, because of the sandwiching of this reading between the other two, today what was a secondary point for Paul takes on priority for us, and that is his call to the service of Jesus. Paul had his own fearful and fascinating encounter with the divine when the risen Christ appeared to him on the road to Damascus. It was there he experienced the call to conversion that he later passed on to the Corinthians.

But, as often happens in any committed group, the Corinthians have lost the initial fervor with which they responded to the Gospel. Paul seeks to abate this erosion of commitment and to fortify the faith of his readers. He begins with the essentials, reaffirming Christ's saving death ("for our sins") and his Resurrection. This is the indispensable ground of faith. Lose that and you've lost everything, because if Christ did not rise from the dead, our

Make eye contact and speak with conviction here.

Indeed, I have toiled **harder** than **all** of them;
　not **I**, however, but the **grace** of God that is **with** me.
Therefore, whether it be **I** or **they**,
　so we **preach** and so you **believed**.

[Shorter: 1 Corinthians 15:3–8, 11]

GOSPEL　Luke 5:1–11

A reading from the holy Gospel according to Luke

They are "pressing in" so that they can hear the word of God.

Gennesaret = geh-NES-uh-ret

They've worked all night and cleaned nets with sore and tired hands.

While the **crowd** was **pressing** in on Jesus and **listening**
　to the word of **God**,
he was standing by the Lake of **Gennesaret**.
He saw two **boats** there alongside the lake;
　the **fishermen** had **disembarked** and were washing their **nets**.
Getting **into** one of the boats, the one belonging to **Simon**,
　he asked him to **put out** a short distance from the **shore**.
Then he sat down and **taught** the crowds from the **boat**.
After he had **finished** speaking, he said to **Simon**,
　"Put out into **deep** water and **lower** your nets for a **catch**."
Simon said in reply,
　"**Master**, we have worked **hard** all **night** and have
　　caught **nothing**,
but at your **command** I will **lower** the nets."
When they had **done** this, they caught a great **number** of fish
　and their nets were **tearing**.

Although he expects the effort will be futile, Peter courteously yields to Jesus' request. Contrast the frustration and the yielding.
Stress the reality of the miraculous catch by emphasizing "great number," "nets were tearing," and "their partners . . . to come to help them."

faith is in vain. Next he stresses the post-Resurrection appearances that irrefutably confirm the resurrection. As you read, strive for greater persuasiveness and convey Paul's growing momentum as he moves through the impressive list of appearances.

Paul stops suddenly to focus on the graced nature of his apostolic calling. He is mindful of his back-door entry into Christ's Church: entered "abnormally," as "*least*" of the apostles." His unworthiness, though more concrete and serious than Isaiah's, was just as surely blotted out by

the grace and initiative of God. But Paul is not hanging his head for he has "toiled harder" than the other apostles, an assertion that might sound arrogant were he not so mindful that even his effective labor was made possible only by God's bountiful and unmerited mercy.

GOSPEL In last week's Gospel, Jesus was rejected by his own neighbors. This week, Jesus is accepted by Peter, James, and John, who abandon all else in favor of him. Like

today's Isaiah reading, this is a *call* text. But instead of a heavenly vision of divine glory, Peter's call occurs amid the smelly nets and sweaty palms of earthly life. The very human context of this story not only provides contrast with Isaiah but, more importantly, makes a statement about God's presence in the world of human affairs. When God calls, it is in the midst of daily life. When our hands are dirty and smelly, Jesus comes and asks us to drop everything to follow him.

Although not yet the friends they will become, Jesus invites himself into Peter's

Shift your tone for Peter's reaction to the miracle. Peter is overwhelmed by his unworthiness.

"Do not be afraid" is Jesus' classic exhortation (especially after the Resurrection).
Pause before proclaiming the final line.

They signaled to their **partners** in the **other** boat
    to come to **help** them.
They came and filled **both** boats
    so that the boats were in danger of **sinking**.
When Simon Peter **saw** this, he fell at the **knees** of Jesus and said,
    "**Depart** from me, Lord, for I am a **sinful** man."
For **astonishment** at the catch of fish they had made **seized** him
    and all those **with** him,
        and likewise **James** and **John**, the sons of **Zebedee**,
    who were **partners** of Simon.
Jesus said to Simon, "Do not be **afraid**;
    from now **on** you will be catching **men**."
When they brought their boats to the **shore**,
    they left **everything** and **followed** him.

boat, making a seemingly simple but, in fact, imposing request. For the fishermen, the workday is over, marked by the washing of their nets. For Jesus it's just beginning. He asks Peter and his crew to put out into deep water with the confidence of one who knows what is about to happen. But Peter knows none of it and must resist fatigue to accede to the request of this man he perceives as "Master." Professional fishermen know where to cast nets and how to find fish, so their willingness to lower nets at Jesus' instruction suggests

their humility and perhaps Peter's burgeoning sense that there is something special about this rabbi from Nazareth.

"When Simon Peter saw this" signals Peter's entry into *mysterium tremendum* (see the First Reading's commentary). Peter is undone by the awesome mystery and power he senses in Jesus, so like Isaiah, he responds by asserting his unworthiness. But the word "astonishment" suggests Peter is as much fascinated as he is terrified. The miracles of Jesus were meant to evoke exactly this kind of response—to spark recognition of the power of God in

Jesus' ministry. But the Pharisees and other religious leaders would not let such events change their hearts. Jesus came down so hard on them precisely because of this refusal to see. But Peter's eyes are wide open; he knows he is in the presence of the holy. Like Isaiah's angel, Jesus reassures him with a tone that also must have offered healing forgiveness. The presence of overwhelming goodness exerts an overwhelming attraction, so finally the fishermen abandon everything and follow him.

6TH SUNDAY IN ORDINARY TIME

Lectionary #78

READING I   Jeremiah 17:5–8

Remember that this is a study in contrasts. Stress those words that convey desolation and emptiness, and don't hold back on the word "Cursed."

The images of "barren bush," "lava waste," and "salt and empty earth" are meant to be jarring. Your tone should convey both distress and warning.

Your tempo and tone on phrases like "stretches out its roots," "leaves stay green," and "shows no distress" contrast with what went before because now you are speaking with the enthusiasm of flowing, surging life that "still bears fruit."

A reading from the Book of the Prophet Jeremiah

Thus says the LORD:
Cursed is the one who trusts in **human beings**,
    who seeks his strength in **flesh**,
    whose **heart** turns **away** from the LORD.
He is like a barren **bush** in the **desert**
    that enjoys no change of **season**,
but stands in a **lava** waste,
    a **salt** and **empty** earth.
Blessed is the one who **trusts** in the LORD,
    whose **hope** is the LORD.
He is like a **tree** planted beside the **waters**
    that stretches out its **roots** to the **stream**:
It fears not the **heat** when it comes;
    its **leaves** stay **green**;
in the year of **drought** it shows no **distress**,
    but **still** bears **fruit**.

READING I Jeremiah uses contrasts to emphasize the need for putting ultimate trust in God rather than in the things of this world. In strong and uncompromising language, this two-stanza poem lays out what constitutes true wisdom. The formula is quite simple: put your faith in God, letting God be your hope, your source of nourishment. Those who do this are "blessed." Like a tree planted beside running water, they put down deep roots and can withstand the fickle seasons.

Fearing neither heat nor drought, they flourish and bear much fruit.

But some do not make God their foundation and nourishment. Instead, they turn to the world of human affairs and put their trust in the things of the flesh. Upon these, the prophet speaks a harsh curse. They bring upon themselves the consequences of their choices: they become like a thirsty, barren bush whose shallow roots provide no protection from the whims of the seasons. They wither away.

Utilizing the same "woe" and "blessing" structure we see in the Gospel (although in reverse order), Jeremiah's extended metaphors provide a stark and sobering message. It is not trees that Jeremiah is describing, but us. The consequences he enumerates result from choices, not from accidents. The pattern of our choices determines whether we survive the inevitable periods of dryness in life. Only if we have placed our faith in God by cultivating a relationship with him as the one who matters most, will we survive life's heat and drought and bear much fruit.

Paul's is an urgent agenda. Don't let this sound unimportant.

"Vain" comes as a surprise after the triple use of "raised." Stress it, and then build in intensity to "you are still . . . ."

Paul is arguing his case. Do the same. The third "if . . . then" clause requires the most intensity. Don't waste the word "pitiable."

There is a shift in tone here. This is the *good* news that contrasts with earlier arguments.

Take time with these details, emphasizing how many came to hear Jesus.

Tyre = tīr
Sidon = SĪ-duhn

READING II   1 Corinthians 15:12, 16–20

A reading from the first Letter of Saint Paul to the Corinthians

Brothers and sisters:
If **Christ** is preached as **raised** from the **dead**,
    how can **some** among you say there **is** no resurrection
        of the dead?
If the dead are **not** raised, neither has **Christ** been raised,
    and if **Christ** has not been raised, your faith is **vain**;
        you are still in your **sins**.
Then those who have fallen **asleep** in Christ have **perished**.
If for **this** life **only** we have hoped in Christ,
    we are the most **pitiable** people of **all**.

But now Christ **has** been raised from the dead,
    the **firstfruits** of those who have fallen **asleep**.

GOSPEL   Luke 6:17, 20–26

A reading from the holy Gospel according to Luke

Jesus came down with the **Twelve**
    and stood on a stretch of **level** ground
    with a **great** crowd of his **disciples**
    and a large **number** of the **people**
    from all **Judea** and **Jerusalem**
    and the coastal region of **Tyre** and **Sidon**.

READING II   When confronted with mis-understanding or blatant error, Paul responds with clear and force-ful teaching. Here he corrects a misunder-standing among some Corinthians who believed that, through the sacraments, they were *already* raised and therefore would experience no further Resurrection of the body. Nonsense, says Paul. Our earthly life is not all there is. Yes, through Baptism each already has died and risen to new life with Christ, but the risen life we live now is only a shadow of what awaits us when we enter eternal life. To limit understand-ing of Resurrection to "this life only" is to deny the benefits of Christ's Resurrection. If Christ's rising yields no eternal conse-quences for us, we are pitiable indeed. Our faith would be absurd if God acted to no purpose in raising Christ from the dead. In fact, Christ is only the first of those who will rise from the dead. "First" implies oth-ers to follow—and we are the others!

Paul's reasoning is compelling. *If* you believe in Christ's Resurrection, *then* how can you deny the resurrection of the dead for the rest of us? Then he moves in reverse: if the *dead* are not raised, then *Christ* was not raised either. Worse, if Christ was not raised, we are all still in our sins and those who have died have truly "perished." Paul's faith is as obvious in these lines as is his scorn for those who deny it. It is the last line that asserts his faith triumphantly, professing that Christ is the first of *many* who will rise, and that believers are not dead for good, but merely "fallen asleep."

GOSPEL   Many may not realize Luke has a counterpart to

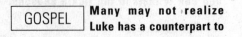

This repetition is intentional. Like a refrain, it draws us in and deepens our experience of what's shared. So stress each "blessed" and each "woe." Remember that you are naming as "blessed" those the world sees as pitiable. Keep your tone hopeful and consoling.

Make eye contact here. Your energy and joy should peak on the first two lines. The third is more sober.

Don't overdo the somber tone. Remember that these lines are directed at those who are already disciples.

Emphasize the word "false." Pause before announcing "The Gospel of the Lord."

And raising his **eyes** toward his **disciples** he said:
  "**Blessed** are you who are **poor**,
    for the **kingdom** of God is **yours**.
  Blessed are you who are now **hungry**,
    for you will be **satisfied**.
  Blessed are you who are now **weeping**,
    for you will **laugh**.
  Blessed are you when people **hate** you,
    and when they **exclude** and **insult** you,
    and **denounce** your name as **evil**
    on account of the Son of **Man**.
Rejoice and leap for **joy** on that day!
Behold, your reward will be **great** in **heaven**.
For their **ancestors** treated the **prophets** in the same **way**.
  But **woe** to you who are **rich**,
    for you have **received** your consolation.
  Woe to you who are **filled** now,
    for you will be **hungry**.
  Woe to you who **laugh** now,
    for you will **grieve** and **weep**.
  Woe to you when all speak **well** of you,
    for their **ancestors** treated the **false** prophets in this **way**."

Matthew's "Sermon on the Mount." That is unfortunate for Luke's beatitudes correspond to "woes" which have no parallels in the other Gospel accounts.

Luke's setting is not Matthew's mountaintop, the usual biblical meeting place of God and people; instead, it is set at the busy crossroads of life where multitudes gather to hear Jesus. This setting corresponds to the more sociological tone of Luke's beatitudes. His underprivileged are simply poor and hungry, not Matthew's more spiritualized poor "in spirit" or hungry "for righteousness."

Note also that Jesus is addressing his "disciples" in the presence of the crowd, not the crowd itself. The fact that these demanding ideals are meant for those already *committed* to Jesus and already drawing on grace should affect your tone. You are not teaching what is demanded of all, but what is offered those who already know grace. That exactly describes your situation: your assembly consists of people who are already "in Christ." Remind them that good fortune consists of receiving God's kingdom blessings, and warn them that confidence placed in the transitory

things of this world makes a disciple unfit for the kingdom. Luke neither extols nor condemns a particular social class, pitting rich against poor. Instead he stresses, as you must, the need for all to recognize their poverty and rely on God rather than on self, remembering that the reversal of life situations is one of the chief characteristics of life in God's kingdom.

ASH WEDNESDAY

Lectionary #219

READING I   Joel 2:12–18

"Even now . . ." means "Even in the midst of this frightening predicament" (the plague of locusts).

In this season of conversion there are two categories of words to stress: The first is words of call and command: "Return," "rend," "blow," "proclaim," "gather," "notify," and "assemble." The second category is words encouraging repentance: "gracious and merciful," "kindness," "relenting," "blessing," "spare," and "pity."

Slow down here. Let your tone become caring and persuasive. You are announcing the goodness and mercy of God.

Imagine a representative of the people speaking these lines, calling neighbors and friends to repentance. Use a quicker pace.

"Children," "bride," and "bridegroom" signal the importance of the entire community's response.

A reading from the Book of the Prophet Joel

Even **now**, says the LORD,
  return to me with your **whole heart**,
  with **fasting**, and **weeping**, and **mourning**;
Rend your **hearts**, not your **garments**,
  and **return** to the LORD, your **God**.
For **gracious** and **merciful** is he,
  slow to anger, **rich** in kindness,
  and **relenting** in punishment.
Perhaps he will **again** relent
  and leave behind him a **blessing**,
Offerings and **libations**
  for the LORD, your **God**.

Blow the **trumpet** in Zion!
  proclaim a **fast**,
  call an **assembly**;
Gather the people,
  notify the congregation;
Assemble the **elders**,
  gather the **children**
  and the **infants** at the breast;
Let the **bridegroom quit** his room,
  and the **bride** her **chamber**.

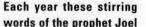 **READING I** Each year these stirring words of the prophet Joel inaugurate the great season of Lent, calling God's people to repentance. Lent's return reminds us of the cyclic nature of all of life. Even our relationship with God has its cycles. Like ancient Israel we wander away from the Lord, but then fear, love, remorse, or some other emotion motivates our return.

What motivated the people of Joel's day was a devastating plague of locusts. Joel interpreted this calamity as a sign that the fearful "Day of the Lord" was imminent. Fearing God's judgment, he calls the people to repentance. The pattern of infidelity, followed by impending danger, resulting in repentance that elicits God's mercy was an oft repeated cycle in the history of Israel. And often, we do the same: roused by some looming disaster or a recent tragedy, we make resolves and turn to God promising never to stray again. But then we do. Remember how full churches were in the weeks following the terrorist attacks of 9/11 and how quickly things went back to "normal"?

Joel appeals to fear, love, and remorse as he urges the people to return to God. The first paragraph throbs with urgent pleading. But throughout, the threat of vengeance is balanced with reminders of God's willingness (even eagerness!) to forgive. That message permeates this text! Joel's words work individually ("fasting," "weeping," and "mourning" describe three *different* actions) and also collectively, to express a call for repentance.

Don't rush the imperatives of the second paragraph—"blow . . . gather . . . assemble!" No one in the community is

Between the **porch** and the **altar**
　　let the **priests**, the **ministers** of the LORD, **weep**,
And say, "**Spare**, O LORD, your **people**,
　　and make not your **heritage** a **reproach**,
　　with the nations **ruling** over them!
Why should they say among the peoples,
　　'**Where** is their **God**?'"

Then the LORD was **stirred** to **concern** for his land
　　and took **pity** on his people.

Don't overdo your proclamation here, but give these lines a sense of urgency.

Imagine scoffing non-believers speaking these lines.

These are crucial lines: repentance brings forgiveness. Speak slowly.

READING II　　2 Corinthians 5:20—6:2

A reading from the second Letter of Saint Paul to the Corinthians

Brothers and sisters:
We are **ambassadors** for **Christ**,
　　as if **God** were **appealing** through **us**.
We **implore** you on behalf of **Christ**,
　　be **reconciled** to **God**.
For **our** sake he made him to **be** sin
　　who did not **know** sin,
　　so that **we** might become the **righteousness**
　　　　of **God** in **him**.

Begin your proclamation slowly. First, get the assembly's attention, and then tell them: 1) who we are and 2) what God is doing through us.

Don't "implore" like a beggar, but rather with the dignity of God's spokesperson.

This is a marvel that should be announced with awe: God allowed Christ to bear the consequences of our sins! Stress that it was done "for our sake."

---

exempted from these commands — not children, not even infants at the breast; priests must respond — even honeymooners aren't excused! Joel's emphasis is on communal response. Although we are individuals, our responses unite into the collective reply of God's people. The final couplet is vital because it presents God's merciful reaction to the people's penitence. "Concern" and "pity" determine your tone as you speak for the compassionate God who forgives.

READING II　Were this another day, we might hear Paul's words differently. But Ash Wednesday determines our focus. We're starting a season of conversion and reconciliation. This day calls us to a change of heart and to the kind of conscious, disciplined effort that leads to holiness, indeed, "the very holiness of God."

　　Joel was God's mouthpiece in the First Reading; now Paul and his companion Timothy embrace that role. In Paul's opening words, we hear an invitation to the entire Christian community to do the same. We, too, are to be "ambassadors for Christ." And the message we are to live and proclaim is simple and clear: "be reconciled to God." At the start of the Lenten season, nothing need be said more clearly!

　　Some have called this text a "Lector's Prayer," since as readers we are, indeed, God's spokespersons. But Paul is saying something much more important here. As Christ's ministers, he and we continue Christ's work in a special way. Everyday,

Again, appeal with dignity and urgency. This is a life-and-death situation.	Working **together**, then,
	    we appeal to you **not** to receive the **grace**
	        of God in **vain**.
	For he says:

Lessen the energy/intensity for the quotation.	*In an **acceptable** time I **heard** you,* *and on the day of **salvation** I **helped** you.*
The double "now" requires a buildup in energy and conviction.	Behold, **now** is a very acceptable time; behold, **now** is the day of ***salvation***.

GOSPEL   Matthew 6:1–6, 16–18

A reading from the holy Gospel according to Matthew

	Jesus said to his **disciples**:
	    "Take **care** not to perform righteous **deeds**
	    in order that people may **see** them;
	    otherwise, you will have no **recompense**
	        from your heavenly **Father**.

Avoid an overly harsh or judgmental tone here.	When **you** give alms,
	    do not blow a **trumpet** before you,
	    as the **hypocrites** do in the **synagogues**
	        and in the **streets**
	    to win the **praise** of others.

Throughout, the text achieves emphasis through contrast, juxtaposing the behavior of hypocrites with that of true disciples ("you").	**Amen**, I say to you, they have **received** their reward. But when **you** give alms,
Is Jesus speaking from anger or frustration?	do not let your **left** hand know what your **right** is **doing**, so that your almsgiving may be **secret**.
Don't vary the stress on this thrice-repeated refrain, but emphasize these same three words each time.	And your Father who **sees** in secret will **repay** you.

God uses us to appeal, to convert, to reconcile! It remains for us to be aware of God's desire to work through us and allow God to use us. Because God's love respects human freedom, God forces no one's conversion, thus the importance of words like "implore" and "appeal."

Paul reminds us of one of the mysteries of the Incarnation: that Jesus willingly became part of sinful humanity. He took our sins upon himself! Lest that has been done for us "in vain," we must realize that *now*—even as you speak the words—God is calling. *Now*—even as we sit and listen—is the time to respond. God's word, in the moment of proclamation, accomplishes that for which it was sent. That means now, on *this* day of salvation.

GOSPEL The First Reading calls for communal and public enactment of remorse and conversion while in the Gospel Jesus calls for privacy and secrecy. Why such a contrast? Because Joel's way had become so institutionalized by Jesus' time that many had turned intended acts of generosity and mortification into the insincere and elaborate displays of hypocrites who sought the admiration of the crowds more than the mercy of God.

Like Joel, Jesus wants hearts converted to God. So, he says, perform your religious acts *only* for God. The acts he names are the three traditional Lenten practices: prayer, fasting, and almsgiving. In the spiritual life, motivation is primary: do the right thing for the wrong reason and you gain nothing. Religious piety and good

Resist the temptation to adopt the superior attitude of the hypocrites as you speak these lines.

Keep the same stresses as before.

Do you hear sarcasm or regret in these lines?

Again, be sure you don't sound as arrogant as the hypocrites and note the third recurrence of the "Father sees/repays" refrain.

Slow down as you approach the words "will repay you."

"When you **pray**,
  do not be like the **hypocrites**,
  who love to **stand** and pray in the **synagogues**
    and on **street** corners
  so that others may **see** them.
Amen, I say to you,
  they have **received** their reward.
But when **you** pray, go to your **inner** room,
  close the door, and **pray** to your Father in **secret**.
And your Father who **sees** in secret will **repay** you.

"When you **fast**,
  do not look **gloomy** like the **hypocrites**.
They **neglect** their appearance,
  so that they may appear to **others** to be **fasting**.
Amen, I say to you, they have **received** their reward.
But when **you** fast,
  anoint your head and **wash** your face,
  so that you may **not** appear to be fasting,
  except to your **Father** who is **hidden**.
And your Father who **sees** what is hidden
      will **repay** you."

works are too often motivated by a desire for the recognition of others rather than by the desire to do good and please God. So, repeatedly, Jesus urges another way: "do not blow a trumpet"; "do not let your left hand know what your right is doing"; "go to your inner room"; "pray . . . in secret"; "do not look gloomy." As he names each spiritual practice, Jesus contrasts his brand of private piety with the ostentatious hypocrites. False piety is its own reward. In fact, the Greek verb Matthew uses to

describe the hypocrites' reward suggests these showoffs are already "paid in full."

But remember that humility requires that we first remove the plank from our own eye. So a sincere and understated delivery, void of judgment or sarcasm, will serve this scripture best. The goal is instruction, not condemnation. Jesus loves even the hypocrites and desires their conversion. Their self-destructive self-deception elicits both wrath and pity from Jesus. His condemnation of false piety is also a warning for disciples that even religion can become a seductive and deadly trap.

Jesus assures the disciples that God rewards true virtue. When *you* give alms or fast or pray, he says, do it in ways opposite those of the hypocrites. The Father will see this and repay you. If Jesus is frustrated or angry here, it is because hypocrites are hurting themselves and giving others a bad example. Jesus cared about the spiritual welfare of *all* his listeners. His frustration is obvious, but so is his desire to protect and encourage.

1ST SUNDAY OF LENT

Lectionary #24

READING I   Deuteronomy 26:4–10

A reading from the Book of Deuteronomy

Moses describes the liturgical setting and the story that is to be retold.

Change vocal quality to signal the quote within a quote.

Aramean = ayr-uh-MEE-uhn

Contrast "small household" with "great, strong and numerous."

Contrast the affliction of slavery with the joy of deliverance.

Emphasize the strong images: "strong hand . . . arm" and "terrifying power . . . signs . . . wonders."

Moses spoke to the **people**, saying:
"The **priest** shall receive the **basket** from you
    and shall set it in front of the **altar** of the LORD, your **God**.
Then you shall **declare** before the LORD, your God,
    'My **father** was a wandering **Aramean**
    who went down to **Egypt** with a small **household**
    and **lived** there as an **alien**.
But **there** he became a **nation**
    great, **strong**, and **numerous**.
When the Egyptians **maltreated** and **oppressed** us,
    imposing hard **labor** upon us,
    we **cried** to the LORD, the God of our **fathers**,
    and he **heard** our cry
    and saw our **affliction**, our **toil**, and our **oppression**.
He brought us **out** of Egypt
    with his strong **hand** and outstretched **arm**,
    with terrifying **power**, with **signs** and **wonders**;
    and bringing us into **this** country,
    he gave us this **land** flowing with **milk** and **honey**.

READING I Liturgy is built on memory. It brings together history and ritual, giving us a context of praise in which to express our faith. That pattern is very old, as witnessed by Moses' use of a harvest thanksgiving festival as the context for his profession of faith. Abraham's history is now also our history, his faith our faith, and Moses' admonition to remember is also addressed to us. When we forget, we cease to be a people of faith. So the practice of our memory-evoking rituals is

not pious religiosity, but a matter of survival. Communicate that urgency when, as Moses, you order the people to retell the story of God's saving action in their lives.

Moses' "creed," his retelling of salvation history, is probably one of the oldest passages in the Bible. Treat it with reverence, but give it life. Together, the people are remembering their common history. The "basket" given to the "priest" contained the "first fruits" offered in gratitude for a successful harvest. In the retelling that follows, take note of the narrative and emotional shifts: the descendants of our

father Abraham multiplied and thrived in Egypt, but the Egyptians enslaved us. God heard our pleas and rescued us and brought us to a land of plenty. Therefore, we now thank God with gifts from the soil. It's a hope-filled retelling of God's constant love and protection. Share it as if it were your own family history, for in fact, it is—and that of all Christians. Let that awareness impact how you speak proudly of Abraham who, though an alien, became a nation great and numerous, and of how you describe the painful oppression and

Speak this phrase ("Therefore . . .") with gratitude for God's goodness. The quote within the quote ends here. Pause briefly.

Here, Moses gives the final liturgical instruction.

Therefore, I have now brought you the **firstfruits**
of the products of the **soil**
which **you**, O LORD, have **given** me.'
And having **set** them before the LORD, your **God**,
you shall **bow down** in his **presence**."

READING II   Romans 10:8–13

A reading from the Letter of Saint Paul to the Romans

Ask this question with a tone that says your listeners should already know the answer to this question.

Is Paul goading or imploring? Is he intense or relaxed?

Slowly balance "confess" and "mouth" with "believe" and "heart."

Pause slightly between words for emphasis: "You . . . will . . . be . . . saved."

Belief justifies; confession saves.

Distinguish the quoted scripture from the sentence that follows.

The universality of Christ's salvation is revolutionary. Announce it with conviction and joy.

Brothers and sisters:
What does **Scripture** say?
*The word is **near** you,*
*in your **mouth** and in your **heart***
—that is, the word of faith that we **preach**—,
for, if you confess with your **mouth** that Jesus is **Lord**
and **believe** in your **heart** that God **raised** him from the **dead**,
you will be **saved**.
For one **believes** with the **heart** and so is **justified**,
and one **confesses** with the **mouth** and so is **saved**.
For the **Scripture** says,
*No one who **believes** in him will be put to **shame**.*
For there is no **distinction** between **Jew** and **Greek**;
the **same** Lord is Lord of **all**,
enriching all who **call** upon him.
For "**everyone** who calls on the name of the **Lord** will be **saved**."

---

affliction in Egypt and the marvel of God's deliverance! But remember that what God did for Israel, God does again in Christ. Christian faith is the conviction that God delivers us from the slavery of sin and brings us to the promised land of grace and salvation. Speak of the land of "milk and honey" with an attitude that anticipates the joy of Easter.

READING II   **What the story of Israel's rescue from slavery in Egypt was to the people of Israel, the story**

of Christ's death and Resurrection is for the new people of God, the Church. Paul reintroduces the theme of confession, that is, the profession of faith we saw in the First Reading. Like Moses, he urges upon his readers the need to *speak* what they believe. Paul says it and then says it again. We must "confess with the mouth" what we "believe with the heart": that Jesus is Lord, and God raised him from the dead. Evangelical Christians are better known than Catholics for citing and relying on this simple formula as the key to salvation.

There's no arguing with Paul on this. It's not enough to simply believe in the heart. Our "mouths" and our whole lives must speak of our faith in Christ. As we saw with Moses, confession on the lips is a matter of survival—even more, *salvation!*

Paul writes with an unassuming and unadorned style that touches us with its simple dignity. He asks the opening question with an expectation that his listeners will *know* the answer, and know it well. Yet he reviews. Why? He is not only *teaching* the formula for salvation but *exhorting* his readers to embrace it! The formula is

Note the repetition of "Spirit" who initiates this encounter with the devil.

Settings affect the mood of each scene, providing clues for delivery of the dialogue. Imagine a barren desert, going "up" a high mountaintop, and the noisy temple precincts. Each influences the tone, volume, and intensity of the dialogue.

Don't resort to stereotypes here.

Although exhausted, Jesus is resolute.

Don't rush the devil's dialogue. He's persuasive.

GOSPEL Luke 4:1–13

A reading from the holy Gospel according to Luke

Filled with the Holy **Spirit**, Jesus **returned** from the **Jordan**
    and was **led** by the Spirit into the **desert** for forty **days**,
    to be **tempted** by the **devil**.
He ate **nothing** during those days,
    and when they were **over** he was **hungry**.
The devil **said** to him,
"**If** you are the **Son** of **God**,
    command this **stone** to become **bread**."
Jesus **answered** him,
"It is **written**, *One does not live on bread alone*."
Then he took him up and **showed** him
    all the **kingdoms** of the **world** in a single **instant**.
The devil **said** to him,
"I shall give to you all this **power** and **glory**;
    for it has been handed **over** to me,
    and I may **give** it to whomever I **wish**.
All this will be **yours**, if you **worship** me."
Jesus said to him in **reply**,
"It is **written**:
    You shall worship the Lord, your God,
        and him alone shall you serve."

two-pronged: belief and confession. Most Christians are better at one than the other, but Paul argues for both. God's word takes root in our hearts when we "believe." But what we first believe in our hearts we must confess with our "mouths." Public witness is meaningless unless it reflects a genuine conviction of the heart. But of what use is inner conviction that is never shared in word or deed?

In the second paragraph, Paul no longer asks, but asserts what scripture says: salvation is for all. This is no small point and Paul works hard to make it, telling us

"no one who believes will be put to shame," and that the Lord of "all" offers the hope of salvation to "everyone"! A people convinced of the eradicable "distinctions" between "Jew" and "Greek" are being told—and persuaded—that Christ is their one foundation and salvation their common hope.

GOSPEL All three synoptics (the Gospel according to Matthew, Mark, and Luke) tell this story. Matthew gives the most detail and orders

the temptations differently. Luke ends with the most subtle, and thus most compelling, temptation: putting God to the test. After all, agreeing to a test demonstrates belief in God—you can't test a god you don't believe in—so what harm could it do? In the context of today's readings, which emphasize salvation through faith, Satan tempts Jesus to abandon faith and instead demand a sign. By putting that temptation last, Luke highlights the importance of placing our trust only in God. Luke is lean on narrative detail, describing neither Jesus' mood nor the personality of the

The intensity heightens; Satan is trying harder.

Satan quotes scripture confidently.

This line resonates with the theme of all of today's readings.

Pause after the words "from him . . ." and then knowingly deliver the final phrase.

Then he led him to **Jerusalem**,
    made him stand on the **parapet** of the **temple**, and said to him,
"If **you** are the **Son** of **God**,
    throw yourself **down** from here, for it is **written**:
        *He will command his **angels** concerning you, to **guard** you,*
    and:
        *With their **hands** they will **support** you,*
        *lest you dash your **foot** against a **stone**."*
Jesus said to him in **reply**,
    "It **also** says,
        *You shall not put the Lord, your **God**, to the **test**."*
When the devil had **finished** every temptation,
    he **departed** from him for a **time**.

tempter. He locates us in the desert—always a place of trial—and emphasizes the initiative of the Spirit. After his long fast, Jesus is obviously hungry, but he hungers for more than food. It is for the word and the ways of God that Jesus hungers. An honest reading of this text requires that you convey these as *real* "temptations," not illustrative scenarios meant to present Jesus as a paradigm of fidelity and endurance. Jesus rejects all the compromises Satan proffers: easily winning the crowds with magic, an earthly kingdom instead of

the kingdom of God, and forcing God's hand to prove Jesus' identity.

Luke consciously deleted Matthew's "high mountain" and the ministering angels—messianic and eschatological signs—in order to cast Jesus as an ordinary man who endures severe temptation. So don't sketch him or his adversary too broadly, using easy stereotypes: Jesus as noble, strong, and Teflon-coated; Satan as dripping with malice. We'll more easily believe Satan could have really tempted Jesus if he is reasonable, logical, and intelligent.

Like Moses and Paul, Jesus makes a confession about how we are to live and whom we are to worship and serve. His faith statements set the course for a life of obedience to God's will that culminates, as the portentous final line suggests, in the garden of last temptation.

2ND SUNDAY OF LENT

Lectionary #27

READING I   Genesis 15:5–12, 17–18

A reading from the Book of Genesis

Don't bury the mystery of this reading under the details.
Abram = AY-br*m.

The Lord **God** took **Abram outside** and said,
    "Look up at the **sky** and count the **stars**, if you can.
Just **so**," he added, "shall your **descendants** be."
Abram put his **faith** in the LORD,
    who **credited** it to him as an act of **righteousness**.

Stress the intimacy between God and Abram. God's voice should reflect the awareness that Abram has waited his whole life to hear this.

He then **said** to him,
    "I am the LORD who brought you from **Ur** of the **Chaldeans**
    to give you this **land** as a **possession**."
"O Lord **GOD**," he asked,
    "how am I to **know** that I shall **possess** it?"

This self-identification is important. Speak slowly and significantly.

Abram is pragmatic here.

He **answered** him,
    "Bring me a three-year-old **heifer**, a three-year-old **she-goat**,
    a three-year-old **ram**, a **turtledove**, and a young **pigeon**."

God is not scolding here; rather, he is answering Abram's question.

Abram **brought** him all these, **split** them in **two**,
    and **placed** each half **opposite** the other;
    but the **birds** he did **not** cut up.

You're describing the transaction of a legal contract that, if broken, will bring dire consequences.
Birds of prey represent potential threats to the covenant.

Birds of prey **swooped** down on the carcasses,
    but Abram **stayed** with them.
As the sun was about to set, a **trance** fell upon Abram,
    and a **deep**, terrifying **darkness enveloped** him.

Speak slowly here. Abram is enveloped in deep mystery.

READING I   The pericopes or reading selections of Lent retell key events in the history of salvation. This text about Abram, soon to become *Abraham*, is wrapped in mystery. At the center of the story, as in the Gospel, is a powerful "theophany" or divine manifestation. God has spoken before to Abram, promising to make him a great and prosperous nation. Just before the start of this passage, however, Abram complains that all his wealth will go to a servant, for God has given him no offspring. In response to his lament, God brings Abram outside to promise descendants as countless as the stars.

In the world of the Bible, a profound and life-changing encounter with God, even one that transforms a desert sheik into the father of a nation and a paradigm of faith, is quite possible. As reader, convince those in *your* world that such transformation indeed can occur. The text begins as if describing the evening stroll of two friends. Even in the Bible such intimacy with God can't be taken for granted. God's promise of immortality through countless descendants fulfills Abram's lifetime of waiting. Immediately, and perhaps contrite over his earlier lament, Abram believes God's promise, and immediately he is crowned with "righteousness."

The second paragraph describes a primitive and elaborate contract ritual foreign to our eyes and ears. The slaughtering of animals and walking between the cleaved carcasses signified each party's willingness to suffer the fate of the butchered animals should either default on their promise. When God makes the first, sublime promise—an aged couple will become parents—Abram takes it on faith. When

The words "fire pot" and "torch" symbolize God. The contract is now sealed.

When the sun had **set** and it was **dark**,
> there appeared a smoking **fire pot** and a flaming **torch**,
> which passed **between** those pieces.

It was on **that** occasion that the LORD made a **covenant** with Abram,
> saying: "To your **descendants** I give this **land**,
> from the Wadi of **Egypt** to the **Great River**, the **Euphrates**."

This is the great promise that Israel still cherishes today.

READING II Philippians 3:17—4:1

This epistle is known as "the letter of joy."

Establish eye contact before you begin. The first sentence is complex, so go slow.

A reading from the Letter of Saint Paul to the Philippians

Join with others in being **imitators** of me, brothers and sisters,
> and **observe** those who thus **conduct** themselves
> according to the **model** you have in us.
For **many**, as I have often **told** you

Use a slower pace for greater emphasis.

> and **now** tell you even in **tears**,
> conduct themselves as **enemies** of the **cross** of **Christ**.
Their **end** is **destruction**.

Pause slightly before the word "is" in each declaration. Proclaim the phrase "Their minds . . . earthly things" more slowly. It's a summary statement.

Their **God** is their **stomach**;
> their **glory** is in their "**shame**."
Their **minds** are occupied with **earthly** things.
But our **citizenship** is in **heaven**,

The mood becomes upbeat and hopeful here. Speak these words slowly.

> and **from** it we also await a **savior**, the **Lord** Jesus **Christ**.
He will **change** our lowly body
> to conform with his **glorified** body
> by the **power** that enables him **also**
> to bring **all** things into **subjection** to **himself**.

God promises the land, instead of believing instantly, Abram boldly asks for proof. God, who self-identifies as the one who beckoned Abram from Ur, offers a covenant which guarantees God's fulfillment. Listing the animals, then, is no rebuke of Abram, but God's patient offer of reassurance. The setting sun, the "trance" and "terrifying darkness" convey the awesome presence of God which envelopes Abram in mystery. The covenant is finally consummated when the divine symbols of "smoking fire pot" and "flaming torch" pass through the animals.

READING II A major theme of Lent is transformation, and this reading introduces that vital process. We are made for heaven, not earth, Paul insists. The ways of the Kingdom are not the ways of this life; therefore, disciples must imitate Paul, who provides a "model" of faithful discipleship. There is no pride in his assertions, for Paul writes from prison where he suffers for the Gospel and where he sheds "tears" because of those who have made themselves "enemies of the cross of Christ." Paul loves the Philippians, whom he himself converted, and so he speaks frankly about the problems he sees and the "destruction" that will inevitably follow if they don't reform. In contrast, Paul offers the hope that Christ will change "our lowly body" to "conform with his glorified body." Paul yearns earnestly for the Philippians, whom he loves and longs for, to experience this transformation. Now a prisoner facing the possibility of death, Paul knows firsthand the changing tides of fortune. But his urgency stems from his personal awareness that while circumstances change, faith can remain stable and unshaken!

Paul multiplies his expressions of affection. Keep it sincere and end with strength.

Therefore, my brothers and sisters,
   whom I **love** and **long** for, my **joy** and **crown**,
   in **this** way stand **firm** in the **Lord**.

[Shorter: Philippians 3:20—4:1]

GOSPEL   Luke 9:28b—36

A reading from the holy Gospel according to Luke

Create a mood of awesome mystery in which we, like the apostles, can share. We need to hear all of the names.

"Behold" is an unusual but arresting word. Use it boldly. Speak of Moses and Elijah with great reverence.

Moses and Elijah appear "in glory" like Jesus.

Although they're waking up, use a faster pace initially to suggest being startled awake, then a slower one.

"Master . . . here" is a classic and memorable line.

Jesus took **Peter**, **John**, and **James**
   and went up the **mountain** to **pray**.
While he was praying, his face **changed** in appearance
   and his **clothing** became dazzling **white**.
And **behold**, two men were **conversing** with him, **Moses**
      and **Elijah**,
   who appeared in **glory** and spoke of his **exodus**
   that he was going to **accomplish** in **Jerusalem**.
Peter and his **companions** had been overcome by **sleep**,
   but becoming fully **awake**,
   they saw his **glory** and the two men **standing** with him.
As they were about to **part** from him, **Peter** said to Jesus,
   "**Master**, it is **good** that we are here;
   let us make three **tents**,
   one for **you**, one for **Moses**, and one for **Elijah**."
But he did not **know** what he was **saying**.

What he desires most is to preserve their faith in Christ as the sole source of salvation. Paul urges them to imitate him because his whole life has become an imitation of Christ. Having abandoned reliance on circumcision ("shame") and dietary laws ("stomach") for his own salvation, Paul now worries that these burdens are being re-imposed on the Philippians by misguided enemies of the cross. Utilize Paul's strong words ("enemies," "tears," "destruction," "shame") to convey his great urgency.

   In opposition to those who "are occupied with earthly things," Paul reminds us

we are meant for heaven, from which comes the Lord Jesus Christ, who will one day conform all things to him.

GOSPEL   The highly symbolic Transfiguration story presents Jesus as the counterpart of God's saving action under the old law. In scripture, mountains are places of divine encounter (and prayer). On Mount Sinai, Moses met with God and came away with a luminous face radiating the presence of the Lord. On Mount Tabor, not only does Jesus' face

change dramatically, but the other details of the theophany closely parallel Moses' Sinai experience. Moses and Elijah, representing the law and prophets, converse with Jesus as their equal. By identifying Jesus with these great figures, Luke asserts that Jesus' path has been given him by God, the same God who led Moses and Elijah in their ministries. Jesus converses with the two men about his "exodus," a reference that looks both backward to the Israelite Exodus from Egypt and forward to his own Passion and Resurrection. But the voice from the cloud speaks only of

The cloud represents God's presence.
See Exodus 24:16–18.

Is the disciples' silence inspired by the
awesome voice or by the Son of whom it
spoke with tenderness?

While he was still **speaking**,
a **cloud** came and cast a **shadow** over them,
and they became **frightened** when they **entered** the cloud.
Then from the cloud came a **voice** that said,
"**This** is my chosen **Son**; **listen** to him."
After the voice had **spoken**, Jesus was found **alone**.
They fell **silent** and did not at that time
tell **anyone** what they had **seen**.

Jesus saying, "Listen to *him*," and when
the cloud disperses, Jesus is found alone.
The law and the prophets now converge in
the one figure of Jesus.

It is no accident that this event occurs
between two predictions of Jesus' Passion
and on the heels of Peter's profession of
faith, to which Jesus responds by asserting that the nature of true discipleship is a
willingness to exchange glory for sacrificial suffering. This awe-inspiring interlude
bolsters the faith of the three apostles by

reaffirming what was heard at Jesus'
Baptism: this man is God's own son.

Twice the narrator comments on
Jesus' reliance on prayer before suddenly
and unexpectedly introducing the super-
natural transformation. Listeners may not
initially make the connection with Sinai,
but your careful attention to details and
allusions will allow listeners to make con-
nections later when the homily mines the
story of its rich meaning. Take time to
describe the waking of the apostles who
must recover from sleep before reacting.

Peter dives in, but with a fumbling suggestion that they pitch tents and stay in this
(safe) place of revelation. The comment
that he didn't know what he was saying
suggests he misinterpreted the event that
could be fully understood only after the
Resurrection.

3RD SUNDAY OF LENT

Lectionary #30

READING I   Exodus 3:1–8a, 13–15

A reading from the Book of Exodus

You are proclaiming a central text of our faith history. It deserves your best effort and requires you to create a mood of mystery and awe. Let your opening tone suggest something significant is about to happen.
Jethro = JETH-roh
Midian = MID-ee-uhn
Horeb = HOHR–ebb

Speak with Moses' sense of puzzlement.

He has no idea what is about to happen.

The repetition of "Moses" gets more emphasis.

Make eye contact with assembly.

"Seeing" God means death.

Stress God's compassion here.

Moses was tending the **flock** of his father-in-law **Jethro**,
    the priest of **Midian**.
Leading the flock across the **desert**, he came to **Horeb**,
    the mountain of **God**.
There an **angel** of the LORD **appeared** to Moses in **fire**
    flaming out of a **bush**.
As he looked **on**, he was **surprised** to see that the **bush**,
    though on **fire**, was not **consumed**.
So Moses decided,
    "I must go **over** to **look** at this remarkable **sight**,
    and see **why** the bush is not **burned**."

When the LORD **saw** him coming over to look at it more **closely**,
    God **called** out to him from the bush, "**Moses! Moses!**"
He answered, "**Here** I am."
God said, "Come **no nearer!**
Remove the **sandals** from your **feet**,
    for the **place** where you **stand** is **holy ground**.
I am the God of your **fathers**," he continued,
    "the God of **Abraham**, the God of **Isaac**, the God of **Jacob**."
Moses hid his **face**, for he was afraid to **look** at God.
But the LORD said,
    "I have witnessed the **affliction** of my people in **Egypt**

READING I   The Exodus deliverance memorialized every Passover begins with this encounter between God and Moses. First and foremost, this is a "call" text that follows the typical pattern: God reaches out to an unsuspecting individual, asking him to embrace a mission or role that the individual has neither anticipated nor feels competent to complete. It is always God's initiative that turns the timid believer into a prophet. An ordinary shepherding scene sets up the encounter. Absorbed with tending sheep—and himself an outcast for having killed an Egyptian—Moses chances upon a sight that simply stirs his curiosity. He knows he's witnessing something "remarkable," but has no idea what awaits him in the bush. Not until God speaks does Moses sense he's in the presence of awesome mystery. He responds in fear and covers his face, not willing to risk death by daring to look at God.

God orders Moses to remove his sandals because he stands on ground made holy by God's presence. Then, remarkably, God identifies himself, not by giving a name, but by naming a relationship: "I am the God of Abraham . . . Isaac . . . and Jacob"—in other words, I am the God who has been in relationship with your ancestors and who now establishes a new relationship with you. We learn the depth of God's relationship with Israel when God reveals "I have witnessed the affliction of my people . . . [and] I know well their suffering." God has never been far from the people, and now God is ready to act on their behalf with mercy and might.

and have heard their cry of **complaint**
against their **slave** drivers,
so I know **well** what they are **suffering**.
Therefore I have come down to **rescue** them
from the **hands** of the **Egyptians**
and lead them **out** of that land into a **good** and **spacious** land,
a land **flowing** with **milk** and **honey**."

Moses said to God, "But when I **go** to the Israelites
and say to them, 'The God of your **fathers** has **sent** me to you,'
if they **ask** me, 'What is his **name**?' what am I to **tell** them?"
God replied, "I **am** who **am**."
Then he added, "This is what you shall **tell** the Israelites:
I AM **sent** me to you."

God spoke **further** to Moses, "**Thus** shall you say
to the Israelites:
The LORD, the God of your **fathers**,
the God of **Abraham**, the God of **Isaac**, the God of **Jacob**,
has **sent** me to you.

"**This** is my **name forever**;
thus am I to be **remembered** through **all generations**."

READING II   1 Corinthians 10:1–6, 10–12

A reading from the first Letter of Saint Paul to the Corinthians

I do not want you to be **unaware**, brothers and sisters,
that our **ancestors** were all under the **cloud**
and all **passed** through the **sea**,

"I have come down" is a figure of speech signaling extraordinary divine intervention.

Don't rush here. Moses insists on some assurance to ease his self-doubt.

This is a bedrock moment in salvation history. Be bold and dignified here.

Speak slowly and tenderly. God again emphasizes relationship.

During the Exodus, a cloud and a pillar of fire led the people through the desert. Start out strong.

Moses responds by asking for signs. This passage leaves out verses in which Moses insists he's unfit for the task thrust upon him. Typically, God responds to such insecurity with a sign intended to encourage the reluctant prophet. But here God promises to give a sign *after* the mission is accomplished. So Moses must ask again.

God responds by revealing the divine name, a gesture that both implies intimacy and asserts God's reality: in the biblical world something is real only if you know

its name, and knowing someone's name puts you on personal terms with that person. The name "I am" reveals God's character: God is an initiator, a cause. God sought out Moses and intervenes on behalf of the enslaved people because God has "[over]heard their cry" against their slave drivers. No one had to persuade God to act. God's words are consistently affirming, reassuring, and compassionate. God's awesome name is shared as a gift and pledge of divine presence and protection—something you can communicate with

uncompromising clarity as you speak God's final affirmation of enduring fidelity.

READING II Paul's theology links Christian Baptism and Eucharist with the events of the Exodus. The "cloud" was the miraculous means God employed to lead the Israelites out of Egypt and the "sea," of course, refers to the miraculous crossing "on dry land" to escape Pharaoh's soldiers. The Israelites were favored and protected in the desert where they ate and drank through God's solicitude.

Run through these items fairly quickly;
they all lead to the word "Yet."

Paul applies the image of a water-
producing rock (said to have followed the
people) to Christ, the source of living water.

In the phrase "Yet . . ." the point is that
they perished anyway! Speak with regret
in your voice.

Here Paul the teacher is making his point.

Your listeners also need to learn this
lesson.

Make eye contact with the assembly.
Speak slowly and soberly.

and all of them were **baptized** into **Moses**
   in the **cloud** and in the **sea**.
All **ate** the same spiritual **food**,
   and all **drank** the same spiritual **drink**,
   for they drank from a spiritual **rock** that followed them,
   and the rock was the **Christ**.
Yet God was not **pleased** with most of them,
   for they were struck **down** in the **desert**.

These things happened as **examples** for us,
   so that **we** might not desire **evil** things, as **they** did.
Do not **grumble** as some of **them** did,
   and suffered **death** by the **destroyer**.
These things happened to them as an **example**,
   and they have been written down as a **warning** to us,
   upon whom the **end** of the **ages** has **come**.
Therefore, whoever thinks he is standing **secure**
   should take **care** not to **fall**.

GOSPEL   Luke 13:1–9

Convey the urgent tone of those relating
the story, implying the victims' guilt.
Galileans = gal-ih-LEE-uhnz

Jesus' tone is somewhat brusque here.

A reading from the holy Gospel according to Luke

Some people told **Jesus** about the **Galileans**
   whose **blood Pilate** had mingled with the blood
     of their **sacrifices**.
Jesus said to them in reply,
   "Do you think that because these Galileans **suffered**
     in this way
   they were greater **sinners** than all **other** Galileans?

(At God's command, Moses struck a desert rock that yielded water. Here Paul alludes to a later legend built upon that incident in which the rock followed the Israelites. He now identifies Christ with that miraculous source of water.) But the care the Israelites received—safe passage through the Red Sea and water and manna in the desert—didn't guarantee God's permanent favor, for eventually "they were struck down." The Corinthians have also been favored with the Good News of the Gospel, preached to them by Paul himself, but they must not

imitate their ancestors in squandering the benefits of Baptism and Eucharist.

Paul has used the Exodus as a cautionary tale because he knows what any wise person understands: those who don't remember the past are doomed to repeat it. The past teaches, warns, and provides a model to follow or avoid. Paul urges his readers not "to be unaware" of the fate of their ancestors who perished despite their many advantages. As a good spiritual father, Paul is anxious for his Corinthian children lest they, too, stumble and fall.

The last sentence is blunt and direct. It might sound too harsh were it not motivated by Paul's genuine affection for the Corinthian community. This kind of talk is pure gift when it comes from a heart that desires our good even more than we do ourselves.

GOSPEL   The central message of Lent echoes here as it did in the letter to the Corinthians: learn from past mistakes and repent before it's too late. Satan's greatest weapon, says C. S. Lewis,

Don't hold back here.	By no **means**! But I tell **you**, if you do not **repent**, you will **all** perish as **they** did!

Jesus provides a second example to illustrate further.	Or those eighteen people who were **killed**
	    when the tower at **Siloam** fell on them—
	    do you think **they** were more guilty
	    than everyone **else** who lived in Jerusalem?

Make eye contact with the assembly. Pause briefly after "repent . . . ."	By no **means**! But I **tell** you, if **you** do not **repent**, you will all **perish** as **they** did!"

Pause to transition into the parable. Your tone should remain solemn.	And he told them this **parable**:
	    "There once was a person who had a **fig** tree planted
	        in his **orchard**,
	    and when he came in search of **fruit** on it but found **none**,
	    he said to the **gardener**,

The owner is disappointed and frustrated.	'For three **years** now I have come in search of **fruit**
	        on this fig tree
	    but have found **none**.
	So cut it **down**.
	Why should it **exhaust** the **soil**?'
	He said to him in **reply**,

The gardener calls for mercy, but ends with a final note of warning.	'Sir, leave it for this year **also**,
	    and I shall **cultivate** the ground around it and **fertilize** it;
	    it **may** bear fruit in the **future**.
	If **not** you can cut it **down**.'"

is convincing us that there is plenty of time. Luke repudiates what was then (and still remains) a popular belief that bad things happen to bad people—that misfortune is a sign of God's disfavor. We're thrown when bad things happen to good people because we expect things to work the other way. To counter such thinking, Luke uses the reported disasters to make an urgent case for *all* to repent. Those killed by Pilate were not Galilee's worst sinners, says Jesus. Those killed by a falling tower were no guiltier than anyone standing in

the crowd. Yet a fate similar to that of those who died in the disasters can befall anyone who fails to repent. Jesus is playing the teacher here, so read the first paragraph with the dual goal of answering questions about the victims' greater guilt ("By no means!") while also warning listeners that tragedy is never far from anyone.

Jesus then offers a parable. What's striking is that the tone remains solemn. This is not the flipside of the coin, for the story is another cautionary tale told to rouse those who are still asleep. The

householder is in a sour mood, disappointed and frustrated over the tree's failure to grow fruit. But in this parable, God is both householder and "gardener." From the latter we hear an appeal for patience and compassion. The parable is clearly intended to evoke a response in weak and vacillating disciples. But note that, even if judgment is delayed, it will surely come, for even the voice of mercy sounds another note of warning in the final line.

3RD SUNDAY OF LENT, YEAR A

Lectionary #28

READING I   Exodus 17:3–7

A reading from the Book of Exodus

In those days, in their **thirst** for **water**,
  the people **grumbled** against **Moses**,
  saying, "**Why** did you ever make us leave **Egypt?**
Was it just to have us **die** here of **thirst**
  with our **children** and our **livestock?**"
So Moses cried out to the LORD,
  "What shall I **do** with this people?
A little **more** and they will **stone** me!"
The LORD **answered** Moses,
  "Go over there in **front** of the people,
  along with some of the **elders** of Israel,
  holding in your **hand**, as you go,
  the **staff** with which you struck the **river**.
I will be standing there in **front** of you on the **rock** in **Horeb**.
Strike the rock, and the water will **flow** from it
  for the people to **drink**."
This Moses **did**, in the presence of the **elders** of Israel.
The place was called **Massah** and **Meribah**,
  because the Israelites **quarreled** there
  and **tested** the LORD, saying,
  "Is the LORD in our **midst** or **not?**"

Start slowly. "Thirst for water" sets up the whole reading.

Recall the sound of your own grumbling. Do you express great anxiety by becoming more strident or more quietly intense?

Moses is angry, but at whom—the people, God, or both?

Like a frustrated parent, be angry at first, but then your words should melt into a tone of loving reassurance.

"Staff . . . river" is a reference to the plague that changed the Nile to blood. The staff that deprived Egypt of water will provide for Israel. The words "in front of the people . . ." convey the public nature of God's reassurance made "in the presence of the elders" who witness the saving miracle.

Speak the words "This . . . did" in a tone that suggests the miracle occurred.

Massah = MAH-sah

Meribah = MAYR-ih-bah

Massah means "the place of the test," and Meribah means "the place of the quarreling." The question can be read with the anxiety of the people or with the narrator's regret at their apparent lack of faith.

READING I   The First Reading often sets the stage for the day's Gospel. "Thirst", "drink," and "water" first introduced in the Exodus account, become the central images of John's story of Jesus' encounter with the Samaritan woman. Desert imagery dominates Lent; there we are more keenly aware of our thirst. Water, so essential to human survival, serves as a powerful symbol of God's place in our lives. The grumbling Israelites thirst not only for water but also for reassurance that the Lord "is in [their] midst." View the entire passage as an affirmative answer to the text's final question.

Uncertainty characterizes the people's grumbling to Moses—uncertainty that soon turns to fear and borders on despair. You're given two questions with which to express it: "Why did you . . . ? Was it just . . . ?" Recall an incident in your life that will help you identify with the Israelites' situation. Their grumbling, although surprising after the miracles they've witnessed, demonstrates the very human tendency to blame someone else for whatever difficulty we're facing. But however human, it is still insufferable. The people's angry, fearful dialogue leaves little room for our sympathy. Moses calls out loudly to God, fearing what the people might do to him, but also frustrated that he's been put in such a difficult situation. It's hard to imagine God would be anything but saddened and angered by the people's lack of faith. Yet God is merciful. God meets the needs of the people, threatens no punishment, and shows sensitivity both to Moses' situation and the people's wants. Your expectant tone as you narrate the words

Don't read this like abstract theology, for the text announces hope, love, and joy.

Paul describes the workings of faith, hope, and love, moving effortlessly from one to the other. Faith brings peace and access to grace, which leads to a hope that will not disappoint. Note that we don't "speak" of hope; instead, we "boast" of it.

There are three distinct ideas in this sentence.

Assume the diction of a teacher making an important point.

It would be unusual to willingly die for a just person, but more unusual is what God did—dying for us while we were still in sin! Proclaim with joy and awe.

READING II   Romans 5:1–2, 5–8

A reading from the Letter of Saint Paul to the Romans

Brothers and sisters:
Since we have been **justified** by **faith**,
    we have **peace** with God through our **Lord** Jesus **Christ**,
    through whom we have gained **access** by faith
    to this **grace** in which we **stand**,
    and we boast in **hope** of the **glory** of **God**.

And **hope** does not **disappoint**,
    because the **love** of God has been **poured** out into our **hearts**
    through the Holy **Spirit** who has been **given** to us.
For **Christ**, while we were still **helpless**,
    died at the appointed time for the **ungodly**.
Indeed, only with **difficulty** does one die for a **just** person,
    though perhaps for a **good** person one might even
        find **courage** to die.
But God **proves** his love for us
    in that while we were still **sinners** Christ **died** for us.

"This Moses did . . ." should suggest he *succeeded* in making the water flow.

    Regret characterizes the final narration. An earlier Lenten Gospel told us we must not put the Lord to the test, but that is what the people did. Speak the names "Massah" and "Meribah" in a way that tells us this was not a proud moment in Israel's history. The last line reminds each of us to trust that God will be always "in our midst."

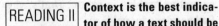 **Context is the best indicator of how a text should be read.** The First Reading presents a grumbling people who, despite witnessing miracles, still doubt God's providence, but God remains patient and merciful. The Gospel presents an adulterous woman whom Jesus refuses to condemn despite knowing "everything [she has] done." Paul's letter is sandwiched in between, explaining "why": "While we were still helpless," God's love was "poured out into our hearts through the Holy Spirit." This text explains and summarizes all that we see illustrated in the other two readings.

    Paul declares that the Christian who has been "justified by faith" is no longer separated from God but instead is given "access by faith" to God's presence. We stand before a God who allows us to boast that one day we will share in God's own glory. This hope is God's free gift, which, although tasted, is as yet unattained, for it will be fully realized only in the Resurrection. But that doesn't mean it's uncertain, as if God might not deliver on the promise. No,

GOSPEL   John 4:5–42

A reading from the holy Gospel according to John

(1) **Jesus** came to a town of **Samaria** called **Sychar**,
    near the plot of land that **Jacob** had given to his son **Joseph**.
Jacob's **well** was there.
Jesus, **tired** from his journey, sat **down** there at the **well**.
It was about **noon**.

(2) A **woman** of Samaria came to draw **water**.
Jesus **said** to her,
   "**Give** me a **drink**."
His **disciples** had gone into the **town** to buy **food**.
The **Samaritan** woman said to him,
   "How can **you**, a **Jew**, ask **me**, a **Samaritan woman**,
      for a **drink**?"
—For **Jews** use nothing in **common** with **Samaritans**.—
(3) Jesus **answered** and said to her,
   "If you **knew** the **gift** of God
   and **who** is saying to you, 'Give me a drink,'
   you would have asked **him**
   and he would have given **you living** water."
The woman **said** to him,
   "**Sir**, you do not even have a **bucket** and the cistern is **deep**;
   where then can you **get** this living water?
Are you **greater** than our father **Jacob**,
   who **gave** us this cistern and **drank** from it **himself**
   with his **children** and his **flocks**?"

Narrate as if you were one of the Samaritans converted at the end of the story. It's your own town that you're describing: the woman is your neighbor, and this incident changed your life.
Samaria = suh-MAYR-ee-uh
Sychar = SĪ-kahr
A slower pace will help suggest his tiredness.

She is stunned that he would ask her for a favor.

Keep the dialogue conversational, not theological.

She bluntly challenges him and his *chutzpah*.

our hope is sure, anchored in God's love for us, simply awaiting its time of completion.
   Someone who has experienced the in-pouring of God's love, like today's woman at the well, would know how to transform Paul's theology into words to live by. Remember the feeling of peace that comes when you reconcile with a loved one. Realize that, although we were the ones who did wrong, it was God who took the first step at reconciliation. Rejoice as you would if someone gave you friendship and then lavished you with gifts as well,

expecting nothing in return. That's what God has done for us!
   Paul is overwhelmed by God's generosity, by the divine initiative that reached out to us while we were still "godless . . . still sinners." That initiative proves God's love. His reasoning is simple, although awkwardly stated: "Look," he argues, always trying to persuade, "when is anyone willing to die for even a good person? Well, all right," he catches himself, "maybe for a *really* good person someone might find the 'courage to die.' But Christ died while we were still helpless and steeped in sin.

There's all the proof anyone could ever need!" First convince yourself of that, and then convince your friends and neighbors.

GOSPEL   This long Gospel, especially evocative for the elect, is instructive for all of us, and is offered as an option during Years B and C because of its power. If you choose this reading, use it in its entirety. The shorter version, though judiciously edited, is weakened. Scholars debate how much of John's story reflects an actual encounter

Contrast his tone with the woman's.	**(4)** Jesus **answered** and said to her, "Everyone who drinks **this** water will be **thirsty** again; but whoever drinks the water **I** shall give will **never** thirst; the water **I** shall give will become in him a **spring** of water **welling** up to eternal **life**."
She's eager for this amazing water.	The **woman** said to him, "Sir, **give** me this water, so that I may not be **thirsty** or have to keep **coming** here to **draw** water."
Speak evenly, with no hint of judgment.	**(5)** Jesus said to her, "**Go** call your **husband** and come **back**." The woman **answered** and said to him, "I do not **have** a husband."
Is her tone wholly transformed, or is this a final brusque reply?	Jesus answered her, "You are **right** in saying, 'I do not have a **husband**.'
Jesus is blunt here, but not harsh.	For you have had **five** husbands, and the one you have **now** is not your **husband**. What you have said is **true**."
His prescient knowledge impresses her, but she abruptly changes the subject.	**(6)** The woman said to him, "Sir, I can **see** that you are a **prophet**. Our **ancestors** worshiped on this **mountain**; but **you** people say that the place to worship is in **Jerusalem**."
Here too, despite the teaching, maintain a conversational tone.	Jesus said to her, "**Believe** me, woman, the hour is **coming** when you will worship the **Father** **neither** on this mountain **nor** in Jerusalem. **You** people worship what you do not **understand**; **we** worship what we **understand**, because **salvation** is from the **Jews**.

of Jesus and a Samaritan woman, and how much is Johannine embellishment expressing various Christological themes. Scholars can define the boundaries of the original narrative and, as homilist, you might consider their conclusions. But as Gospel reader, your only concern is the story, which that you must tell convincingly.

There are three uneven acts to this drama, each with its distinctive mood: first, the sometimes pointed, sometimes ironic repartee between Jesus and the woman; second, the return of the apostles, characterized by their surprise and confusion and Jesus' urgency; third, the enthusiastic response of the Samaritans.

(1, 2) Your tone should signal that passing through Samaria was uncommon for a Jew. Though it provided the shortest route from Judea to Galilee, most Jews bypassed Samaria. Jesus passed through for theological, not geographical reasons. Speak of "Jacob's well" with familiarity since it was an ancient holy place. Jesus approaches the well in the noontime heat, and he is tired, hot, and thirsty, which may explain why he shatters custom. The woman's reaction comes from her surprise that a man, and a rabbi at that, would speak to a woman in public, especially a ritually unclean Samaritan! She, however, has nothing to lose. She, too, is countercultural—and an outcast: after all, she has lived with more than one man to whom she was not married.

(3) Jesus refers to himself as "the gift of God," insinuating his identity as the source of "living water." The woman misses that cloaked reference and takes Jesus literally. This exchange is central to the story. Jesus means "water of life," but she hears, "flowing water," as opposed to

	But the hour is **coming**, and is now **here**, 　　when **true** worshipers will worship the Father 　　　in **Spirit** and **truth**; 　　and **indeed** the Father **seeks** such people to worship him. God is **Spirit**, and those who **worship** him 　　must worship in **Spirit** and **truth**."
She begins to sense who she is talking to.	(7) The woman **said** to him, 　　"I know that the **Messiah** is coming, the one called the **Christ**; 　　when he **comes**, he will tell us **everything**." Jesus said to her,
His self-identification is a gesture of love to the woman.	"**I am he**, the one who is **speaking** with you."
The second act begins here. The return of the disciples shatters the mood. They seem suspicious.	(8) At that moment his disciples **returned**, 　　and were **amazed** that he was talking with a **woman**, 　　but **still** no one said, "What are you **looking** for?" 　　or "Why are you **talking** with her?"
The woman undertakes her missionary journey. Speak the phrase "Could he be . . . ?" with expectant joy.	The woman **left** her water jar 　　and went into the **town** and said to the **people**, 　　"**Come** see a **man** who told me **everything** I have **done**. Could he possibly be the **Christ**?" They went out of the town and **came** to him.
They're prodding: "Rabbi, *eat!*" His response summarizes his ministry.	(9) Meanwhile, the disciples **urged** him, "Rabbi, **eat**." But he said to them, 　　"I have **food** to eat of which you do not **know**." So the disciples **said** to one another, 　　"Could someone have **brought** him something to eat?" (10) Jesus said to them,
Note the ample harvest imagery.	"My **food** is to do the **will** of the one who **sent** me 　　and to **finish** his work. Do you not say, 'In four months the **harvest** will be here'? I **tell** you, look **up** and see the fields **ripe** for the **harvest**.

a stagnant well. She mocks Jesus as might a school girl who has mistaken the new principal for the janitor. But in her attempt to mock his naiveté, she only mocks herself. What she presumes impossible, that Jesus could be greater than Jacob, is the very truth she'll shortly learn.

(4) Jesus is persuasive in his next discourse. (She should begin to sense that this man speaks well for a janitor!) She becomes excited, but only because of her misunderstanding (as if the school girl thought the janitor had access to copies of the final exams). Contrast is the key to

Jesus' dialogue: Everyone who drinks *this* water will thirst *again;* but those who drink the water *I* shall give will *never* thirst. Jesus will be water that requires no cup to drink, for he will bubble-up like a "spring." The woman enthuses because of another misunderstanding. Her naiveté is showing, setting the stage for the crisis that follows.

(5) Jesus calmly prepares the way for her conversion. Her admission is surprising in one so contentious. Jesus' blunt assertion of her sinfulness fails to drive her away. Obviously, his honesty is tempered with compassion.

(6) Probably shocked by his knowledge of her private life, the woman acknowledges Jesus as "prophet." But immediately she shifts to a less embarrassing subject. Jesus' answer minimizes the importance of where one worships ("mountain" versus "Jerusalem"), and announces a new universalism where worship transcends place.

(7) The realization that has been growing in the woman through Jesus' last speech now flowers. She speaks with confidence of the coming "Messiah" and Jesus

The **reaper** is already receiving **payment**
> and gathering crops for eternal **life**,
> > so that the **sower** and **reaper** can rejoice **together**.

For here the saying is verified that 'One **sows** and another **reaps**.'

I sent you to **reap** what you have not **worked** for;
> **others** have done the work,
> > and **you** are sharing the **fruits** of their work."

<table>
<tr><td>

This is the final act. Maintain high energy when speaking "the word of the woman."

</td><td>

(11) Many of the **Samaritans** of that town began to **believe** in him
> because of the **word** of the **woman** who testified,
> > "He told me **everything** I have **done**."

When the Samaritans **came** to him,
> they invited him to **stay** with them;
> > and he **stayed** there two **days**.

</td></tr>
</table>

They are urging him to remain with them.

Many **more** began to believe in him because of his **word**,
> and they **said** to the woman,
> > "We no longer believe because of **your** word;
> > for we have heard for **ourselves**,
> > and we **know** that this is **truly** the **savior** of the **world**."

There should be joy and gratitude in their comment to the woman responsible for their faith. Place special emphasis on the title given to Jesus.

[Shorter: John 4:5–15, 19b–26, 39a, 40–42]

---

rewards her by revealing himself to her—echoes of the divine "I am" sound in his self-identification.

(8) The return of the disciples signals a mood change. In their surprise, they murmur about what they see. The tone of their unasked questions can suggest confusion—or perhaps disapproval. The woman, transformed and freed of shame, runs off to share her discovery with the townspeople.

(9, 10) Now it is the disciples who misunderstand, taking literally Jesus' reference to food. Their confusion is probably best spoken is a hushed tone, contrasting with the urgency of their appeal to "eat." But Jesus does not let them leave confused. His "food," he says, is doing the will of God. What better summary of his ministry? With urgency, and using harvest imagery, he speaks on the theme of evangelization.

(11) This narration reveals the woman's success as a missionary, for the Samaritans believed "because of the word of the woman." Stress that narration and speak "He told me everything . . ." in her excited voice. Remember that, as narrator, you are one of these who "began to believe in him." Speak with energy and excitement and let the last sentence be your personal statement of faith.

4TH SUNDAY OF LENT

Lectionary #33

READING I   Joshua 5:9a, 10–12

Joshua = JOSH-oo-uh

Stress "Today," pause slightly, and then continue.

The narrator is aware of a new moment in Israel's life.

Gilgal = GIL-gahl

Jericho = JAYR-ih-koh

Speak joyfully here; they are eating food from their own land.

"Manna ceased" is not bad news.

"No longer. . ." means that now, with God's help, they will provide for themselves.

A reading from the Book of Joshua

The LORD said to Joshua,
    "Today I have **removed** the reproach of **Egypt** from you."

While the **Israelites** were encamped at **Gilgal** on the plains
        of **Jericho**,
    they celebrated the **Passover**
    on the evening of the **fourteenth** of the **month**.
On the day **after** the Passover,
    they ate of the **produce** of the land
    in the form of unleavened **cakes** and parched **grain**.
On that **same** day after the Passover,
    on which they ate of the **produce** of the land, the **manna ceased**.
No **longer** was there **manna** for the Israelites,
    who that year ate of the **yield** of the **land** of **Canaan**.

READING II   2 Corinthians 5:17–21

This reading is jubilant good news. Maintain the joy throughout, but don't rush.

A reading from the second Letter of Saint Paul to the Corinthians

Brothers and sisters:
Whoever is in **Christ** is a **new creation**:
    the **old** things have passed **away**;
    behold, **new** things have come.

READING I   This is Laetare Sunday, a day of intentional rejoicing during this penitential season as we draw closer to the victory of Easter. Joy permeates all of today's readings. Joshua's reason for rejoicing is the celebration of Israel's first Passover in the *Promised Land,* a significant milestone in the life of Israel. God had sworn that, as punishment for their disobedience, none of the circumcised warriors who left Egypt would enter the new land. Only those born during the desert wanderings would see the land of milk and honey. Joshua has just circum-

cised all these younger men, thus leaving behind the "reproach of Egypt," the slavery and misery that nation represented.

In the new land, the "manna ceased." During the desert sojourn, this bread from heaven signified God's provident care. Its termination now signals not God's disfavor, but Israel's coming of age. The chosen people will henceforth eat the fruit of their own labor. Their exodus is over and they begin a new moment in the life of the nation. Each year, through our Lenten observance, we too experience the drama

of being lost and wandering, and finally finding our way back home to God.

As you read, stress those phrases that speak of transition from dependence to mature independence: "they ate . . . *produce* of the *land* . . . the manna *ceased* . . . ate of the yield of the *land* of *Canaan.*" Israel now fends for itself, so the people's joy is well founded, but in no way does it border on arrogance. For we discover God's loving sustenance even in what comes from our own labor.

Stress God's initiative.	And **all** this is from **God**, • who has **reconciled** us to himself through **Christ** and given us the **ministry** of reconciliation,
Breathe as if starting a new sentence.	**namely**, God was reconciling the **world** to himself in **Christ**, not counting their **trespasses** against them and **entrusting** to us the **message** of reconciliation.
Make eye contact with the assembly. Suggest the importance of being "ambassadors." Don't read "implore" without sounding like you mean it. Speak slowly here. This is a difficult concept, but it's good news. Stress the words "be" and "know."	So **we** are **ambassadors** for Christ, as if **God** were **appealing** through **us**. We **implore** you on behalf of **Christ**, be **reconciled** to **God**. For **our** sake he made him to **be** sin who did not **know** sin, so that **we** might become the **righteousness** of **God** in **him**.

GOSPEL   Luke 15:1–3, 11–32

	A reading from the holy Gospel according to Luke
Stress the context of the sinners and Pharisees. Does the "complaining" give Jesus an agenda to pursue or persuade him to entice his detractors with a story lovingly told?	**Tax collectors** and **sinners** were all drawing near to **listen** to Jesus, but the **Pharisees** and **scribes** began to **complain**, saying, "**This** man welcomes **sinners** and **eats** with them." So to **them** Jesus addressed this **parable**:
Here are memorable, human characters who speak realistic, moving dialogue.	"A man had **two sons**, and the **younger** son said to his father, '**Father** give me the **share** of your **estate** that should **come** to me.'
Read the words "So the father divided . . ." slowly. Suggest the father's inner struggle as he divides his property, convinced that his son may never return. Don't overdramatize the boy's demise, but stress words like "squandered," "dissipation," "dire," "longed," and especially "pods" and "swine."	So the father **divided** the property between them. After a few **days**, the younger son **collected** all his belongings and **set** off to a **distant** country where he **squandered** his inheritance on a life of **dissipation**.

READING II The most arresting aspect of the father's behavior in Jesus' parable of the prodigal is his initiative in forgiving his wayward son. Paul revels in that same initiative here as he announces a God who "has reconciled us to himself" and made all things "new!" Paul joyously announces that "the old things have passed away." The spiritual life is built on such experiences—God constantly remaking us, reversing our distortions, forgiving us, and restoring our original likeness. Recall your own experiences of forgiveness, whether from God or

people. With whatever tone and pace you select, help us desire forgiveness and convince us it makes a difference!

Paradoxically, Paul implores reconciliation from those he calls a new creation. Reconciliation requires constant renewal—hence, the urgency of the second half of the reading. Paul speaks passionately of God's refusal to count our transgressions against us. Paul is an "ambassador," imploring that we not miss the opportunity to become the "righteousness" of God. Christ, the sinless one,

"became sin," that is, accepted the condition of alienation common to humanity, to make possible this reconciliation. Through today's liturgy, Paul reaches across the centuries and, through you, addresses to your assembly the same message of hope he addressed to the Corinthians.

Although "reconciliation" is the key word of the passage, it can't be stressed every time it occurs. Instead, emphasize new words and ideas rather than words that echo what was said before. For example, after stressing "God . . . who has *reconciled* us," shift the stress to "and has

Here the tone shifts, as if this were a new chapter of the story.	When he had freely spent **everything**,
	    a severe **famine** struck that country,
	    and he found himself in dire **need**.

This is the ultimate humiliation.	So he **hired** himself out to one of the local **citizens**
	    who sent him to his **farm** to tend the **swine**.
	And he **longed** to eat his fill of the **pods** on which the **swine** fed,
	    but nobody **gave** him any.

The tone shifts here. The light of grace is breaking through.	Coming to his **senses** he thought,
	    'How many of my father's hired **workers**
	    have **more** than enough food to eat,
	    but here am **I**, **dying** from **hunger**.

This "rehearsal" is unemotional. Save the emotional intensity for the actual encounter with his father.	I shall **get** up and **go** to my father and I shall **say** to him,
	    "**Father**, I have **sinned** against **heaven** and against **you**.
	I no longer **deserve** to be called your **son**;
	    treat **me** as you would treat one of your **hired workers**."'
	So he got up and went **back** to his father.

The father can't wait to greet the boy.	While he was still a **long** way off,
	    his father caught **sight** of him, and was filled with **compassion**.
	He **ran** to his son, **embraced** him and **kissed** him.
	His son **said** to him,
	    '**Father**, I have **sinned** against **heaven** and against **you**;
	    I no longer **deserve** to be called your **son**.'

The father's interest is in unconditional welcome, not recrimination. The "ring" is a sign of household authority.	But his **father** ordered his **servants**,
	    '**Quickly** bring the finest **robe** and put it **on** him;
	    put a **ring** on his **finger** and **sandals** on his **feet**.
	Take the fattened **calf** and **slaughter** it.
	Then let us **celebrate** with a **feast**,
	    because this **son** of mine was **dead**, and has come to **life** again;
	    he was **lost**, and has been **found**.'
	Then the **celebration began**.

given us the *ministry* of reconciliation," since ministry introduces the new idea.

 GOSPEL This is not simply the tale of a repentant son, but a two-act drama of a *father* and *two* sons. The section focusing on the *prodigal* son is followed by the equally profound and potentially more important section concerning the *elder* son. Most who gather in church probably resemble the older son more than the younger. But it's the father who dominates the story with his eagerness to dole out prodigious love to both offspring.

Jesus' audience is familiar with stories that juxtapose brothers: Esau and Jacob, Joseph and his brothers. In those stories, the younger brother always comes out on top. But this story will be more nuanced. Begin by stressing the *setting* in which the parable is told. The text describes the very situation in which Jesus finds himself—the company of sinners who, according to common belief, should be excluded from inheriting the kingdom.

According to Jewish law, eldest sons inherited a double share of the estate, so the younger brother's portion is only a third. A father would normally deed property to his sons while continuing to collect rent until his death. But the brash younger son demands everything *now*, effectively depriving father and brother of potential revenue. The events in the "distant country" are significant: the son's gradual dissolution, and his loss of identity. By the end, he's become more Gentile than Jew as he resorts to tending pigs. He reeks of

This is a new beat. Your tone can telegraph the coming confrontation.

Now the **older** son had been out in the **field**
and, on his way **back**, as he **neared** the house,
he heard the sound of **music** and **dancing**.
He called one of the **servants** and asked what this might **mean**.
The servant said to him,

The servants have caught the spirit of the father's rejoicing.

'Your **brother** has returned
and your **father** has slaughtered the fattened **calf**
because he has him **back** safe and **sound**.'
He became **angry**,

This is another new beat, and the mood becomes tense.

and when he **refused** to enter the house,
his **father** came **out** and **pleaded** with him.
He said to his father in reply,
'**Look**, all these years I **served** you
and not **once** did I disobey your **orders**;
yet you never gave me even a young **goat**
to feast on with my friends.

His resentment is unchecked.

But when your son **returns**
who **swallowed** up your property with **prostitutes**,
for **him** you slaughter the fattened **calf**.'
He **said** to him,
'My **son**, you are here with me **always**;
everything I have is **yours**.

Proclaim slowly here. You're speaking to most of the members of the assembly.

But now we must **celebrate** and **rejoice**,
because your brother was **dead** and has come to **life** again;
he was **lost** and has been **found**.' "

self-pity and self-hatred as he rehearses what he will say to his father.

"While . . . a long way off" is the most important information we have about the father. That he runs to meet and kiss the boy is a great revelation of his character. Sincerely, the son begins his rehearsed speech, but the father stops him and instead orders a celebration. "Robe" and "ring" signal that the boy will not return as a servant but as a son.

"Now the older son . . ." introduces the second half of the drama. The naive

excitement of the servants contrasts with and exacerbates the son's anger. Whether explosive or seething, his anger is expressed with self righteousness ("all these *years* I served you"), absolutes ("not once"), and jealousy ("for *him* you slaughter . . ."). He fails to realize that he, too, has dined with swine and eaten freely the husks of bitterness and hate.

The father reminds him that "everything" (the remaining two-thirds of the property) is already deeded to him. But that is irrelevant now. There is no choice but to celebrate: brother can't disown brother

any more than father can disown son. Give equal weight to both sections of the story and invest energy in the father's exchanges with both sons. Help us recognize ourselves in both brothers.

4TH SUNDAY OF LENT, YEAR A

Lectionary #31

READING I   1 Samuel 16:1b, 6–7, 10–13a

A reading from the first Book of Samuel

The LORD said to **Samuel**:
   "**Fill** your horn with **oil**, and be on your **way**.
I am sending you to **Jesse** of **Bethlehem**,
   for I have chosen my **king** from among his **sons**."

As Jesse and his sons came to the **sacrifice**,
   Samuel looked at **Eliab** and thought,
   "**Surely** the LORD's anointed is **here** before him."
But the LORD said to Samuel:
   "Do not **judge** from his **appearance** or from his lofty **stature**,
   because I have **rejected** him.
Not as **man** sees does **God** see,
   because **man** sees the **appearance**
   but the LORD looks into the **heart**."
In the **same** way Jesse presented **seven sons** before Samuel,
   but Samuel said to Jesse,
   "The LORD has not chosen any **one** of these."
Then Samuel **asked** Jesse,
   "Are these **all** the sons you have?"
Jesse replied,
   "There is still the **youngest**, who is tending the **sheep**."
Samuel said to Jesse,
   "**Send** for him;
   we will not begin the sacrificial **banquet** until he **arrives** here."

The voice of God is authoritative and resolute.

Speak of Eliab with Samuel's conviction that this is God's anointed.
Eliab = ee-LĪ-uhb

Give God's dialogue the tone of a patient teacher rather than a disciplinarian. God uses this opportunity to teach a valuable lesson about God's ways and ours.

Suggest the tediousness of this lengthy process. Stress the word "seven."

Samuel is confused, perhaps worried, and somewhat exasperated.

Jesse is not hopeful that his youngest will be the one.

READING I **Perhaps the best connection between this reading** and today's other texts is found in God's instruction to Samuel not to judge from appearance, a lesson the disciples will also learn in the Gospel narrative.

    God has repented of choosing Saul as king of Israel and sends Samuel to consecrate his successor. The result is this intriguing story about the anointing of Israel's greatest king. Samuel is in a double bind: first, he must secretly discern and anoint Saul's successor—all the while

fearing he may be put to death if his mission is discovered. Secondly, he is sent "blind" to recognize the one among Jesse's eight sons whom God has chosen to be the new king. He doesn't know who he's looking for, yet he is the seer who must announce God's choice to the anxious family. The verses missing from this Lectionary selection say the elders of Bethlehem "came trembling to meet" Samuel; considering the circumstances, he may be doing some trembling of his own!

    Samuel invites Jesse's family to a "sacrifice" specially arranged so he can survey the eight brothers and select the "Lord's anointed." When he sees the tall and sturdy Eliab, Samuel seems to think his mission is accomplished. But God's admonition to "not judge from appearance" stops Samuel from jumping to conclusions. That admonition constitutes the heart of the reading. It's a theme we hear elsewhere in the Old Testament: God's ways are not our ways; we judge from appearance, God judges the heart.

Speak with great respect and admiration for David.

God is pleased with this choice.

Slowly, as he is anointed, David is filled with the Spirit.

Jesse **sent** and had the young man **brought** to them.
He was **ruddy**, a youth **handsome** to behold
   and making a **splendid** appearance.
The LORD said,
  "**There**—anoint **him**, for **this** is the one!"
Then **Samuel**, with the horn of **oil** in hand,
  anointed David in the presence of his **brothers**;
  and from **that** day on, the **spirit** of the LORD
    rushed upon David.

READING II Ephesians 5:8–14

A reading from the Letter of Saint Paul to the Ephesians

Brothers and sisters:
You were once **darkness**,
  but **now** you are **light** in the **Lord**.
Live as **children** of light,
  for **light** produces every kind of **goodness**
  and **righteousness** and **truth**.
Try to learn what is **pleasing** to the Lord.
Take no **part** in the **fruitless** works of **darkness**;
  rather **expose** them, for it is shameful even to **mention**
  the things done by them in **secret**;
  but everything **exposed** by the light becomes **visible**,
  for everything that becomes visible **is** light.
Therefore, it says:
  "**Awake**, O sleeper,
  and **arise** from the **dead**,
  and **Christ** will give you **light**."

The good news of the opening and closing sentences undergirds the teaching tone in the body of the reading. Speak one line at a time. You must not blur these ideas.

"Goodness," "righteousness," and "truth" are three distinct virtues.

"Try" sets the tone of this line: exhortation softened by an understanding that doing right is not an easy process to learn.

Imagine speaking these words to a beloved young person in your charge.

Hear the cadence in this line. Speak it with joyous hope.

A lengthy process of examining and rejecting each of seven sons forces Samuel to ask if these are "all" of Jesse's sons. It was God who rejected each of the seven and it will be God who chooses the worthy candidate, but even Jesse doesn't seem to hold much hope for the one remaining son who is off "tending the sheep." Jesse's tone can betray his skepticism about David's candidacy. But Samuel appears immediately hopeful that this last may be the one, and eagerly commands they send for him!

As soon as David appears, the tempo of the piece quickens: short, clipped phrases describe the boy who was "ruddy," "handsome," and "splendid." Samuel knows instantly this is God's chosen. Slowly and with dignity, narrate David's anointing in front of his father and brothers. "Rushed" is one of those great words that surprises *and* communicates. But remember that it's the Spirit who rushes, not you.

READING II Lent is the period of purification and enlightenment for those preparing for Baptism. This text appears in Lent because of the baptismal allusions expressed in the light and darkness references and in the excerpt from an early baptismal hymn that closes the passage. Our passage also complements today's Gospel that proclaims Jesus as "light of the world." In a text that repeats the word "light" six times in the span of a dozen-plus lines, there can be little question where our emphasis must go.

GOSPEL   John 9:1–41

A reading from the holy Gospel according to John

Stress the words "blind from birth," for it is later questioned.

(1) As **Jesus** passed by he saw a man **blind** from **birth**.
His disciples **asked** him,
   "Rabbi, who **sinned**, **this** man or his **parents**,
   that he was born **blind**?"
Jesus answered,
   "Neither **he nor** his parents sinned;
   it is so that the **works** of **God** might be made **visible**
      through him.
We have to **do** the works of the one who sent me while it is **day**.
Night is coming when **no** one can **work**.
While I am in the **world**, I am the **light** of the world."

Jesus' answer is unexpected and new. Don't rush.

(2) When he had said this, he **spat** on the ground
   and made **clay** with the saliva,
   and **smeared** the clay on his **eyes**, and said to him,
   "Go **wash** in the **Pool** of **Siloam**"—which means **Sent**—.
So he **went** and **washed**, and came back able to **see**.

Enjoy the graphic details!

Siloam = sig-LOH-uhm

Relate the miracle with a sense of awe. Pause to shift to a new scene.

(3) His **neighbors** and those who had **seen** him earlier
      as a **beggar** said,
   "Isn't **this** the one who used to **sit** and **beg**?"
Some said, "It **is**,"
   but **others** said, "**No**, he just **looks** like him."
He said, "I **am**."
So they said to him, "**How** were your eyes opened?"
He replied,
   "The man called **Jesus** made **clay** and **anointed** my **eyes**
   and told me, 'Go to **Siloam** and **wash**.'
So I **went** there and **washed** and was able to **see**."
And they said to him, "Where **is** he?"

The man is insistent: "I am!"

He relates the details joyfully.

The passage starts and ends with the same good news: once you were darkness, now you are light. Paul's use of metaphor ("you *were* darkness . . . you *are* light") makes an important point about the spiritual life: we become what we do consistently. Live in darkness long enough and you will become darkness. Live in the light of Christ and you will be light! Through Baptism each of us has been liberated from fruitless and shameful deeds done in darkness and empowered to live in the light of Christ.

If you were speaking to college freshmen away from home for the first time, reminding them to use their newfound freedom responsibly, warning them that shameful behavior eventually comes to light, how might you deliver Paul's exhortation to "take no part in fruitless works of darkness"? If one of those young people were your own child, might you complement the strong directives ("Try to learn . . . take no part . . . expose them . . .") with underlying compassion so that after focusing on the dangers of living in the dark you

could also offer an invitation to embrace the light which is Christ?

The closing lines were originally sung as part of an early baptismal hymn. They conclude with a promise of light. Light symbolizes oneness with Christ; darkness represents separation from him. By stressing "arise from the dead" you'll remind us of the perennial possibility of being overcome by darkness and death. Then, by contrast, the final "light" will shine more brightly.

It suddenly dawns on him that he doesn't know Jesus' whereabouts. Pause briefly.

Your tone as you read the phrase "So the Pharisees . . ." should hint at where they're going with this.

Proclaim the phrase "He put clay. . ." in a matter-of-fact way, but do so joyfully.

One of the Pharisees is angry, the other reasonable.

He must decide if he will make this confession of faith, and he does it boldly.

They feel they've been duped, so they look further.

Their speech is guarded. They say only what they must.

He said, "I don't **know**."

(4) They **brought** the one who was once blind to the **Pharisees**.
Now Jesus had made clay and opened his eyes on a **sabbath**.
So then the **Pharisees** also asked him **how** he was able to see.
He said to them,
   "He put **clay** on my eyes, and I **washed**, and **now** I can **see**."
So some of the **Pharisees** said,
   "**This** man is not from **God**,
   because he does not keep the **sabbath**."
But **others** said,
   "How can a **sinful** man do such **signs**?"
And there was a **division** among them.
So they **said** to the blind man **again**,
   "What do **you** have to say about him,
   since he opened your eyes?"
He said, "He is a **prophet**."

(5) Now the Jews did not **believe**
   that he had been **blind** and gained his **sight**
   until they summoned the **parents** of the one
      who had gained his sight.
They **asked** them,
   "Is this your **son**, who you say was **born blind**?
How does he now **see**?"
His parents answered and said,
   "We **know** that this is our **son** and that he **was** born blind.
We do **not** know how he sees **now**,
   nor do we know **who** opened his eyes.
Ask **him**, he is of **age**;
   he can speak for **himself**."

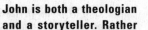

GOSPEL   John is both a theologian and a storyteller. Rather than subordinate the narrative to his theologizing, John has so integrated his ideas into this storyline that deleting any part of the story would destroy aspects of both the artistry and the theology.

   The narrator, who is critical in this story, needs a personality to match the tone of the several asides in the text. Perhaps the person is an eyewitness turned believer, perhaps the apostle; the narrator is mainly an invested, caring observer.

   (1) By assuming that the man's blindness is the result of sin, the disciples reflect the accepted wisdom of their culture. John uses their ignorance to set up one of his misunderstanding/illumination sequences that reveal his key insight into who Jesus is, namely, the light of the world. Jesus surprises the disciples with his answer. Contrast their assumption ("Who sinned, *this* man or his *parents*?") with Jesus' announcement: "Neither he nor his parents sinned . . . it is so that the works of God might be made visible." Jesus speaks of the advance of "night"

with urgency for he knows the time grows short to do the will of the one who sent him.

   (2) The words are graphic: "spat," "clay," "saliva," "smeared." Use these pungent images that accent the "hands-on" nature of this healing. Jesus is not afraid to touch human pain. His instructions to wash may be a test of faith which the man gladly accepts. Note that the meaning of "Siloam" refers back to Jesus' self-description as one "sent" by the Father.

Offer this aside as an excuse for the parents' behavior.

His parents said this because they were **afraid**
    of the Jews, for the Jews had **already** agreed
    that if anyone **acknowledged** him as the **Christ**,
    he would be **expelled** from the **synagogue**.
For this **reason** his parents said,
    "He is of **age**; question **him**."

Speak the narration as if through clenched teeth, suggesting the exasperation of the leaders.

(6) So a **second** time they called the man who had been blind
    and said to him, "Give God the **praise**!
We **know** that this man is a **sinner**."
He replied,
    "If he is a **sinner**, I do not **know**.

The tone here should be "Don't entangle me in your politics. All I know is that I'm healed!"

One thing I **do** know is that I was **blind** and now I **see**."
So they said to him,
    "What did he **do** to you?
    How did he open your eyes?"
He answered them,
    "I told you **already** and you did not **listen**.

He's becoming impatient, and bold!

Why do you want to hear it **again**?
Do **you** want to become his disciples, **too**?"
They **ridiculed** him and said,
    "**You** are that man's disciple;
    we are disciples of **Moses**!

The leaders' anger is mounting.

We **know** that God spoke to **Moses**,
    but we do not know where **this** one is **from**."
The man **answered** and said to them,
    "This is what is so **amazing**,
    that you do not know where he is **from**,

First he mocks them, and then he instructs them.

      yet he **opened** my **eyes**.
We know that God does **not** listen to **sinners**,
    but if one is **devout** and does his **will**, he **listens** to him.

(3) Imagine the various reactions of the crowd to the miracle: amazement, confusion, doubt, jealousy. The crowd speculates about the beggar's identity and how he was healed, though some insist they know the truth. The beggar simply reviews events without editorial comment. His own enlightenment will grow, but here his healer is just "the man called Jesus." Perhaps he surprises even himself when he realizes he doesn't know the whereabouts of this Jesus, whom he has yet to see.

(4) With the tone used to speak the aside about healing on the Sabbath you can signal that the encounter with the Pharisees will be controversial. Under these intimidating circumstances the beggar's responses are more guarded. The Pharisees are as divided as the crowd, some calling Jesus "sinner" and others countering that the evidence speaks of godliness. Stressing their sharp division will avoid presenting the Pharisees as uniformly sinister. The beggar reaches another stage of illumination when he risks the confession that Jesus is a "prophet."

(5) The scene with the man's parents prepares for the judgment Jesus later levels at the religious leaders who refused to believe. The parents, fearful, play their cards close to the chest, saying only what they must. Unlike their son, they are unwilling to risk. Indications of their fear may reflect the time in which the story was written rather than the situation during Jesus' time. Later decades would see real animosity develop between Jews and Christians resulting in the latter's expulsion from synagogues, but it was not a reality of Jesus' day. However, that detail

It is **unheard of** that anyone ever **opened** the eyes
> of a person born **blind**.
If this man were not from **God**,
> he would not be able to do **anything**."
They **answered** and said to him,
> "You were born totally in **sin**,
> and are **you** trying to teach **us**?"
Then they **threw** him **out**.

They take refuge in the false assumption that his blindness was the result of sin. Pause before the final scene with Jesus.

(7) When Jesus **heard** that they had thrown him out,
> he **found** him and said, "Do you **believe** in the Son of **Man**?"
He answered and said,
> "Who **is** he, sir, that I **may** believe in him?"
Jesus said to him,
> "You have **seen** him,
> the one **speaking** with you is **he**."
He said,
> "I **do** believe, Lord," and he **worshiped** him.
Then Jesus said,
> "I came into this world for **judgment**,
> so that those who do **not** see **might** see,
> and those who **do** see might become **blind**."

As yet, he has not seen Jesus. He's anxious to "see" him.

Pause after the words "he said" to suggest his moment of decision.

Jesus' tone attracts the attention of the Pharisees.

Some of the **Pharisees** who were with him **heard** this
> and said to him, "Surely **we** are not also blind, **are** we?"
Jesus said to them,
> "If you **were** blind, you would have no **sin**;
> but **now** you are saying, 'We **see**,' so your sin **remains**."

[Shorter: John 9:1, 6–9, 13–17, 34–38]

This is strong, uncompromising language, but it's motivated by his desire that they truly "see."

is well motivated within the context of the story. You might read the parenthetical aside ("His parents said this . . .") as the narrator's attempt to make fear an excuse for the parents' aberrant behavior.

(6) Good literature builds and peaks consistently and contains variety in rhythm and intensity. Don't make this second encounter between man and Pharisees a carbon of the first. The leaders' anger and frustration, even any sincere desire for the truth, must have intensified by now. That

Jesus is a "sinner" is a given for them. But the beggar disagrees with brilliantly animated and witty dialogue. Despite himself, he launches into a lecture proclaiming Jesus to be "from God." The response of the leaders is swift and harsh.

(7) A concerned Jesus seeks out the beggar, inviting more than questioning his belief in "the Son of Man." Remember, the beggar has yet to *see* Jesus, so a pause before the beggar's response will allow us to imagine him remembering Jesus' voice before falling down to worship.

Jesus' final speeches contain uncompromising truth. But how would a good shepherd who loves all his sheep speak such words of judgment?

You'll need much practice to tell this story well. No doubt it will take time. No doubt it will be worth it.

5TH SUNDAY OF LENT

Lectionary #36

READING I   Isaiah 43:16–21

A reading from the Book of the Prophet Isaiah

With poetic imagery and brevity the opening lines recall how God saved Israel during the Exodus from Egypt.

Don't drop your voice until the end of this sentence, building one relative clause upon another.

Here begin the words of God. Use a more solemn tone and slower pace.

Speak joyfully, as if you expect your listeners to "see" the vision with you.

Again, build one clause upon another with growing energy.

Your words should sound like joyous praise.

Thus says the LORD,
    who opens a **way** in the **sea**
    and a **path** in the mighty **waters**,
who leads out **chariots** and **horsemen**,
    a **powerful** army,
till they lie **prostrate** together, never to **rise**,
    snuffed out and **quenched** like a **wick**.
Remember **not** the events of the **past**,
    the things of long ago **consider** not;
see, I am doing something **new**!
    Now it **springs** forth, do you not **perceive** it?
In the **desert** I make a **way**,
    in the **wasteland**, **rivers**.
Wild **beasts honor** me,
    jackals and **ostriches**,
for I put **water** in the desert
    and **rivers** in the wasteland
    for my chosen **people** to **drink**,
the people whom I **formed** for myself,
    that they might **announce** my **praise**.

READING I | This week we focus on God's redemptive acts in history, especially the Exodus, as a foreshadowing of the salvation God will achieve in Christ. This text from Isaiah is addressed to exiles, promising them the joy of restoration and homecoming. But it also contains strong Exodus imagery which, as we approach the Triduum, can remind us that the Christian's "exodus" is achieved only by those who taste Christ's suffering, and cross over with him from death to new life.

The six lines that follow "Thus says the Lord" are poetic descriptors telling us who the Lord is. The lines are a confessional statement, declaring the goodness and power of God, so powerfully manifested in the deliverance of Israel from slavery. So don't mistake these statements for questions. To paraphrase, the text says: "Thus says the Lord, the Lord who *opens* . . . the Lord who *leads* . . . ." And note that what the Lord "says" does not begin until the word "Remember."

In this passage, God promises a new exodus to a people who have survived the exile. "Events of the past" and "things of long ago" refer to the first Exodus. They conjure up images of God's power and love. But God is planning something even greater! For the prophet, it is already tangible and visible: "*Now* it springs forth, do you not *perceive* it?" To prove that God's future action will surpass the miracles of the past, Isaiah describes the coming wonders: a road paved through the desert and rivers transforming the desert into an endless oasis. But the ultimate fulfillment will be the transformation of the exiles themselves into people "formed for myself." Save your best effort for that gorgeous image.

READING II   Philippians 3:8–14

A reading from the Letter of Saint Paul to the ...

Brothers and sisters:
I consider **everything** as a **loss**
    because of the supreme **good** of knowing Christ **Jesus** my **Lord**.
For **his** sake I have accepted the loss of **all** things
    and I consider them so much **rubbish**,
    that I may gain **Christ** and be found in **him**,
    not having any righteousness of my **own** based on the **law**
    but that which comes through **faith** in **Christ**,
    the righteousness from **God**,
    depending on faith to **know** him and the power
        of his **resurrection**
    and the sharing of his **sufferings** by being **conformed**
        to his **death**,
    if somehow I may attain the **resurrection** from the dead.

It is not that I have already taken **hold** of it
    or have already attained perfect **maturity**,
    but I **continue** my pursuit in **hope** that I may **possess** it,
    since I have **indeed** been taken **possession** of by Christ **Jesus**.
Brothers and sisters, I for **my** part
    do **not** consider myself to have taken **possession**.
Just one thing: **forgetting** what lies **behind**
    but straining **forward** to what lies **ahead**,
    I **continue** my pursuit toward the **goal**,
    the **prize** of God's upward **calling**, in Christ **Jesus**.

Remember that you are telling us that nothing in life is as valuable as a relationship with Christ.

"Rubbish" is a colorful word ("garbage!").

My only righteousness is what I have received from Christ.

For Paul, "suffering" and "death" must be mentioned in the same breath as "resurrection."

"It" is the Resurrection, that is, the fullness of resurrected life that comes only after death.

Although he does not possess it fully now, he continues to strive for it.

He has not "arrived," but continues to move toward the goal.

The "goal" is eternal life with Christ.

READING II   Paul, in jail and in danger of death, writes with exuberant energy about his commitment to Jesus and the transformation Christ has made in his life. Paul has learned that to reach the Resurrection we must climb the ladder of the cross. That may not seem like cause for rejoicing, but Paul has matured to the point of realizing that compared to "knowing Christ" everything else is worthless ("loss").

From his jail cell Paul composes a strong polemic against false teachers who insist salvation comes either from dependence on the law (Paul's own former error!) or from special, secret knowledge given to a select few (as done in the Gnostic sects that often corrupted Christian teaching). In response to those who say they have reached perfection by means other than Christ, Paul asserts that his own justice comes *only* "through faith in Christ." Anything else is "rubbish!" Paul further stresses that his pursuit of perfection is ongoing. He knows that Christ has taken "possession" of him. But he understands that we never really surrender ourselves fully to Christ. The more we grow in the spiritual life the more we discover layers of ourselves we are still holding back. It is this reality to which Paul refers when he says, "I for my part do not consider myself to have taken possession." In other words, he's saying: I'm still in the race; I have not yet reached the finish line.

"Forgetting what lies behind" Paul sets his eye on "what lies ahead," which is eternal life in Christ. Paul speaks with passion and energy. It will take great effort on your part to communicate the meaning of this difficult text.

GOSPEL   John 8:1–11

A reading from the holy Gospel according to John

Jesus went to the Mount of **Olives**.
But early in the **morning** he arrived again in the **temple** area,
     and all the people started **coming** to him,
     and he sat down and **taught** them.
Then the **scribes** and the **Pharisees** brought a **woman**
     who had been caught in **adultery**
     and made her stand in the **middle**.
They said to him,
     "**Teacher**, this **woman** was caught
     in the very **act** of committing adultery.
Now in the **law**, **Moses** commanded us to **stone** such women.
So what do **you** say?"
They said this to **test** him,
     so that they could have some **charge** to bring against him.
Jesus **bent** down and began to **write** on the ground with his **finger**.
But when they continued **asking** him,
     he **straightened** up and said to them,
     "Let the **one** among you who is **without** sin
     be the **first** to throw a **stone** at her."
Again he bent down and **wrote** on the **ground**.
And in **response**, they went **away one** by **one**,
     beginning with the **elders**.
So he was left **alone** with the woman **before** him.
Then Jesus **straightened** up and **said** to her,
     "**Woman**, where **are** they?
Has no one **condemned** you?"
She replied, "**No one**, sir."
Then Jesus said, "Neither do **I** condemn you.
Go, and from now **on** do not **sin** any **more**."

Remember that when you proclaim, you are believer first and public reader second. Your belief renders your art artless: simple, natural, uncontrived.

Take time to establish the setting.

Select a point of view for your narrator: a neutral bystander watching events unfold, a sympathetic disciple very invested in the unfolding events? Emphasize the treatment of the woman, exposed and humiliated in front of everyone.

The religious leaders appear low-key. Are they coy or blatant in their efforts to snare Jesus?

This aside shares an "insider's" point of view.

Pause before and after reading about him bending down. When Jesus straightens up, let his question seem a sincere invitation for a non-sinner to step forward.

Create a sense of mystery about Jesus' finger tracing. Not even the narrator knows what Jesus wrote.

This is a new beat. The tone shifts here.

Ask these questions with compassion.

This is the highpoint of the story.

GOSPEL   Earlier in John's Gospel account (3:17), Jesus says God did not send the Son to judge the world but to save it. In this story of the woman caught in adultery, we see that text lived out. The story doesn't dwell on whether we should or should not "judge" one another. Rather, it is enjoining us from being judgmental, from assuming we can read the heart of the other or, as we see here, from "condemning" the other. Only God can condemn. But even God's Son came not to condemn, but to save.

When the religious leaders push him for a decision about the woman's fate, Jesus' response expresses the great truth embedded in this encounter: all are sinners; all are in need of God's mercy; none can point the finger, or they'll find it pointing right back at them. At the heart of this story is the merciful love of God. Everyday, God comes not to condemn, but save. That's why Jesus came. That why the Church was formed—to be an agent of that divine mercy.

In memory, this story seems much longer than the span of a few paragraphs.

That's because so much happens during the silences. Take time to create the dramatic scenes that comprise the drama.

Take time to narrate the drifting away of the crowd, the dropping of stones, the woman standing alone with Jesus. Employ the greatest care with Jesus' final question. His final words forgive, heal, and pull the woman away from her past, propelling her into a future where God is doing something new.

5TH SUNDAY OF LENT, YEAR A

Lectionary #34

READING I   Ezekiel 37:12–14

A reading from the Book of the Prophet Ezekiel

Thus says the Lord GOD:
O my **people**, I will **open** your graves
    and have you **rise** from them,
    and bring you **back** to the land of Israel.
Then you shall **know** that I am the LORD,
    when I **open** your graves and have you **rise** from them,
    O my **people**!
I will put my **spirit** in you that you may **live**,
    and I will **settle** you upon your **land**;
    thus you shall **know** that I am the LORD.
I have **promised**, and I will **do** it, says the LORD.

"Thus says the Lord" is meant to get our attention. Speak it with authority. Pause briefly before narrating the intense vision.

The same idea is stated twice, with word order reversed. This is a poetic technique meant to give emphasis.

Use a quieter tone here. This is God's promise of restoration. The fulfillment of the promise will persuade Israel of God's great love for them. "And I will do it" must be spoken with strength and conviction.

READING I The old liturgical calendar designated this Sunday as the start of Passiontide. Though that designation is gone, these readings propel us toward the climactic events of Holy Week and Easter. Together they help us to contemplate Resurrection and new life.

The First Reading is not addressed to individuals, but to the nation of Israel, languishing in exile without hope of restoration. Their situation seemed as hopeless as the end of apartheid, the reunification of Germany, or the end of the Cold War. It is just such hopelessness that the prophecy seeks to dispel.

Spoken in a battlefield over the dry and barren bones of long-dead soldiers, this prophecy proclaims the death of despair, the inevitability of the impossible, the advent of new hope. God's voice, not the prophet's, makes the promise (twice!) that graves will be opened and the dead will walk again in the land of Israel. The exclamation "O my people" frames God's promise. Can you hear the urgency, the sincerity that kind of repetition conveys? There are many ways to suggest such direct and earnest feeling—with full-throated conviction, with quiet intensity, with subdued emotion, but always as if the events were unfolding right before you. Choose your tone and use it to persuade us.

Written long before belief in life after death became common among the Israelites, the stark images of this passage speak, nonetheless, of God's love and protection accompanying us to the grave and beyond. During the exile, being resettled "upon [their] land" was the only form of resurrection that mattered. "I will put my spirit in

READING II   Romans 8:8–11

A reading from the Letter of Saint Paul to the Romans

A short text calls for a slow reading. Paul's logic is filled with joy.

Brothers and sisters:
Those who are in the **flesh** cannot **please** God.
But **you** are not in the flesh;
    on the **contrary**, you are in the **spirit**,
    if only the **Spirit** of God **dwells** in you.

The negative tone of "Those in the flesh . . ." immediately turns positive at the words "But you are not . . . ."

Whoever does **not** have the Spirit of Christ
        does not **belong** to him.

The negative tone of "does not belong to him . . ." immediately turns positive at the words "But if Christ . . . ."

But if **Christ** is in you,
    although the body is **dead** because of **sin**,
    the **spirit** is **alive** because of **righteousness**.

Contrast "dead/sin" with "alive/ righteousness."

If the **Spirit** of the One who **raised** Jesus from the dead
        dwells in you,
    the One who **raised** Christ from the dead
    will give life to **your** mortal bodies **also**,
    through his **Spirit** dwelling in you.

This is an "if/then" clause with an implied "then." Proclaim these words with joy.

GOSPEL   John 11:1–45

A reading from the holy Gospel according to John

For the narrator, these are familiar names and places. Speak of the anointing with tenderness.

Bethany = BETH-uh-nee

(1) Now a man was **ill**, **Lazarus** from **Bethany**,
    the village of **Mary** and her sister **Martha**.
Mary was the one who had **anointed** the Lord with perfumed **oil**
    and dried his **feet** with her **hair**;
    it was her **brother** Lazarus who was ill.

---

you that you may live . . ." is a promise of such restoration. So save your best emphasis for that line. Stressing the word "spirit" will help prepare us for the Second Reading where God's spirit is the central motif. In this text Ezekiel presents one of scriptures most striking images to offer his message of hope. Speak that message to each individual in the assembly, for many wounded hearts long to hear such words of promise.

READING II Count the number of times Paul uses the word "Spirit." Like Ezekiel, Paul draws a contrast between what is and is not life, and that difference is the Spirit of God who alone can transform "flesh" into "spirit." "Flesh" for Paul represents those who have not embraced new life in Christ, who live only to please themselves. "Spirit" refers to those who have accepted newness of life and live selflessly, pleasing both God and neighbor.

Paul rejoices that his listeners are in this second camp. Although he starts with bad news ("Those who are in the flesh cannot please God"), he qualifies himself immediately: "But you are not . . ." part of that bad news. You are living the good news of life in the Spirit! Walk your listeners slowly through the text. There is clear logic and nice progression throughout. Contrasting "dead" and "sin" with "alive" and "righteousness" will add to the clarity.

Say the word "Master" with anxiety in your tone of voice.

Don't get philosophical here. Keep the tone low-key and conversational.

Proclaim the words "Jesus loved" slowly. Everything else builds on this.

The disciples are immediately anxious and incredulous.

Again, avoid a lofty tone and keep it conversational.

Here, speak as if you were really going to wake a sleeping friend.

The tone here should be "Master, you're not making sense!"

Speak with some gravity, but not sadness.

So the sisters sent **word** to Jesus saying,
  "**Master**, the one you **love** is **ill**."
When Jesus **heard** this he said,
  "This illness is **not** to end in **death**,
  but is for the **glory** of **God**,
  that the **Son** of God may be **glorified** through it."
(2) Now Jesus **loved** Martha and her sister and Lazarus.
So when he **heard** that he was ill,
  he **remained** for two **days** in the place where he **was**.
Then **after** this he said to his disciples,
  "Let us go back to **Judea**."
The disciples said to him,
  "**Rabbi**, the Jews were just trying to **stone** you,
  and you want to go **back** there?"
Jesus answered,
  "Are there not **twelve** hours in a day?
If one walks during the **day**, he does not **stumble**,
  because he sees the **light** of this world.
But if one walks at **night**, he **stumbles**,
  because the light is not **in** him."
He said this, and then told them,
  "Our friend **Lazarus** is **asleep**,
  but I am going to **awaken** him."
So the disciples said to him,
  "**Master**, if he is **asleep**, he will be **saved**."
But Jesus was talking about his **death**,
  while **they** thought that he meant **ordinary** sleep.
So then Jesus said to them **clearly**,
  "**Lazarus** has **died**.
And I am **glad** for you that I was not **there**,
  that you may **believe**.
Let us **go** to him."

"Although the body is dead . . ." is not a literal statement, of course. Paul means that, despite being saved through Christ's Resurrection, the fullness of salvation won't be ours until after death. For now, our bodies are subject to the signs of death—illness, aging, pain—because we live in a world still under death's influence. But our spirit already enjoys a foretaste of what will be ours fully in eternity.

Paul's conclusion announces hope of *physical* Resurrection for those who possess Christ's spirit. The same spirit who makes it possible for Christians to live holy lives now will also bring their "mortal bodies to life" on the last day. The same attitude of joy that has pervaded the text proclaims this final good news.

GOSPEL Fascinating as it is, this story means little unless it tells us that death still yields to life, unless it says that Jesus walks among us ready to repeat the words that beckoned Lazarus from the tomb, unless we learn he's willing still to brave the stench of death and call the living back to life. That's a tall order for a proclaimer—to convince us of all that. But that's why we tell and retell the stories of scripture. So prepare by deciding what you need to do to make this a proclamation of hope rather than a recitation of history. That may mean spending time with these characters until they're as real to you as those from a favorite piece of literature—or as real as people you encounter on your daily rounds. That may mean imagining yourself in the same situation—watching

So **Thomas**, called **Didymus**, said to his fellow **disciples**,
   "Let us **also** go to **die** with him."

(3) When Jesus **arrived**, he found that Lazarus
   had already been in the **tomb** for **four days**.
Now Bethany was **near** Jerusalem, only about two miles **away**.
And many of the **Jews** had **come** to Martha and Mary
   to **comfort** them about their brother.
When Martha **heard** that **Jesus** was coming,
   she went to **meet** him;
   but **Mary** sat at home.
Martha said to Jesus,
   "**Lord**, if you had **been** here,
   my brother would not have **died**.
But even **now** I know that **whatever** you ask of God,
   God will **give** you."
Jesus said to her,
   "Your brother will **rise**."
Martha said to him,
   "I **know** he will rise,
   in the **resurrection** on the last **day**."
Jesus told her,
   "**I** am the resurrection and the **life**;
   whoever **believes** in me, even if he **dies**, will **live**,
   and everyone who **lives** and believes in me will **never** die.
Do **you** believe this?"
She said to him, "**Yes**, Lord.
I have come to believe that you are the **Christ**, the Son of **God**,
   the one who is **coming** into the **world**."

He's willing to pay the price of discipleship.

"Four days" reflects the Jewish belief that the spirit left the body after three days: hence Lazarus is "fully" dead.

Martha exhibits mixed emotions: disappointment and hopefulness.

Martha has missed his point. Jesus' explanation and self-identification are the key points of this Gospel passage.

Speak slowly here. This parallels the "light of the world" pronouncement in last week's Gospel.

Martha's confession is sincere and unreserved.

a loved one die, hoping for a remedy that comes too late. You might read the story several times picturing yourself a different character each time—a disciple, one of the sisters, a mourner, Jesus, even Lazarus. Is there someone you know for whom this story has been a source of hope? Could you question that person about how the story touches them? These strategies will take time and effort.

(1) In the opening lines, the narrator speaks with familiarity and affection about these people and places, about perfume and hair-dried feet. The sisters send for Jesus, confident that he will hasten to comply. As with the healing of the blind man, Jesus announces the divine purposes to be achieved through "this illness" and betrays no sense of urgency.

(2) The scene in which Jesus receives the news of Lazarus' illness sets up a paradox: Jesus loves Lazarus' family, yet he tarries intentionally before setting out. Jesus' announcement that they will return to Judea disturbs the disciples who immediately appear afraid and seem to think the decision is irresponsible. Jesus replies using a familiar Johannine motif: day and night. "Day" refers to the time of Jesus' presence on the earth—a time for doing God's work and a time to be free of fear, because "if one walks during the *day*, he does not stumble." Jesus' announcement of Lazarus' death need not be emotional; simplicity better hints at his depth of inner feeling. The disciples misunderstand his use of "asleep." Jesus clarifies and reiterates the divine purpose behind these events. Thomas might outdo even Peter's Last Supper grandstanding ("I will lay

Use a quieter tone here. Martha may have been coaxing Mary to go, but now Mary goes eagerly.

Her line echoes Martha's, but vary the delivery for variety.

Jesus experiences genuine sorrow here. A note in the NAB says that in Greek this is a startling image: "He snorted in spirit."

Jesus' reply to John's disciples ("Come and see . . .") is the start of his ministry.

Convey the contrasting moods of the crowd.

Proclaim these simple but dramatic statements slowly.

Concern about the stench is a very practical one.

(4) When she had **said** this,
　she went and called her sister Mary **secretly**, **saying**,
　"The **teacher** is here and is **asking** for you."
As soon as she **heard** this,
　she rose **quickly** and **went** to him.
For Jesus had not yet come into the **village**,
　but was still where Martha had **met** him.
So when the Jews who were **with** her in the house **comforting** her
　saw Mary get up quickly and go out,
　they **followed** her,
　presuming that she was going to the **tomb** to **weep** there.
When Mary came to where **Jesus** was and **saw** him,
　she fell at his **feet** and said to him,
　"**Lord**, if you had **been** here,
　my brother would not have **died**."
When Jesus saw her **weeping** and the Jews who had come
　　with her weeping,
　he became **perturbed** and deeply **troubled**, and said,
　"**Where** have you **laid** him?"
They said to him, "**Sir**, come and **see**."
(5) And Jesus **wept**.
So the Jews said, "See how he **loved** him."
But some of them said,
　"Could not the one who opened the eyes of the **blind** man
　have **done** something so that **this** man would not have **died**?"

So **Jesus**, perturbed **again**, came to the **tomb**.
It was a **cave**, and a **stone** lay across it.
Jesus said, "Take away the **stone**."
Martha, the dead man's **sister**, said to him,
　"Lord, by **now** there will be a **stench**;
　he has been dead for **four days**."

down my life for you!" [John 13:37]) in his own eagerness for martyrdom.

(3) Jesus arrives at Bethany and the physical reality of Lazarus' death is starkly emphasized. His arrival creates a stir and changes the mood of the town. The sisters are clearly distressed by Jesus' delay: while Martha goes to meet him, Mary sits "at home." Yet Martha declares her faith that God will grant whatever Jesus asks. Jesus' response is cryptic and not what Martha wants to hear. The Gospel reaches a high point in Jesus' great pronouncement that he is the source of life. Martha responds with a clear declaration of faith.

(4) Martha (secretly) tells Mary that Jesus is *asking* for her, so Mary runs to Jesus, falls at his feet and weeps over the loss of her brother, laying responsibility squarely on Jesus. Jesus demonstrates rare emotion when he becomes "deeply troubled" by Mary's sorrow. "Where have you laid him?" Jesus asks. You play this scene each time you visit a funeral home. "Come and see."

(5) "And Jesus wept": build toward that moment for it is the most striking. Some bystanders are impressed by his emotion, while others join the Mary/Martha chorus, questioning why Jesus could do nothing for this friend when he could heal strangers. "It was a cave" is the haunting reference to the tomb. Jesus speaks with authority but Martha's concern ("there will be a stench") betrays a lack of confidence, so he reproaches her gently.

(6) Jesus prays "because of the crowd," addressing the Father with confidence and gratitude, asking that the crowds

This should be a very gentle reproach.	Jesus said to her,
	  "Did I not **tell** you that if you **believe**
	  you will see the **glory** of **God**?"
	(6) So they **took away** the stone.
	And Jesus raised his **eyes** and said,
	  "**Father**, I **thank** you for **hearing** me.
	I know that you **always** hear me;

Jesus prays for others here, not himself.	but because of the **crowd** here I have said this,
	  that they may **believe** that you **sent** me."
	And when he had **said** this,
	  he **cried** out in a **loud** voice,

Use great authority here.	"**Lazarus**, come **out**!" The **dead** man **came** out, tied **hand** and **foot** with **burial** bands,
See the commentary for possible phrasings of this line.	and his **face** was wrapped in a **cloth**. So Jesus said to them, "**Untie** him and let him **go**."
Hearing this Gospel should arouse deeper faith in the assembly.	(7) Now **many** of the Jews who had come to **Mary** and **seen** what he had done began to **believe** in him. [Shorter: John 11:3–7, 17, 20–27, 33b–45]

be brought to faith. Throughout, Jesus has been in charge, the master of circumstances. The extent of his power and authority is shown nowhere else better than in this dramatic moment. In John, it is this event that finally prompts the religious leaders to move against him.

    Speak "Lazarus" as if it were the name of those most in need of renewed life: your city's homeless poor, an oppressed country, a friend suffering from depression, a long-dead part of you. The appearance of Lazarus can be read without much inflection. If you really *witness* the event, the assembly will see and *feel* it with you. But for that to happen, you must read slower than you've ever read. Try phrasing like this: "The dead man / came out / bound / hand / and foot / with burial bands / and his face / was wrapped in a cloth." Practice until it sounds and feels right.

    (7) Build on each phrase of this final sentence. In contrast with the epilogue of the blind man story, "many" come to faith in Bethany. Through this dramatic narrative, you bring your assembly in contact with a side of Jesus' humanity we rarely see. The Lord of life, who healed the blind and raised the dead, was one of us, mourning the death of a friend, comforting his family, shedding real tears.

PALM SUNDAY OF THE LORD'S PASSION

Lectionary #37

GOSPEL AT THE PROCESSION   Luke 19:28–40

Suggest the fuller meaning of the movement toward Jerusalem.
Bethpahge = BETH-fuh-gee
Bethany = BETH-uh-nee

His confident tone regarding the "colt" can be spoken with strength or with such matter-of-factness that no one would think to question it.

Is this what they expected or are they surprised?

The owners' question could be either a challenge or a non-threatening request for an explanation.

Deliver the words "The master has need of it" either with confidence in the adequacy of the rehearsed response, or parroted with uncertainty about its efficacy.

A reading from the holy Gospel according to Luke

Jesus proceeded on his **journey** up to **Jerusalem**.
As he drew near to **Bethphage** and **Bethany**
  at the place called the Mount of **Olives**,
  he sent two of his **disciples**.
He said, "Go into the **village** opposite you,
  and as you **enter** it you will find a **colt** tethered
  on which **no** one has ever **sat**.
Untie it and **bring** it here.
And if anyone should **ask** you,
  '**Why** are you untying it?'
  you will answer,
  'The **Master** has **need** of it.'"
So those who had been **sent** went **off**
  and found **everything** just as he had **told** them.
And as they were **untying** the colt, its **owners** said to them,
  "Why are you **untying** this colt?"
They answered,
  "The **Master** has need of it."
So they **brought** it to Jesus,
  threw their **cloaks** over the colt,
  and helped Jesus to **mount**.

PROCESSION GOSPEL The two Gospel readings on Passion Sunday proclaim first a triumphal entry, then a walk of pain to Calvary. But there is greater unity between these readings than is immediately evident. The liturgy asks us to see more than a triumphal procession in this first Gospel. It is *here* that Christ initiates his journey to Calvary, where he will lay down his life in a supreme act of love and redemption.

The first line clarifies the single focus of today's liturgy by speaking of how Jesus "proceeded on" to Jerusalem. That phrase holds paradoxical connotations of the painful yet triumphant destiny that awaits him there. "At the place called the Mount of Olives" suggests Luke doesn't expect his readers to be familiar with the geography; you certainly can make the same assumption about your listeners and deliver the line with an explanatory tone. The task Jesus gives the disciples may well have made them feel anxious or awkward. The confident tone of Jesus' voice must erase any insecurity in the disciples.

To reflect the mounting excitement of the crowd, increase the energy of your reading. While the contrast with what will follow in the Passion reading is stark and ironic, the rightness of recounting this triumphal entry cannot be denied. It is only on the throne of the cross that Jesus will assume his rightful kingship. The praise and adulation of the crowd anticipate the worship of saints and angels and all creation when Jesus enters fully into his glory. With typical irony, Jesus' glorious entry comes on the back of a humble colt.

Express the mounting excitement and joy. They spread "cloaks", not "palms."

As he **rode** along,
　　the people were spreading their **cloaks** on the road;
　　and now as he was approaching the **slope** of the Mount
　　　　of **Olives**,
　　the whole **multitude** of his disciples
　　began to praise God **aloud** with **joy**
　　for all the mighty **deeds** they had seen.
They proclaimed:
　　"**Blessed** is the **king** who comes
　　　　in the **name** of the **Lord**.

"Peace in heaven . . ." is Luke's version of "hosannah."

　　Peace in **heaven**
　　　　and **glory** in the **highest**."
Some of the **Pharisees** in the crowd said to him,

They are fearful.

　　"**Teacher**, **rebuke** your disciples."
He said in reply,

Jesus is saying that it's is out of his hands. Proclaim with energy.

　　"I **tell** you, if **they** keep silent,
　　the **stones** will cry out!"

Lectionary #38

READING I   Isaiah 50:4–7

A reading from the Book of the Prophet Isaiah

Speak slowly and with confident joy at the mission God has given you.

The Lord **GOD** has **given** me
　　a well-**trained** tongue,
　　that I might **know** how to **speak** to the **weary**
　　a word that will **rouse** them.
Morning after **morning**

Again, speak confidently. It is God who daily rouses the prophet to listen and speak.

　　he opens my **ear** that I may **hear**;
　　and I have not **rebelled**,
　　have not turned **back**.

The people express their praise by spreading their "cloaks," not palm branches on the ground. The intensity peaks in shouted "hosannas" that Luke (without ever using the word) uniquely translates as "Peace in heaven and glory in the highest," an obvious allusion to the angels' song at the Nativity. The Pharisees protest out of fear of Roman vengeance for "we have no king but Caesar" (John 19:15). Without anger Jesus responds that, like an uncapped champagne bottle, this flow of spontaneous jubilation simply cannot be stopped.

READING I This third "servant-song" of Isaiah's proclaims the prophet's ceaseless efforts to speak "a word" to a people that has apparently grown tired of hearing it. The "suffering servant" is Isaiah's characterization of the faithful steward whose service for the Lord brings little more than persecution and suffering upon him. This passage presumes that Israel languishes in exile, grown "weary" of hearing promises of deliverance that remain unfulfilled. But the prophet is resolute in his determination to "rouse" this people to hope and to reignite

their faith. His resolve mirrors that of the Lord who "morning after morning" opens the prophet's ear to hear God's word. Unlike the people, the prophet doesn't resent God's persistence. In fact, he strenuously asserts his openness to God's discipline in phrases like "I have not rebelled, have not turned my back."

As noted earlier, the prophet is paid in pain for his willingness to serve. The early Church clearly saw a connection between Isaiah's suffering servant and the suffering Jesus, whose Passion we memorialize

No sense of self-pity here. It's in the past tense. What remains is the quiet joy of having done God's will.

Joy undergirds this final declaration of confidence in God's vindication.

I gave my **back** to those who **beat** me,
     my **cheeks** to those who plucked my **beard**;
my **face** I did not **shield**
     from **buffets** and **spitting**.

The Lord **GOD** is my **help**,
     therefore I am not **disgraced**;
I have set my face like **flint**,
     knowing that I shall **not** be put to **shame**.

READING II   Philippians 2:6–11

A reading from the Letter of Saint Paul to the Philippians

Begin slowly, but with solid energy.

"Rather" signals a shift. Speak more slowly and with greater solemnity.

These are not detractions; speak them with gratitude that Christ became one of us.

Here is another shift; the tempo should quicken. You can get louder, or softer but more intense.

Speak slowly here.

Gradually slow down at the words ". . . of God the Father."

Christ **Jesus**, though he was in the form of **God**,
     did not regard **equality** with God
          something to be **grasped**.
Rather, he **emptied** himself,
     taking the form of a **slave**,
     coming in **human** likeness;
     and found **human** in **appearance**,
     he **humbled** himself,
     becoming **obedient** to the point of **death**,
          even death on a **cross**.
Because of this, God greatly **exalted** him
     and bestowed on him the **name**
     which is above **every** name,
     that at the name of **Jesus**
     every **knee** should **bend**,
     of those in **heaven** and on **earth** and **under** the earth,
     and every **tongue confess** that
Jesus Christ is **Lord**,
     to the **glory** of God the **Father**.

---

today. The past tense softens a bit the impact of the strong language that describes his pain. "Beat me," "plucked my beard," and "buffets and spitting" all speak of suffering *willingly* endured—an especially important detail today, so your reading should have less lament and more peaceful determination. While "I gave my back . . . my face I did not shield" are more important expressions than the details of torture that follow them.

The last four lines change the mood for they focus on God's "help" by speaking of trust in God's ultimate vindication ("I am

not disgraced . . . not put to shame")—a trust that strengthens the prophet against future pain.

    Note that the opening sentence describes the lector's ministry: to employ a well-trained tongue to announce the Good News of the Lord in a way that will rouse listeners to hope-filled life!

READING II We established above that pain is far from being the only focus of this day. The authors of Christian scriptures see Jesus' suffering

and death always through the filter of his glorious Resurrection and Ascension. Theirs is never a lop-sided emphasis on agony, so the incorporation of this magnificent hymn of praise and exultation into today's liturgy is most appropriate.

    We learn the content of the hymn by studying its structure: the first half (up to "death on a cross") refers exclusively to Christ, telling us *who* he is—equal with God, born as a man, humble, and obedient. In the second half the subject becomes God, and we learn what God has done for Christ: exalted him, given him the name above

PASSION   Luke 22:14—23:56

The Passion of our Lord Jesus Christ according to Luke

"Hour" refers to the hour of Jesus' death, not the time of the meal. In other words, the time of fulfillment has been inaugurated.

Only Luke includes this line. Jesus anticipates the suffering ahead.

(1) When the **hour** came,
Jesus took his place at **table** with the **apostles**.
He **said** to them,
"I have **eagerly** desired to eat this **Passover** with you
before I **suffer**,
for, I **tell** you, I shall not eat it **again**
until there is **fulfillment** in the **kingdom** of God."
Then he took a **cup**, gave **thanks**, and said,
"**Take** this and **share** it among yourselves;
for I tell you that from this time **on**
I shall not **drink** of the fruit of the **vine**
until the kingdom of God **comes**."
Then he took the **bread**, said the **blessing**,
broke it, and **gave** it to them, saying,
"This is my **body**, which will be **given** for you;
do this in **memory** of me."
And likewise the **cup** after they had **eaten**, saying,
"This **cup** is the **new covenant** in my **blood**,
which will be **shed** for you.

The mood here should be intimate but solemn.

Take time with these sacred words. Don't speak them as a formula, but convey the love they embody.

The sense of betrayal is deep here.

(2) "And yet **behold**, the hand of the one who is to **betray** me
is with me on the **table**;
for the Son of Man indeed **goes** as it has been **determined**;
but **woe** to that man by whom he is **betrayed**."
And they began to **debate** among themselves
who among them would **do** such a deed.

These words shatter the mood.

The apostle's insensitivity turns into self-absorption.

(3) Then an **argument** broke out among them
about **which** of them should be regarded as the **greatest**.

every other, that all might worship him. As reader, note how the hymn first speaks of Christ's humbling himself to become human, and then abruptly changes key and tempo and swells into symphonic praise.

Speak the opening line with conviction, your tone guided by the emptying and humbling of which you speak. Here the hymn stresses Christ's oneness with humanity: "taking the form of a slave, coming in human likeness and found human in appearance," but the last line of the section, "death on a cross," asserts what makes him unique.

"Because of this" is the fulcrum on which the hymn shifts. The mood changes with the tempo. Like Isaiah's servant, Jesus is not put to shame but "exalted" (note how insistently the hymn tells where the exaltation occurs: heaven, earth, and under the earth). "Exalted" flavors all that follows. Express this either by quickening and amplifying your proclamation, or by softening but intensifying it. Either way, a blend of joy and gratitude for what God has done for Christ carries you to the concluding exclamation. And note that Jesus is

"Lord" not for his own glory, but for the "glory of God the Father."

PASSION   Because the story of Christ's death is essentially "good news," no reading of the Passion can ever cross over into a mood of sad sentimentality. A Christian can never speak of the tomb without simultaneously hearing the rumbling of the moving stone. As you bring this story to life with its pathos unfolding in numerous scenes of anger, hatred, fear, guilt and sorrow, you must remember the

Jesus continues his teaching ministry to the end.

He said to them,
  "The kings of the **Gentiles lord** it over them
  and those in **authority** over them are addressed as '**Benefactors**';
  but among **you** it shall not **be** so.
Rather, let the **greatest** among you be as the **youngest**,
  and the **leader** as the **servant**.
For who is **greater**:
  the one **seated** at table or the one who **serves**?
Is it not the one **seated** at table?
I am among you as the one who **serves**.

Don't rush past this significant line.

It is **you** who have **stood** by me in my **trials**;
  and I confer a **kingdom** on you,
  just as my **Father** has conferred one on **me**,

Jesus speaks with gratitude and hope.

  that you may **eat** and **drink** at my **table** in my **kingdom**;
  and you will sit on **thrones**
  judging the twelve tribes of **Israel**.

This is a sudden shift, as if Jesus responds to seeing Peter with urgent caution.

(4) "**Simon, Simon**, behold **Satan** has demanded
  to **sift** all of you like **wheat**,
  but I have **prayed** that your own **faith** may not **fail**;
  and once you have turned **back**,

This is a solemn instruction to Peter.

  you must **strengthen** your **brothers**."
He said to him,

Peter is fully sincere here.

  "**Lord**, I am prepared to go to **prison** and to **die** with you."
But he replied,
  "I **tell** you, Peter, before the cock **crows** this day,

Don't use a judgmental tone here. Jesus will forgive.

  you will deny three **times** that you **know** me."

(5) He said to them,

The mood shifts here. The tone becomes instructing, but more urgent.

  "When I sent you **forth** without a **money** bag or a **sack**
    or **sandals**,
  were you in **need** of anything?"

---

surprise that awaits the third day. Let that flavor all the scenes no matter how turbulent, for the light of the Resurrection penetrates the darkness even of the garden, Peter's denial, and Jesus' final moments on the cross.

As you prepare, be aware of the unique character of this story. While the rest of the Gospel consists of story units or episodes passed on individually by word-of-mouth before they were collected into a Gospel, the Passion was always told, not in pieces, but as one continuous story. It is the longest unit because you really cannot

tell one part without telling the others. This seamless narrative challenges you to understand what it means to be a *story-teller*. Storytellers don't simply remind us of past events; in the act of telling, they make those events present and real so their power can touch us once again. Stories unfold one episode at a time, just like real life events.

Although we read the Passion by the light of the Resurrection, that light does not rob the individual moment of its suspense and drama. That's the magic of stories—even when we know the ending

(Hamlet will be dead by the end of the evening, for example), the knowledge does not cancel the possibility of hoping as we watch that *this* time events will unfold differently, that *this* time Hamlet *won't* die. Let this story first work its magic on you, the proclaimer. Be the first to be moved by the events and emotions you describe.

It will be helpful, as you prepare, to note the unique features of Luke's Passion: Jesus' innocence is asserted often; his disciples, even his enemies, receive kinder treatment here than in the other Passion

Jesus is urging them to be ready for anything, including hostile opposition.

"**No**, **nothing**," they replied.
He said to them,
"But **now** one who has a **money** bag should **take** it,
    and likewise a **sack**,
    and one who does not have a **sword**
    should sell his **cloak** and **buy** one.
For I tell you that this **Scripture** must be **fulfilled** in me,
    namely, *He was counted among the **wicked***;
    and indeed what is **written** about me is coming to **fulfillment**."
Then they said,

It's as if they're saying, "Lord, we're ready to fight!" And Jesus says, "That's enough!" They've missed his point.

"**Lord**, **look**, there are **two** swords here."
But he replied, "It is **enough**!"

The garden is a familiar place of prayer.

(6) Then going **out**, he **went**, as was his **custom**, to the Mount
        of **Olives**,
    and the disciples **followed** him.
When he **arrived** at the place he **said** to them,
    "**Pray** that you may not undergo the **test**."

Jesus is not in anguish here.

After withdrawing about a **stone's** throw from them and **kneeling**,
    he **prayed**, saying, "**Father**, if you are **willing**,
    take this cup **away** from me;
    still, not **my** will but **yours** be done."
And to **strengthen** him an **angel** from heaven **appeared** to him.

Now the agony begins in earnest.

He was in such **agony** and he prayed so **fervently**
    that his **sweat** became like drops of **blood**
    falling on the ground.
When he **rose** from prayer and returned to his **disciples**,
    he found them **sleeping** from **grief**.

Luke makes excuses for the disciples' lack of vigilance. Jesus is forceful in his urging.

He **said** to them, "Why are you **sleeping**?
Get **up** and **pray** that you may not undergo the **test**."

narratives, Jesus is not so regal as in John, nor so forsaken as in Matthew/Mark. Instead he calmly accepts his death as a fulfillment of God's will. Jesus arrives at Calvary not abandoned but with companions, forgiving those who crucify him and characteristically showing more concern for others' needs than for his own.

The reading of the Passion has a long and varied history. To enhance the dynamic interplay of voices and characters, it may be done with three readers. However, an excellent solo reader can also deliver a riveting proclamation, so that option

should not be ruled out. If the participation of the assembly is to be encouraged, remember the downside is the need for all to "read along" so they know when to speak their lines. In this instance, active participation is better achieved by active *listening*, that results in a spiritual involvement with the story. So consider seriously the merits of letting the assembly simply listen. Readers must be well-prepared, having studied and rehearsed the entire Passion, not only their assigned lines. Movement during the proclamation should

be discouraged. But familiarity and practice with microphones and lecterns are a must. The Passion only seems long when those proclaiming it are not "telling the story." Storytelling requires more than reading words. It takes an intimate knowledge of the characters, their motivations, their relationships to each other, and a clear sense of how the parts comprise the whole. Pray that you might proclaim worthily and that the experience will draw you closer to Christ.

(1) *The Last Supper.* The juxtaposition of "eagerly desired" and "before I suffer"

The pain of betrayal is palpable.

Peter is eager to defend here.

Jesus says, "Don't interfere." Only Luke records this compassionate healing.

There is judgment in his voice.

She's too loud to ignore.

(7) While he was still **speaking**, a **crowd** approached
   and in **front** was one of the **Twelve**, a man named **Judas**.
He went up to Jesus to **kiss** him.
Jesus said to him,
   "**Judas**, are you **betraying** the Son of Man with a **kiss**?"
His disciples **realized** what was about to happen, and they asked,
   "**Lord**, shall we strike with a **sword**?"
And **one** of them struck the high priest's **servant**
   and cut off his right **ear**.
But **Jesus** said in reply,
   "**Stop**, no **more** of this!"
Then he **touched** the servant's ear and **healed** him.
And Jesus said to the chief **priests** and temple **guards**
   and **elders** who had come for him,
   "Have you come out as against a **robber**, with **swords**
      and **clubs**?
Day after **day** I was with you in the **temple** area,
   and you did not **seize** me;
   but this is **your** hour, the time for the **power** of **darkness**."

(8) After **arresting** him they led him **away**
   and took him into the house of the high **priest**;
   Peter was following at a **distance**.
They lit a **fire** in the middle of the **courtyard** and **sat** around it,
   and **Peter** sat down **with** them.
When a **maid** saw him seated in the **light**,
   she looked **intently** at him and said,
   "This man **too** was with him."
But he **denied** it saying,
   "**Woman**, I do not **know** him."

sets the tone. Jesus' mood blends awareness of his coming agony (his "hour") with joy over celebrating this final meal with his friends. Meals often occasioned Jesus' ministry. Though intimate, this one also has a solemn quality, anticipating the stylized ritual it will become for the assembly of believers. To the end, Jesus pours himself out for his disciples: "Do this . . . this cup . . ." are poignant lines, filled and spoken with love.

(2) *The Betrayal Foretold.* That his betrayer is one who shares the fellowship of the "table" rubs salt into the wound, but

it is no surprise for it has been "determined." "But woe . . ." might express more grief than warning. Judas is never named or exposed, leading the others to engage in insensitive disputes.

(3) *The Role of the Disciples.* Without ever addressing Jesus on the question of betrayal, the disciples launch into another dispute. Again, instead of receiving care, Jesus gives it, identifying himself as "one who serves." He teaches through the example of his humility and tenderness—evident in the tone of your reading. Although facing execution, Jesus guarantees these men

who have stood by him the reward of seats at the heavenly banquet. His voice must communicate love for these friends, as well as assurance.

(4) *Peter's Denial Foretold.* "Simon, Simon" is a challenging repetition. Sincerity is the goal; whether you raise or lower your volume on the second naming, the intensity must increase. Before placing the mantle of leadership on Peter (characterized as *strengthening*), Jesus alludes to danger, but assures Peter of efficacious prayer. Typically overconfident, Peter responds

Peter still remains calm.

A short while **later** someone **else** saw him and said,
"You **too** are one of them";
but Peter answered, "My friend, I am **not**."
About an hour **later**, still **another** insisted,
"**Assuredly**, this man **too** was with him,
for he **also** is a **Galilean**."
But Peter said,

Speak with a hostile tone here, as if through clenched teeth.

"My **friend**, I do not **know** what you are **talking** about."
Just as he was **saying** this, the cock **crowed**,
and the Lord **turned** and **looked** at Peter;

Jesus' look releases bitter tears. Luke alone relates this detail.

and Peter **remembered** the word of the Lord,
how he had **said** to him,
"Before the cock **crows** today, you will **deny** me **three** times."

Pause briefly here.

He went **out** and began to weep **bitterly**.

As narrator, you are angered by this treatment of Jesus.

(9) The men who held Jesus in **custody** were **ridiculing** and
beating him.
They **blindfolded** him and **questioned** him, saying,

"prophesy = PROF-uh-sī

"**Prophesy!** Who is it that **struck** you?"
And they **reviled** him in saying many **other** things against him.

(10) When **day** came the council of **elders** of the people **met**,
both chief **priests** and **scribes**,
and they brought him before their **Sanhedrin**.

"Sanhedrin" = san-HEE-druhn

There is tension throughout the scene.

They said, "If you are the **Christ**, **tell** us,"
but he **replied** to them, "If I **tell** you, you will not **believe**,
and if I **question**, you will not **respond**.
But from this time **on** the Son of **Man** will be seated
at the **right** hand of the power of **God**."
They all asked, "**Are** you then the Son of **God**?"
He replied to them, "**You** say that I am."

He's a blasphemer!

Then they said, "What further **need** have we for **testimony**?
We have **heard** it from his own **mouth**."

with overstated loyalty. Why does Jesus predict Peter's denial? To prepare him for that failing? To soften his inevitable guilt? To temper his pride? Jesus' reply is blunt and direct, but given the context of the meal, it probably carries no judgment.

(5) *Future Trials.* Jesus shifts to figurative language and the disciples miss his purpose entirely. They respond eagerly to his inquiry, "were you in need . . . ?" but they assume his talk of "money bag" and "sword" are warnings of imminent danger which they can repel with violence rather than symbolic references to future trials and opposition. They present their swords with too much eagerness to use them, so Jesus abruptly ends the discourse with a single word that betrays his sadness, perhaps even a sense of failure or disgust.

(6) *The Garden.* Never alone in this Passion, Jesus seeks the refuge of a customary retreat in the company of his disciples. Immediately he commands *them* to pray that they not succumb to temptation. Drinking from the "cup" symbolizes a fearsome and difficult task. Although not as abjectly agonized as in Mark's Gospel account, the garden experience is a great ordeal for Jesus. Phrases like "strengthen him," "in such agony," "so fervently," and "drops of blood" suggest the struggle. Luke makes excuses for the disciples' inability to remain awake by attributing their exhaustion to "grief." Jesus rouses them with a second, more insistent, call to prayer.

(7) *The Betrayal and Arrest.* Again Judas is identified as "one of the twelve," but Luke distances his readers from Judas by referring to him as "a man *named* Judas." When Jesus interrogates Judas about the

They're on the offensive here, accusing him of political crimes.

(11) Then the whole **assembly** of them **arose** and brought him
    before **Pilate**.
They brought **charges** against him, saying,
  "We found this man **misleading** our people;
  he **opposes** the payment of **taxes** to **Caesar**
  and maintains that he is the **Christ**, a **king**."
Pilate asked him, "**Are** you the **king** of the **Jews**?"
He said to him in reply, "**You** say so."

Pilate comes across as sympathetic. His interest in Jesus grows steadily.

Pilate then addressed the chief **priests** and the **crowds**,
  "I find this man **not guilty**."
But they were **adamant** and said,
  "He is **inciting** the people with his **teaching**
    throughout all **Judea**,
  from **Galilee** where he **began** even to **here**."

"Galilean" = gal-ih-LEE-uhn
Pilate is eager to be rid of Jesus.

(12) On **hearing** this Pilate asked if the man was a **Galilean**;
  and upon learning that he was under **Herod's** jurisdiction,
  he **sent** him to Herod, who was in **Jerusalem** at that time.

Herod is expecting to be entertained.

Herod was very **glad** to see Jesus;
  he had been **wanting** to see him for a long **time**,
  for he had **heard** about him
  and had been hoping to **see** him perform some **sign**.
He **questioned** him at **length**,
  but he gave him no **answer**.
The chief priests and **scribes**, meanwhile,
  stood by **accusing** him **harshly**.

Again, you are not an impartial narrator.

Herod and his **soldiers** treated him **contemptuously**
  and **mocked** him,
  and after clothing him in **resplendent** garb,
  he sent him **back** to **Pilate**.

Don't rush this detail.

Herod and Pilate became **friends** that very **day**,
  even though they had been **enemies** formerly.

kiss, we almost sense he's using the question to stall or prevent the gesture of false affection. "Judas," then could be spoken abruptly, as if to stop his move toward Jesus. The disciples are eager for violence; the tone of their question betraying a thirst for blood which "one of them" actually draws when he severs the servant's ear. Jesus orders them to stop the violence, but he will not derail his destiny. Still the compassionate healer, Jesus restores the servant's ear. In Luke, it's not the crowd but the leaders who are hostile. Of these

he asks scornfully, "Have you come out as against a robber?" He accepts his fate at their hands ("This is *your* hour"), but he speaks with judgment ("the time . . . of *darkness!*").

   (8) *Peter's Denials.* With characteristic deference, Luke omits the detail of the disciples dispersing after the garden scene, yet only Peter follows to the trial. Probably cowed and anguished, he sits until the servant girl notices and observes him "intently." Increase your energy on each of Peter's three denials. Wanting to minimize attention, his first response is

low-key. The servant's second accusation builds on her first: "You, too, are one of them." With five words you must express Peter's insistent second denial. "Assuredly" and "Galilean" convey the intensity of the final accusation. Luke expunges Peter's cursing and swearing but allows Peter a fiery response to the equally intense third accusation. "My friend" barely disguises his hostility, which becomes evident in the remainder of the sentence, spoken as if through clenched teeth. Immediately twin

Pilate makes his best effort, arguing logically and convincingly.	(13) **Pilate** then summoned the chief **priests**, the **rulers** and the **people** and said to them, "You **brought** this man to me and **accused** him of **inciting** the people to **revolt**. I have **conducted** my investigation in your **presence** and have not found this man **guilty** of the charges you have brought **against** him, nor did **Herod**, for he sent him **back** to us. So no **capital** crime has been **committed** by him. **Therefore** I shall have him **flogged** and then **release** him."
The crowd turns ugly here.	But all **together** they **shouted** out, "**Away** with this man! Release **Barabbas** to us."
Barabbas offers a glimmer of hope. Read as if you're hoping Pilate might persuade them.	—Now **Barabbas** had been imprisoned for a **rebellion** that had taken place in the city and for **murder**.— **Again** Pilate addressed them, still wishing to **release** Jesus, but they **continued** their shouting, "**Crucify** him! **Crucify** him!" Pilate addressed them a **third** time, "What **evil** has this man done?
Pilate becomes more emotional now.	I found him guilty of **no** capital crime. Therefore I shall have him **flogged** and then **release** him." With loud **shouts**, however,
Their anger persuades him.	they **persisted** in calling for his **crucifixion**, and their voices **prevailed**. The **verdict** of Pilate was that their **demand** should be **granted**. So he **released** the **man** who had been imprisoned
This is a very reluctant decision.	for rebellion and murder, for whom they **asked**, and he handed **Jesus** over to them to deal with as they **wished**.

daggers pierce Peter's heart: "the cock crowed" and "the Lord turned and looked"—twin reminders of his predicted infidelity. "He went out" will best reveal the depth of his remorse if read slowly, perhaps softly, but simply, without overdramatizing.

(9) *Jesus Is Mocked.* You might narrate the mockery in the persona of a loyal follower of Jesus distressed by this degrading treatment. "Ridiculing," "blindfolded," "struck," "reviled," conjure images of mistreated prisoners of war. Luke presents Jesus as a martyr.

(10) *Jesus before the Council.* Tension characterizes this scene. Jesus' hostile response to the council's question suggests it was asked with hostility. His confident, authoritative posture regarding the "Son of Man" is sure to rouse more anger. In chorus the leaders again ask Jesus about his identity and he gives them what they need, and this supreme irreverence (to even suggest that he is God's anointed!) unleashes an avalanche of righteous indignation.

(11) *Trial before Pilate.* Pilate is Luke's foil for presenting the innocence of Jesus to his Gentile audience. Luke places deceit in the mouths of the religious leaders who accuse Jesus of *political* crimes though they have just concluded a *religious* trial. They know Pilate is well aware of the proliferation of military messianic pretenders, so they use the catchwords "Messiah, a king" to grab the governor's attention. Pilate seems disinterested at first and questions Jesus as he might any prisoner. He takes Jesus' reply as a denial and pronounces his innocence only to provoke

"Cyrenian" = sĭ-REE-nee-uhn

Jesus ministers even as he goes to his death. He is speaking through exhaustion and pain.

Speak these words slowly.

Pause briefly after this poignant line.

(14) As they led him **away**
   they took hold of a certain **Simon**, a **Cyrenian**,
   who was coming in from the **country**;
   and after laying the **cross** on him,
   they made him **carry** it behind Jesus.
A large crowd of **people** followed Jesus,
   including many **women** who **mourned** and **lamented** him.
Jesus **turned** to them and said,
   "**Daughters** of Jerusalem, do not **weep** for **me**;
   weep instead for **yourselves** and for your **children**
   for **indeed**, the days are **coming** when people will say,
   '**Blessed** are the **barren**,
   the wombs that never **bore**
   and the breasts that never **nursed**.'
At that time people will say to the **mountains**,
   '**Fall** upon us!'
   and to the **hills**, '**Cover** us!'
   for if these things are done when the wood is **green**
   what will happen when it is **dry**?"
Now two **others**, both **criminals**,
   were led away with him to be **executed**.

(15) When they came to the place called the **Skull**,
   they **crucified** him and the **criminals** there,
   one on his **right**, the other on his **left**.
Then **Jesus** said,
   "**Father**, **forgive** them, they **know** not what they **do**."
They **divided** his **garments** by casting **lots**.

another salvo of angry accusations from the leaders. Pilate seems relieved to defer the case to Herod.

(12) *Jesus before Herod.* Luke downplays the complicity of the Romans in the death of Jesus by avoiding references to Roman soldiers. Suddenly we're in Herod's court. Your tone as narrator can suggest a small-minded, self-indulgent monarch who views Jesus as a source of exotic entertainment. Disappointed that Jesus won't do tricks, he turns mean and ridicules him, but never condemns him. Ironically,

Jesus' presence even heals the rivalry between enemies ("Herod and Pilate became friends").

(13) *The Sentence of Death.* Now Luke uses Pilate to play defense lawyer. He pleads Jesus' case with logic and detachment, even covering his bases by offering to "release him" after he has "taught him a lesson." The crowd joins the call for Jesus' blood. Luke clearly infuses Pilate with Jesus bias, but to no avail. "Crucify him, crucify him" requires that you build from one expression to the next. A third time Pilate pleads Jesus' innocence. He opts

for compromise once more offering to "have him flogged and then release him." The intense demands and "loud shouts" of the crowd should suggest that for political expediency Pilate had no choice but to concede.

(14) *The Way of the Cross.* Throughout his Gospel account Luke stresses the need for disciples to follow after Jesus. That motif surfaces here in the persons of Simon and the large crowd who follow Jesus to Calvary. All the evangelists are sparse in their descriptions of the Crucifixion.

The people are watching. It's the leaders and soldiers who jeer: speak with their voices.

The **people** stood by and **watched**;
the **rulers**, meanwhile, **sneered** at him and said,
"He saved **others**, let him save **himself**
if he is the **chosen** one, the **Christ** of **God**."
Even the **soldiers** jeered at him.
As they approached to offer him **wine** they called **out**,
"If you are **King** of the **Jews**, **save** yourself."
Above him there was an **inscription** that read,
"**This** is the **King** of the **Jews**."

Speak these words in Pilate's voice empathetically.

(16) Now one of the **criminals** hanging there **reviled** Jesus, saying,
"Are you not the **Christ**?
Save yourself and **us**."
The **other**, however, **rebuking** him, said in reply,
"Have you no **fear** of **God**,
for you are **subject** to the **same** condemnation?
And indeed, **we** have been condemned **justly**,
for the **sentence** we received corresponds to our **crimes**,
but **this** man has done **nothing** criminal."
Then he said,
"**Jesus**, **remember** me when you come into your **kingdom**."
He replied to him,
"**Amen**, I **say** to you,
today you will be **with** me in **Paradise**."

Remember that he too is exhausted and dying, but sincere.

This is a prayer, as if murmured over and over.

Take time with these words.

(17) It was now about **noon** and **darkness** came
over the whole **land**
until **three** in the afternoon
because of an **eclipse** of the **sun**.
Then the **veil** of the **temple** was **torn** down the **middle**.
Jesus **cried** out in a **loud** voice,
"**Father**, into your **hands** I commend my **spirit**";
and when he had **said** this he breathed his **last**.

The powers of darkness are raging.

Speak the words "Father / into your hands / I commend my spirit" deliberately and peacefully.

Besides the Roman soldiers, Luke also deletes the crown of thorns to focus instead on a compassionate Jesus who, even in his direst need, ministers to others. "Do not weep for me . . . [but] for your children" is spoken by one who is both exhausted and in great pain.

(15) *The Crucifixion.* With the little crucifixion narration you have, communicate the narrator's attitude toward Jesus: are you neutral, skeptical, or a firm believer? Luke's grammar in the original Greek suggests Jesus repeated the "Father forgive them . . ." prayer many times over.

The people simply watch; it is the leaders and soldiers who jeer and taunt. Subtle shifts can distinguish the leaders' voices from those of the soldiers whom Luke finally introduces. The "inscription" might be spoken in the voice of a sincere Pilate.

(16) *The Two Thieves.* The thieves offer an opportunity for contrast: one is angry, maybe even half-serious in his request for help. The other (unique to Luke) shouts his convincing defense of Jesus, but perhaps whispers his pleas for remembrance. In this Gospel of pardons and com-

passion, Jesus' moving reply requires special attention.

(17) *The Death of Jesus.* A Roman soldier, symbolizing the Gentile occupiers, oversees the Crucifixion. The veil of the temple that separated the people from God's abode is torn in two! Then, amid cosmic cataclysm, fully aware and deliberately, Jesus surrenders his life.

(18) *Jesus' Innocence.* The centurion's confession is significant for, as we've seen often in Luke's Gospel, it is the non-Jew who penetrates Jesus' identity. Don't fail to draw attention to the repentant Jewish

[Here all kneel and pause for a short time.]

Jesus' innocence is declared again. The crowd experiences a change of heart. The women watch prayerfully.

(18) The **centurion** who **witnessed** what had happened glorified
    God and said,
  "This man was **innocent** beyond **doubt**."
When all the people who had **gathered** for this spectacle **saw**
    what had happened,
  they returned **home** beating their **breasts**;
  but all his **acquaintances** stood at a **distance**,
  including the **women** who had followed him from **Galilee**
  and **saw** these events.

Joseph is obviously a believer.

(19) Now there was a **virtuous** and **righteous** man
    named **Joseph**, who,
  though he was a member of the **council**,
  had not **consented** to their plan of action.

Arimathea = ayr-ih-muh-THEE-uh

He came from the Jewish town of **Arimathea**
  and was **awaiting** the kingdom of **God**.
He went to **Pilate** and asked for the **body** of Jesus.

Don't rush through these important details.

After he had taken the body **down**,
  he **wrapped** it in a linen **cloth**
  and **laid** him in a rock-hewn **tomb**
  in which **no** one had yet been **buried**.
It was the day of **preparation**,
  and the **sabbath** was about to begin.

It is the women who take notice and prepare.

The **women** who had come from **Galilee** with him
    followed behind,
  and when they had **seen** the tomb
  and the **way** in which his body was **laid** in it,
  they **returned** and prepared **spices** and perfumed **oils**.
Then they **rested** on the sabbath according to the **commandment**.

[Shorter: Luke 23:1–49]

crowd. They reveal the power of the cross by returning home "beating their breasts." Jesus has touched and transformed the world of both Jew and Gentile.

(19) *The Burial.* Your tone can betray bias toward the saintly Joseph, a "virtuous and righteous . . . member of the Council." No group is without its singular members. Describe Jesus' descent from the cross with tenderness, as if your words were the "linen cloth" wrapped lovingly around his body. Due to the necessity of concluding the burial before the approaching Sabbath,

the scene ends abruptly. Stress the women's taking notice of the place of burial and their home preparation of "spices and perfumed oils" which will be used later to anoint the body. The Sabbath rest was surely needed by the friends of Jesus to recover from this shocking ordeal . . . and to prepare for the greater shock of the third day.

HOLY THURSDAY: MASS OF THE LORD'S SUPPER

Lectionary #39

READING I   Exodus 12:1–8, 11–14

A reading from the Book of Exodus

The LORD said to **Moses** and **Aaron** in the land of **Egypt**,
    "This **month** shall stand at the **head** of your **calendar**;
    you shall reckon it the **first** month of the year.
Tell the whole **community** of Israel:
    On the **tenth** of this month every one of your **families**
    must procure for itself a **lamb**, one **apiece** for each **household**.
If a family is too **small** for a whole lamb,
    it shall **join** the **nearest** household in procuring one
    and shall **share** in the lamb
    in **proportion** to the number of **persons** who **partake** of it.
The lamb must be a year-old **male** and without **blemish**.
You may take it from either the **sheep** or the **goats**.
You shall keep it until the **fourteenth** day of this month,
    and **then**, with the whole assembly of Israel **present**,
    it shall be **slaughtered** during the evening **twilight**.
They shall take some of its **blood**
    and **apply** it to the two **doorposts** and the **lintel**
    of every **house** in which they **partake** of the lamb.
That same **night** they shall **eat** its roasted flesh
    with unleavened **bread** and bitter **herbs**.

These instructions are given to Israel while still in slavery. Suggest the importance of this solemnity, for this night is like no other night, this meal like no other meal.

God is the speaker—a voice of authority and compassion.

The ritual makes community.

Attention to minutia reinforces the importance of the ritual. Vary energy and pace; maintain interest by *being* interested in the details.

Blood, the sign of death, becomes a sign of new life.

The bread was unleavened because there was no time for dough to rise; the bitter herbs bring to mind the bitterness of slavery.

READING I The Easter Triduum, from Holy Thursday evening to Easter Sunday evening, constitutes a single act of worship celebrating the single act of salvation. Each of the Three Days highlights individual aspects, but without ever surrendering a sense of the whole. Jesus' last meal with his disciples was a Passover meal much like the one described in this text. Although filled with intricate details about how to eat a certain meal, the passage evokes the roots of our faith. Through the details, we cannot only conjure up mental images of a past event, but we actualize and experience that event in the present. When we remember, we are there. That's a basic liturgical principle you should remember whenever you proclaim.

All of this night's readings speak of communities gathered for a ritual meal. Communities gather for meals because meals make community and community and family are central in this text. The "whole community" and "every family" must procure a lamb, but families too small for a whole lamb join larger families. Not only is the law not meant to be a burden, but it fosters the community life of the nation. Graphic images of slaughtered lambs and blood smeared on doorposts add color to the instructions, but they also draw a clear connection between this ancient ritual and the Lamb of God whose blood removes the sin of the world.

"Loins girt," "sandals on the feet," and "staff in hand" lead to a key announcement: "you shall eat *like those who are in flight.*" The meal was to be eaten hurriedly, with a sense of expectation. Later centuries identified this expectation with the attitude with which one awaits the Messiah,

Maintain a brisk pacing. They are to be ready to go at a moment's notice.

"This is **how** you are to eat it:
> with your loins **girt**, **sandals** on your **feet** and your **staff**
> > in **hand**,
> you shall **eat** like those who are in **flight**.

It is the **Passover** of the LORD.
For on this **same** night I will go through **Egypt**,
> **striking** down every **firstborn** of the land, both **man** and **beast**,
> and executing **judgment** on all the **gods** of Egypt—**I**, the LORD!

Speak with authority here, not vengeance.

But the **blood** will mark the **houses** where **you** are.
Seeing the blood, I will pass **over** you;
> **thus**, when I **strike** the land of **Egypt**,
> no destructive **blow** will come upon **you**.

Speak more slowly here; explain these details carefully.

"This day shall be a **memorial feast** for you,
> which all your **generations** shall celebrate
> with **pilgrimage** to the LORD, as a **perpetual** institution."

Pause here as the mood shifts. Take a breath and look over the heads of the assembly as you solemnly mandate this perpetual institution.

A reading from the first Letter of Saint Paul to the Corinthians

Brothers and sisters:
I **received** from the Lord what I also handed on to **you**,
> that the Lord **Jesus**, on the night he was handed **over**,
> took **bread**, and, after he had given **thanks**,
> **broke** it and said, "This is my **body** that is for **you**.
Do this in **remembrance** of me."
In the same way also the **cup**, after supper, saying,
> "This **cup** is the new **covenant** in my **blood**.

This text is also discussed with the readings for the solemnity of The Most Holy Body and Blood of Christ.
Speak with reverence and gratitude here.
Pause after "you"; an implied "namely" precedes what follows. "Handed over" refers to Jesus' betrayal. Help us understand that. Stress Jesus' actions: he "took," gave "thanks," and "broke" the bread.

---

and which characterizes Christian anticipation of the return of Christ. The brutal imagery ("striking down every firstborn") reveals the seriousness of this event. There can be no doubt that the people are in the hands of a powerful God, but this God both threatens *and* protects. "I will pass over you . . . no destructive blow will come upon you" are like words of reassurance spoken in the midst of a terrible storm. It is the blood, the sign of life, that wards off death. The final sentence reaffirms the importance of the prescribed ritual which is to be remembered and celebrated forever.

READING II Nowhere else can we see more clearly than at a eucharistic liturgy that "remembering" makes past events present: Eucharist is not a recalling of Christ's death and Resurrection, it is an experience of it in the here and now. Paul's words describe the very things we are engaged in at this celebration: "receiving" and "handing on." That what we have is "received from the *Lord*" assures us of the ever-present guidance of the risen Christ within the community that preserves and hands on his memory per his own instructions.

Rather than narrate the entire Last Supper meal, Paul has *selected* the elements to recall here, so all the chosen details are important. "On the night he was handed over" alludes to his betrayal, and thus casts the shadow of the cross on the meal and suggests its *sacrificial* dimension. This sacred meal proclaims an embarrassing truth: it is from Christ's death that we draw life. Every Eucharist celebrates how Christ became our paschal lamb, offered up on the cross. Only here and in Luke's Gospel is the command to

> Do this, as often as you **drink** it, in **remembrance** of me."
> For as often as you **eat** this bread and **drink** the cup,
>   you proclaim the **death** of the **Lord** until he **comes**.

Pause before last sentence. Make eye contact with the assembly and speak slowly.

GOSPEL John 13:1–15

A reading from the holy Gospel according to John

Emphasize Jesus' awareness and the lateness of the "hour."

Before the feast of **Passover**,
     Jesus **knew** that his hour had **come**
     to pass from **this** world to the **Father**.
He loved his **own** in the world, and he **loved** them to the **end**.
The **devil** had already induced **Judas**, son of Simon the **Iscariot**,
          to hand him **over**.
So, during **supper**,
     fully **aware** that the Father had put **everything** into his power
     and that he had **come** from God and was **returning** to God,
     he **rose** from supper and took **off** his outer garments.
He took a **towel** and **tied** it around his waist.
Then he poured **water** into a basin
     and began to **wash** the disciples' **feet**
     and **dry** them with the **towel** around his waist.
He came to Simon **Peter**, who said to him,
     "**Master**, are you going to **wash** my **feet**?"
Jesus **answered** and said to him,
     "What I am **doing**, you do not **understand now**,
     but you **will** understand **later**."
Peter **said** to him, "You will **never** wash my feet."

As Jesus shares a last intimate moment with friends, he's aware one of them will betray him.

Iscariot = is-KAYR-ee-uht

John again stresses Jesus' self-awareness.

You might suggest how unexpected this was, or the tender and loving humility it embodies.

Don't caricature Peter. His protests are as sincere as his compliance.

"Do this . . . in remembrance of me" mentioned. It's a critical line, for it is Jesus' guarantee that by remembering him we will always remain in his presence. Spoken here in the Liturgy of the Word, rather than where we're used to hearing it, it may catch our ears anew. The final sentence reminds us that we always celebrate the Eucharist with a twin focus: by looking backward to the act of redemption (death) made present is this liturgy, and by gazing forward to the day when the Lord comes in all his glory.

GOSPEL It may be surprising that only John's Gospel records this special moment between Jesus and his disciples. Where the synoptics place their description of Jesus' last meal, recording the "words of institution" and all they signify, John places an enacted parable that embodies the essence of Jesus' life and ministry, and even suggests participation in his death.

The arrival of Jesus' "hour" is a major dimension of this text. John makes a point of stressing Jesus' awareness of the lateness of the hour. In fact, it's that awareness that prompts him to demonstrate his love for his disciples in a dramatic way; he puts on an apron and washes their feet. Jesus often reversed expectations, and here he does it by bathing the feet of disciples who ought to be washing his. The devil has already done his work on Judas, so Jesus must act now if he is to give his friends a final lesson in service and humility.

Take plenty of time with the details of "outer garments," "towel," and "basin" to emphasize the exemplary nature of this

This is not a rebuke, but a lesson.

Jesus answered him,
   "Unless I **wash** you, you will have no **inheritance** with me."
Simon Peter said to him,

His enthusiasm brims over here.

   "**Master**, then not only my **feet**, but my **hands**
      and **head** as **well**."
Jesus said to him,

Convey Jesus' love for Peter here.

   "Whoever has **bathed** has no **need**
      except to have his **feet** washed,
   for he is **clean** all **over**;
   so **you** are clean, but not **all**."
For he **knew** who would **betray** him;
   for this **reason**, he said, "Not **all** of you are clean."

Ask your listeners, too.

So when he had **washed** their feet
   and put his **garments** back on and reclined at **table** again,
   he **said** to them, "Do you **realize** what I have **done** for you?
You call me '**teacher**' and '**master**,' and **rightly** so, for indeed I **am**.

Jesus speaks with affection for his friends. The pronouns are the key to the meaning of this sentence.

If **I**, therefore, the **master** and **teacher**, have washed **your** feet,
   you ought to wash one **another's** feet.
I have given you a **model** to follow,
   so that as **I** have done for **you**, you should **also** do."

behavior. Only Peter protests the apparent inappropriateness of the master washing disciples' feet, but much of what Jesus did in life was understood only after his death; Jesus indicates this deed will be no different. Peter grows bolder in his resistance only to be rebutted by Jesus' insistence that this kind of humility typifies his ministry and if Peter is to share in that ministry he must be comfortable with this symbol. Typically naive and overzealous, Peter overreacts, asking to be washed head to toe. But his overreaction indicates he's

understood that belonging to Christ means holding *nothing* back from him. This exchange is touching and human. Jesus tolerates Peter's naiveté and even admires his zeal, assuring him "*you* are clean."

Having given the example, Jesus makes sure the disciples have not missed the point. Pose Jesus' questions for the disciples directly to your own assembly. Make sure your assembly understands that Jesus' command to follow his example is meant for all believers, not only those in leadership. Jesus' parable-in-action demonstrates the integrity of his teaching. Unlike

those who hide behind "Do as I say, not as I do," Jesus always asks others to do only what he did first.

RIDAY OF THE LORD'S PASSION

Lectionary #40

READING I   Isaiah 52:13—53:12

A reading from the Book of the Prophet Isaiah

The voice of God should be strong and proud.	**See**, my servant shall **prosper**, he shall be raised **high** and greatly **exalted**.

There is a sudden mood shift as the narration about the suffering of God's servant begins.	Even as many were **amazed** at him—
	   so **marred** was his look beyond human **semblance**
	   and his **appearance** beyond that of the sons of **man**—

The sense of this verse is this: In the same way that many were amazed at him—because he was so disfigured he didn't even look human—others will be startled and astonished.	so shall he **startle** many **nations**,
	   because of him **kings** shall stand **speechless**;
	for those who have not been **told** shall **see**,
	   those who have not **heard** shall **ponder** it.

	Who would **believe** what we have heard?
	   To **whom** has the arm of the LORD been **revealed**?
	He grew up like a **sapling** before him,
	   like a **shoot** from the parched **earth**;
	there was in him no **stately** bearing to make us **look** at him,
	   nor **appearance** that would **attract** us to him.

This is a new voice: that of the people.	He was **spurned** and **avoided** by people,
	   a man of **suffering**, accustomed to **infirmity**,
	one of those from whom people **hide** their faces,
	   spurned, and we **held** him in no **esteem**.

Much lamenting here. People hid their faces because he was not pleasing to look at.	Yet it was **our** infirmities that he bore,
	   our **sufferings** that he endured,
	while we thought of him as **stricken**,
	   as one **smitten** by God and **afflicted**.

READING I This fourth Song of the Suffering Servant achieves a fusion of sound, contrast, and balance seldom found in the Bible. The cumulative impact of so many strong words speaking of pain, rejection, and affliction is one of heaviness, like the impact of a dirge. In poetry, sound communicates meaning. Imagine hearing a plaintive song in a foreign language. Would you need a translator to interpret the lyrics, or might the sound of the words and music be enough to communicate the emotion in the lines?

Part of any song's meaning rests in the sound of the words; even without music, the words of a poem make melodies that communicate its meaning.

This Isaiah text is a powerful dirge that takes a long, repetitive look at the bruised and bleeding face of God's sinless servant. Bible scholars believe Isaiah was either describing all of God's people, Israel, who have endured the ordeal of exile, or he was speaking of himself as God's servant. But Christian tradition, and certainly today's liturgy, allows us to discern Jesus' face in these lines, and view him as the perfect

fulfillment of this prophecy. So it is of Jesus that we sing this day. In God's voice, the song begins announcing the future victory of the servant. Though a dirge typically speaks of past glory and future sorrow, this song reverses the pattern and proclaims a glory *born* of sorrow. So the timbre of our song soon shifts to the sorrow (cast in the past tense) out of which the victory will arise. In your reading, stress what the servant will do: "prosper," "be raised high," "startle," and make kings "speechless"! Though the servants' sorrow is in the past,

Emphasize how he bore *our* guilt.

"Stripes" are the marks left behind from a whipping.

Use a softer tone here. The two images ("lamb," "sheep") make the same point so the pace can be a bit quicker, although your intensity should not wane.

"Oppressed" and "condemned" are *two* distinct words; don't rush them together.

Perhaps use a tone of anger and regret over this indignity.

Use a tone of resignation here.

The voice of God returns—energetic, proud, and proclaiming.

Use a quieter tone now, but a persuasive one.

But he was **pierced** for our **offenses**,
  crushed for our sins;
upon **him** was the **chastisement** that **makes us whole**,
  by his **stripes** we were **healed**.
We had **all** gone astray like **sheep**,
  each following his **own** way;
but the LORD laid upon **him**
  the **guilt** of us **all**.

Though he was **harshly** treated, he **submitted**
  and opened **not** his **mouth**;
like a **lamb** led to the **slaughter**
  or a **sheep** before the **shearers**,
  he was **silent** and opened not his **mouth**.
Oppressed and **condemned**, he was taken **away**,
  and who would have thought any **more** of his destiny?
When he was cut **off** from the land of the **living**,
  and **smitten** for the sin of his **people**,
a **grave** was assigned him among the **wicked**
  and a **burial** place with **evildoers**,
though he had done **no wrong**
  nor spoken any **falsehood**.
But the LORD was **pleased**
  to **crush** him in **infirmity**.

If he gives **his** life as an offering for **sin**,
  he shall see his **descendants** in a **long** life,
  and the **will** of the LORD shall be **accomplished** through him.

Because of his **affliction**
  he shall see the **light** in **fullness** of **days**;

it is described as graphically and intensely as if it were happening now.

In the next section, it is not God but the people who speak; perhaps it is the Gentile nations or grieved disciples of the prophet who look on and utter this startled question: "Who would believe?" What we hear is the terrible regret of looking back and realizing a great opportunity was missed: He grew up among us, yet because there was nothing extraordinary about him ("no stately bearing") we "spurned" him and gave him no respect. Stupidly, we

thought he was smitten by God for his *own* failings, but now we see it was for *our* sins he was pierced! *We* went "astray" and *he* paid the price. Rejection from one's own people is bitter sorrow indeed. "Spurned," "suffering," "hide their faces" are words that help express that singular pain. "Smitten," "pierced," and "crushed" are also powerful words that sound like what they mean and suggest the weight of injustice hurled at God's servant.

The servant's silence is striking. He accepts his fate resolutely. Again, close attention to words will help you effectively

proclaim this text: "lamb" contrasts powerfully with "slaughter." "Oppressed," "condemned," "cut-off," and "smitten" all add to a sense of loneliness that borders on despair. The final humiliation hurled at God's servant is burial "among the wicked . . . though he had done no wrong." You can speak for all who innocently endure injustice when you defend the servant's innocence with that line. The word "pleased" is surprising but it suggests the servant's fate was somehow within the will of God.

through his **suffering**, my servant shall justify **many**,
and their **guilt** he shall **bear**.
Therefore I will give him his **portion** among the **great**,
and he shall divide the **spoils** with the **mighty**,
because he **surrendered** himself to **death**
and was **counted** among the **wicked**;
and he shall take **away** the sins of **many**,
and win **pardon** for their **offenses**.

This is the high point of the reading. The servant is honored, but notice that it's because he suffered willingly!

Use *ritardando* (slowing toward the end) on the words "and win pardon . . . offenses."

READING II   Hebrews 4:14–16; 5:7–9

A reading from the Letter to the Hebrews

Brothers and sisters:
Since we have a **great** high **priest** who has passed
through the **heavens**,
Jesus, the Son of **God**,
let us hold **fast** to our **confession**.
For we do not have a high priest
who is **unable** to **sympathize** with our **weaknesses**,
but one who has **similarly** been **tested** in every **way**,
yet without **sin**.
So let us **confidently** approach the throne of **grace**
to receive **mercy** and to find **grace** for timely **help**.

In the days when Christ was in the **flesh**,
he offered **prayers** and **supplications** with loud **cries** and **tears**
to the one who was able to **save** him from **death**,
and he was **heard** because of his **reverence**.

Begin with confident rejoicing.

He was one of us. He can sympathize and knows our pain.

Confidently persuade us of his sinlessness.

Christ truly suffered: that's why he understands our suffering.

We hear God's voice again in the closing sections ("If he gives his life . . . Because of his affliction . . . Therefore I will give . . .") proclaiming another oracle of future glory for the servant and announcing hope for the many for whom his voluntary suffering has won pardon. Biblical tradition viewed suffering as punishment for sin, but Isaiah will have none of that. The positive, expiatory value he finds in suffering lays the foundation for Christianity's understanding of human pain. The voice of God strongly affirms the value of the servant's voluntary suffering. His affliction

was not wasted for it brings reward for the servant ("I will give him his portion among the great") and justification and healing for others.

Who could fail to see the aptness of this reading in a Good Friday liturgy? No other text better describes the suffering Christ we memorialize today. To conclude with sadness would be inappropriate. Hope, even pride, might serve better. The servant who suffered is now the risen Lord who reconciles.

READING II There is a marvelous harmony between these words of Hebrews and those in the First Reading from Isaiah. As in Isaiah, we find in Hebrews a companion in suffering, a mediator who has tasted struggle and temptation, who is one with all who wear the weak flesh of humanity—made unique only by his innocence and his total dedication to the will of God. But there is none of Isaiah's lamentation in these lines. The opening sentence exclaims with confident joy that we can be fully confident in Christ's

Note that Jesus "learned" obedience through his suffering.

Son though he **was**, he learned **obedience** from what he **suffered**;
and when he was made **perfect**,
he became the **source** of eternal **salvation** for all who
obey him.

Jesus modeled obedience. We imitate him and find salvation. Use *ritardando* **(slowing toward the end) on the words "for . . . obey him."**

PASSION   John 18:1—19:42

The Passion of our Lord Jesus Christ according to John

Kidron = KID-ruhn.

The garden is a peaceful, familiar place.

(1) **Jesus** went out with his **disciples** across the Kidron **valley**
to where there was a **garden**,
into which he and his disciples **entered**.

The shadow of Judas suddenly shifts the mood.

Judas his **betrayer also** knew the place,
because Jesus had **often** met there with his disciples.
So Judas got a band of **soldiers** and **guards**
from the chief **priests** and the **Pharisees**
and went there with **lanterns**, **torches**, and **weapons**.

"Lanterns" are symbolic of the hour of darkness.

Jesus, knowing **everything** that was going to happen to him,
went out and said to them, "Whom are you **looking** for?"
They **answered** him, "**Jesus** the **Nazorean**."

Jesus moves forward fully aware and in charge of his destiny.

He said to them, "**I AM**."
Judas his betrayer was **also** with them.
When he said to them, "I **AM**,"
they turned **away** and fell to the **ground**.

Jesus' power overwhelms the guards. He'll be taken only when he permits it.

So he **again** asked them,
"**Whom** are you looking for?"
They said, "**Jesus** the **Nazorean**."
Jesus answered,
"I **told** you that I **AM**.
So if you are looking for **me**, let **these** men **go**."

---

intercession. The author will later call this letter "a message of encouragement" (13:22). And that must be what sounds in your voice. We have every reason to cling to confident hope, for our "great high priest" (an assertion of Christ's superiority to the priests of the old law) knows our "weaknesses" and dispenses mercy and grace, and help in time of need. The second paragraph presents Jesus at Gethsemane and powerfully portrays Jesus' humanness. "Loud cries and tears" convey that humanness, but let that be a brushstroke on the portrait you are painting, not a reen-

actment of Christ's garden agony. "He was heard" says not that Jesus was saved from death but that he was delivered *through* it.

In the concluding reflection we read that Jesus "learned obedience." He did that by willingly enduring suffering and thus teaches us how to obey. Jesus was "made perfect" by his suffering. That may sound strange to our ears, but it tells us that Jesus was not some robot who automatically fulfilled God's will. No. He was so fully human that he achieved his earthly mission despite struggle and temptation. And the result is "eternal salvation for all."

Can there be greater reason to celebrate? Hebrews calls us to hope and to celebrate that all "who obey him" will also move through suffering to perfection. It is a great mystery, and yet Christ persuades us that even our own suffering can bring holiness and life.

 PASSION John has a clear agenda in presenting his passion narrative. His is a story of Christ's irrevocable movement toward glory. Everything in the narrative is subordinated to this. Episodes

Violence expressed with "struck" and "cut off."

Malchus = MAL-kuhs

Jesus rebukes Peter.

Annas = AN-uhs

Caiaphas = KĪ-uh-fuhs

This is a significant quote attributed to Caiaphas.

Is Peter kept out or staying out from fear?

Peter doesn't want to be overheard denying Jesus.

This was to **fulfill** what he had said,
   "I have not lost **any** of those you **gave** me."
(2) Then Simon **Peter**, who had a **sword**, **drew** it,
   struck the high priest's slave, and **cut** off his right **ear**.
The slave's name was **Malchus**.
Jesus said to Peter,
   "Put your **sword** into its **scabbard**.
Shall I not **drink** the cup that the Father **gave** me?"

So the band of **soldiers**, the **tribune**, and the Jewish **guards**
      seized Jesus,
   bound him, and brought him to **Annas** first.
He was the **father**-in-law of **Caiaphas**,
   who was **high** priest that year.
It was **Caiaphas** who had **counseled** the Jews
   that it was better that **one** man should die
      rather than the **people**.

(3) Simon **Peter** and **another** disciple **followed** Jesus.
Now the **other** disciple was **known** to the high priest,
   and he entered the **courtyard** of the high priest with **Jesus**.
But **Peter** stood at the gate **outside**.
So the other **disciple**, the **acquaintance** of the high priest,
   went out and spoke to the **gatekeeper** and brought Peter **in**.
Then the **maid** who was the **gatekeeper** said to Peter,
   "You are not one of this man's **disciples**, **are** you?"
He said, "I am **not**."
Now the **slaves** and the **guards** were standing
      around a charcoal fire
   that they had made, because it was **cold**,
   and were **warming** themselves.
Peter was **also** standing there keeping **warm**.

mentioned by the synoptics that detract from the image of a Christ fully in control of his destiny, are deleted by John. The garden agony, the help of Simon, the mourning women, the ridicule hurled at the crucified Jesus: all are missing from this account so that the appearance of a Jesus who is completely in charge is never compromised. Here he is not the abused, abandoned martyr of Matthew, Luke and Mark, but a man self-possessed, who moves intentionally toward Calvary where he will mount the cross as a king mounts his throne.

John introduces the Roman occupiers' complicity with the Jewish authorities earlier than the synoptic writers, but for some readers, John's persistent use of the term "the Jews" suggests hostility toward the Jewish people and seems to brand them as solely responsible for Christ's death—a responsibility passed on to each successive generation. Of course, that is not the belief of the Church. Papal and episcopal statements have made it clear that, when these texts are used, listeners should be made aware that the Church does not hold the Jewish people guilty. To

counter potential misinterpretations, you might consider addressing the issue in a part of the homily.

A lector once remarked that, as a child, each time he heard the Passion he hoped it would end differently—that this time the crowds would not choose "Barabbas" and Pilate would not "[hand] him over to be crucified." Therein lies the power of story, there is the hope for every lector who fears proclaiming words that have been heard too often. Stories have the power to awaken in us the hope that this time things will work out differently. So read the Passion

This is a new scene, so renew your energy.

(4) The high priest **questioned** Jesus
    about his **disciples** and about his **doctrine**.
Jesus **answered** him,
    "I have spoken **publicly** to the world.
I have always taught in a **synagogue**
    or in the **temple** area where all the Jews **gather**,
    and in **secret** I have said **nothing**. Why ask **me**?
Ask those who **heard** me what I **said** to them.
They know what I said."

Jesus is strong in his self-defense, showing the weakness of their "case."

Deliver line like a slap—fast and hard.

When he had **said** this,
    one of the temple **guards** standing there **struck** Jesus and said,
    "Is **this** the way you answer the high **priest**?"
Jesus answered him,
    "If I have spoken **wrongly**, **testify** to the wrong;
    but if I have spoken **rightly**, why do you **strike** me?"

Jesus holds his ground.

Then Annas sent him **bound** to **Caiaphas** the **high** priest.

This is another new scene.

(5) Now Simon **Peter** was **standing** there keeping **warm**.
And they **said** to him,
    "**You** are not one of his **disciples**, **are** you?"
He **denied** it and said,
    "I am **not**."

Peter gets angry here.

One of the **slaves** of the high priest,
    a **relative** of the one whose **ear** Peter had cut off, said,
    "Didn't I see you in the **garden** with him?"
Again Peter denied it.

The denials are brief, but with this line suggest the lasting impact on Peter.

And **immediately** the **cock** crowed.

(6) Then they brought Jesus from **Caiaphas** to the **praetorium**.
It was **morning**.
And they **themselves** did not **enter** the praetorium,
    in order not to be **defiled** so that they could eat the **Passover**.

---

with that awareness, not as someone who knows the ending and lets that knowledge color all the telling, but as someone who watches the action unfold, allowing yourself to be drawn in and to move with the ebb and flow of emotions.

As mentioned in the commentary for the Palm Sunday Passion reading, there is more than one option for effective proclamation of this lengthy narrative. A single, excellent reader could make for a powerful and riveting proclamation. But the operative word is "excellent," and that level of

excellence is rare. Participation of the assembly has its merits, but also many liabilities, foremost of which is the need for members of the assembly to read along with the lectors—so that they are ready for their part. Three fine readers may be the best option. The lines can be variously divided: a voice for Jesus, a voice for the narrator, and a third voice for all the others speakers, or some such arrangement.

But the method of proclamation is not as important as your relationship with the story. Remember that in the liturgical assembly, the proclamation of scripture

brings the saving events of the past into the present moment. That's an awesome responsibility. Don't trivialize it by lack of preparation or over-dramatization. The Jesus of the Gospel according to John knows who he is, speaks openly of his relationship to the Father, and is always firmly in charge of his destiny. Let that awareness infuse your delivery of this story of passion and triumph.

(1) The peaceful mood of the familiar garden is immediately shattered by the shadow of Judas who arrives with a noisy

This is a spat among political adversaries. Each is annoyed with the other.

So **Pilate** came out to **them** and said,
    "What **charge** do you bring against this man?"
They **answered** and said to him,
    "If he were not a **criminal**,
    we would not have handed him **over** to you."
At **this**, Pilate said to them,
    "Take him **yourselves**, and **judge** him according to your **law**."
The Jews **answered** him,
    "We do not have the right to **execute** anyone, "
    in order that the word of **Jesus** might be **fulfilled**
    that he said indicating the kind of **death** he would die.

The scene shifts here. Pilate is "starting over" and is not presented as a villain.

(7) So Pilate went **back** into the praetorium
    and **summoned** Jesus and said to him,
    "Are you the **King** of the **Jews**?"
Jesus answered,
    "Do you say this on your **own**
    or have **others** told you about me?"
Pilate answered,
    "I am not a **Jew**, **am** I?

Pilate is becoming impatient again.

Your own **nation** and the chief **priests** handed you over to me.
What have you **done**?"
Jesus answered,
    "My **kingdom** does not **belong** to **this** world.
If my kingdom **did** belong to this world,
    my attendants would be **fighting**
    to **keep** me from being handed over to the Jews.
But as it **is**, my kingdom is not **here**."
So Pilate said to him,
    "Then you **are** a king?"

Stressing the words "are" or "king" changes the meaning of the question.

Jesus answered,
    "**You** say I am a king.

---

crowd of soldiers bearing "lanterns, torches and weapons." It's a double irony that those who bring on the "hour of darkness" come bearing *light*, and so large a cohort comes against the unarmed Jesus. Remember that, in John, Jesus has not just emerged from the garden agony. He is not spent, but speaks with authority, *aware* of what will unfold. He takes the initiative, challenging the mob with his question. Their response is less self-assured. In fact, they are bowled over by Jesus' "I AM." John paints a mob emboldened only by

their numbers. Jesus is still playing shepherd. "Let these men go" reveals his willingness to accept the crowd's designs against him, but not against his friends.

(2) Peter's response is violence. "Struck" and "cut off" convey his rage. But Jesus matches Peter's energy: "Put your sword into its scabbard" echoes "Get behind me, Satan." Once again, stress that it is Jesus' *choice* to "drink the cup." And take note that it is the Roman soldiers and their tribune, as well as the Jewish guards who arrest Jesus. Don't gloss over this reference to Roman complicity. Proclaim

"that it was better that one man die . . ." in the voice of Caiphas.

(3) Peter's first denial can be underplayed. It would seem he has quickly forgotten his grandiose Last Supper protestations of undying loyalty. He'll remember it soon enough. For now, your narration suggests his frustration at being unable to get close to the action. When "the other disciple" gets him through the gate, he makes an over-the-shoulder response to the girl's question (perhaps trying to keep the "disciple" from over-hearing him).

Jesus speaks with confidence here.

For this I was **born** and for this I came into the **world**,
  to **testify** to the **truth**.
Everyone who **belongs** to the truth **listens** to my voice."
Pilate said to him, "What is **truth**?"

(8) When he had **said** this,
  he **again** went out to the Jews and said to them,
  "I find no **guilt** in him.
But you have a **custom** that I release one **prisoner**
    to you at **Passover**.

He is seeking a quick resolution. Is he trying to put words in their mouths?

Do you want me to release to you the **King** of the **Jews**?"
They cried out **again**,
  "Not **this** one but **Barabbas**!"

Barabbas = buh-RAB-uhs

Now Barabbas was a **revolutionary**.

Then Pilate took Jesus and had him **scourged**.
And the soldiers wove a **crown** out of **thorns**
    and placed it on his **head**,
  and clothed him in a **purple** cloak,
  and they came to him and said,

This is a greatly understated scene, but the pain is real.

  "**Hail**, **King** of the **Jews**!"
And they **struck** him **repeatedly**.
(9) Once **more** Pilate went out and said to them,

Perhaps he is saying, "Look at what you made me do!"

  "**Look**, I am bringing him **out** to you,
  so that you may **know** that I find no **guilt** in him."
So Jesus came out,
  wearing the crown of **thorns** and the purple **cloak**.
And he said to them, "**Behold**, the man!"
When the chief priests and the guards **saw** him they **cried** out,
  "**Crucify** him, **crucify** him!"
Pilate said to them,

When a phrase is repeated, give greater stress to second utterance.

  "Take him **yourselves** and **crucify** him.

---

(4) Jesus' composure before the high priest is remarkable. He is not intimidated. But his confidence is taken for disrespect, earning him a slap. The violent anger of the guard should be heard in your voice when you *narrate,* as well as when you speak his dialogue. Jesus is recovering from the "sharp blow" as he begins his answer. His second clause, then, is spoken with more intensity than the first.

(5) Surely Peter cringed at the sight of Jesus slapped. But suddenly *he* is slapped with a question: "You are not one of his disciples, are you?" His answer is short and quick. The persistent "relative of the one whose ear Peter had cut off" (probably out of malice!) tries to get an admission from Peter. But he responds with yet another denial. Deliver the words "And again Peter denied it" as if they were Peter's actual words of denial. After the third denial, though not predicted in this Gospel, the cock crows. Report the crowing of the cock with the regret that must have flooded Peter's heart.

(6) The scene before Pilate is cast as a drama between good and evil. John's portrait of the Jewish authorities is not monochromatic. Together with men who became chief instigators in the plot against Jesus there are men of unquestioned integrity and sincerity—Nicodemus and Joseph of Arimethea. In proclaiming this Passion we must deal with the characters John has created, and it cannot be denied that, in their tug-of-war, Pilate comes off looking better than the religious authorities. The struggle between them lends life and excitement to this part of the narrative.

I find no **guilt** in him."
The Jews **answered**,
    "We have a **law**, and according to that **law** he ought to **die**,
    because he **made** himself the **Son** of **God**."
(10) Now when Pilate **heard** this statement,
    he became even **more** afraid,
        and went back into the **praetorium** and said to **Jesus**,
    "Where are you **from**?"
Jesus did not **answer** him.
So Pilate said to him,
    "Do you not speak to me?
Do you not **know** that I have **power** to **release** you
    and I have power to **crucify** you?"
Jesus answered him,
    "You would have **no** power over me
    if it had not been **given** to you from **above**.
For **this** reason the one who handed me **over** to you
    has the **greater** sin."
(11) **Consequently**, Pilate tried to **release** him;
    but the **Jews** cried out,
    "If you **release** him, you are not a **Friend** of **Caesar**.
Everyone who makes himself a **king** opposes **Caesar**."

When Pilate **heard** these words he brought Jesus out
    and **seated** him on the **judge's** bench
        in the place called **Stone Pavement**, in **Hebrew**, **Gabbatha**.
It was **preparation** day for **Passover**, and it was about **noon**.
And he said to the **Jews**,
    "**Behold**, your **king**!"
They **cried** out,
    "**Take** him away, **take** him away! **Crucify** him!"

Pilate's frustration turns on Jesus.

"Friend of Caesar" is a title of honor bestowed by Rome on high-ranking officials, which Pilate might lose if he mishandles this situation.

Gabbatha = GAB-uh-thuh

John spends more time with the interaction between Pilate and Jesus than do the synoptics, giving us additional details, like their exchange about "truth."

Very likely, Pilate was not overjoyed at being dragged from his bed at early morning to hear a religious case. The exchange between Pilate and the Jewish leaders indicates there's no love lost between them. Only John tells us that the motive for seeking recourse with Pilate was the fact that the religious body lacked "the right to execute anyone."

(7) Pilate questions Jesus and is annoyed at being questioned back by this Jew who has disturbed his sleep. Slowly, Pilate seems to be drawn over to Jesus, but he does not yet take him seriously. He spars with him: "Then you are a king? . . . What is truth?"

(8) The exchange regarding Barabbas might be seen as Pilate's effort to resolve the problem quickly—and favorably for Jesus. It doesn't work. So his effort intensifies. Maybe a good flogging will satisfy these zealots! John provides fewer details of the flogging and mockery of Jesus than

the other evangelists, yet the few words of narration provided must suggest the awful violence of the scourging and the crowning with thorns.

(9) Pilate's tone addressing the chief priests after the scourging seems to be saying: Look, I've listened to you. I've punished him for you. That's all I'm going to do. The calls for crucifixion both anger and frighten Pilate. He didn't expect that. He's not done with this mess after all. Pilate offers to hand him over while again asserting Jesus' innocence. The Jewish leaders insist Jesus *is* guilty . . . for religious reasons.

This is a final effort to forestall.

Pilate said to them,
 "Shall I crucify your **king**?"
The chief **priests** answered,
 "We have **no** king but **Caesar**."
Then he **handed** him over to them to be **crucified**.

This is another new scene. Speak slowly.

Golgotha = GOL-guh-thh

(12) So they **took** Jesus, and, **carrying** the cross **himself**,
 he went out to what is called the **Place** of the **Skull**,
  in **Hebrew**, **Golgotha**.
There they **crucified** him, and with him two **others**,
 one on either **side**, with Jesus in the **middle**.
Pilate also had an **inscription** written and put on the **cross**.
It read,

Proclaim the inscription slowly.

 "**Jesus** the **Nazorean**, the **King** of the **Jews**."
Now **many** of the Jews **read** this inscription,
 because the place where Jesus was **crucified** was near the **city**;
 and it was written in **Hebrew**, **Latin**, and **Greek**.
So the chief **priests** of the Jews said to **Pilate**,
 "Do not **write** 'The **King** of the Jews,'
 but that he **said**, 'I am the King of the Jews'."
Pilate answered,
 "What I have **written**, I have written."

(13) When the soldiers had **crucified** Jesus,
 they took his **clothes** and **divided** them into four **shares**,
 a share for each **soldier**.
They also took his **tunic**, but the tunic was **seamless**,
 woven in one **piece** from the top **down**.
So they said to one another,
 "Let's not **tear** it, but cast **lots** for it to see whose it will **be**,"

(10) Pilate responds with fear. His mounting frustration and growing anger at the religious leaders, he now directs at Jesus: "Where do you come from? Do you refuse . . . . Do you not know . . . ?" Jesus' composure is disconcerting but persuasive. The intensity builds. Sensing that Pilate is weakening, the religious men pressure and threaten him. In the conversation about "power," Jesus says the blame for his death will fall less on Pilate than on those religious leaders who have falsely accused him.

(11) Pilate does not surrender Jesus easily. He redoubles his effort to "release him" but is immediately rebuffed with barely veiled threats. Pilate "hears" the threats to report him to Caesar and responds by parading their false king before them, with a taunting "behold your king." Ironically, the people respond claiming as their only king, Caesar, who rules the occupying forces they so despise. After making a final effort to win pity for Jesus ("Shall I crucify your king?") Pilate finally relents.

(12) John has Jesus carry the cross "himself" and offers no details of the

Crucifixion, save that he was crucified with two others. Take time with the short narration, stressing that Jesus carried the cross alone, with a tone that speaks of sorrow and the great horror of the Crucifixion. Proclaim Pilate's inscription as might a herald reading from a scroll. The dialogue between Pilate and priests is animated and angry, but this time Pilate gets the last word.

(13) The soldiers are greedy and insensitive, but they are pragmatic about the seamless tunic, recognizing value when

Use a tone shift when quoting scripture.

in order that the passage of **Scripture** might be **fulfilled**
   that says:
     *They divided my **garments** among them,*
      *and for my **vesture** they cast **lots**.*
This is what the soldiers **did**.

In this new scene, the women are much grieved. *Four* **women are identified: "his mother's sister" is different from "Mary the wife of Clopas."**

Clopas = KLOH-puhs

Magdala = MAG-duh-luh

(14) Standing by the **cross** of Jesus were his **mother**
   and his mother's **sister**, **Mary** the wife of **Clopas**,
   and Mary of **Magdala**.
When Jesus **saw** his mother and the **disciple** there whom he **loved**
   he said to his mother, "**Woman**, behold, your **son**."
Then he said to the **disciple**,
   "Behold, your **mother**."
And from **that** hour the **disciple** took her into his **home**.

In this new scene, stress Jesus' awareness and control.

(15) **After** this, aware that **everything** was now **finished**,
   in order that the **Scripture** might be **fulfilled**,
   Jesus said, "I **thirst**."
There was a **vessel** filled with common **wine**.

Hyssop = HIS-uhp

So they put a **sponge** soaked in wine on a sprig of **hyssop**
   and put it up to his **mouth**.
When Jesus had **taken** the wine, he said,
   "It is **finished**."

Jesus' "spirit" is the Holy Spirit, the spirit of the new creation. Jesus' death is the giving of the Spirit.

And **bowing** his **head**, he handed **over** the **spirit**.

[Here all kneel and pause for a short time.]

(16) Now since it was **preparation** day,
   in order that the **bodies** might not **remain** on the cross
     on the **sabbath**,
   for the sabbath day of **that** week was a **solemn** one,

Breaking legs assured quicker death—by asphyxiation.

   the Jews asked **Pilate** that their legs be **broken**
   and that they be taken **down**.

---

they see it. Your tone should suggest their hard selfishness, but the quotation of scripture ("they divided my garments . . .") requires a tone of sadness and resignation, as does the summary statement: "This is what the soldiers did."

(14) Introduce "his mother" in a more animated and hopeful tone, as if they are trying with their energy to sustain Jesus' failing strength. Name each of the women as if you know her. Remember that Jesus is dying as he speaks, but the "behold your son . . . mother" dialogue carries a singular expression of love.

(15) No despair fills his voice on "I thirst." He has mustered his last strength to fulfill scripture. The scene is brief, void of final anguish or abandonment. Instead, after taking a sip of wine, with strength and full awareness he utters his last words: "It is finished." Pause briefly after those words and then, imagining Jesus dropping his head in death, quietly read the narration. Here, take a longer pause for silence and prayer.

(16) What remains is denouement, but with a few peaks. The talk of "preparation day" and "sabbath" is important, so don't rush past this information. Although the predominant tone is subdued, increase your intensity when speaking of the soldiers who "broke the legs" and "thrust [the] lance." "Blood and water" is both a sure biological sign of death and a powerful theological symbol, traditionally seen to represent Baptism and Eucharist. Don't rush it. Speak in a subdued but confident

Blood and water are important symbols.

Speak these words with conviction.

Arimathea = ayr-ih-muh-THEE-uh

Speak with tender respect for Joseph, and later Nicodemus.

Nicodemus = nik-oh-DEE-muhs

myrrh = mer

aloes = AL-ohz

Use a slow pace here.

So the **soldiers** came and **broke** the legs of the **first**
and then of the **other** one who was crucified with Jesus.
But when they came to **Jesus** and saw that he was already **dead**,
they did **not** break his legs,
but one soldier thrust his **lance** into his **side**,
and immediately **blood** and **water** flowed out.
An **eyewitness** has **testified**, and his testimony is **true**;
he **knows** that he is speaking the **truth**,
so that you **also** may come to **believe**.
For this **happened** so that the **Scripture** passage might be **fulfilled**:
*Not a **bone** of it will be **broken**.*
And again **another** passage says:
*They will **look** upon him whom they have **pierced**.*

(17) After **this**, **Joseph** of **Arimathea**,
secretly a **disciple** of Jesus for **fear** of the **Jews**,
asked **Pilate** if he could **remove** the body of Jesus.
And Pilate **permitted** it.
So he came and **took** his body.
Nicodemus, the one who had first come to him at **night**,
also came bringing a mixture of **myrrh** and **aloes**
weighing about one hundred **pounds**.
They took the **body** of Jesus
and bound it with **burial cloths** along with the **spices**,
according to the Jewish **burial** custom.
Now in the **place** where he had been crucified there was a **garden**,
and in the garden a **new tomb**, in which no one
had yet been **buried**.
So they laid Jesus **there** because of the Jewish **preparation** day;
for the **tomb** was close **by**.

tone of the eyewitness testimony regarding these events. You aren't making a courtroom presentation but presenting the faith of a believer.

(17) Speak of Joseph as of a revered member of the community, the secrecy surrounding his discipleship understandable because of "fear of the Jews." Nicodemus, another secret disciple, now also identifies himself fully with Jesus by coming to care for his body, anointing it with oils and spices. Speak the burial details with reverence and tenderness, grief held mostly in

check. Imagine what it might be like telling a friend about the funeral of a dear loved one she was unable to attend. Without overwhelming her with sorrow, you would state the facts with obvious love for the one who died. This impromptu tomb was the best they could do for Jesus but, *mirabile dictu* (wonderful to tell!), it didn't have to do for long.

EASTER VIGIL

Lectionary #41

READING I Genesis 1:1—2:2

A reading from the Book of Genesis

Speak the first three words with all that is in you. Remember the five-part pattern of each day. Use the repeated refrains to draw your listeners deeper and deeper into the *pattern* of God's creative work. The pattern should be obvious, so it is better to *stress* the repetitions than to hide them with novel readings on each day. Their regularity, familiarity, and predictability give the passage much of its power. So don't rush them.

In the **beginning**, when God created the **heavens** and the **earth**,
    the earth was a formless **wasteland**, and **darkness**
        covered the **abyss**,
    while a mighty **wind** swept over the **waters**.

Then God **said**,
    "Let there be **light**," and there **was** light.
God saw how **good** the light was.
God then **separated** the light from the **darkness**.
God called the light **"day"** and the darkness he called **"night."**
Thus **evening** came, and **morning** followed—the **first** day.

Then God said,
    "Let there be a **dome** in the **middle** of the waters,
    to **separate one** body of water from the **other**."
And so it **happened**:
    God **made** the dome,
    and it separated the water **above** the dome
        from the water **below** it.
God called the dome **"the sky."**
Evening came, and **morning** followed—the **second** day.

The declaration that creation is "good" and the accomplishment of God's command are stressed each time they recur.

Then God said,
    "Let the **water** under the sky be gathered into a single **basin**,
    so that the dry **land** may appear."

Renew your energy with each "Then God said."

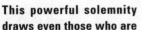 This powerful solemnity draws even those who are disconnected from the liturgical flow during the rest of the year. Lent is ended, this night is a beginning. And so we begin at the beginning and tell the story of God's tireless efforts to fashion a people with a mother's nurturing love and a father's protective power.

Many have encountered James Weldon Johnson's compelling rendering of the creation story. Johnson speaks of a God who "spits out" the seven seas, hollows out the valleys and bulges up the mountains with the soles of his feet and, like a "mammy" tending her baby, molds clay into human life. The poem paints an image of a God who deeply cares for and is intimately involved with all creation. God looks at moon, sun and stars and says "that's good!" Genesis presents a dignified God of power rather than a "mammy." But here, too, we see God working with a mother's love to fashion a home for the man and woman who will fill and subdue it. So your proclamation must leave your listeners with an image of a caring God.

Narration of the days of creation follows a consistent pattern that includes five repeated refrains. Each day contains 1) an *introduction:* "Then God said . . ."; 2) God's spoken *command:* "Let there be . . ."; 3) announcement of the *accomplishment* of the command: "And so it happened . . ."; 4) an *affirmation* of goodness after each day's work: "God saw how good it was . . ."; and 5) an *identification* of the day: "Evening came and morning followed the first day . . . the second . . . and so forth." The most important refrains are the last two. The affirmation of goodness is

Identify each creation ("the earth . . . the sea") with tenderness.

And so it **happened**:
> the water under the sky was **gathered** into its basin,
> and the dry **land** appeared.
God called the dry land "the **earth**,"
> and the basin of the **water** he called "the **sea**."
God saw how **good** it was.

There is much detail here: use the words marked for emphasis to guide you in placing your stress. Every word isn't important. Here it's the energy and enthusiasm that matter most.

Then God said,
> "Let the **earth** bring forth **vegetation**:
> every kind of **plant** that bears **seed**
> and every kind of **fruit tree** on earth
> that bears fruit with its **seed** in it."
And so it **happened**:
> the earth brought forth every **kind** of plant that bears **seed**
> and every kind of **fruit tree** on earth
> that bears fruit with its **seed** in it.
God saw how **good** it was.
Evening came, and morning **followed**—the **third** day.

Then God said:
> "Let there be **lights** in the dome of the sky,
> to separate **day** from **night**.

Here as before, it's more important to convey a sense of joy and wonder rather than overemphasizing details.

Let them mark the fixed **times**, the **days** and the **years**,
> and serve as **luminaries** in the dome of the sky,
> to shed **light** upon the earth."
And so it **happened**:
> God made the **two** great lights,
> the **greater** one to govern the **day**,
> and the **lesser** one to govern the **night**;
> and he made the **stars**.
God **set** them in the dome of the **sky**,
> to shed **light** upon the earth,
> to **govern** the day and the night,
> and to separate the **light** from the **darkness**.

Proclaim the words "and he made the stars" quickly, with excitement, or slowly, with amazement. Note that the purpose of each of the lights somehow serves humanity.

as sincere as parents' affirmation of their child. The identification of each day does not sound like a tired worker checking off the day's accomplishments but like a woman counting off the months of her pregnancy, aware of her movement toward the full ripening of the life she carries.

Before the "beginning" there was chaos—dark, terrifying chaos. If you've seen a large lake or ocean at night you know the look of water "swept" by that "mighty wind." The God who creates is awesome and sovereign, creating not with the wave of a hand but with the utterance

of a word. Without overdramatizing, find an appropriate level of majesty and power. There is a sense of *joy* in all the work of creation.

"Then God said . . ." moves us through the sequence of events and each repetition of the phrase requires fresh energy. Before each "And so it happened," pause as if watching the birth of a child and then, with wide-eyed wonder, describe what you've just seen.

Days 1 and 2: God creates light with a command! Then God separates the waters

above from those below, creating earth and sky!

Day 3: God separates earth and sea and dry land appears. And God calls it good. Those who love the earth and wish to protect its resources do so, in part, because they realize this planet was entrusted to us by the God who designed every detail—from the "plant that bears seed" (a pine or maple) to the "fruit tree . . . that bears fruit with its seed in it" (peaches and pears). "And it was good . . ." recurs with ever deepening conviction, "and evening came and morning followed . . ." could be

Each time it recurs, this refrain should convey the end of an epoch of time and creation. Speak with a sense of accomplishment, joy, and peace. This "day" teems with life; there is much excitement and energy in creation.

God saw how **good** it was.

Evening came, and **morning** followed—the **fourth** day.

Then God said,
"Let the water **teem** with an **abundance** of living **creatures**,
and on the **earth** let **birds** fly beneath the **dome** of the sky."
And so it **happened**:
God created the great **sea** monsters
and all kinds of **swimming** creatures with which
the water **teems**,
and all kinds of winged **birds**.

Notice that God "blesses" the creatures. End this section with calm satisfaction.

God saw how **good** it was, and God **blessed** them, saying,
"Be **fertile**, **multiply**, and **fill** the water of the seas;
and let the birds **multiply** on the earth."
Evening came, and morning **followed**—the **fifth** day.

Renew your energy once again with joy at the thrill of creating life.

Then God said,
"Let the **earth** bring forth all kinds of living **creatures**:
cattle, **creeping** things, and wild **animals** of all **kinds**."
And so it **happened**:
God made all **kinds** of wild **animals**, all kinds of **cattle**,
and all kinds of **creeping** things of the earth.

The reading reaches a sub-climax here. *All* creation is good!

God saw how **good** it was.

Then God said:
"Let us make **man** in our **image**, after our **likeness**.

Use a nobler, slower pace here. Humans are made in God's own likeness! Use, don't rush, the repetitions. They deepen our sense of these great truths.

Let them have **dominion** over the **fish** of the sea,
the **birds** of the air, and the **cattle**,
and over all the wild **animals**
and all the creatures that **crawl** on the **ground**."
God created **man** in his **image**;
in the image of **God** he created him;
male and **female** he created them.

the journal entry of an expectant mother who delights in the growing child within.

Day 4: Rejoice in the gift of lights: The sun that makes things grow. The romantic moon that makes dark places less fearful. And the stars! They are many, magnificent, and mysterious. It will be the freshness in your voice that keeps listeners from tuning out thinking, "I've heard this all before." Speak with the peace and confidence of a mother singing to her growing child. And it was good; and evening came.

Day 5: "Winged birds . . . sea monsters . . . swimming creatures . . . ." In a frenzy of creativity, God makes them all. The waters teem and the skies fill with fluttering wings. "And God blessed them." And evening came, and morning followed.

Day 6: A zoo of living creatures, "wild" and "creeping" fills the earth. God is as excited as a child watching a parade of circus animals of "all kinds . . . all kinds . . . all kinds." And they're *really* good.

Finally, comes God's greatest good: a creature made "in our image, after our likeness." Imagine expectant parents moving

from the excitement of preparing the nursery to the reality of the imminent birth. This is the most solemn moment: the voice slows and assumes a tender and noble quality. In the way parents bequeath all their worldly goods to their children God bestows all the world's riches on man and woman. God gives dominion and blessing and the command to "Be fertile . . . multiply." Like a grandparent who can't pack enough treats for the grandkids to take home, God continues the litany of giving, telling the woman

Speak this as a blessing. All the beauty and good that God has created is entrusted to humanity.

God **blessed** them, saying:
"Be **fertile** and **multiply**;
fill the earth and **subdue** it.
Have **dominion** over the fish of the **sea**, the birds of the **air**,
and all the **living** things that **move** on the earth."
God **also** said:
"**See**, I give you every **seed**-bearing plant all over the **earth**
and every **tree** that has seed-bearing **fruit** on it to be your **food**;
and to all the **animals** of the land, all the **birds** of the air,
and all the living creatures that **crawl** on the **ground**,
I give all the **green** plants for **food**."
And so it **happened**.

This is the summary statement: God's creation is *very* good!

God looked at **everything** he had made, and he found it
very good.
Evening came, and **morning** followed—the **sixth** day.

With a sense of accomplishment and pride, pause after the word "completed."

Thus the **heavens** and the **earth** and all their array
were **completed**.
Since on the **seventh** day God was **finished**
with the work he had been doing,

"Rested" suggests more than not working; it means delighting in the "work," that is, the beloved creation God has now completed.

he **rested** on the seventh day from all the **work**
he had **undertaken**.

[Shorter: Genesis 1:1, 26–31a]

READING II Genesis 22:1–18

A reading from the Book of Genesis

The opening line both introduces and summarizes the entire story. Pause slightly after "Abraham." "Here I am" is eager.

God put **Abraham** to the **test**.
He called to him, "**Abraham**!"
"**Here** I am," he replied.

and man to fill the earth and have dominion, and giving them every plant and tree and every living creature. Speak with the generosity and the love of a parent praying a baptismal blessing over a new-born child. God looks at *all* of creation and finds it very good. And evening comes again.

Day 7: Pride fills your declaration that the work was completed. The announcement of Sabbath rest is very important. It ends the reading on a note of peace and joy—what a new father might feel as he goes home to tell the family that the new

mother and child are resting well in each other's arms.

READING II This is a hard story. It forces a couple of obvious questions upon us: What kind of God would put anyone through such a trial? What kind of person would take such a request seriously? These questions would not have been so obvious to the culture from which the author of Genesis comes. At that time, it was not uncommon to offer human sacrifice to the gods of various ancient cults. So

for Abraham to take God's brutal request seriously is quite believable. Now you must make it believable to your listeners. On this night, as we tell the story of salvation and celebrate the new covenant initiated in Christ, we look back to the beginnings. In Abraham we find the beginning of God's covenant with Israel, and in Isaac—so innocent of what is to come that he carries the wood for his own sacrifice—we find a type, or symbol, of the innocent Christ who willingly gave his life for all.

Then God said:
"Take your son **Isaac**, your **only** one, whom you **love**,
and **go** to the land of **Moriah**.
There you shall **offer** him up as a **holocaust**
on a **height** that I will point **out** to you."
Early the next **morning** Abraham saddled his **donkey**,
took with him his son **Isaac** and two of his **servants** as well,
and with the **wood** that he had cut for the holocaust,
set out for the place of which God had **told** him.

On the **third** day Abraham got **sight** of the place from **afar**.
Then he **said** to his servants:
"Both of you stay **here** with the **donkey**,
while the **boy** and I go on over **yonder**.
We will **worship** and then come **back** to you."
Thereupon Abraham took the wood for the holocaust
and laid it on his son **Isaac's** shoulders,
while he **himself** carried the **fire** and the **knife**.
As the two walked on **together**, Isaac **spoke**
to his father Abraham:
"**Father**!" Isaac said.
"**Yes**, son," he replied.
Isaac continued, "Here are the **fire** and the **wood**,
but where is the **sheep** for the holocaust?"
"**Son**," Abraham answered,
"God **himself** will provide the sheep for the holocaust."
Then the two **continued** going forward.

When they **came** to the place of which God had **told** him,
Abraham built an **altar** there and arranged the **wood** on it.
Next he **tied** up his son Isaac,
and put him on **top** of the wood on the **altar**.

Don't give away what's coming at the end. God's voice is solemn, not stern. Emphasize the gravity of God's command by stressing "only" and "love."

Abraham works hard to hide his pain. Don't let this sound like a trip to the mall.

This image foreshadows Jesus' carrying his own cross. Don't waste it.

This dialogue is poignant: Isaac is sincerely curious and unaware. Abraham speaks intentionally and his words are pained and weighty.

Speak slowly here, as the scene grows tense and darker. Share one image at a time. Tying up the boy can't sound like he's buttoning his jacket.

The word "test" tips us off from the start that nothing awful will really happen in this story. The horror in the narrative lies not in Isaac's close call, but in the turmoil experienced by Abraham as he prepares to carry out his gruesome mission. The enduring spiritual value of the story results from our efforts to come to grips with the emotions of a man preparing to take the life of his own son for the sake of a God who demands we hold nothing back. Remember that, through Isaac, God's promise to make Abraham a great nation would be fulfilled.

How can that happen if Isaac is killed? No wonder Abraham is called our father in faith.

To lift up as a model of faith a man who willingly surrenders what he holds most precious in life, you must relate convincingly the human dimensions of this chilling story. Abraham's naiveté ("Here I am!") quickly turns to anguish as God's powerful voice surprises him with the request for a human holocaust. Abraham responds immediately, but he obviously has hinted to neither son nor family the true nature of the mission he undertakes

the very next day. The objective tone of your narration, as he saddles donkey and takes servants, paints for us Abraham's stoic face. The dialogue, in particular, both with the servants and with Isaac, shows his determination to avoid alarming his son. The boy's question is genuine. He's confused and says so. Abraham covers his pain as he answers, ironically, that God will provide the sheep. We know a ram waits in the brambles. Abraham thinks only of Isaac.

Don't speak like you're describing a "near-miss," but as if you were relating the actual slaughter. "But" breaks the mood. The second "Abraham" is louder, stronger than the first.

"Here I am . . ." has no sense of relief yet, just terror. The "Do not . . ." commands can be spoken with calm and tender compassion. Speak the words "I now know . . ." with solemnity. Pause after "beloved son."

Here the mood becomes faster and more upbeat. The "ram" is replacement for Isaac. Don't rush.

Yahweh-yireh = YAH-way-YEER-ay
Yahweh-yireh means "The Lord will see [to it]."

In a long passage like this, variety in pacing is urgent. Although it is "God" speaking, you must not adopt a monotone or an overly slow delivery. Speak like a parent announcing good news to an anxious child—both reassuring and praising.

The fulfillment of these promises is what tonight's readings and tonight's liturgy are all about.

If you've given proper emphasis and not rushed the preceding, the final line will call us all to obedience.

Then he **reached** out and took the **knife** to **slaughter** his son.
But the LORD's **messenger** called to him from **heaven**,
    "**Abraham**, **Abraham**!"
"**Here** I am," he answered.
"Do not lay your **hand** on the boy," said the messenger.
"Do not do the least **thing** to him.
I **know** now how **devoted** you are to **God**,
    since you did not **withhold** from me your own beloved **son**."
As Abraham looked **about**,
    he spied a **ram** caught by its horns in the **thicket**.
So he went and **took** the ram
    and offered **it** up as a holocaust in **place** of his son.
Abraham **named** the site **Yahweh-yireh**;
    hence people now say, "On the **mountain** the LORD will **see**."

Again the LORD's messenger **called** to Abraham from heaven
    and said:
    "I **swear** by myself, declares the LORD,
    that because you **acted** as you **did**
    in not **withholding** from me your beloved **son**,
    I will **bless** you **abundantly**
    and make your **descendants** as **countless**
    as the **stars** of the sky and the **sands** of the seashore;
    your descendants shall take **possession**
    of the **gates** of their **enemies**,
    and in your **descendants** all the nations of the **earth**
        shall find **blessing**—
    all **this** because you **obeyed** my **command**."

[Shorter: Genesis 22:1–2, 9a, 10–13, 15–18]

Almost robotically, Abraham continues preparing for the sacrifice. Your voice must suggest the immense (but unseen) effort it took to prepare the altar and arrange the wood. The emotional strain is more apparent as you describe him placing the boy "on top of the wood." When you relate how Abraham took the knife "to slaughter his son," remember that he thought he was really going to do it. That should send a shiver down everyone's spine. A pause before announcing that God's messenger intervened will give the shiver time to do its work. "But" is like a

heavenly hand reaching out and catching Abraham's wrist just in time. God's voice is at first urgent and authoritative. Then it mellows into tenderness and compassion. Relate quickly, and with relief, the incident with the ram.

The closing section presents the moral of the story. God never wanted human sacrifice, only the unflinching obedience demonstrated by Abraham. In tender and compassionate tones, God's messenger swears abundant and enduring blessings, blessing meant not only for

Abraham, but also for us, his "descendants" in faith.

READING III This is a story best told around a campfire where eager young faces ask: tell us again about Moses and how he made the waters part so our people could get through safely but our enemies didn't. Then an equally eager face begins: "The Lord said to Moses . . . ." That's how stories like this are meant to be told—with a sure sense that this is *our* story, not that of a people who lived long

READING III   Exodus 14:15—15:1

A reading from the Book of Exodus

Don't fear the repetitions in this text and have confidence in the power of this story to move your listeners. Be eager to tell it to people eager to hear it again. Begin with the strong voice of God.

The LORD said to **Moses**, "**Why** are you crying **out** to me?
Tell the Israelites to go **forward**.
And **you**, **lift** up your **staff** and, with hand **outstretched**
      over the **sea**,
   split the sea in **two**,
   that the Israelites may pass **through** it on dry **land**.
But I will make the **Egyptians** so **obstinate**
   that they will go in **after** them.
Then I will receive **glory** through **Pharaoh** and all his **army**,
   his **chariots** and **charioteers**.
The Egyptians shall **know** that **I** am the **LORD**,
   when I receive **glory** through **Pharaoh**
   and his **chariots** and **charioteers**."

"Pharaoh . . . army . . . chariots . . . charioteers" will become a much repeated refrain. Use all the words each time it recurs.

The **angel** of **God**, who had been **leading** Israel's camp,
   now **moved** and went around **behind** them.
The column of **cloud** also, leaving the **front**,
   took up its place **behind** them,
   so that it came **between** the camp of the **Egyptians**
   and that of **Israel**.
But the **cloud** now became **dark**, and thus the **night** passed
   without the rival **camps** coming any closer **together**
      all night long.
Then Moses **stretched** out his hand over the **sea**,
   and the LORD **swept** the sea
   with a **strong** east **wind** throughout the night
   and so **turned** it into **dry** land.

"Column of cloud" and the "angel" are manifestations of God's presence and protection. The action intensifies. Build suspense.

Slow your pace to suggest the passage of time over the long night. Pause briefly.

Speak with renewed vigor here. See what you describe.

ago. When we tell stories with enthusiasm and eyewitness ownership we give them life and variety that keeps them from seeming redundant or boring. Can you imagine Moses, years later, retelling these events in the first person: "The Lord said to me, 'Moses, why are you crying out . . . lift up your hand . . . split the sea!' " As narrator, be as involved in the story as Moses was.

This is the story of Israel's great deliverance, the exodus from slavery to freedom. After Pharaoh permitted the Israelites to leave Egypt, he repented of the decision and mustered a vast army to bring them

back. Seeing the Egyptian cohort about to descend upon them, the Israelites panic, and blame Moses for leading them into this danger. Then, as Moses urges them to keep still and abandon fear, the mighty voice of God orders Moses to "Go forward . . . lift up your staff"! God is stating facts, not trying to persuade Moses: "I will make the Egyptians obstinate . . . I will receive glory." The words fill Moses' heart with a vision of the future God has promised and the confidence to move forward.

The events of this night not only bring salvation to the Israelites, they foreshadow

our own deliverance in Christ's Passover from death to life, and symbolize our salvation in the waters of Baptism. As reader you must convincingly narrate these events that led to the fulfillment of God's promise. First there's activity: the angel and the column of cloud—both manifestations of God—move and shield the people from the advancing army. Then there is darkness and waiting all through the night. Suddenly, Moses takes action. Let your voice convey the sound of the wind that sweeps the sea by emphasizing the "s" sounds in "swept," "sea," "strong," "east," and the "n" of

This is a marvelous sight.

When the **water** was thus **divided**,
    the **Israelites** marched into the **midst** of the sea on **dry** land,
    with the water like a **wall** to their **right** and to their **left**.

The Egyptians **followed** in **pursuit**;
    all Pharaoh's **horses** and **chariots** and **charioteers**
      went after them
    right into the **midst** of the sea.

Use a faster pace here.

In the **night** watch just before **dawn**
    the LORD **cast** through the column of the fiery cloud
    upon the Egyptian force a **glance** that threw it into a **panic**;
    and he so **clogged** their chariot wheels
    that they could hardly **drive**.

You are aware that it was God who saved. Speak slowly and quietly.

With **that** the Egyptians sounded the **retreat** before Israel,
    because the LORD was fighting for them **against** the Egyptians.

Then the LORD told **Moses**, "**Stretch** out your hand over the **sea**,
    that the water may flow **back** upon the Egyptians,
    upon their **chariots** and their **charioteers**."

God's justice is uncompromising.

So Moses **stretched** out his hand over the **sea**,
    and at **dawn** the sea flowed **back** to its normal **depth**.

"Dawn" is the moment of liberation.

The Egyptians were **fleeing** head **on** toward the sea,
    when the LORD **hurled** them into its midst.

Narrate these lines without any hint of vindictiveness.

As the water flowed **back**,
    it **covered** the **chariots** and the **charioteers**
      of Pharaoh's whole **army**
    which had **followed** the Israelites into the **sea**.
Not a single **one** of them escaped.
But the **Israelites** had marched on dry **land**
    through the **midst** of the sea,
    with the water like a **wall** to their **right** and to their **left**.

Speak these words with gratitude and relief.

Thus the LORD **saved** Israel on that day
    from the **power** of the **Egyptians**.

"wind" to suggest the sound of the storm. The power of God's command splits the sea. Relate with wonder and absolute conviction the marvel of the walls of water through which the people march on *dry* land. See it as you tell it.

The Egyptians follow in vain. Your tone betrays the futility of their action as the Egyptians foolishly pursue "right into the midst of the sea." Describe the "night watch before dawn" in hushed tones, but then build volume and intensity as the Egyptians "panic" and sound "the retreat."

Scripture is often unambiguous in relating actions with consequences. Here we see how Pharaoh's obstinacy sealed the fate of the Egyptian forces. In a sober voice, not angry or vindictive, speak of their utter destruction. God's justice is uncompromising: "Not a single" Egyptian is spared. Again, no vindictiveness but no apologies either.

In stark contrast, you announce with amazement how the Israelites marched on dry land through the miraculous corridor of water. With profound gratitude, and not a little pride, relate how God showed such

favor and granted such wonders! Then with reverential awe tell how the people "feared . . . and believed."

Hushed awe at seeing the great power of God turns into jubilant song. The joyous gratitude of those who sang must be your joy, too, as you invite *all* to rejoice over God's saving power.

READING IV We could easily introduce this passage saying: A reading from the book of the *poet* Isaiah,

God's power inspires a reverential fear. Use a hushed tone.

When Israel **saw** the Egyptians lying **dead** on the **seashore**
  and beheld the great **power** that the LORD
  had shown **against** the Egyptians,
  they **feared** the LORD and **believed** in him
    and in his **servant Moses**.

The joy of this song should ring in your voice and show on your face.

Then **Moses** and the **Israelites** sang this **song** to the LORD:
  I will **sing** to the LORD, for he is **gloriously triumphant**;
  horse and **chariot** he has **cast** into the **sea**.

READING IV Isaiah 54:5–14

A reading from the Book of the Prophet Isaiah

"Husband" and "maker" are meant to express tenderness and compassion. Persuade us God can love us this much.

The One who has become your **husband** is your **Maker**;
  his name is the LORD of **hosts**;
your **redeemer** is the **Holy** One of **Israel**,
  called **God** of all the **earth**.
The LORD calls you **back**,

Use a brisk pace with "like a wife forsaken . . ." and increase the intensity of "a wife married . . . ."

  like a wife **forsaken** and grieved in **spirit**,
  a wife married in **youth** and then cast **off**,
  says your God.

Contrast the regret of "For a brief moment . . ." with the joy of "but with great tenderness . . . ." The same point is made twice. Maintain your energy and conviction throughout.

For a brief **moment** I **abandoned** you,
  but with great **tenderness** I will take you **back**.
In an outburst of **wrath**, for a **moment**
  I **hid** my **face** from you;
but with enduring **love** I take **pity** on you,
  says the LORD, your **redeemer**.

for here we have a reading that is all imagery and tone. Using dramatic metaphors, Isaiah speaks of Israel's return from exile, her restoration after a time of great turmoil and humiliation. The time of deliverance draws near, and the prophet describes what God has in store for Israel when her people return to the city of Jerusalem, which, although destroyed and desolate, will be rebuilt and soon will resonate with jubilant laughter.

Although we know God to be a transcendent spirit whose ways are completely different from ours, scripture repeatedly paints a God who thinks and acts much the way we do. When we piece together scripture's many images of God we find that, though each is incomplete in itself, together they comprise a striking portrait. The primary image Isaiah offers here is that of a husband. Not a newlywed in the thrall of first love, but a middle-aged lover old enough to know betrayal and young enough to forgive and love with renewed passion. And God's passion is abundant and life-giving.

Most of the passage is an elaboration of the analogy of God as husband and Israel (us) as estranged wife. It is God's voice we hear throughout the reading speaking of anger, forgiveness, and tender love. Your tone must be as persuasive as Isaiah's poetry. Convince us that God loves us, longs for us, like a husband loves a wife. That God can forgive like some rare and special spouses forgive their partner's infidelity. All the emotions are here. First, the initial anger: "For a brief moment I abandoned you . . . . In an outburst of wrath . . . I hid my face." Then a forgiveness that's

The exile is compared to Noah's flood. God is saying, "As I swore then, so I swear now never to punish you again."

These words represent the excess of love. Don't hold back.

These words are spoken directly to Jerusalem. Say them lovingly, as if embracing the one with whom you are reconciling.
carnelians = kahr-NEEL-yuhnz
Carnelians are reddish quartz and carbuncles are smooth, round deep-red garnets.
God is making a promise here. Speak with reassuring strength and conviction.

This is for me like the days of **Noah**,
  when I **swore** that the **waters** of Noah
  should never **again deluge** the earth;
so I have sworn not to be **angry** with you,
  or to **rebuke** you.
Though the **mountains** leave their **place**
  and the **hills** be **shaken**,
my **love** shall never **leave** you
  nor my covenant of **peace** be **shaken**,
  says the LORD, who has **mercy** on you.
O **afflicted** one, **storm-battered** and **unconsoled**,
  I lay your **pavements** in **carnelians**,
  and your **foundations** in **sapphires**;
I will make your **battlements** of **rubies**,
  your **gates** of **carbuncles**,
  and all your **walls** of precious **stones**.
All your **children** shall be taught by the LORD,
  and **great** shall be the **peace** of your children.
In **justice** shall you be **established**,
  far from the fear of **oppression**,
  where **destruction** cannot come **near** you.

READING V   Isaiah 55:1–11

A reading from the Book of the Prophet Isaiah

Thus says the LORD:
All you who are **thirsty**,
  come to the **water**!
You who have no **money**,
  come, receive **grain** and **eat**;

Note the imperatives, but the tone is like inviting hungry, homeless children to a feast.

nothing short of miraculous: "but with great tenderness I will take you back . . . with enduring love I take pity on you."

God is in love with us and wants to say so. The depth of that love is reinforced with the memory of Noah. At the time of the flood God promised Noah never again to destroy the earth. Just so, says the Lord, I will never again be angry with you or reject you. Today you are God's messenger chosen to speak those words of promise— a promise that even our own infidelity can't cancel.

A new image expresses God's compassion in the final section of the text. With "O afflicted . . . and unconsoled" God speaks directly to the city of Jerusalem assuring her she will be rebuilt and restored to her original grandeur. Speak the words as if you were drawing a person you've forgiven into your embrace. God will restore the people like a workman rebuilds a city. Only, in place of bricks, God will use precious stones glowing blue as the sky and red as the burning sun. God further promises that all needs will be met, all fears removed.

At this Easter Vigil, we see in Israel's return from the enslavement of exile the Church's own deliverance from the slavery of sin through Christ's death and Resurrection. Let your proclamation capture the fire in the heart of a God who offers precious stones as a sign of love, a love more solid and enduring than the mountains from which the stones were mined.

READING V **On Thanksgiving or Christmas you sometimes hear of a philanthropic restaurant owner**

Ignore the comma after "come."

Ask the questions sincerely as if expecting an answer.

To be nourished, it is necessary to heed and listen to the Lord. "That you may have life . . ." is the heart of God's promise. Use a slower pace here.

"Him" refers to David. The nation will be restored.

Renew your energy here. Imagine those you are trying to persuade getting up to leave. Your words must catch and hold them.

This is not a condemnation, but an earnest call for conversion.

This section explains why God can be so "generous in forgiving": God's plans are not our plans; God's methods not our methods. Speak slowly and with great dignity.

come, without **paying** and without **cost**,
　　drink **wine** and **milk**!
Why spend your **money** for what is not **bread**,
　　your **wages** for what **fails** to **satisfy**?
Heed me, and you shall eat **well**,
　　you shall **delight** in rich fare.
Come to me **heedfully**,
　　listen, that you may have **life**.
I will **renew** with you the everlasting **covenant**,
　　the **benefits** assured to **David**.
As I made him a **witness** to the peoples,
　　a **leader** and commander of **nations**,
so shall you **summon** a nation you knew **not**,
　　and nations that knew you not shall **run** to you,
because of the LORD, your **God**,
　　the **Holy** One of Israel, who has **glorified** you.

Seek the LORD while he may be **found**,
　　call him while he is **near**.
Let the **scoundrel** forsake his **way**,
　　and the **wicked** man his **thoughts**;
let him turn to the LORD for **mercy**;
　　to our **God**, who is **generous** in **forgiving**.
For **my** thoughts are not **your** thoughts,
　　nor are **your** ways **my** ways, says the LORD.
As high as the **heavens** are above the **earth**,
　　so high are **my** ways above **your** ways
　　and my **thoughts** above **your** thoughts.

For just as from the **heavens**
　　the **rain** and **snow** come down

who throws open his doors to all in need of a good meal. On this greatest of solemnities, God reminds us that the doors of God's place of rest and nourishment are always open. And admission is free. God addresses us directly in this passage that is a continuation of the text of tonight's fourth reading. "You who are thirsty . . . come! You, who have no money, come . . . come, without paying .\. . drink wine and . . . delight in rich fare!" Imagine God, apron tied round the waist, rounding up those who've spent "wages" (and their lives!) on "what fails to satisfy."

Of course, what God promises is not food for the belly, but for the soul. As the time of exile draws to an end, God promises new life with all the "benefits assured to David." The covenant God made with David is not nullified; despite the faithlessness that brought exile upon the people, God's promises will be renewed and the nation restored. But the people must repent. God is urgent and insistent, pleading with the people to make a change of heart and forsake their wrongdoing. God works hard to persuade the listener of the urgency of the situation: do it now, God says, while

there is time, before it's too late! No one is unworthy; no one will be turned away. Neither the "scoundrel" nor the "wicked"; for ours is a God "generous in forgiving," whose "thoughts" and "ways" are as different from ours as earth is from sky.

The final section makes a point perhaps best understood by children. For a child who is receptive to imaginative play, even without mask or costume, a speaker can become a vivid character by simply saying so. God's words also actualize what they represent. God says it and it is! (Remember tonight's First Reading!) God

and do not **return** there
  till they have **watered** the earth,
  making it **fertile** and **fruitful**,
giving **seed** to the one who **sows**
  and **bread** to the one who **eats**,
so shall my **word** be
  that goes **forth** from my **mouth**;
my word shall not **return** to me **void**,
  but shall do my **will**,
  achieving the end for which I **sent** it.

This is an important teaching about the efficacy of the word of God: it accomplishes what it sets out to do! Go slowly. This is a long comparison. Just as rain and snow don't evaporate and return to the sky until after they have watered the earth, helping seed to grow and yielding bread for the hungry, the word that goes forth from my mouth does not return without having accomplished the purpose for which it was sent. Speak with conviction and authority.

READING VI   Baruch 3:9–15, 32—4:4

A reading from the Book of the Prophet Baruch

Hear, O Israel, the **commandments** of **life**:
  listen, and know **prudence**!
How **is** it, Israel,
  that you are in the **land** of your **foes**,
  grown **old** in a **foreign** land,
defiled with the **dead**,
  accounted with those **destined** for the **netherworld**?
You have **forsaken** the fountain of **wisdom**!
  Had you **walked** in the way of **God**,
  you would have **dwelt** in enduring **peace**.
Learn where **prudence** is,
  where **strength**, where **understanding**;
that you may know **also**
  where are length of **days**, and **life**,
  where light of the **eyes**, and **peace**.

Baruch = buh-ROOK

This is exhortation motivated by love.

You are asking, "Do you know why?"

The answer is "I'll tell you why!" Still, love is the motive.

Here is the better way: follow it and find peace! You are cajoling, exhorting, and wanting to spur a change in behavior. There is a lilting cadence in these lines. Don't rush them. "Days" and "peace" can be sustained.

urges us to hear these offers of life and renewal not as things hoped for, but as things assured. So speak with confidence, knowing the truth of what you say. That truth is comfort for your listeners, for God says, "My word . . . shall do my will." In tonight's liturgy, as in every liturgy, God's promise of rich fare is fulfilled beyond all expectation at the table of the Eucharist.

READING VI Baruch's basic premise is very simple: Wisdom is the source of all prosperity; without it one finds only disaster. No one finds wisdom on their own, for it is a gift only God can give. The problem is, Israel has forsaken wisdom and as a result she is now exiled "in the land of [her] foes." The Babylonian exile is seen as punishment for Israel's abandonment of God's law. The path back to grace, the road that leads from the land of the dead to a land of life and peace is wisdom herself. Wisdom is personified as a woman. But more significantly, wisdom is identified with the law, "the book of the precepts of God," that is, the commandments given by God as pure gift.

The Israelites' understood law not as an oppressive burden restraining their freedom, but as a gift that taught them God's will. Following the law not only meant pleasing God; it saved them from self-destruction. But Israel went astray, ignored the law and brought evil upon itself. Baruch's beautiful poetry—filled with rich imagery and deliberate repetition—urges the people to embrace the wisdom embodied in the commandments, and thus find their way back to God.

Who has **found** the place of **wisdom**,
   who has **entered** into her **treasuries**?

The One who knows all **things** knows **her**;
   he has **probed** her by his **knowledge**—
the One who established the **earth** for all **time**,
   and **filled** it with four-footed **beasts**;
he who **dismisses** the light, and it **departs**,
   calls it, and it **obeys** him **trembling**;
before whom the **stars** at their posts
   shine and **rejoice**;
when he **calls** them, they answer, "Here we **are**!"
   shining with **joy** for their **Maker**.
Such is our **God**;
   no **other** is to be **compared** to him:
He has traced out the whole way of **understanding**,
   and has given her to **Jacob**, his **servant**,
   to **Israel**, his beloved **son**.

Since then she has **appeared** on earth,
   and **moved** among people.
She is the **book** of the **precepts** of **God**,
   the **law** that endures **forever**;
all who **cling** to her will **live**,
   but those will **die** who **forsake** her.
Turn, O Jacob, and **receive** her:
   walk by her **light** toward **splendor**.
Give not your **glory** to **another**,
   your **privileges** to an **alien** race.
Blessed are we, O Israel;
   for what **pleases** God is **known** to us!

There is a dramatic shift in mood here. This is a poetic song of praise to Wisdom.

"The One" refers to God. You are retelling the story of creation. Use a faster, joyous tempo.

"Dismisses light" is an order for the sun to go down. "Calls it" indicates the sunrise. Maintain high energy here.

Let your voice ring with joy at God's goodness!

This is a new beat. Use a more sober tone. "Given her" indicates understanding. "Jacob" and "Israel" represent the whole people.

"She has appeared on earth" refers to Wisdom, now personified as the book of the law.

Use a contrasting tone for those who "live" and those who "die." Pause before the next line.
Imagine yourself saying, "Oh, my dear child, turn and receive . . . ."

"Glory" indicates the law. "Privileges" refer to knowing and observing the law. You are saying, "Don't throw away the riches you've been given." End on a note of joy.

Christian faith has always seen Jesus as the embodiment of wisdom, the true teacher of what pleases God. Can you imagine him quoting these lines in one of his exhortations? The words are rich and powerful, but full of love. To proclaim them well, imagine yourself a teacher confronting a student who has somehow run afoul of the system. Motivated by love, you begin your exhortation: "Hear . . . listen, and know prudence!" (Note the exclamation point.) How did you get into this mess, you ask, living "in the land of your foes, grown old . . . defiled . . . accounted with those

destined for the nether world?" As if leaning over the offender, your whole presence asks: you *know* why, don't you? "You have forsaken the fountain of wisdom," that's why! If you had "walked in the way of God" you wouldn't have these problems. So "learn where prudence is" that you may also find peace!

The best teachers do this: After pointing out where we have failed, they teach us the advantages of right behavior. And they give us hope that we *can* change, that help is available. Baruch is a good teacher. His exhortation to "learn" is followed by

an exultant song of praise to the God who is our only hope of finding the wisdom we need. The questions "Who has found . . . ? Who has entered . . . ?" are really declarations that God is the answer to all our questions. The God "who knows all things," the creator of sun and moon and stars, knows wisdom. With joy and a quickened tempo describe this God who "established the earth . . . and filled it," whom the sun and the stars obey gladly. The luminous stars tell you how to sound and look as you proclaim: "shining with joy for [your] maker."

READING VII   Ezekiel 36:16–17a, 18–28

A reading from the Book of the Prophet Ezekiel

The **word** of the LORD came to me, saying:
  Son of **man**, when the house of **Israel** lived in their **land**,
  they **defiled** it by their **conduct** and **deeds**.
Therefore I poured out my **fury** upon them
  because of the **blood** that they poured out on the **ground**,
  and because they **defiled** it with **idols**.
I **scattered** them among the **nations**,
  dispersing them over **foreign** lands;
  according to their **conduct** and **deeds** I judged them.
But when they came among the nations **wherever** they came,
  they served to **profane** my holy name,
  because it was said of them: "**These** are the people of the LORD,
  yet they had to **leave** their **land**."
So I have **relented** because of my holy **name**
  which the house of Israel **profaned**
  among the **nations** where they **came**.
Therefore **say** to the house of Israel: **Thus** says the Lord **GOD**:
  Not for **your** sakes do I act, house of Israel,
  but for the sake of my holy **name**,
  which you **profaned** among the nations to which you **came**.
I will prove the **holiness** of my great name,
    profaned among the **nations**,
  in whose **midst** you have profaned it.
Thus the nations shall **know** that I am the LORD,
    says the Lord **GOD**,
  when in their sight I prove my **holiness** through **you**.

"Their land" is their own land. Ezekiel's tone is blunt. Don't dilute his anger. "Fury," "scattered," "dispersing," "judged," and "profane" are all strong words that convey God's wrath. Let them work.

"Because of the blood . . ." refers to worshipping false idols.

The exile is God's punishment for Israel's infidelity.

But the punishment "backfired" because it gave God a bad name.

Speak the taunt in the voice of the foreigners.

Pause at this new beat. Frustrated, God reluctantly adopts a new approach. Note that the words "profaned among the nations" are repeated three times.

God must restore his "good name."

God's anger slowly yields to mercy and love. Speak this as a promise.

The final section focuses on the personification of wisdom as the book of the law that has been given to Jacob (the Hebrew people) and still is present on the earth. Contrary to the sometimes negative modern attitudes toward the law, Baruch announces that clinging to God's law yields life. He pleads (and so must you) that, for our own good we must "receive her (and) walk by her light." By teaching us what pleases God, the law gives us reason to rejoice. What better response than to say, "Blessed are we"?

READING VII The just punishment God has levied against the unfaithful "house of Israel" is having a negative impact on God's reputation. Foreigners among whom Israel was dispersed are questioning God's fidelity to the covenant. This is an embarrassment to God who decides, for the sake "of my holy name," to relent and start new with these stubborn children, despite their unworthiness. Such anthropomorphism should not surprise us, for scripture regularly ascribes human attributes to God.

Except for the first line, it is exclusively God's voice heard throughout the reading. But, unlike the Fifth Reading where God beckons tenderly, here God's voice is full of justifiable anger because the people have "defiled" the land by worshipping idols. Exile was the consequence, but the promise of forgiveness and return are clearly heard in this reading.

Halfway through the text, God orders the prophet to announce a shift in policy. "I have relented," God says. But at the same time God insists "Not for your sakes do I act." The exile made it look like God

The tone becomes more reassuring and loving here.

God will purify the people. This is an important image of Baptism for tonight's liturgy.

Make eye contact with the assembly. This is a classic and memorable line. Speak slowly and sincerely.

Imagine saying this to a child whom you love in order to ensure the child's success and prosperity. Say the words "You shall be . . . God" like a spouse vowing fidelity.

For I will take you **away** from among the nations,
    gather you from all the foreign **lands**,
    and bring you **back** to your **own** land.
I will sprinkle **clean water** upon you
    to **cleanse** you from all your **impurities**,
    and from all your **idols** I will cleanse you.
I will give you a **new** heart and place a new **spirit** within you,
    taking from your bodies your **stony** hearts
    and giving you **natural** hearts.
I will put my **spirit** within you and make you live by my **statutes**,
    careful to observe my **decrees**.
You shall **live** in the land I gave your **fathers**;
    you shall be my **people**, and **I** will be your **God**.

EPISTLE   Romans 6:3–11

A reading from the Letter of Saint Paul to the Romans

Brothers and sisters:
Are you **unaware** that we who were **baptized** into Christ **Jesus**
    were baptized into his **death**?
We were indeed **buried** with him through baptism into **death**,
    so that, just as Christ was **raised** from the dead
    by the glory of the **Father**,
    we **too** might live in **newness** of **life**.

For if we have grown into **union** with him
    through a **death** like his,
    we shall also be **united** with him in the **resurrection**.

Paul's literary device is a rhetorical question. Let it sound like a question. Make eye contact with the assembly and speak as directly as Paul writes.

Take the time to understand Paul's point: what happened to Christ will happen to us. He died and was buried, then rose. We die and are buried in Baptism; we, too, will rise to new life.

Paul develops the idea: we were made one with Christ by sharing a death (Baptism) like his; so we also will be made one with him by experiencing Resurrection.

didn't keep the promise to be Israel's God and protector; so now God must act to restore the divine reputation. But we quickly sense that God's mercy and love overwhelm the call of justice. God will purify the people and give them new hearts—made of flesh, not stone. Love triumphs. We knew it would. God always takes the initiative. By the time we hear the tender "you will be my people and I will be your God" we know God has not only saved a "name," but a people who will be empowered to keep God's statutes back home "in the land of [their] fathers."

EPISTLE   The first seven readings carried us through salvation history; Paul now projects us into our future, theologizing on the implications of Christ's death and Resurrection for all people and for all time.

The elect among us (those who will be baptized on this night) hear Paul's words with special clarity. For them, death and burial have become synonyms for life, because their "death" and "burial" in the waters of Baptism will be their pathway to

"new life." But Paul's words also speak directly to all of us who have come this night to renew our baptismal promises. "Are you not aware . . ." he asks, that our old self died and was buried with Christ? He expects us to know the answer and to realize that this "death" is good news, not bad, for having died with Christ, now we also may rise with him. Though Resurrection is a future hope, it is also a present reality, for by being crucified with Christ in Baptism we were freed from "slavery to sin" and began to live the risen life we will know fully after our physical death.

We know that our **old** self was **crucified** with him,
    so that our **sinful** body might be done **away** with,
    that we might no longer be in **slavery** to sin.
For a **dead** person has been **absolved** from sin.
If, then, we have **died** with Christ,
    we believe that we shall also **live** with him.
We know that **Christ, raised** from the dead, dies no **more**;
    death no longer has **power** over him.
As to his **death**, he died to sin **once** and for **all**;
    as to his **life**, he lives for **God**.
Consequently, you **too** must think of yourselves
        as being **dead** to **sin**
    and **living** for **God** in Christ **Jesus**.

GOSPEL   Luke 24:1–12

A reading from the holy Gospel according to Luke

At **daybreak** on the **first** day of the week
    the **women** who had come from **Galilee** with **Jesus**
    took the **spices** they had prepared
    and went to the **tomb**.
They found the **stone** rolled **away** from the tomb;
    but when they **entered**,
    they did not find the **body** of the Lord Jesus.
While they were **puzzling** over this, **behold**,
    two **men** in dazzling **garments appeared** to them.
They were **terrified** and bowed their **faces** to the **ground**.

The men want to build faith, not reprimand. Give them a soothing, persuasive voice meant to calm the women's fears.

Your energy should be greatest at the words "he has been raised." The intensity dips as they gently remind the women, but it rises again on the reference to "third day."

Much is suggested by the words "they remembered."

Speak excitedly and breathlessly. Take time with the list of women. Your tone should suggest their integrity and reputation for reliability, making the apostles' judgment of "nonsense" a surprise.

Surprise us with Peter's response.

Peter believes instantly. Your tone must indicate the "burial cloths" were proof enough to inspire his amazement.

They said to them,
    "Why do you seek the **living** one among the **dead**?
He is not **here**, but he has been **raised**.
Remember what he **said** to you while he was still in **Galilee**,
    that the Son of **Man** must be handed over to **sinners**
    and be **crucified**, and rise on the third **day**."
And they **remembered** his words.
Then they **returned** from the tomb
    and **announced** all these things to the **eleven**
    and to all the **others**.
The women were **Mary Magdalene**, **Joanna**,
    and **Mary** the mother of **James**;
    the **others** who accompanied them **also** told this
    to the apostles,
    but their **story** seemed like **nonsense**
    and they did not **believe** them.
But **Peter** got up and **ran** to the tomb,
    bent down, and saw the **burial** cloths **alone**;
    then he went home **amazed** at what had **happened**.

The women, who are to be the privileged heralds of the Resurrection, approach the tomb with no miraculous expectations. But then they see the rolled-away stone, the empty tomb, and the men in dazzling robes! Terrified and confused, they bow before the angelic messengers who remind them that Jesus had foretold his Passion and death. The risen one is not to be found in the place of death, they announce. Death is vanquished and the one who vanquished it is out among the living. "And they remembered his words" is a statement of searing insight and faith! The women need investigate no further.

The women rush from the tomb and share "all these things" with the disciples. They are credible witnesses, but their story is too good to be true and the disciples refuse to believe. Yet Peter seems to contemplate the *possibility* of Resurrection, then bolts as his heart *leaps* at the possibility. The empty tomb and "burial cloths" are enough for him. Convinced, he leaves amazed! Speak with Peter's hushed intensity. There is nothing in the world as overwhelming as this empty tomb.

EASTER SUNDAY

Lectionary #42

READING I   Acts 10:34a, 37–43

Except for the first six words, the entire reading is spoken in the voice of Peter. Rhetorical questions are a device meant to capture listener attention. Remember that Peter is making a public address.

"Spirit" and "power" are important characteristics of Jesus' ministry.

Jesus' healing ministry and exorcisms are important signs of who he is. Don't rush any of this first paragraph.

Pause to establish eye contact with the assembly. Peter is saying, "I was there!" There is a personal, intimate quality to this entire text.

The announcement of Jesus' Crucifixion is followed immediately by the announcement of his Resurrection. Pause after "tree" and again after "This man." Use a more upbeat tone for the balance of the paragraph.

Speak the words "the witnesses chosen by God . . ." humbly. This emphasizes Peter's credibility.

The tone continues to be energetic and earnest. "Preach" and "testify" will be redundant unless you build energy from one to the other.

A reading from the Acts of the Apostles

Peter proceeded to **speak** and said:
"You know what has **happened** all over **Judea**,
   beginning in **Galilee** after the **baptism**
   that **John** preached,
   how God **anointed** Jesus of **Nazareth**
   with the Holy **Spirit** and **power**.
He went about doing **good**
   and **healing** all those oppressed by the **devil**,
   for **God** was with him.
We are **witnesses** of all that he did
   both in the country of the **Jews** and in **Jerusalem**.
They put him to **death** by hanging him on a **tree**.
This man God **raised** on the **third** day and granted
      that he be **visible**,
   not to **all** the people, but to **us**,
   the witnesses **chosen** by God in **advance**,
   who **ate** and **drank** with him **after** he rose from the dead.
He **commissioned** us to **preach** to the people
   and **testify** that **he** is the one appointed by God
   as **judge** of the **living** and the **dead**.
To him all the **prophets** bear witness,
   that everyone who **believes** in him
   will receive **forgiveness** of **sins** through his **name**."

READING I

Easter is a beginning, a new first day of creation. With this liturgy we initiate the period of "fifty days" until the great solemnity of Pentecost. During this "week of weeks" (seven times seven, plus one, makes 50!) we will reflect on the post-Easter manifestations of Jesus, the consequences for us of his death and Resurrection, and his continuing presence in his body the Church, through which he continues to live and act in the world. A more self-confident and articulate Peter than we are used to incorporates all these elements into the address he delivers to the household of the new convert, Cornelius.

Peter's self-confidence is rooted in what he later asserts; he has witnessed everything he describes. What he relates is a basic catechism of early Christian faith. Peter begins with a review of Jesus' earthly ministry. First he recalls the Baptism and Jesus' anointing with "the Holy Spirit and power." Then he clarifies why power was given to Jesus—not to lord it over anyone, but to manifest God's love in concrete terms by doing good, heal-ing, and driving out demons. Peter knows this is true. He saw it!

The fact that Peter and the apostles "are witnesses" to the healing ministry of Jesus assures Luke's audience that what they hear proclaimed accurately reflects what Jesus himself preached. This is no minor issue for the infant church (or for us who follow them), so work hard to bring these points to our attention.

Then Peter directly takes on the scandal of Jesus' ignominious death. He speaks without melancholy or embarrassment. And he can do that because he knows how

This short text requires a slow reading.

"If then you were raised . . ." means "because you were raised up . . . ."

The tone is firm, yet encouraging.

Tell us two things: who will appear and what will happen.

READING II Colossians 3:1–4

A reading from the Letter of Saint Paul to the Colossians

Brothers and sisters:
If then you were **raised** with Christ, seek what is **above**,
    where Christ is **seated** at the right hand of **God**.
Think of what is **above**, not of what is on **earth**.
For you have **died**, and your life is **hidden** with Christ in **God**.
When Christ your life **appears**,
    then you **too** will appear with him in **glory**.

Or:

READING II 1 Corinthians 5:6b–8

This short text requires a slow reading.

Listeners are expected to know the answer to the rhetorical question. Pause before giving the following command.

You will become a batch of "unleavened," that is, uncorrupted, dough.

Be more energetic with the second "yeast" clause. Use *ritardando* (slowing toward the end) with the words "of sincerity and truth."

A reading from the first Letter of Saint Paul to the Corinthians

Brothers and sisters:
Do you not **know** that a little **yeast** leavens **all** the dough?
Clear out the **old** yeast,
    so that you may become a **fresh** batch of dough,
    inasmuch as you are **unleavened**.
For our paschal **lamb**, **Christ**, has been **sacrificed**.
Therefore, let us **celebrate** the feast,
    not with the **old** yeast, the yeast of **malice** and **wickedness**,
    but with the **unleavened** bread of **sincerity** and **truth**.

the story ends: God raised the man Jesus from the dead! This, too, he knows from experience. Without pride, Peter asserts his credibility by claiming to be among the few who saw the risen Jesus, a claim he concretizes by insisting they "ate and drank with him" after his Resurrection. Finally, Peter asserts an evangelistic mission entrusted to him and the others by Jesus. Although he stresses future divine judgment (an important aspect of early preaching to pagans), Peter ends with his most hopeful message by recalling the

words of the prophets that promise forgiveness of sins for everyone "who believes in him."

There is a choice of readings today. Speak with the liturgy coordinator to find out which readings will be used.

READING II COLOSSIANS. This is such a short reading, and yet so much spiritual and theological truth! Brief readings always require more effort on the part of the reader, because no word can be

wasted or the meaning may be lost. Jesus has not risen alone: we, who have died with him in Baptism, have also risen to new life! That is the good news of Easter. In addition to celebrating a historical event, Easter announces the present, mysterious reality that we "were raised with Christ." But the Easter celebration also reminds us we must never take that reality for granted. Faith is not magic. It always requires of us a response to God's generous initiative. Paul insists there is something *we* must do and we must do it *now:*

GOSPEL   John 20:1–9

A reading from the holy Gospel according to John

On the **first** day of the week,
  Mary of **Magdala** came to the **tomb** early in the **morning**,
  while it was still **dark**,
  and saw the **stone removed** from the tomb.
So she **ran** and went to Simon **Peter**
  and to the **other** disciple whom Jesus **loved**, and **told** them,
  "They have taken the **Lord** from the **tomb**,
  and we **don't** know where they **put** him."
So **Peter** and the **other** disciple went out and **came** to the tomb.
They both **ran**, but the **other** disciple ran **faster** than Peter
  and arrived at the tomb **first**;
  he bent **down** and saw the **burial** cloths there, but did
    not go **in**.
When Simon Peter arrived **after** him,
  he went **into** the tomb and **saw** the burial cloths there,
  and the **cloth** that had covered his **head**,
  not **with** the burial cloths but **rolled** up in a **separate** place.
Then the other disciple **also** went in,
  the one who had arrived at the tomb **first**,
  and he **saw** and **believed**.
For they did not yet **understand** the Scripture
  that he had to **rise** from the **dead**.

Take us through the text by allowing us to experience the characters' various emotions: Mary's panic, the disciples' instant anxiety, Peter's confusion before the empty wrappings and folded cloth, and John's silent assent in faith.

Magdala = MAG-duh-luh

Speak slowly here; the mood is a bit melancholy.

Your pace should quicken here. Mary is fearful and distressed.

Let Peter and John do the racing, not you. Convey their haste without rushing the lines. Say "but the other disciple . . . did not go in" in a hushed tone.

Stress Peter's activity: he enters, sees, and examines. Speak the words "saw and believed" with quiet reverence.

It's understandable that they would not yet fully "understand."

"seek what is above . . . ." In other words, we must put our sinful ways behind us and embrace instead the risen life that we are privileged to taste, even if only partially, here in this life. Paul contrasts that which "is on earth"—material values and passing concerns—with the higher, spiritual values to which we aspire. "For you have died, and your life is hidden with Christ . . ." is in many ways a shocking statement that tells a double truth: we already are living the risen life of the kingdom, but its fullness is not yet entirely realized in our lives.

Help us hear the joy of that reality *and* the imperative for moral living it places on us.

The full realization of what Christ accomplished through his death and Resurrection will become apparent at some point in the future when Christ "appears." Twice Paul uses that word to suggest coming glory and to peak his listener's eagerness for it. Perhaps you can do the same for us if, instead of visualizing the "glory," you envision him whom Paul poignantly calls "our life."

1 CORINTHIANS. The text from Colossians used baptismal imagery while this Corinthians text focuses on eucharistic images. Yeast is commonly known to cause fermentation, so it serves as a natural symbol for anything that spreads, whether good or ill. In this case, Paul uses yeast as a symbol for the insidious spread of wickedness and corruption. The moral life is fragile and subject to many influences, some of which are evil and corrupting. Among the community of Christians in Corinth there was in fact an individual who was spreading error.

Lectionary #46

AFTERNOON GOSPEL Luke 24:13–35

A reading from the holy Gospel according to Luke

The "day" of this occurrence is important.

Emmaus = eh-MAY-uhs

Let your tone convey the irony of their failure to recognize the very one they're discussing.

Jesus is "playing dumb" here.

Cleopas = KLEE-oh-puhs
He responds with annoyance.

Jesus coaxes further. Initially their response might sound like "How could you not know this?" But soon they are into the story.

We can't help but feel sorry for them and their sense of loss.

That **very** day, the **first** day of the week,
  two of Jesus' **disciples** were going
  to a village seven **miles** from Jerusalem called **Emmaus**,
  and they were **conversing** about all the things
    that had **occurred**.
And it **happened** that while they were **conversing** and **debating**,
  Jesus **himself** drew near and **walked** with them,
  but their **eyes** were **prevented** from **recognizing** him.
He asked them,
  "What are you **discussing** as you walk along?"
They **stopped**, looking **downcast**.
One of them, named **Cleopas**, said to him in **reply**,
  "Are you the **only** visitor to Jerusalem
  who does not **know** of the things
  that have taken **place** there in these days?"
And he replied to them, "What **sort** of things?"
They **said** to him,
  "The things that happened to **Jesus** the **Nazarene**,
  who was a **prophet** mighty in **deed** and **word**
  before **God** and all the **people**,
  how our chief **priests** and **rulers** both handed him over
  to a sentence of **death** and **crucified** him.
But **we** were hoping that he would be the one to **redeem** Israel;
  and **besides** all this,
  it is now the **third** day since this took place.

Here, Paul draws on Jewish custom that mandated the removal of every crumb of leavened bread in the house before the Passover so that no trace of the old could corrupt the new. Paul urges the same scrupulous removal of the old leaven of "malice and wickedness" and calls the Corinthians to celebrate the feast with the unleavened bread (that is, bread that has no yeast) of "sincerity and truth." Help us hear his logic: even a pinch of old yeast pollutes the loaf, he says, so celebrate with something worthy of the feast! For us, Christ is the

unleavened bread we share at this and at every celebration. It is by eating this bread of life that we acquire strength to resist the spread of evil among us and within us. On this day of great rejoicing, no anger or judgment need color your words of exhortation, only sincere joy.

GOSPEL | The shock of Easter begins in the early, still dark hours of the morning. A tinge of Friday's death and gloom lingers in the air as Mary approaches the tomb, but the narration

gives no hint of the dramatic reversal soon to be revealed. When she finds the stone removed from the tomb's entrance, Magdalene immediately assumes Jesus' body has been stolen and runs to alert the disciples. Significantly, it is Peter and "the other disciple Jesus loved" (most likely John) to whom she reports Jesus' disappearance. Peter and the disciple react immediately, racing to the tomb—Peter outrun by the younger John. Since many commentators see John's waiting for Peter to enter the tomb first as a sign of Peter's

Are they dismissing the testimony because it came from women?

Some **women** from our group, however, have **astounded** us:
they were at the **tomb** early in the **morning**
and did not find his **body**;
they came back and reported
that they had indeed seen a **vision** of **angels**
who announced that he was **alive**.

They just can't add two and two: the tomb was empty and angels announced his rising, but this does not yet add up to Resurrection.

Then some of those with us **went** to the tomb
and found things **just** as the women had **described**,
but **him** they did not **see**."
And he said to them, "Oh, how **foolish** you are!

Jesus' emotion is real: frustration and some sadness.

How **slow** of heart to believe all that the **prophets** spoke!
Was it not **necessary** that the Christ should **suffer** these things
and enter into his **glory**?"

This is a new beat, so don't rush.

Then beginning with **Moses** and all the **prophets**,
he **interpreted** to them what **referred** to him
in all the **Scriptures**.
As they approached the **village** to which they were **going**,
he gave the impression that he was going on **farther**.

They plead with him to stay!

But they **urged** him, "**Stay** with us,
for it is nearly **evening** and the day is almost **over**."
So he went in to **stay** with them.

Slowly narrate this eucharistic scene. Pause after the words "gave it to them."

And it **happened** that, while he was with them at **table**,
he took **bread**, said the **blessing**,
broke it, and **gave** it to them.

Speak the words "With that [pause] their eyes were open . . ." with energy and awe.

With **that** their eyes were **opened** and they **recognized** him,
but he **vanished** from their **sight**.

preeminence in the apostolic brotherhood, these lines should be carefully highlighted. John bends down to peer into the empty tomb and waits. Peter's arrival is significant; as he observes the burial cloths we sense a slow realization dawning on him that the carefully "rolled up" cloth negates the possibility that grave robbers or even the authorities stole the body.

John's suspenseful text describes a melancholy scene until "faith" bursts open the door to belief in the Resurrection. When "the other disciple" (carefully identified as the one who "arrived at the tomb

first") finally enters the tomb, he sees and believes. But actually John believes without "seeing," for in the Gospel according to John it will be Mary who first lays eyes on the risen Lord. The final sentence might be confusing: if John has just "believed," why are we told they did not yet understand "he had to rise from the dead"? Often, belief comes in stages. We witness the impossible but then go away wondering if what we saw was real. The reality of Resurrection takes time to sink in. So the parenthetical closing is delivered in a joyful, not judgmental tone, for it speaks with present

faith about a previous (and not unreasonable) lack of understanding.

AFTERNOON GOSPEL This Gospel text is one of the key Christian stories. Downcast and discouraged because their hero and hoped for messiah was betrayed by one of his own and murdered in the most shameful way, two disciples make their way home leaving behind the events of the Passion and all the hopes and dreams they had pinned on Jesus. Their hearts ache for him

Use a quickened pace here, but keep it natural and realistic.

Remember this is a story. Tell it as if for the first time, with enthusiasm and suspense.

Speak with great reverence and awareness of the significance of these lines. Use *ritardando* (slowing toward the end) on the words "in the breaking of the bread."

Then they **said** to each other,
"Were not our **hearts burning** within us
while he **spoke** to us on the way and opened the **Scriptures**
to us?"
So they set out at **once** and returned to **Jerusalem**
where they found gathered **together**
the **eleven** and those with them who were saying,
"The Lord has **truly** been **raised** and has appeared to **Simon**!"
Then the **two** recounted
what had taken **place** on the way
and how he was made **known** to them in the **breaking** of **bread**.

and yet, when he approaches, they fail to recognize him. Jesus plays dumb and coaxes them into telling him his own story. He marvels at their lack of faith, their ignorance, their inability to see in the very story they've just told the outlines of the one who stands before them. They report everything—Jesus' powerful preaching, his arrest and Crucifixion, the women's report of the empty tomb and visions of angels, and the men's confirmation of what the women announced. And to all that Jesus says, "How foolish you are!" How could they have experienced and seen and heard so much and have so little faith?

But Jesus plays the teacher once again as he accompanies them to Emmaus, opening up and explaining the scriptures all the while. At their destination, Jesus pretends to be going further and allows himself to be coaxed into staying. He gathers them at table, a familiar setting for him and friends, then takes, blesses and breaks. And suddenly their eyes are open. He departs from their midst. Now any thinking person would have said, "Where'd he go?" But the disciples are still so filled with the presence of Jesus that they barely notice his departure. With hearts still burning, they realize that their whole journey to Emmaus had been blessed with his presence. And they know they'll never again be without it. That awareness propels them back to Jerusalem where they proclaim what the disciples know already. In all of scripture, there is no more important ecclesiological line than the one that ends this text: they knew him "in the breaking of the bread."

2ND SUNDAY OF EASTER   DIVINE MERCY SUNDAY

Lectionary #45

READING I   Acts 5:12–16

A reading from the Acts of the Apostles

Many **signs** and **wonders** were done among the people
    at the hands of the apostles.
They were all **together** in Solomon's **portico**.
None of the others dared to **join** them, but the people
    esteemed them.
Yet more than **ever**, **believers** in the Lord,
    great **numbers** of men and women, were **added** to them.
Thus they even carried the **sick** out into the streets
    and laid them on **cots** and **mats**
    so that when **Peter** came by,
    at least his **shadow** might fall on one or **another** of them.
A large **number** of people from the towns
    in the vicinity of **Jerusalem also** gathered,
    bringing the **sick** and those disturbed by unclean **spirits**,
    and they were **all cured**.

Distinguish "signs" from "wonders."

Contrast "dared to join them" from "esteemed them."

Stress with joy the steady growth of believers.

Relate these details with a sense of reverence and awe.

In the New Testament, "shadow" always demonstrates divine power (see Luke 1:35; 9:34).

Don't be an uninvolved commentator, but rejoice in these tidings.

READING I   From Easter to Pentecost, we take our First Reading not from the Old Testament but from the Acts of the Apostles. These texts chronicle the life of the early Church. They note the rapid spread of faith in Jesus without glossing over the conflicts within the community and the obstacles from without, culminating in the martyrdom of Stephen. In the previous chapter of Acts the community joined Peter and John in praying that "signs and wonders" would accompany their bold proclamation of the Gospel (4:30). Here Luke recounts an answer to

that prayer. Although not all the members of the community had "dared to join them" in Solomon's portico, the crowds are greatly impressed with the apostle's healing and preaching ministry, and "great numbers" join the community of believers. This growing number of believers deserves special emphasis because it highlights God's initiative in adding new members to an already existing community. This growth not only swells the number of believers, it also provides tangible evidence of the efficacy of the apostles' teaching and of their own faith in Christ.

Because of the unusual power they manifested, the apostles are clearly presented as the cornerstones of the community, and foremost among them is Peter, whose very shadow summons divine healing power. The description of people bringing their sick is a poignant story of faith. Move slowly through that narration, speaking with the conviction of someone who witnessed one of these miracles of healing. Distinguish the "sick" from those "disturbed by unclean spirits", but rejoice in the fact that they "all" were cured.

READING II   Revelation 1:9–11a, 12–13, 17–19

A reading from the Book of Revelation

I, **John**, your **brother**, who **share** with you
   the **distress**, the **kingdom**, and the **endurance** we have
     in **Jesus**,
found myself on the island called **Patmos**
because I proclaimed God's **word** and gave **testimony** to **Jesus**.
I was caught up in **spirit** on the **Lord's** day
   and heard behind me a **voice** as loud as a **trumpet**, which said,
   "**Write** on a **scroll** what you **see**."
Then I turned to see **whose** voice it was that **spoke** to me,
   and when I **turned**, I saw **seven gold lampstands**
   and in the **midst** of the lampstands one like a **son** of **man**,
   wearing an ankle-length **robe**, with a gold **sash**
     around his chest.

When I caught **sight** of him, I fell down at his **feet** as though **dead**.
He **touched** me with his right **hand** and said, "Do not be **afraid**.
I am the **first** and the **last**, the one who **lives**.
Once I was **dead**, but now I am **alive** forever and **ever**.
I hold the **keys** to **death** and the **netherworld**.
Write down, therefore, what you have **seen**,
   and what is **happening**, and what will happen **afterwards**."

This is the first of six consecutive weeks we read from Revelation. Note that there is no "s" at the end of the word.

His self-identification as "brother" is important.

Patmos = PAT-muhs

As in the first sentence, many details are packed into one sentence: 1) it's the Lord's day, 2) he had a vision, and 3) he heard a loud voice.

Remember, you are describing a divine vision, not some mundane dream. "Seven lampstands" refer to the seven churches that represent the whole Church. "Robe" and "sash" represent Christ as priest and king.

"Fell down . . ." indicates reverence and awe.

The voice of the son of man conveys a blend of power and comfort.

This is a command. Don't rush; there are three things to write down.

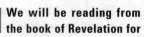 We will be reading from the book of Revelation for six consecutive weeks, so knowledge of the literary style that distinguishes this book—apocalyptic literature—is very important. Always written in times of distress, apocalyptic writing offers hope while exhorting firm faith in the face of struggle. That is what John does here.

The complex first sentence sets the scene and tone for what follows: exiled to the island of Patmos because he "gave testimony to Jesus," John experiences distress, but waits with patient endurance for the fullness of Christ's kingdom. And because he shares this fate with other Christians, he calls himself their "brother"—a kinship with his audience that he wears not as grounds for self-pity but as a badge of honor. The context of tribulation is important because it points to the purpose of the entire book—strengthening those in the midst of trial. John's elaborate imagery and symbolism offer assurances of God's constant presence to a people who, in the midst of persecution, feel God's absence and even abandonment.

The symbolism that powers the vision speaks of the presence of God: "trumpets" frequently accompany divine apparitions. "Son of Man," a term borrowed from the book of Daniel, suggests a heavenly being who exercises power and authority. Clearly, the vision is of Jesus the Alpha and Omega, "the first and last," the living one who once was dead, but now lives forever. Even his attire—"an ankle-length robe" and golden "sash"—symbolize the eternal priesthood and kingship of Christ. John's symbolism was intended for an audience that would understand the imagery and would find

GOSPEL   John 20:19–31

A reading from the holy Gospel according to John

On the evening of that **first** day of the week,
  when the doors were **locked**, where the **disciples** were,
  for **fear** of the Jews,
  Jesus came and stood in their **midst**
  and said to them, "**Peace** be with you."
When he had **said** this, he showed them his **hands** and his **side**.
The disciples **rejoiced** when they saw the Lord.
Jesus said to them **again**, "**Peace** be with you.
As the **Father** has sent **me**, so **I** send **you**."
And when he had **said** this, he **breathed** on them and said
    to them,
  "**Receive** the Holy **Spirit**.
Whose **sins** you **forgive** are **forgiven** them,
  and whose sins you **retain** are **retained**."

Thomas, called **Didymus**, one of the **Twelve**,
  was not **with** them when Jesus came.
So the **other** disciples said to him, "We have **seen** the **Lord**."
But **he** said to them,
  "Unless I **see** the mark of the **nails** in his **hands**
  and put my **finger** into the nailmarks
  and put my **hand** into his **side**, I will not **believe**."

Now a week **later** his disciples were again inside
  and Thomas **was** with them.
Jesus **came**, although the doors were **locked**,
  and stood in their **midst** and said, "**Peace** be with you."

Speak slowly so that the many details won't be missed. The tone should be somewhat hushed and subdued.

Jesus' entrance is surprising. He speaks in tones both authoritative and comforting.

"The disciples rejoice . . ." conveys their agitated response that Jesus must calm with his next "Peace be with you."

Pause and then slowly narrate both his "breathing" and what he said. Pause again before introducing Thomas.

Didymus = DID-ih-muhs

You are setting up the scene that follows. Don't rush the details and create some suspense.

Don't make Thomas mean-spirited. The others *did* see Jesus; he's only asking for what they've already received.

Maintain energy here and stress that Thomas is present this time.

This second "Peace be with you" should not be rushed.

---

comfort and reassurance in it. Your assembly, on the other hand, won't be familiar with this metaphoric lexicon, but your tone can convey to them the same reassurance and comfort it conveyed to its first hearers. In biblical literature, seeing the face of God meant certain death. Although the "son of man" tells the visionary there is "nothing to fear," still your tone should suggest a powerful, awe-inspiring presence, not a sentimental one.

In a voice different from John's, speak the first person lines of the Son of Man, who not only lives again, but also holds

"keys to death and the netherworld" — another image of power and dominion. For Christians suffering intense persecution, this vision offers much hope: the oppressive powers of this world will be overcome; God is still in charge and able to act decisively. When you prepare and proclaim, think of people persecuted or disenfranchised—victims of war, citizens of oppressive dictatorships, the hungry poor — and imagine yourself speaking these hopeful words to them.

GOSPEL   Jesus penetrates the gloom and fear of the group of disciples hiding behind locked doors, gives them his "peace" and fills them with rejoicing. It is the "first day of the week," an apt time for a new creation to begin. As God breathed on Adam, Jesus now breathes on his disciples giving new life in the Spirit. A transformed Jesus in turn transforms frightened disciples into apostles, that is, "those sent" to give witness. And this commissioning occurs within the context of an apparition that is meant to affirm the historical reality of Jesus' Resurrection.

Jesus is answering his plea, not judging him.

Speak Thomas' words with great sincerity. "My Lord . . ." can be spoken slowly. Pause slightly and then quickly say, "and my God!" John's Gospel account consistently identifies Christ with God.

He's not criticizing Thomas, but praising all to follow who will believe without seeing.

The denouement contains an important faith statement: Jesus is the Christ.

Then he said to **Thomas**, "Put your **finger** here and see my **hands**,
    and bring your **hand** and put it into my **side**,
    and do not be **unbelieving**, but **believe**."
Thomas **answered** and said to him, "My **Lord** and my **God!**"
Jesus said to **him**, "Have you come to **believe**
    because you have **seen** me?
Blessed are those who have **not** seen and have **believed**."

Now Jesus did many **other** signs in the presence of his **disciples**
    that are not **written** in this book.
But **these** are written that you may come to **believe**
    that **Jesus** is the **Christ**, the Son of **God**,
    and that **through** this belief you may have **life** in his **name**.

It's no accident that John pays so much attention to physical detail: Jesus appears despite "locked" doors; he shows his wounded hands and side to prove his identity and to demonstrate that he is physically, not just spiritually, present. All this is part of John's agenda in narrating this appearance, so find appropriate stresses to help him make this point. Jesus' tone with the disciples stands in stark contrast to the fear that has bound them both to each other and to that place. With solemn authority, Jesus imparts his Spirit of peace and confers upon them the power to forgive sins.

A contentious mood shatters the previous harmony as Thomas' skepticism matches the disciples' insistence that they've "seen the Lord." This second apparition is as important as the first for here, through Thomas, the commissioning of the disciples is extended to each of us. Again, John spends much time detailing the physical circumstances. Thomas insists on physical evidence for faith, but he's asking for no more than what the other disciples already received, so don't cast him too negatively. His unique confession of faith can be nuanced to reveal the repentance it also voices. Jesus' climactic beatitude assures any of John's readers (and us!) that faith without "seeing" is not only possible, but even more virtuous.

3RD SUNDAY OF EASTER

Lectionary #48

READING I   Acts 5:27b–32, 40b–41

A reading from the Acts of the Apostles

When the **captain** and the court **officers** had brought
     the **apostles** in
and made them stand before the **Sanhedrin**,
     the high **priest** questioned them,
     "We gave you **strict orders**, did we **not**,
     to stop **teaching** in that **name**?
Yet you have filled **Jerusalem** with your teaching
     and want to bring this man's **blood** upon us."
But **Peter** and the **apostles** said in reply,
     "We must obey **God** rather than **men**.
The God of our **ancestors raised** Jesus,
     though **you** had him **killed** by hanging him on a **tree**.
God **exalted** him at his right **hand** as **leader** and **savior**
     to grant Israel **repentance** and **forgiveness** of **sins**.
We are **witnesses** of these things,
     as is the Holy **Spirit** whom God has given to those who
          obey him."

The Sanhedrin **ordered** the apostles
     to stop **speaking** in the name of **Jesus**, and **dismissed** them.
So they **left** the presence of the Sanhedrin,
     rejoicing that they had been found **worthy**
     to suffer **dishonor** for the sake of the **name**.

A sense of frustration at having to replay the arrest and interrogation.

Sanhedrin = san-HEE-druhn

The high priest is angry at their disobedience and at being implicated in Jesus' death. For him, "that name" isn't worth the breath it takes to say it.

Peter's tone contrasts with the high priest's. He speaks with the familiarity and conviction of one who lived with and would die for Jesus. Remember "repentance" and "forgiveness" are distinct words.

Stress both "we" and "Holy Spirit" as witnesses.

The Sanhedrin angrily dismisses prisoners they've just flogged.

The last sentence is spoken with the attitude of the rejoicing (and suffering) apostles.

READING I Because of the jealousy of the religious leaders, the apostles were jailed, but then miraculously freed; whereupon they resume the preaching that got them in trouble in the first place. When the Sanhedrin discovers that the apostles are *again* teaching in the temple area, they arrest and interrogate them anew. The high priest is not only affronted by their disobedience, he fears being implicated in Jesus' death. But Peter boldly defies him and blames him nonetheless. Peter's speech provides an early form of the Christian proclamation of salvation through Jesus. For him, this is more a teaching opportunity than a confrontation. He insists that even "the Holy Spirit" witnesses to Jesus, who was raised by the very God of their ancestors and whose mission was to bring them "forgiveness of sins." (The latter might suggest the tone of Peter's exhortation.)

Verses omitted from our text narrate how a prudent council member deterred the Sanhedrin from ordering the deaths of the apostles, suggesting instead they wait and see what becomes of this movement. The leaders concur, but flog the disciples before releasing them. Despite their narrow escape and severe beating, the apostles go forth rejoicing over the privilege of suffering for the name of Jesus. The name of Jesus manifests the authority of God in powerful, concrete ways. One of the most concrete is the disciples' own willingness to die for it.

READING II During the weeks of the Easter season, the book of Revelation presents the risen Christ reigning supreme in the eternal Jerusalem

This is the second of six consecutive weeks we read from Revelation.

The entire text is spoken in the first person. This is a vision, which means it must sound different from other readings. "Creatures" and "elders" are important symbols.

Use all six words ("power . . . blessing") to paint a portrait of the Lamb. Each is a different quality. Don't rush.

Distinguish the locations: "heaven," "earth," and "under the earth."

"Blesing," "honor," "glory," and "might" are four distinct words.

See and hear these images before you describe them.

READING II   Revelation 5:11–14

A reading from the Book of Revelation

I, **John**, **looked** and heard the voices of many **angels**
   who surrounded the **throne**
   and the living **creatures** and the **elders**.
They were **countless** in number, and they **cried** out
      in a **loud** voice:
   "**Worthy** is the **Lamb** that was **slain**
         to receive **power** and **riches**, **wisdom** and **strength**,
         honor and **glory** and **blessing**."
Then I heard every creature in **heaven** and on **earth**
   and **under** the earth and in the **sea**,
   everything in the **universe**, cry out:
   "To the one who sits on the **throne** and to the **Lamb**
         be **blessing** and **honor**, **glory** and **might**,
         forever and **ever**."
The four living **creatures** answered, "**Amen**,"
   and the **elders** fell down and **worshiped**.

GOSPEL   John 21:1–19

You might tell the story from the perspective of one close to these events who wants to persuade others of their truth and relevance. That he "revealed himself" is obviously important.

Didymus = DID-ih-muhs

A reading from the holy Gospel according to John

At that time, Jesus **revealed** himself **again** to his disciples
      at the **Sea** of **Tiberias**.
He revealed himself in this **way**.
Together were Simon **Peter**, **Thomas** called **Didymus**,
   Nathanael from Cana in **Galilee**,
   Zebedee's sons, and two **others** of his disciples.

where one day we, too, will celebrate the everlasting liturgy of praise and adoration. Apocalyptic literature like this speaks in symbols often obscure to us but familiar to its intended audience. With rich and melodic poetry, John speaks today of a heavenly liturgy where the "four creatures" (symbolizing all creation) and the "elders" (symbolizing the Church) gather to offer God unending praise. Christ, the triumphant Lamb, is enthroned in glory beside the Father. Every creature imaginable joins the hymn of praise in this divine liturgy.

John is immersed in a profound mystical experience in which creatures of heaven, on earth, and under the earth form a single chorus of praise to the omnipotent God and to the Lamb. Your voice should reveal the impact that witnessing this overwhelming scene has on the prophet. John is immersed in divine reality, steeped in the mystery, the majesty, the infinite goodness of the Lamb who "was slain" for us. Gratitude and awe are fused. Use the repetitions and the rhythm of the poetry to help us glimpse this profound moment of religious ecstasy. John uses six words to describe the worthiness of the Lamb. Each of them means something different, so don't rush them, but let them sing a melody of praise. The couplet that ends the reading is an opportunity for you to voice your own love of God and gratitude for God's mercy. *Hear* the "Amen" before you report it, and *visualize* the church falling down in fervent adoration.

GOSPEL Because they offered convincing evidence of Jesus' victory over death, the post-Resurrection

Decide the mood of Peter's "I'm going fishing." Is it restlessness, anxiety, or depression? "Caught nothing" ends on a somber note.

"Dawn" brings new energy and hope. Are the "children" here insecure and in need of a final reassurance before they can be left on their own?

Speak the words "So they cast it . . ." with a sense of surprise that they'd obey this stranger. Then, the surprise of the catch!

Your energy and pace should increase with the physical activity. There are many details here, and all of them are important. The clothing details are rather humorous.

This is a new beat.

Stress the number of fish.

Perhaps they don't "dare" because none wants to risk being scolded by Jesus for lack of faith. Describe the meal with tenderness. There are eucharistic overtones here.

Simon **Peter** said to them, "I am going **fishing**."
They said to him, "We **also** will come with you."
So they **went** out and got into the **boat**,
  but that night they caught **nothing**.
When it was already **dawn**, **Jesus** was standing on the **shore**;
  but the disciples did not **realize** that it was Jesus.
Jesus said to them, "**Children**, have you **caught** anything to eat?"
They answered him, "**No**."
So he said to them, "Cast the net over the **right** side of the boat
  and you will **find** something."
So they **cast** it, and were not **able** to pull it **in**
  because of the **number** of fish.
So the disciple whom Jesus **loved** said to Peter, "It is the **Lord**."
When Simon Peter **heard** that it was the Lord,
  he **tucked** in his garment, for he was **lightly** clad,
  and **jumped** into the sea.
The **other** disciples came in the **boat**,
  for they were not **far** from shore, only about a hundred **yards**,
  dragging the **net** with the **fish**.
When they **climbed** out on **shore**,
  they saw a charcoal **fire** with **fish** on it and **bread**.
Jesus said to them, "**Bring** some of the **fish** you just caught."
So Simon Peter went over and **dragged** the net ashore
  full of one **hundred fifty-three** large fish.
Even though there were so **many**, the net was not **torn**.
Jesus **said** to them, "**Come**, have **breakfast**."
And **none** of the disciples dared to **ask** him, "Who **are** you?"
  because they **realized** it was the **Lord**.
Jesus came over and took the **bread** and **gave** it to them,
  and in like **manner** the **fish**.

appearances were of paramount importance to the early Church that was still establishing the authenticity of the Resurrection. Hence John's detailed description and his stress on the fact that this is Jesus' third revelation of himself. All the details, from time of day to number of fish, insist on the reality of the incident.

Commentators suggest the return of Peter and the disciples to their former work, despite their commissioning in John's previous chapter, is plausible only if one assumes this chapter existed independently of the rest of the Gospel and was

later added on. But one need only remember human nature, and the fact that the Spirit of Pentecost has not yet descended upon the disciples igniting the zeal demonstrated in today's First Reading, to realize how plausible it is that the disciples might return to what was safe and familiar. John's nighttime setting and the unsuccessful fishing set a tone of hopelessness. But with Jesus comes dawn and success. He calls them "Children" and dares ask these professionals if they've caught anything. Without shame, they admit failure. Then Jesus offers advice and suddenly every fish

in the sea leaps into their net. Recognition stirs in the beloved disciple's heart.

Surprisingly, and not without humor, upon hearing "it is the Lord," Peter first covers up and then dives into the sea. (The scene alone with Jesus will remind us of what Peter really needs to cover up.) The number of fish is probably symbolic of the apostles' universal mission, but it stresses the more literal details regarding the size and number of fish held by a net that, amazingly, was not torn. Amid the frenzy of the stunning catch, the disciples discover that Jesus—ever the caretaker—has already

"Third time" should be stressed.

This is another new beat. Each scene is important. Don't rush them.

Perhaps he winces with the pain of guilt at remembering his denials.

Finally, Peter lets down all his defenses.

Jesus is possibly using a proverb about old age to hint at Peter's death as a martyr.

Address the words "Follow me" to the entire assembly.

This was now the **third** time Jesus was **revealed** to his disciples
   after being **raised** from the **dead**.

When they had **finished** breakfast, Jesus said to Simon **Peter**,
   "**Simon**, son of **John**, do you **love** me **more** than these?"
Simon Peter answered him, "**Yes**, Lord, you **know** that
   I love you."
Jesus said to him, "**Feed** my **lambs**."
He then said to Simon Peter a **second** time,
   "**Simon**, son of **John**, do you **love** me?"
Simon Peter answered him, "**Yes**, Lord, you **know**
   that I love you."
Jesus said to him, "**Tend** my **sheep**."
Jesus said to him the **third** time,
   "**Simon**, son of **John**, do you **love** me?"
Peter was **distressed** that Jesus had said to him a **third** time,
   "Do you **love** me?" and he said to him,
   "**Lord**, you know **everything**; you **know** that I **love** you."
Jesus said to him, "**Feed** my **sheep**.
Amen, **amen**, I say to you, when you were **younger**,
   you used to dress **yourself** and go where you **wanted**;
   but when you grow **old**, you will **stretch** out your **hands**,
   and someone **else** will dress you
   and **lead** you where you do not **want** to go."
He said this signifying by what kind of **death** he would
   glorify God.
And when he had **said** this, he said to him, "**Follow** me."

[Shorter: John 21:1–14]

prepared their meal. John's emphasis (and yours) is on the fact that *none* "dared to ask him" his identity, because they "realized" who he was.

The second act of this drama entails reconciliation and commission. Peter has likely concealed knowledge of his recent triple denial, so imagine how great is his need to right the wrong he publicly committed. Jesus provides the opportunity. Each of Peter's responses arises from a different motivation. Perhaps the first lacks

much forethought; the second might be tinged with the painful memory of his denials; while the third could represent surrender of all his armor, even his guilt, to Jesus. Each poignant response is met with a commissioning to feed Jesus' lambs and sheep.

Jesus' solemn pronouncement to Peter that he will no longer be master of his fate prepares the disciple for the destiny he embraced through his three-fold profession of love. Use the contrasts in those lines ("younger"/"grow old"; "where you wanted"/"where you do not want to go") to heighten the bittersweet tone of

Jesus' prediction about Peter's death. Jesus asks Peter to walk a difficult road, but simultaneously assures him he'll not walk it alone. That's why the last two words are so important.

4TH SUNDAY OF EASTER

Lectionary #51

READING I   Acts 13:14, 43–52

A reading from the Acts of the Apostles

Paul and **Barnabas** continued on from **Perga**
    and reached **Antioch** in **Pisidia**.
On the **sabbath** they entered the **synagogue** and took their **seats**.
Many **Jews** and worshipers who were **converts** to Judaism
    followed Paul and Barnabas, who **spoke** to them
    and **urged** them to remain **faithful** to the grace of **God**.

On the **following** sabbath almost the whole **city** gathered
    to **hear** the word of the **Lord**.
When the **Jews** saw the **crowds**, they were filled with **jealousy**
    and with violent **abuse contradicted** what Paul said.
Both Paul and Barnabas spoke out **boldly** and said,
    "It was **necessary** that the word of God be spoken to you **first**,
    but since you **reject** it
    and **condemn** yourselves as **unworthy** of eternal **life**,
    we now turn to the **Gentiles**.
For so the **Lord** has **commanded** us,
    *I have made you a **light** to the **Gentiles**,*
    *that you may be an **instrument** of **salvation***
    *to the **ends** of the **earth**."*

The Gentiles were **delighted** when they heard this
    and **glorified** the word of the Lord.

This is the fourth of eight consecutive weeks we read from Acts.

Perga = PER-guh

Antioch = AN-tee-ahk

Pisidia = pih-SID-ee-uh

The words "Many . . . followed Paul" suggest the fiery preaching that brought huge crowds the following week.

If he's exaggerating, it's intentional. The crowd was huge: emphasize it. Stress that jealousy is the motive for the opposition.

Sustain a declamatory tone here.

He's quoting Isaiah 49:6.

READING I   On the previous Sabbath, Paul and Barnabas had spoken in this same synagogue with such compelling vigor and authority that "almost the whole city" has come to hear the preaching you will proclaim today. "Urged them to remain faithful to the grace of God" is a fragment of that *earlier* homily. Use it, and the surrounding narration, to suggest the spirited energy of Paul's previous sermon.

During this Easter season, the First Readings celebrate the Christian *kerygma,* that is, the proclamation of Jesus' saving death and Resurrection, and the spread of that Gospel message from the Jewish cities where it was first preached to the Gentile nations. Though the Jews rightly were first to hear the Good News, many squandered that privilege, says Paul, so now the Spirit prompts him to bring the message to Gentiles who, we are told, receive it with delight. There is much work for the homilist here to offer a corrective that will prevent an anti-Semitic understanding of these lines.

Today's text alternately reports the forward and unstoppable movement of the Good News and its consistent opposition by the Jewish authorities. Three clear ideas emerge: the Good News is meant for all, it will be resisted, and its spread can be hindered but not stopped. You must suggest the joy, courage, and zeal with which Paul and Barnabas approach their ministry, while also capturing the jealous opposition that fails to thwart their progress. Despite the obstacles that send them off to another town at the end of this reading, they are Spirit-filled and joyful.

Announce these words joyfully.

"The women . . . and the leading men" is one thought. Keep it connected.

Your tone can convey the hostility of Paul's opponents. Pause after the word "territory."

Ioonium = ī KOH noo uhm

The narrative ends with joy in the Spirit.

All who were destined for eternal **life** came to **believe**,
   and the word of the **Lord** continued to **spread**
      through the whole **region**.
The **Jews**, however, incited the women of **prominence**
      who were **worshipers**
   and the leading **men** of the city,
      stirred up a **persecution** against Paul and Barnabas,
      and **expelled** them from their territory.
So they shook the **dust** from their **feet** in **protest** against them,
   and went to **Iconium**.
The **disciples** were filled with **joy** and the Holy **Spirit**.

READING II   Revelation 7:9, 14b–7

A reading from the Book of Revelation

I, **John**, had a vision of a great **multitude**,
   which no one could **count**,
   from every **nation**, **race**, **people** and **tongue**.
They stood before the **throne** and before the **Lamb**,
   wearing white **robes** and holding **palm** branches
      in their hands.

Then one of the **elders** said to me,
   "**These** are the ones who have **survived** the time
      of great **distress**;
   they have **washed** their robes
   and made them **white** in the **blood** of the **Lamb**.

   "For this **reason** they stand before God's **throne**
      and **worship** him **day** and **night** in his **temple**.

This is the third of six consecutive weeks we read from Revelation.

Read slowly. Remember this is a unique form of writing meant to comfort those in distress.

"Nation," "race," "people," and "tongue" are four different images. Don't run them together.

Speak with admiration of these "survivors."

READING II | Throughout the Easter season, we read John's dramatic vision of the heavenly liturgy—a very special kind of literature we must approach with great care. In his vision, John sees the whole world. (The words "nation, race, people and tongue" suggest the universality of his "great multitude.") Assembled before the throne of God and Christ the Lamb, they worship in unison with the angelic host. Remember you are relating a mystical experience, not something you saw while riding the bus. Here is awe and reverence of the highest order. Although "white robes" and "palm branches" symbolize victory and joy, we sense that the prophet sees through the joyous scene to a deeper reality that shuts out the celebrating crowd and offers instead a mystical silence.

The elder identifies the makeup of the crowd: those who survived not just any trial, but the *great* trial. He explains what brought them before the throne with imagery that's especially attractive to people in a hot climate: they will find "shelter," and never again know "hunger" or "thirst," or the sun's ravaging "heat," for they shall find "life giving water." The most striking image is that of the "Lamb" turned "shepherd." Such a role reversal must have been arresting and poignant for people used to seeing real shepherds caring for helpless lambs.

John borrows lyrics from Isaiah, another great poet, for his hymn of comfort, which promises that all sorrow will be blotted out and every tear wiped "from their eyes." Make these images your own by envisioning the relief of hunger, thirst, and grief that caring people today dispense in the name of that same glorious and gentle Lamb.

Make eye contact with the assembly. These lines will be meaningless if the people don't sense these words of comfort are meant for them.

Proclaim the last line slowly. There are those in the assembly who long for God to wipe away their tears. Give them hope.

The one who sits on the throne will **shelter** them.
They will not **hunger** or **thirst** anymore,
    nor will the sun or any heat **strike** them.
For the **Lamb** who is in the **center** of the throne
    will **shepherd** them
    and **lead** them to springs of life-giving water,
    and God will wipe **away** every **tear** from their **eyes**."

GOSPEL   John 10:27–30

A short reading relies on every word to achieve its effect. Do not waste any of these words.

Remember that Jesus is responding to opponents here. Proclaim his words with strength and conviction.

Pause before "and they shall never perish."

Communicate the power of the God who is "greater than all." Pause before the final line. Speak it slowly.

A reading from the holy Gospel according to John

Jesus said:
"My **sheep** hear my **voice**;
    I **know** them, and they **follow** me.
I give them eternal **life**, and they shall never **perish**.
No one can take them out of my **hand**.
My **Father**, who has **given** them to me, is greater than **all**,
    and **no** one can take them out of the **Father's** hand.
The **Father** and I are **one**."

GOSPEL   Just prior to this beautiful testimony to the oneness of the good shepherd and his "sheep," the Jewish authorities command Jesus to speak plainly and tell them whether or not he is the Messiah. Jesus counters that he *already* has told them, but they have not believed him because they "are not among [his] sheep." Then, with the words of today's text, he declares who *are* his sheep: those who "hear" and "follow" him. Awareness of the controversial context of this scene should help you deliver Jesus'

words with vigor and energy—he's not being pietistic; he's refuting his enemies. Jesus' language suggests an affinity between sheep and shepherd that equals oneness. His sheep are safe in his care and never will be snatched from his hand. If the encounter with the hostile authorities makes Jesus defensive, it's not for himself but for those who follow him. No one will rob his sheep of the gift of "eternal life" he intends for them because the omnipotent Father guarantees the gift.

    The text ends with Jesus' most candid public declaration yet of his identity: "The

Father and I are one." His perceived blasphemy almost gets him stoned. This statement of oneness with the Father is how Jesus declares that when he speaks and acts it is the Father who speaks and acts.

Lectionary #54

READING I   Acts 14:21–27

A reading from the Acts of the Apostles

After **Paul** and **Barnabas** had proclaimed the good **news**
   to that city
   and made a considerable number of **disciples**,
      they returned to **Lystra** and to **Iconium** and to **Antioch**.
They strengthened the **spirits** of the disciples
      and **exhorted** them to **persevere** in the **faith**, saying,
      "It is **necessary** for us to undergo many **hardships**
      to enter the kingdom of **God**."
They appointed **elders** for them in each **church** and,
      with **prayer** and **fasting**, commended them to the **Lord**
      in whom they had put their **faith**.
Then they traveled through **Pisidia** and reached **Pamphylia**.
After proclaiming the word at **Perga** they went down to **Attalia**.
From there they sailed to **Antioch**,
      where they had been commended to the grace of **God**
      for the **work** they had now **accomplished**.
And when they **arrived**, they called the church **together**
      and **reported** what God had **done** with them
      and how he had opened the door of **faith** to the **Gentiles**.

This is the fifth of eight consecutive weeks we read from Acts.

"That city" is Derbe. Don't rush the names and stress the missionary effort.

Iconium = ī-KOH-nee-uhm
Antioch = AN-tee-ahk

Stress their effort to reassure the struggling community. Remember that they *know* what it means to suffer for the faith.

There are three actions here: 1) they appointed elders, 2) they prayed and fasted, and 3) they commended them to God.

Pisidia = pih-SID-ee-uh
Pamphylia = pam-FIL-ee-uh
Perga = PER-guh
Attalia = uh-TAHL-ee-uh

They were "commended," that is, they had been "prayed" into their assignment.

They gather the community to share good news.

READING I   On the surface of this reading we have a report of the missionary activities of Paul and Barnabas. But the details express a deeper truth—a conviction that God is doing a new and mighty work through the disciples of Jesus. This work is so compelling that it spreads quickly, despite opposition, throughout the Greco-Roman world. Knowing something about the cities mentioned will help you speak of them familiarly. Try "visiting" these towns by referring to a map (found in most Bibles) of Paul's missionary journeys, noting the geographical relationship of the cities and the part of Asia they occupied. Paul and Barnabas have been to Lystra before: Paul healed a crippled man there. The people at first wanted to worship him, but as if to prove that no good deed goes unpunished, the healing was used against him by opponents and he was stoned and left for dead (Acts 14:8–20). Now, amazingly, Paul returns to this city where he nearly lost his life to monitor the growth of his recent converts. So when he exhorts the disciples that "It is necessary for us to undergo many hardships to enter the kingdom of God" he is speaking from hard experience. One who has come so close to martyrdom can speak convincingly of the need "to persevere" in the face of opposition.

Throughout the Easter season we reflect on the spread of the Gospel. This list of cities must be read (joyfully!) with awareness that God's will was accomplished in these towns through the work (preaching and the appointing of elders) and suffering of the early missionaries. If you had recently returned from a successful peace mission to the Middle East, with

READING II   Revelation 21:1–5a

A reading from the Book of Revelation

Then **I**, **John**, saw a **new** heaven and a new **earth**.
The **former** heaven and the former **earth** had passed **away**,
    and the **sea** was no **more**.
I also saw the holy **city**, a new **Jerusalem**,
    coming down out of **heaven** from **God**,
    prepared as a **bride** adorned for her **husband**.
I heard a loud **voice** from the throne saying,
    "**Behold**, God's **dwelling** is with the human **race**.
He will **dwell** with them and they will be his **people**
    and God **himself** will **always** be with them as their **God**.
He will wipe every **tear** from their **eyes**,
    and there shall be no more **death** or **mourning**, **wailing** or **pain**,
    for the **old** order has passed **away**."

The One who sat on the **throne** said,
    "**Behold**, I make **all** things **new**."

This is the fourth of six consecutive weeks we read from Revelation. "See" the vision as John sees it. Don't rush; persuade us that what you describe is possible.

"Sea" is an archetypal symbol of chaos and death.

Read these lines slowly; this is gorgeous poetry.

The excitement builds. The "voice from the throne" speaks with majesty and authority.

Speak more softly here. Make eye contact with the assembly and give this a very personal quality.

Speak strongly again here. This is the promise of Easter. Announce it with conviction.

---

what kind of energy would you report that news to anxious ears back home?

READING II   **The faithful reading of scripture can render any situation tolerable, for the truths we encounter in its pages foster joyful faith and confident hope, even in people facing grief or crisis. Today's reading is a sample of "apocalyptic" literature written especially to bolster the faith of people living through hard times. But one need not be facing crisis to appreciate it. The key word**

in this text is a word overused and cheapened by advertising media that ceaselessly proclaim, "New and improved!" But your belief in the impossible news of Easter morning should help you speak of the newness promised here with special meaning and conviction. John's vision is not of life beyond, but of life renewed and infused with hope here on earth. It is a message for now, not for the end. The Resurrection inaugurated a new age; the one who died and rose had lived in human flesh among us, but now through word and sacraments, God lives with us forever. Granted, what

John "sees" is not yet fully realized; tears, mourning, pain, and death are still among us, but faith helps us see God at work transforming and renewing and allows us to hope for the day when all those signs of death are gone for good.

John clothes his message in jubilant imagery: Jerusalem is a "bride adorned for her husband!" See the vision as John does, one scene at a time, as if frame after gorgeous frame of the revelation were displayed before you.

A reading from the holy Gospel according to John

When **Judas** had **left** them, **Jesus** said,
   "**Now** is the Son of Man **glorified**, and **God** is glorified **in** him.
If God is **glorified** in him,
   God will **also** glorify him in **himself**,
   and God will glorify him at **once**.
My **children**, I will be with you only a little while **longer**.
I give you a **new commandment: love** one another.
As **I** have loved **you**, so you **also** should love one **another**.
This is how all will **know** that you are my **disciples**,
   if you have **love** for one another."

Proclaim this reading slowly. Listeners *must* hear the allusion to Judas.

Two words distinguish this text: "glorify" and "love." Go slowly to clarify the meaning, or this will sound like gibberish.

The salutation sets the tone. Speak lovingly.

Stress "I" and "you" so we hear the comparison. The tone is personal and intimate, but ramifications are universal.

GOSPEL   Why does mention of Judas open a Gospel of the Easter season? Set in the context of the Last Supper, this soliloquy anticipates Jesus' final glorification which Judas' departure now sets in motion. John equates suffering and glory, for the one leads to the other, hence Judas' ominous departure prompts Jesus' confident assertion that he will be exalted by the Father.

The connection between the seemingly disjointed first and second halves of the reading is provided by Jesus' injunction to "love one another." Not really a new commandment (compare Leviticus 19:18), Jesus, nonetheless, makes it the distinguishing sign of the new people of God. Jesus will be "glorified" not in a palace or on a regal throne, but in the love his followers share for one another. Jesus' announcement of glorification is full of expectant hope. The news that he will remain with them "only a little while longer" is not a melancholic lament, but a promise of better things to come, for as Jesus states later in the discourse, his departure makes possible the coming of the Paraclete.

Jesus offers the hope with which he faces trial as a model for the disciples. He also offers himself as model for the love that must characterize their community. "As I have loved you . . ." reaffirms *his* love for the disciples (and us); "So you also should love . . ." challenges them (and us) to love as he does. In John, this command to love parallels the synoptics' institution of the Eucharist at the Last Supper.

Lectionary #57

READING I   Acts 15:1–2, 22–29

A reading from the Acts of the Apostles

"Some" refers to Jerusalem Pharisees who converted to Christianity.

Their tone may be legalistic and unyielding.

Paul opposed them fiercely, but could not win the argument.

Some who had come down from **Judea** were **instructing**
      the brothers,
   "Unless you are **circumcised** according to the Mosaic **practice**,
   you cannot be **saved**."
Because there arose no little **dissension** and **debate**
      by **Paul** and **Barnabas** with them,
      it was **decided** that Paul, Barnabas, and some of the **others**
      should go up to **Jerusalem** to the **apostles** and **elders**
      about this question.

There is a jump in the narrative here. Start out slowly.

Antioch = AN-tee-ahk

Barsabbas = bar-SAH-buhs

Silas = SI-luhs

The **apostles** and **elders**, in agreement with the whole **church**,
      decided to choose **representatives**
      and to send them to **Antioch** with **Paul** and **Barnabas**.
The ones **chosen** were **Judas**, who was called **Barsabbas**,
      and **Silas**, **leaders** among the brothers.
This is the **letter** delivered by them:

The tone of the letter is conciliatory and pastoral.

Cilicia = sih-LISH-ee-uh

"The **apostles** and the **elders**, your **brothers**,
      to the brothers in **Antioch**, **Syria**, and **Cilicia**
      of **Gentile** origin: **greetings**.
Since we have heard that **some** of our number
      who went out without any **mandate** from us
      have **upset** you with their teachings
      and **disturbed** your peace of **mind**,
   we have with one **accord** decided to choose **representatives**

Those who created the controversy were not speaking for us, but now we *will* speak, and with authority!

READING I   Today's First Reading is challenging for several reasons: it is very long, it has been truncated and robbed of what elements of suspense it contained, and it deals with a controversy known vaguely if at all by most Catholics. But despite these drawbacks, the text is significant for it gives insights into the early Church and underscores the universality of the salvation made possible by Jesus. Here we learn that the early Church experienced controversy from within as well as without, that the spread of the Gospel was sometimes impeded by

those who most desired its growth, and that without the Holy Spirit it might not have spread at all.

   The controversy concerns whether Gentile converts to Christianity must first "become Jews" by submitting to circumcision. On their own authority, some Jewish Christians were instructing Paul's converts that they *must* submit to circumcision. An argument ensues and Paul finally takes the question to a higher authority in Jerusalem. How you speak "it was decided that Paul . . . about this question" can

reveal whether this was an easy decision or a tough compromise.

   The text jumps to the solution offered by the Jerusalem elders. The process they followed and the compromise and unanimity they achieved (no doubt it was difficult letting go of the ancient tradition of circumcision!) are of historical interest because they offer a telling glimpse of the workings of the early Church. Throughout Acts, Jerusalem serves as a center of authority for the Christian communities. Even Paul, who often asserts his equal status with the original twelve, defers to the

and to **send** them to you along with our beloved **Barnabas**
      and **Paul**,
   who have dedicated their **lives** to the name
      of our Lord Jesus **Christ**.
So we are sending **Judas** and **Silas**
   who will also convey this same **message** by word of **mouth**:
   'It is the decision of the Holy **Spirit** and of **us**
   not to place on you any **burden** beyond these **necessities**,
   namely, to abstain from **meat** sacrificed to **idols**,
   from **blood**, from meats of **strangled** animals,
   and from unlawful **marriage**.
If you keep free of **these**,
   you will be doing what is **right. Farewell.'"

Stress the Holy Spirit as source of the decision. You can move through the directives rather quickly.

Speak slowly and with benevolent authority here.

READING II   Revelation 21:10–14, 22–23

A reading from the Book of Revelation

The **angel** took me in **spirit** to a great, high **mountain**
   and showed me the holy city **Jerusalem**
   coming down out of **heaven** from **God**.
It **gleamed** with the splendor of **God**.
Its **radiance** was like that of a precious **stone**,
   like **jasper**, clear as **crystal**.
It had a massive, high **wall**,
   with twelve **gates** where twelve **angels** were stationed
   and on which **names** were inscribed,
   the names of the twelve **tribes** of the **Israelites**.

This is the fifth of six consecutive weeks we read from Revelation.

These words will catch your listeners by surprise, so read them slowly.

Remember that tone is everything. Speak with enthusiasm and joy. Gems suggest the beauty and uniqueness of the Church.

"Gates/tribes" suggests continuity with Israel. The new city is built to last for it has strong gates and a solid foundation.

Jerusalem elders, James, and Peter. When Paul and Barnabas return to Antioch, they will not go back alone, but with representatives who will announce the decision of the Jerusalem Church.

The letter sent to Antioch reviews events with honesty and expresses concern for the disruption caused in the community. Unanimity is again stressed, Paul and Barnabas are diplomatically mentioned, and the decision, ascribed to the Spirit's guidance, is shared. Some clear directives are laid out regarding dietary

practice and avoidance of idolatry and incestuous marriage. But emphasis is placed less on the individual directives than on the desire not to burden the new believers—meaning that this authoritative statement must balance challenge with comfort.

READING II   You are given a text that is layered with symbolism and many descriptive details that could easily be forgotten as soon as the reading ends. So you have two tasks: 1) visualize

all you relate so that your listeners will have clear images that won't fade when you finish reading and 2) realize that here mood is as important as the meaning of individual words. Classical music doesn't rely on spoken words but on rhythm, tempo, intensity and tone color to make an impact on the listener. In the same way, the sound of this reading can communicate the sense of majesty and awe the seer John intended.

By the time of the writing of Revelation, the earthly Jerusalem, Israel's heart, had

There were **three** gates facing **east**,
three **north**, three **south**, and three **west**.
The **wall** of the city had twelve courses of **stones**
as its **foundation**,
on which were inscribed the twelve **names**
of the twelve **apostles** of the **Lamb**.

I saw no **temple** in the city
for its temple is the Lord God **almighty** and the **Lamb**.
The city had no need of **sun** or **moon** to **shine** on it,
for the glory of **God** gave it **light**,
and its **lamp** was the **Lamb**.

Speak of the "apostles" with great reverence.

This is unexpected! The explanation that God is the temple is spoken with rising joy and confidence.

GOSPEL John 14:23–29

A reading from the holy Gospel according to John

Jesus said to his **disciples**:
"Whoever **loves** me will keep my **word**,
and my **Father** will love **him**,
and we will **come** to him and make our **dwelling** with him.
Whoever does **not** love me does **not** keep my words;
yet the word you **hear** is not **mine**
but that of the **Father** who **sent** me.

"I have **told** you this while I am **with** you.
The **Advocate**, the Holy **Spirit**,
whom the **Father** will send in my **name**,
will teach you **everything**
and **remind** you of **all** that I **told** you.

A slow delivery and eye contact are essential. The dialogue hints at the mood: "my Father will love him . . . we will come to him" suggest intimacy and "make our dwelling [home] with him" indicates warmth.

"Dwelling" means "home." "Whoever does not love . . ." reinforces, through contrast, the theme of love and loyalty.

When you have two equivalent terms ("Advocate . . . Holy Spirit"), an increase in intensity is needed on the second term.

been destroyed by the Romans. John witnesses a new, dazzling Jerusalem descending from heaven. Its gates bear the names of Israel's twelve tribes, but the foundation stones are inscribed with the names of the twelve apostles. Speak with affection as you mention them and the Lamb they followed. Of course, John is describing the Church of Christ that stands on the foundation of the apostles and the rich tradition of Israel.

Use the words "gleamed," "splendor," "radiance," "massive," and "high" to suggest the wonder the vision inspires. The oft

repeated number "twelve" connotes the perfection of the new believing community. Shift your focus from one part of the vision to another as you describe it, as if it were there before you.

The last paragraph presents the most startling realization: "no temple" adorns the city. Stone and mortar aren't needed here, for "the Lord God almighty" takes the place of the temple. And Christ, the Lamb, so pervades his Church that no building could contain him and no light, not even the sun or moon, could shine as bright as he!

GOSPEL If you didn't know this dialogue was spoken in the context of the Last Supper, you might think it was a farewell discourse issuing from the mouth of the risen-though-not-yet-ascended Jesus who prepares to return to the Father. But despite its original context, and given its use in this pre-Ascension liturgy, a farewell tone would not be inappropriate for your proclamation.

Jesus begins by contrasting those who do and do not love him. The difference is simple: they do or don't keep his words, which are not really his words, but the

Speak this classic line slowly and with great warmth.

Jesus takes great care to explain what he is doing to spare them misunderstanding or fear and to build their faith.

Peace I leave with you; my peace I **give** to you.
Not as the **world** gives do **I** give it to you.
Do not let your hearts be **troubled** or **afraid**.
You heard me **tell** you,
  'I am going **away** and I will come **back** to you.'
If you **loved** me,
    you would **rejoice** that I am going to the **Father**;
    for the Father is **greater** than I.
And now I have **told** you this before it **happens**,
    so that **when** it happens you may **believe**."

Father's. Jesus reminds the disciples, and all listening today, that his departure does not leave us orphaned. The word of the Father remains, and the Paraclete will come. He speaks of the sending of the Spirit in a way that suggests an *imminent* departure. There is a sense of commissioning in his words, an implied "Be ready!" for what the Spirit will do among them— remind them of all that Jesus taught them.

Jesus then imparts his peace, *his* peace, not the world's, for his is a peace that penetrates the heart and cancels fear.

This conferral of peace can be experienced by your assembly as a "now" moment, not a distant memory. After all, doesn't Christ offer us that same peace in every liturgy? As he imparts this final gift, Jesus seems to be saying: You would *rejoice* if you knew what I know and could see what I see. By opening the eyes of the apostles to truth they only dimly perceive, he offers them hope and comfort. Jesus' final words demonstrate the concern of a true teacher and friend: "I have told you before it happens . . . so that you may believe." Jesus is ensuring the very peace he earlier promised, guard-

ing it against the fear and troubled hearts that could so easily snatch it from them. It's just another sign of his great love for them and us. We, too, are believers whose vision sometimes blurs. So speak Jesus' words reassuringly to every person in the assembly who glimpses the truth while longing for its fulfillment.

MAY 13

180 ASCENSION OF THE

This is wha
they ask
and ins
cont

ASCENSION OF THE LORD

Lectionary #58

READING I   Acts 1:1–11

A reading from the beginning of the Acts of the Apostles

You are communicating a faith story, not a history. Speak with great intentionality: Luke is trying to persuade.
Theophilus = thee-OF-uh-luhs

In the **first** book, Theophilus,
    I dealt with all that Jesus **did** and **taught**
    until the day he was taken **up**,
    after giving **instructions** through the Holy **Spirit**
    to the **apostles** whom he had **chosen**.

Stress the work of the Spirit here.

He presented himself **alive** to them
    by many **proofs** after he had **suffered**,
    appearing to them during **forty** days
    and **speaking** about the kingdom of **God**.
While **meeting** with them,
    he enjoined them not to depart from **Jerusalem**,

"Forty" is a number that expresses an indeterminate, but sacred, period of time during which Jesus appeared to and instructed the disciples.

    but to **wait** for "the promise of the **Father**
    about which you have heard me **speak**;
    for **John** baptized with **water**,
    but in a few days **you** will be baptized with the Holy **Spirit**."

Note that "the promise of the Father . . . " is a quotation of Jesus. Adjust the tone to convey the mid-sentence shift.

When they had gathered **together** they asked him,
    "**Lord**, are you at **this** time going to restore
    the **kingdom** to Israel?"

Although they should know better, it's an innocent question.

He **answered** them, "It is not for **you** to know the **times**
    or **seasons**
    that the Father has established by his own **authority**.

If the Ascension of the Lord is celebrated next Sunday, today's readings are used in place of those for the Seventh Sunday of Easter.

READING I   Luke is responsible for much of what we know of Jesus and the early Church. Today he speaks to us in both the First Reading and the Gospel, relating two different versions of Jesus' Ascension. The shorter, simpler version recounted in the Gospel *concludes* and reviews Jesus' earthly ministry; but in this account from Acts, Jesus *inaugurates*

the Church's mission, urging on the disciples the work of advancing the kingdom of God. In the Gospel, Jesus speaks of "staying" and "returning," but the language of Acts is all about action: "you will be baptized," "you will receive power," "you will be my witnesses," "why are you standing there looking at the sky?" Acts presents the embryonic Church beginning to realize: we're here to stay and we've work to do! By the time Acts was written, the belief that the world would soon end and Jesus would return in glory had faded. So the young Church rolled up its sleeves to

tackle the work Jesus gave them. There is no gloom or despondency in these lines, only confidence that this young community will carry on in Jesus' name.

The stately and polished writing of Acts is addressed to "Theophilus," apparently a person of some political or social consequence (although some commentators suggest the name refers to anyone who loves God, as "Theophilus" means "lover of God"). Remember that this is a narrative, not a newscast. The story it tells has shaped our faith and deserves our greatest respect and reverence. According

he gives in place of what
d for. His words both reassure
pire his friends. This prophecy
ues being fulfilled to this day.

Speak slowly and with a sense of awe.
This is not an ordinary occurrence.
"While they were . . . " retains the mood
of the previous line. Break the mood on
"Suddenly . . . ."

The angels' tone is not berating, but
"nudging." The word "return" should
alert your assembly to the need to
be ready.

But you will receive **power** when the Holy **Spirit** comes upon you,
   and you will be my **witnesses** in **Jerusalem**,
      throughout **Judea** and **Samaria**,
      and to the **ends** of the **earth**."
When he had **said** this, as they were **looking** on,
   he was **lifted** up, and a cloud **took** him from their **sight**.
While they were looking **intently** at the **sky** as he was **going**,
   suddenly two **men** dressed in white **garments**
      stood **beside** them.
They said, "Men of **Galilee**,
   why are you **standing** there looking at the **sky**?
This **Jesus** who has been taken **up** from you into **heaven**
   will **return** in the same way as you have seen him
      going into heaven."

READING II   Ephesians 1:17–23

A reading from the Letter of Saint Paul to the Ephesians

Brothers and sisters:
May the **God** of our Lord Jesus **Christ**, the Father of **glory**,
   give you a Spirit of **wisdom** and **revelation**
   resulting in **knowledge** of him.
May the eyes of your **hearts** be **enlightened**,
   that you may know what is the **hope** that belongs to his call,
   what are the riches of **glory**
   in his **inheritance** among the holy **ones**,
   and what is the surpassing **greatness** of his **power**
   for us who **believe**,
   in accord with the **exercise** of his great **might**:

This is a prayer.

You want us to know three things (hope,
riches, and power), so build your energy
from the first to the last.

God exalts us in the way he first exalted
Christ. You are praising Christ with
these words.

to Luke, it is a story of the Holy Spirit guid-
ing the new community and spreading the
good news of Jesus. So the two references
to the Spirit in the text need to be highlighted. A striking feature of the story is
the question the disciples put to Jesus;
even to the end they do not understand that
Jesus has not come to establish an earthly
kingdom, and to the end Jesus must be the
patient teacher. Rather than the special
knowledge they seek, Jesus promises the
"power" of the Spirit, and then disappears
before them.

The exhortation of the "two [angelic]
men" reinforces the "Let's get to it!"
feel of this passage. The angels' promise
that Jesus "will return," is a hint to the
disciples — and us! — that they must
always be ready.

There is a choice of readings today.
Speak with the liturgy coordinator or the
homilist to find out which reading will
be used.

READING II   EPHESIANS. This jubilant
hymn of praise begins as a
greeting and continues as a prayer. The
author first prays that the reader will be
blessed with "wisdom" and "knowledge"
of God. He goes on to pray that every
believer be granted insight into the mighty
plan of God that unfolded in the life of
Jesus, who died and rose, and now sits in
power at the right hand of God. This Jesus,
who made available to humanity the riches
of God's glory—our salvation—sits on a
heavenly throne with "all things beneath
his feet" and reigns there as head of his

which he worked in **Christ**,
raising him from the **dead**
and **seating** him at his right **hand** in the **heavens**,
far **above** every **principality**, **authority**, **power**, and **dominion**,
and every **name** that is **named**
not only in **this** age but **also** in the one to **come**.
And he put all **things** beneath his **feet**
and gave him as **head** over all things to the **church**,
which is his **body**,
the **fullness** of the one who fills **all** things in every **way**.

Or:

"Principality," "authority," "power," and
"dominion" are four distinct images.
Don't speed through them.

"He" is the Father; "him" is Christ. "Gave
him as head" means that the Father made
Christ the head of the Church. Speak with
joy and gratitude.

READING II Hebrews 9:24–28; 10:19–23

A reading from the Letter to the Hebrews

Christ did not enter into a sanctuary made by **hands**,
  a **copy** of the true one, but heaven **itself**,
  that he might now appear before **God** on our **behalf**.
Not that he might offer himself **repeatedly**,
  as the high **priest** enters each **year** into the sanctuary
  with **blood** that is not his **own**;
  if **that** were so, he would have had to suffer **repeatedly**
  from the **foundation** of the **world**.
But **now** once for **all** he has appeared at the **end** of the ages
  to take away **sin** by his **sacrifice**.
Just as it is appointed that men and women die **once**,
  and **after** this the **judgment**, so also **Christ**,
  offered **once** to take away the **sins** of **many**,

Throughout this reading, you are persuading, teaching, and making strong the faint of heart.

Stress the contrast between the repeated sacrifice of the high priest and Christ's "once for all" sacrifice.

You are making a comparison here. Just as we live and die only once, so Christ lived and died only once to save us from our sins.

body, the Church. That announcement, found in the closing lines, climaxes the reading and is the point toward which all the beautiful language and compelling imagery flow.

The passage consists of only three sentences, but each is complex and easily could become a labyrinth in which you and your listeners get lost. Identify the ideas in each sentence, then use pauses and slow pacing to present one thought at a time as you build toward the conclusion—remembering, all the while, you're speaking a prayer.

The first sentence is easiest: two identifications for God and a request for "wisdom" and "revelation." The second sentence asks that the reader be enlightened about *three* things: "the hope" that results from God's call, the "riches of glory," and "the greatness of [God's] power." In Baptism, God raised all of "us who believe" to positions of glory in the same way God raised Jesus from the dead and exalted him above every creature in heaven and on earth. The final sentence asserts that, as his body, we share in the exaltation and lordship of Jesus, our head,

who fills us at every moment with his presence. The message of this text is quite beautiful, but it will take practice and hard work to make the sound of the words as beautiful as their meaning.

HEBREWS. Addressed to Jewish Christians who were in danger of abandoning their faith in Christ—not because of persecution or danger, but because they had grown tired of living the Christian life and had begun to grow cold in their commitment to Christ—this letter seeks to encourage and strengthen its readers, firm up their faith, and give them hope. Here,

Here's what it all adds up to: we can approach God with confidence and hope.

"Flesh" is not the "way" he opened; it is the "veil" that stood in the way.

Look at the assembly and offer them the conviction that Christ's promises are trustworthy.

will appear a **second** time, not to take away **sin**
but to bring **salvation** to those who eagerly **await** him.

Therefore, brothers and sisters, since through the **blood** of **Jesus**
we have confidence of **entrance** into the **sanctuary**
by the **new** and **living** way he **opened** for us through the **veil**,
that is, his **flesh**,
and since we have "a **great** priest over the house of **God**,"
let us approach with a **sincere** heart and in absolute **trust**,
with our hearts sprinkled **clean** from an evil **conscience**
and our bodies **washed** in pure **water**.
Let us hold **unwaveringly** to our **confession** that gives us **hope**,
for he who made the **promise** is **trustworthy**.

GOSPEL   Luke 24:46–53

A reading from the holy Gospel according to Luke

Jesus said to his **disciples**:
"Thus it is written that the **Christ** would **suffer**
and **rise** from the dead on the third **day**
and that **repentance**, for the forgiveness of **sins**,
would be **preached** in his **name**
to all the **nations**, beginning from **Jerusalem**.
You are **witnesses** of these things.
And **behold** I am sending the **promise** of my Father upon you;
but stay in the **city**
until you are clothed with **power** from on **high**."

There are eleven "disciples," not twelve. Jesus reviews two features of his ministry: suffering and preaching repentance.

Make eye contact with the assembly and include them among the "witnesses."

The "promise of my Father" is the Spirit. Speak with conviction. Jesus' dialogue ends here.

---

the author compares the "once for all" unique sacrifice of Christ with the animal sacrifices offered over and over by the high priests of Jewish ritual. As sacred as the Holy of Holies was in Jewish tradition, the author says this "sanctuary made by hands" is nothing compared to where Christ has entered—heaven itself and the very presence of the almighty God. His sacrifice, in which he offered his *own* blood, is eternally valid. Christ took away sin by taking it upon himself; no other sacrifice will ever be needed. Just as death is a door we can pass through only once in

human life, so Christ's sacrifice is an offering that can be made only once for all eternity. Christ will come again, but when he does, it will not be to once more cleanse us of our sins, but to bring salvation to all who await him.

The consequences of Christ's priesthood and sacrifice are stated in the long first sentence of the final paragraph. Because of Christ, Christians can now enter confidently into the house of God. We have been washed clean in the waters of Baptism. We have a great high priest who intercedes before God's throne. Therefore,

we should enter the sanctuary with pure bodies, sincere hearts, and clear consciences. Those who have grown lukewarm should hold fast to the promises they embraced in Baptism. Such is the encouragement of this letter. Speak it with conviction for surely some in your assembly have grown weary with living the demands of the faith. Assure them that Christ's promises are solid and trustworthy.

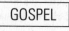 **GOSPEL** The verse that immediately precedes today's Gospel

This is a new scene. Narrate it slowly. It would seem that, as he ascends, Jesus is revealed in all his glory, for the disciples respond by falling down and worshipping.

Then he **led** them out as far as **Bethany**,
    raised his hands, and **blessed** them.
As he **blessed** them he **parted** from them
    and was **taken** up to **heaven**.
They did him **homage**
    and then returned to **Jerusalem** with great **joy**,
    and they were continually in the **temple** praising **God**.

passage reveals Jesus' objective in this encounter: "Then he opened their minds to understand the scriptures." One last time Jesus reviews two of the salient features of his ministry: suffering, which led to death and Resurrection, and proclamation of the Good News of the forgiveness of sins. The review is intended to prepare the disciples to be better "witnesses" of all they have seen and heard from Jesus. Once reminded, Jesus assures them that the Holy Spirit will "clothe" and confirm them in this knowledge and understanding, but "stay in

the city" indicates the new chapter will begin only after this last one has ended.

Unlike the account related in Acts that depicts the Ascension as the inaugural moment of the time of the Church, this account concludes the time of Jesus. The first half of the reading looks forward to the Spirit-guided work of the Church, but the Ascension narrative itself is a farewell scene. The mood, therefore, differs from that of the Acts account. We don't sense here the excitement of new efforts and directions. It is a slower scene. More time is spent on the departure than in the Acts

version: "He led them . . . blessed them . . . parted from them, and was taken up." The disciples respond by falling down to do him "homage" ("worship" in other translations), the only instance of such reverence in Luke.

The disciples don't mourn Jesus' departure. Instead, buoyed by his blessing and perhaps eager for the coming of the promised Spirit, they return "with great joy" to the temple, the place where Luke's Gospel began.

7TH SUNDAY OF EASTER

Lectionary #61

READING I   Acts 7:55–60

A reading from the Acts of the Apostles

Stephen, filled with the Holy **Spirit**,
    looked up intently to **heaven** and saw the glory of **God**
    and **Jesus** standing at the right **hand** of God,
    and Stephen said, "**Behold**, I see the heavens **opened**
    and the Son of **Man** standing at the right **hand** of **God**."
But they **cried** out in a **loud** voice,
    covered their ears, and **rushed** upon him **together**.
They **threw** him out of the **city**, and began to **stone** him.
The **witnesses** laid down their **cloaks**
    at the **feet** of a young man named **Saul**.
As they were **stoning** Stephen, he **called** out,
    "Lord **Jesus**, receive my **spirit**."
Then he fell to his **knees** and cried out in a loud **voice**,
    "**Lord**, do not hold this sin **against** them";
    and when he **said** this, he fell **asleep**.

You can hardly describe this scene as a disinterested narrator. Imagine yourself a believer for whom Stephen is a faith hero and use the story to inspire your listeners.

Without over-dramatizing, create the reality of his vision, stressing the Holy Spirit. Awesome realities sometimes overwhelm us into hushed tones.

They cover their ears to block out his supposed blasphemy. Does the narrator relate the stoning with regret or with righteous anger?

Although the text doesn't say so, your tone can reveal that "Saul" is not just another member of the mob.

The narrative bridge in the middle of Stephen's prayer ("then he fell . . . loud voice") can retain the emotional intensity of the prayer itself. Here, volume and intensity are not necessarily synonymous.

Your announcement of Stephen's death should not move us to outrage but to prayer. Note the euphemism for his death: "he fell asleep."

If the Ascension of the Lord is celebrated today, please see pages 179–183 for the appropriate readings.

READING I   In its first martyr, Stephen, the early Church learns the full cost of discipleship. Stephen has been brought before the Sanhedrin on charges of denigrating Moses and the temple, of which, in a way, he was guilty for he elevated Jesus over Moses and the temple. In response to his accusers, Stephen launches into an impassioned discourse, which Luke ascribes, in his trademark way, to the inspiration of the Holy Spirit. In mid-speech, Stephen receives a vision of the glorified Christ. Jesus, the Son of Man, he announces, is standing at the right hand of God! In effect, he's telling the Sanhedrin that what Jesus prophesied at his own trial has now been fulfilled. To the authorities, this affront is nothing short of blasphemy; they react quickly and with great vengeance, leading him out of the city to stone him. Significantly, some lay their robes at the feet "of a young man named Saul," who, of course, will later become Paul the apostle.

In imitation of his Lord, Stephen forgives the very ones who take his life. When he first appeared before the Council, all who looked at him saw that "his face was like the face of an angel." Here Stephen proves his profound spirituality in making his dying prayer that Christ would receive his spirit and forgive his killers.

READING II   After listening to Stephen's last words, we now hear the final words of John's great vision.

READING II   Revelation 22:12–14, 16–17, 20

A reading from the Book of Revelation

I, **John**, heard a **voice** saying to me:
　"**Behold**, I am coming **soon**.
I bring with me the **recompense** I will give to **each**
　according to his **deeds**.
I am the **Alpha** and the **Omega**, the **first** and the **last**,
　the **beginning** and the **end**."

Blessed are they who **wash** their robes
　so as to have the **right** to the tree of **life**
　and enter the **city** through its **gates**.

"**I, Jesus**, sent my **angel** to give you this **testimony**
　for the churches.
I am the **root** and offspring of **David**,
　the bright morning **star**."

The **Spirit** and the **bride** say, "**Come**."
Let the **hearer** say, "**Come**."
Let the one who **thirsts** come **forward**,
　and the one who **wants** it receive the **gift** of life-giving **water**.

The one who gives this **testimony** says, "**Yes**, I am coming **soon**."
Amen! **Come**, Lord Jesus!

Although we are not in crisis in the way the original audience of this message was, can we fail to be comforted by assurances of reward, or perhaps somewhat shaken by the promise of receiving what we deserve.

Use a vocal shift from "John" to voice of the vision.

Alpha = AHL-fuh
Omega = oh-MAY-guh

Build on each pair of titles. They serve as promises of assistance, as if he were saying, "Call on me."

"The city" is the heavenly Jerusalem.

The tone is personal and full of comfort.

Each sentence is a separate thought. Speak with conviction.

"I am coming soon" is spoken with joy! "Amen, come . . ." is a final hope-filled prayer.

Parting words often possess urgency, more overt feeling, and greater honesty.

After the first line, the majority of the text is spoken entirely by Jesus in a tone reminiscent of Advent watchfulness: "Behold, I am coming soon!" As a message intended for people in crisis, the words of Jesus offer comfort and hope, but also warning: Jesus comes "with recompense," but it will be given to each "according to his deeds." Let Jesus' words comfort anyone in the assembly who faces personal crises or worries over the problems of the world. Jesus' self-identification is spoken not to say who he is but what he offers—he is the source of life, the beginning and the end, all we want and need are found in him! Let your tone assure us that Jesus can and will answer our hearts' desire. The second set of self-identifications is also spoken as promises, each of them positive, each offering life (he grants access to the "tree of life" and to "life-giving water!"). In "Blessed are they . . ." it's possible to hear both promise and warning—some will wash their robes, but perhaps not all.

It's the voice of John that concludes the passage and the entire New Testament with a beautiful prayer in which the Spirit and the whole Church ("the bride") long for Christ's return. Jesus promises to come "soon" (that is, "swiftly" or "suddenly"). John's "Amen" is, in every age, the constant prayer of the Church. Make it yours as you say, "Come, Lord Jesus!"

GOSPEL Jesus' "high priestly prayer" to his Father is overheard by the disciples just before Jesus' arrest. The prayer expresses Jesus' deepest feelings for his disciples, and for those who

A reading from the holy Gospel according to John

Lifting up his eyes to **heaven**, Jesus **prayed** saying:
"Holy **Father**, I pray not only for **them**,
   but **also** for those who will **believe** in me through their **word**,
   so that they may all be **one**,
   as **you**, Father, are in **me** and **I** in **you**,
   that **they** also may be in **us**,
   that the **world** may **believe** that you **sent** me.
And I have given them the **glory** you gave **me**,
   so that **they** may be one, as **we** are one,
   I in **them** and **you** in **me**,
   that they may be brought to **perfection** as one,
   that the **world** may know that you **sent** me,
   and that you loved **them** even as you loved **me**.
Father, they are your **gift** to me.
I wish that where **I** am they **also** may be with me,
   that they may see my **glory** that you **gave** me,
   because you **loved** me before the **foundation** of the **world**.
Righteous **Father**, the **world** also does not **know** you,
   but **I** know you, and they know that you **sent** me.
I **made** known to them your **name** and I **will** make it known,
   that the **love** with which you loved **me**
   may be in **them** and I in them."

Looking to heaven and addressing God as Father are characteristic of Jesus at prayer.

Almost every line states a new idea. Don't rush. The language is simple and direct, yet its impact is poetic and uplifting.

Our oneness testifies to Christ.

"They are your gift. . . " requires careful stress. Express his longing that we who love him could be forever with him.

Address God with the tenderness that suggests the intimacy of Father and Son.

He will "make it known" by sending the Holy Spirit.

Make sure this has had the feel of a prayer. Pause before announcing the words "The Gospel of the Lord."

---

will come to faith through them. Since today's liturgy retains an Ascension Day flavor, the farewell tone of the prayer is most apropos. Jesus has thoroughly identified with his followers and now he wishes for them the same unity with each other and with God that he himself enjoys. The prayer is very dense—almost every line contains a new thought or petition. Because it is a prayer and because of how much is packed into the lines, you must proceed very slowly. Jesus' voice rings with strength and with concern for the welfare of the

friends he leaves behind, yet the prayer is never maudlin. Sentimentality would rob the text of its beauty and pervasive dignity.

The frequent use of "I" and "me" and the familiarity with which Jesus addresses the Father reveal the immensely personal character of the prayer. Jesus speaks of his followers as God's *gift* to him and prays that they might come to share in the glory God gave him from before the world began. Recall that this prayer is spoken shortly before Jesus' arrest. In John, the connection is strong between Jesus' glorification and his Passion.

Jesus prays with tremendous confidence in God, his disciples, and in us who believe because of them. Let this be a prayer for the kind of oneness that makes the world say: "See how they love one another."

PENTECOST: VIGIL

Lectionary #62

READING I   Genesis 11:1–9

A reading from the Book of Genesis

The whole **world** spoke the same **language**, using the same **words**.
While the people were **migrating** in the **east**,
    they came upon a **valley** in the land of **Shinar** and **settled** there.
They **said** to one another,
    "**Come**, let us mold **bricks** and **harden** them with **fire**."
They used bricks for **stone**, and bitumen for **mortar**.
Then they said, "**Come**, let us build ourselves a **city**
    and a **tower** with its top in the **sky**,
    and so make a **name** for ourselves;
    otherwise we shall be **scattered** all over the **earth**."

The LORD came down to **see** the city and the **tower**
    that the people had built.
Then the LORD said: "If **now**, while they are **one** people,
    all speaking the **same** language,
    they have started to do **this**,
    nothing will **later** stop them from doing
        whatever they **presume** to do.
Let us then go **down** there and **confuse** their language,
    so that one will not **understand** what another **says**."
Thus the LORD **scattered** them from **there** all over the **earth**,
    and they **stopped** building the city.

Side notes (left margin):

As narrator, you know this innocent age is lost.

Shinar = SHĪ-nahr

Speak with the arrogance that motivates their defiance.

bitumen = bih-TYOO-m*n

Their plan is in direct defiance of God's order to "fill the earth." They plan to enhance their own reputation without any help from God.

This is a new scene. Suggest the disapproval with which God views the city and tower.

God is not being vindictive, but rather protecting humanity from itself.

This would be the reply if an ancient child asked, "Why do people speak different languages?"

There is a choice of readings today. Speak with the liturgy coordinator or the homilist to find out which reading will be used.

READING I   GENESIS. The first 11 chapters of Genesis chronicle the spread of sin and its alienating consequences: the sin of Adam leads to the sin of Cain that leads to Babel that leads to Noah's flood. The solemnity of Pentecost celebrates God's undoing of what is powerfully depicted in this passage — the alienation of neighbor from neighbor and nation from nation. In one sense, the story functions like many ancient folk tales, explaining how people came to speak different languages. But it is also a theological exploration of sin, addressing why nations are divided.

To our industrial age these ambitious builders may seem more virtuous than sinful. But this is a story of human ambition competing with divinity, men and women wanting to be like gods. The people's sin consists in wanting to "make a name" for themselves, that is, on their own, independent of God who will later promise Abraham "*I* . . . will make your name great" (12:2). Further, although God had commanded humanity to "fill the earth" (1:28), they now defiantly refuse to "be scattered." And with their tower, the people seek to invade the very domain of God. Plainly, human pride has swelled to a point that God can no longer tolerate. But what is sinful in the people's behavior will not be immediately apparent to your listeners, so your tone will have to suggest that what you describe is in opposition to God's will. Do that on phrases like "Come, let us mold . . . . Come, let us build . . . ." Speak the lines

Speak with conviction that what God has accomplished is just.

That is why it was called **Babel**,
    because there the LORD **confused** the speech of all the **world**.
It was from that **place** that he **scattered** them all over the **earth**.

Or:

READING I   Exodus 19:3–8a, 16–20b

With the opening narration you must intimate that Moses' ascent up the mountain is no ordinary climb; he is about to meet his God.

God recounts Israel's deliverance from slavery with incredible intimacy: God brings Israel not to the mountain, but "to myself." The covenant is "my covenant" and Israel is God's "special possession," the nation that is "holy."

Stress the conditions God sets.

"Kingdom of priests" refers to the nation as a whole. Among the nations, Israel is as special as are the priests among the people.

This is a solemn yet joyful statement of assent to God's conditions.

A reading from the Book of Exodus

Moses went up the **mountain** to **God**.
Then the LORD **called** to him and said,
    "**Thus** shall you say to the house of **Jacob**;
    tell the Israelites:
    You have seen for **yourselves** how I treated the **Egyptians**
    and how I **bore** you up on **eagle** wings
    and **brought** you here to **myself**.
Therefore, if you **hearken** to my voice and **keep** my **covenant**,
    you shall be my **special possession**,
    dearer to me than all **other** people,
    though **all** the earth is **mine**.
You shall be to me a **kingdom** of **priests**, a holy **nation**.
That is what you must tell the **Israelites**."
So Moses **went** and **summoned** the elders of the people.
When he **set** before them
    all that the LORD had **ordered** him to tell them,
    the people all answered **together**,
    "**Everything** the LORD has **said**, we will **do**."

---

with the pride that motivates their efforts. "Otherwise, we shall be scattered" conveys their intent to thwart God's will: they would rather build a great city than go to their appointed homelands.

God's response is decisive and swift, but the divine emotions are surprisingly human. God appears almost frightened or jealous. The Bible is never uncomfortable with ascribing human emotions to God, so don't you be either. God acts not out of vindictiveness, but for the good of humanity, like a parent chastising a presumptuous child. God's sovereign will prevails, but

humanity has paid the price of rebellion with confused speech and shattered unity.

EXODUS. The events described in this reading are but a climactic prelude to an even more significant moment in salvation history, the giving of the commandments at Mount Sinai and the sealing of the covenant that established Israel as God's Chosen People. In this event, Israel (in the person of Moses) experiences a very significant encounter with God. So important is this encounter that Exodus devotes an entire chapter to the preparations for it. Everything about this face to face meeting

with God suggests awe—fear, wonder, and reverence.

God tells Moses to remind the people of how God delivered them from Egyptian slavery. Next comes an "if/then" proposition: *If* you keep my law, says God, *then* I will make you the apple of my eye. The "scandal" of such favoritism—God choosing this one people from among all the people of the earth—is asserted boldly and with no apology. Not only that, but God will make the people a nation of "priests" consecrated to God's service. The God of

Describe the great theophany (manifestation of God's powerful presence) with a sense of awe.

Fire and smoke are common manifestaions of God. Wind and fire imagery dominate Pentecost.

"Trumpet" may be a metaphor for a strong, driving wind.

Speak slowly here. There is great suspense in this line.

On the morning of the **third** day
    there were peals of **thunder** and **lightning**,
    and a heavy **cloud** over the mountain,
    and a very loud **trumpet** blast,
    so that all the people in the camp **trembled**.
But **Moses** led the people **out** of the camp to meet **God**,
    and they **stationed** themselves at the **foot** of the mountain.
Mount **Sinai** was all wrapped in **smoke**,
    for the LORD came down upon it in **fire**.
The smoke **rose** from it as though from a **furnace**,
    and the whole mountain trembled **violently**.
The **trumpet** blast grew **louder** and **louder**,
      while Moses was **speaking**,
    and God **answering** him with **thunder**.

When the LORD came **down** to the top of Mount Sinai,
    he **summoned** Moses to the **top** of the mountain.

Or:

READING I   Ezekiel 37:1–14

A reading from the Book of the Prophet Ezekiel

The hand of the LORD came upon me,
    and he **led** me out in the **spirit** of the LORD
    and **set** me in the center of the **plain**,
    which was now **filled** with **bones**.
He made me **walk** among the **bones** in every **direction**
    so that I saw how **many** they were on the surface of the plain.
How **dry** they were!

To enhance rather than slight the unique features of this text (the refrain-like repetitions and the extraordinary visions), you will need extra preparation time. The style and content of this writing is quite different from contemporary prose, so prepare until you are comfortable with and enjoying the rich imagery and poetic flow of the language.
Ezekiel finds himself transported into the midst of this scene of devastation.

thunder and lightening comes later in the reading, in this first encounter God is awesome, yet comforting and caring. God's tender love, as relayed to the people by Moses, evokes their heartfelt assent: "Everything . . . we will do!"

    Fire and smoke are common Old Testament signs of God's presence. The awe-inspiring, fireworks-filled scene at the foot of the mountain brings together the two parties who are about to transact a covenant—Israel and their awesome God.

But the atmospheric display that powerfully manifests God's presence so overwhelms Moses and the people that they must overcome fear to approach God. The final, suspenseful, line should insinuate that the real excitement waits at "the top of the mountain."

    EZEKIEL. Some events can shake a nation to its core. September 11, 2001, was such an event in United States history. For ancient Israel the exile was a disorienting trauma that truly tested its faith. The most unthinkable part of the tragedy was the

utter destruction of the city of Jerusalem and its temple. This profound shock brought the people to despair. Ezekiel prophesied *during* the exile, predicting the restoration of Israel at this time when all hope had been abandoned. God challenges that despair by granting Ezekiel this vision of the dry bones. Ezekiel is made to linger among the bones so that he comprehends fully the utter destitution they represent. Then God asks, "Can these bones come to life?" He wants to awaken hope in the

God orders Ezekiel to prophesy. Speak these words with authority.

He **asked** me:

Son of man, can these **bones** come to **life**?

I answered, "Lord GOD, you **alone** know that."

Then he said to me:

Prophesy over these bones, and **say** to them:

Dry **bones**, hear the word of the LORD!

Thus says the Lord GOD to these bones:

See! I will bring **spirit** into you, that you may come to **life**.

I will put **sinews** upon you, make **flesh** grow over you,

cover you with **skin**, and put **spirit** in you

so that you may come to **life** and know that I am the LORD.

I, **Ezekiel**, **prophesied** as I had been **told**,

Don't overdramatize these events; they should have an air of reality.

and even as I was **prophesying** I heard a **noise**;

it was a **rattling** as the bones came **together**, **bone** joining **bone**.

I saw the **sinews** and the **flesh** come upon them,

and the **skin** cover them, but there was no **spirit** in them.

Then the LORD said to me:

These repetitions, like the repeated phrases of a song, add beauty to the text and etch its message in our memories. Don't treat them like redundancies to be gotten around as quickly as possible. Only when they receive God's spirit do the bones come alive.

Prophesy to the **spirit**, **prophesy**, son of man,

and **say** to the spirit: Thus says the Lord GOD:

From the four winds **come**, O spirit,

and **breathe** into these **slain** that they may come to **life**.

I prophesied as he **told** me, and the spirit **came** into them;

they came **alive** and stood **upright**, a vast **army**.

Then he said to me:

Son of **man**, these bones are the whole **house** of **Israel**.

They have been saying,

"Our bones are **dried up**,

our **hope** is **lost**, and we are cut **off**."

prophet and the people. But hope is hard to kindle in Ezekiel's heart and his faint-hearted response ("You alone know that") only deepens the hopelessness of the scene. Help us hear his despondency in the way you speak the line.

God takes charge, ordering Ezekiel to speak God's Spirit into the very bones. The ensuing scene is heart-stopping. Amid the roar of wind and rattling bones, flesh, sin-ews and skin appear on the skeletons. But the restoration happens in stages: first comes "life," and then "spirit" follows. The powerful symbolism is a promise to Israel

that the ordeal of exile will come to an end: the nation will be restored, the temple rebuilt, for God may chastise but never abandon the chosen people. The Spirit that restores these dry bones is the same Spirit that descends on the disciples at Pentecost and still guides the Church. Don't cheapen the beauty of the vision by being embar-rassed by its starkness or by overdramatiz-ing. God's command ("Prophesy, son of man, prophesy") is the breath that sustains the passage. Experience these amazing

events through Ezekiel's eyes and describe them with his attitude of wonder.

JOEL. The nation was beset by a dev-astating plague of locusts, and the prophet Joel viewed this as God's judgment against the people who had grown cold in their faith. When Joel called the nation to repen-tance, the people responded with genuine contrition. In answer to their repentance, God had already promised the material blessing of a restored land. But now God promises even more significant blessings that are to take three forms.

Therefore, **prophesy** and say to them: **Thus** says the Lord **GOD**:
    O my **people**, I will open your **graves**
    and have you **rise** from them,
    and bring you **back** to the land of **Israel**.
Then you shall **know** that I am the LORD,
    when I **open** your graves and have you **rise** from them,
    O my **people**!
I will put my **spirit** in you that you may **live**,
    and I will **settle** you upon your **land**;
    thus you shall **know** that I am the LORD.
I have **promised**, and I will **do** it, says the LORD.

Or:

READING I   Joel 3:1–5

A reading from the Book of the Prophet Joel

Thus says the LORD:
I will pour out my **spirit** upon all **flesh**.
Your **sons** and **daughters** shall **prophesy**,
    your **old** men shall dream **dreams**,
    your **young** men shall see **visions**;
even upon the **servants** and the **handmaids**,
    in those **days**, I will pour out my **spirit**.
And I will work **wonders** in the **heavens** and on the **earth**,
    blood, **fire**, and columns of **smoke**;
the **sun** will be turned to **darkness**,
    and the **moon** to **blood**,

This promise should arouse hope in the listener.

The fulfillment of the promise will prove God's sovereignty.

Make sure you have given proper attention to words like "spirit," "life," "winds," and "breathe." The last lines contains two ideas: "I promised" and "I will do it." Don't run them together.

This text forms the basis of much of Peter's Pentecost sermon (see Acts 2:17–21).

prophesy = PROF-uh-sī
Stress the variety of those who will receive the Spirit.

This is unexpected: "Even upon the servants . . .". Stress these words appropriately.

There is a more sober mood here. The images are not terrifying, but awe inspiring.

First, there is an outpouring of God's spirit on all flesh. The spirit will be given liberally, to a great diversity of people: sons and daughters, old men and young, even servants and handmaids. In a religious tradition that believed God's spirit could only be imparted to great charismatic leaders like Moses or David, this promise is truly remarkable. The spirit brings even servants to equality. An enthusiastic, generous tone pervades these lines. Speak them with joy.

Second, there are awesome cosmic signs. The tone here is more sober, but terrifying as they may be, these signs in earth and sky are actually blessings that point the believer to the "great and terrible day" of the Lord, a day when new, unexpected wonders will occur. "Terrible" captures the mood of these lines for it suggests not an awful, but an *awesome* experience. It's like an eclipse—too fascinating not to watch, but blinding if you linger too long. Infuse the marvelous Pentecost images ("fire," "smoke," and "the coming of the day") with positive urgency.

Third, there is a promise of deliverance. Notice who will be rescued: "Everyone . . . who calls on the name of the Lord." They will be given a home in "Jerusalem" and "Mount Zion," much loved images of hope and comfort. "Remnant" and "survivors" point to a future when the spirit will make all God's people prophets.

READING II   Paul's reflection focuses on the almost-but-not-yet aspect of the workings of the Spirit. The coming of God's Holy Spirit ushered in a

Those who call on God need not fear the "terrible day" of the Lord.

"Zion" and "Jerusalem" combine with "remnant" and "survivors" to create a sense of joyful hope.

at the coming of the **day** of the LORD,
the **great** and **terrible** day.
Then everyone shall be **rescued**
who calls on the **name** of the LORD;
for on Mount **Zion** there shall be a **remnant**,
as the LORD has **said**,
and in **Jerusalem survivors**
whom the LORD shall **call**.

READING II   Romans 8:22–27

A reading from the Letter of Saint Paul to the Romans

Brothers and sisters:
We **know** that all **creation** is **groaning** in **labor** pains
even until **now**;
and not only **that**, but we **ourselves**,
who have the **firstfruits** of the **Spirit**,
we **also** groan within ourselves
as we wait for **adoption**, the **redemption** of our **bodies**.
For in **hope** we were **saved**.
Now hope that **sees** is **not** hope.
For who **hopes** for what one **sees**?
But if we hope for what we do **not** see, we wait with **endurance**.

In the **same** way, the Spirit **too** comes to the aid of our **weakness**;
for we do not know **how** to **pray** as we **ought**,
but the Spirit **himself** intercedes with inexpressible **groanings**.

The "labor pains" are unexpected. Don't rush past the image.

While we have already tasted life in the Spirit, we long for the fullness only the kingdom can offer.

There is a lively, colloquial feel to Paul's logic here.

The Spirit even prays within us when we don't know how to pray.

---

new age that still moves toward completion. We taste but the first fruits of it now; its fullness awaits the coming kingdom. As we wait, we long for that fullness. With the rest of creation we "groan" as if experiencing the travail of childbirth because our full adoption as God's children is not yet realized. Any heart that truly seeks God knows this longing, this wanting now what can never be ours while we still live. It is "hope" that enables us to bear this longing and to "wait with endurance." Paul defines hope as expecting what we cannot see. If we can see something, we don't need to

hope for it. But when the object of our desire is out of sight, then we can truly hope. Paul is not arguing like a lawyer, but as a believer sharing his own faith. From the depths of your own longing for what you cannot see—health of loved ones, a just society, a child's success, inner peace—invite us to yearn patiently for what eyes fail to perceive.

The final paragraph emphasizes the Spirit's role in strengthening faith. Our understanding is weak; we don't even know how to pray as we ought. But the Spirit, who understands what we cannot, comes

to our aid and presents our prayers to God in "groanings" that transcend speech.

The reading closes with a splendid image: God, "the one who searches hearts," understands our Spirit-led prayers even better than we do. With a sense of confidence, offer that assurance to your assembly.

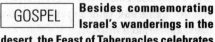 GOSPEL   **Besides commemorating Israel's wanderings in the** desert, the Feast of Tabernacles celebrates with much thanksgiving the gathering of

Don't rush past this beautiful image: "The one who searches hearts."

And the one who searches **hearts**
> **knows** what is the **intention** of the Spirit,
> because he **intercedes** for the holy ones
> according to God's **will**.

Suggest that he rose and spoke with great vigor at the words "Let anyone . . . ." Make eye contact with the assembly.

"From within him . . ." is one of those rare instances when you should stress the preposition.

Although this sounds parenthetical, sustain the energy. It's important.

Jesus' glorification was his death and Resurrection.

A reading from the holy Gospel according to John

On the **last** and **greatest** day of the **feast**,
> **Jesus** stood up and **exclaimed**,
> "Let anyone who **thirsts** come to **me** and **drink**.
As Scripture says:
> *Rivers of **living** water will flow from **within** him*
> > *who **believes** in me."*

He said this in reference to the **Spirit**
> that those who came to **believe** in him were to **receive**.
There was, of course, no Spirit **yet**,
> because **Jesus** had not yet been **glorified**.

the harvest. For seven days water was carried into the city from the Pool of Siloam to remind the people of the water from the rock in the desert and to symbolize the hope of Messianic deliverance. Prayers were then offered for plentiful rain. On the eighth day, a full holiday, when no water was carried, and in the midst of prayer and rejoicing, Jesus "cried out" offering *himself* as the source of even greater rejoicing. He will be the yield of our spiritual harvest. Through the gift of the Spirit he

imparts, Jesus brings to an end our spiritual wanderings, even our thirst. Jesus offers "rivers of living water," an image of inexhaustible abundance.

Scholars are divided on the question of whether Christ or the believer is the source of "living water." But clearly the water represents the wisdom of the Spirit that Jesus would send upon those who believe in him. Place your stress on "rivers of living water" rather than "him" and you will highlight the central image of the passage. Because the passage is short, read at a slower pace or you might be finished

before your listeners have fully tuned in. The closing sentence must not sound anticlimactic. It's an important statement that connects the coming of the Spirit with the glorification of Jesus through his Passion and Resurrection. Read in a quiet tone, as if taking the assembly into your confidence and sharing special information, all with the awareness that anticipating the "Spirit" is the purpose of this vigil.

PENTECOST: DAY

Lectionary #63

READING I   Acts 2:1–11

A reading from the Acts of the Apostles

When the time for **Pentecost** was **fulfilled**,
    they were all in one place **together**.
And **suddenly** there came from the **sky**
    a noise like a **strong** driving **wind**,
    and it **filled** the entire **house** in which they were.
Then there appeared to them **tongues** as of **fire**,
    which **parted** and came to **rest** on each **one** of them.
And they were all **filled** with the **Holy Spirit**
    and began to speak in different **tongues**,
    as the Spirit **enabled** them to **proclaim**.

Now there were **devout** Jews from every **nation** under heaven
    staying in Jerusalem.
At this **sound**, they gathered in a large **crowd**,
    but they were **confused**
    because **each** one heard them **speaking** in his own **language**.
They were **astounded**, and in **amazement** they asked,
    "Are not all these people who are speaking **Galileans**?
Then how does **each** of us hear them in his **native** language?
We are **Parthians**, **Medes**, and **Elamites**,
    inhabitants of **Mesopotamia**, **Judea** and **Cappadocia**,

---

The opening sentence gives no hint of the excitement that follows. Even "Pentecost," which refers to the Jewish harvest festival, not the Christian solemnity we celebrate today, doesn't suggest the explosive events about to unfold.

"Suddenly" breaks the calm mood and introduces the spectacular. See the story of the Sinai covenant and you'll find similarities between that event and the driving wind and the flames of Pentecost that automatically signal the Spirit (see Exodus 19:1–15). In both instances, the Spirit's compelling energy announces a new moment in God's plan of salvation.

The "tongues of fire" appeared, parted, and rested on each one. There are three separate moments here. Renew your energy on the words "And they were filled . . . ."

Drop your energy level for the narration about the devout Jews, and then raise it again on "At the sound."

The words "astounded" and "amazement" should tell you how to proclaim here.

Name each nation carefully. Together they express the universality of the Christian message.

Galileans = gal-ih-LEE-uhnz
Parthians = PAHR-thee-uhnz
Medes = meedz
Elamites = EE-luh-mīts
Mesopotamia = mes-uh-poh-TAY-mee-uh
Judea = joo-DEE-uh
Cappadocia = cap-uh-DOH-shee-uh

READING I   With tremendous energy this passage relates the amazing events of the day of Pentecost. We sense the building excitement and confusion of the crowd that experienced this miraculous theophany, or manifestation of God. In the form of driving wind and tongues of fire, God becomes powerfully, unmistakably present to the small band of disciples.

The Spirit's arrival attracts the attention of many besides the disciples. Devout Jews from many parts of the world had come to Jerusalem to participate in the festival that celebrated both the grain harvest and the covenant God made with Israel at Sinai (that moment filled with fireworks inaugurated the original covenant in the same way this moment inaugurates the *new* covenant). Many commentators find in today's story a striking reversal of the events that occurred at the tower of Babel, where people with a common language suddenly were unable to understand one another. On Pentecost, people from many different lands are suddenly pulled together and, despite different languages, are able to hear the same message at the same time, each in their own tongue.

But Pentecost's reversal of Babel is not total, for there is no indication that the foreigners are made to understand *each other;* they only understand the apostles. Nor are the different people assembled here given a new common language with which to communicate with each other. But in the drawing together of so many people in one place, the universality of Christ's Church is foreshadowed: all people will hear the message of salvation and

Pontus = PON-thus
Phrygia =FRIJ-ee-uh
Pamphylia = PAM-fil-ee-uh
Libya = LIB-ee-uh
Cyrene = sī-REE-nee
Cretans = KREE-tuhns

The final line summarizes the amazement that builds throughout the listing of the nations. There are two ideas here: "our own tongues" and "mighty deeds of God."

Paul's balance and logic mustn't make you neglect the emotional understructure of the text. Remember Paul's love for the Corinthians and his desire for harmony among them. Recall the need for harmony in your own world—whether local or global—and perhaps you'll find a proper balance between logic and passion.

Don't stress the repetitions of "different"; instead, stress "service," "Lord," "workings," and "God."

This line concludes and summarizes the first section.

Speak the body analogy carefully and slowly. Paul says much with just a few words. Stress the contrasts. Note the suggestions for when to stress the word "one." The oneness of the body is maintained with the glue of the Spirit: "Jews or Greeks, slaves or free" reinforces that idea, saying no matter how large or diverse the community, it remains one body in the Spirit.

Pontus and **Asia**, **Phrygia** and **Pamphylia**,
Egypt and the districts of **Libya** near **Cyrene**,
as well as travelers from **Rome**,
both **Jews** and **converts** to Judaism, **Cretans** and **Arabs**,
yet we hear them **speaking** in our own **tongues**
of the mighty **acts** of **God**."

READING II   1 Corinthians 12:3b–7, 12–13

A reading from the first Letter of Saint Paul to the Corinthians

Brothers and sisters:
No one can say, "**Jesus** is **Lord**," except by the Holy **Spirit**.
There are different **kinds** of spiritual **gifts** but the same **Spirit**;
   there are different forms of **service** but the same **Lord**;
   there are different **workings** but the same **God**
   who produces **all** of them in **everyone**.
To **each** individual the **manifestation** of the Spirit
   is given for some **benefit**.

As a body is **one** though it has many **parts**,
   and **all** the parts of the body, though **many**, are **one** body,
   so also **Christ**.
For in **one** Spirit we were all **baptized** into **one body**,
   whether **Jews** or **Greeks**, **slaves** or **free** persons,
   and we were all given to **drink** of one **Spirit**.

Or:

all will find a home in the Church of Christ. Perhaps it can even be said that in the Church there *is* a common language. Christ's Church must be a spirit-speaking Church. Our common language is God's Holy Spirit.

> There is a choice of readings today. Speak with the liturgy coordinator to find out which readings will be used.

READING II   **1 CORINTHIANS.** Paul's opening is strong, uncompromising, and authoritative. Why so dra-

matic a start? Paul writes to a divided community splintered by the very reality that should be the source of unity, the Spirit. Only God's Spirit, he insists, not the false spirits of pagan experience, enables one to profess Jesus as Lord. These Corinthians had created discord over God's generosity. They had received the gifts of the Spirit but, instead of rejoicing with each other, they became like selfish siblings comparing their gift to what the others got, feeling they did better or came up short.

So Paul tackles the question of gifts. Gifts can bring out the best or worst in others—the worst is jealousy and rivalry, and that's the trap into which the Corinthians fell. Although given to individuals, gifts are to be exercised as "forms of service" for the benefit of all. Even the insight to acknowledge Jesus as the Lord comes from the Spirit. So, all of you who claim Jesus as Lord, he argues, do so by the grace of the very *same* Spirit. Knowing what you have in common, he continues, you must realize that you also have differences.

READING II   Romans 8:8–17

A reading from the Letter of Saint Paul to the Romans

Brothers and sisters:
Those who are in the **flesh** cannot **please** God.
But **you** are not in the flesh;
   on the **contrary**, **you** are in the **spirit**,
   if only the Spirit of God **dwells** in you.
Whoever does **not** have the Spirit of Christ does not **belong**
     to him.
But if **Christ** is in you,
   although the **body** is **dead** because of **sin**,
   the **spirit** is **alive** because of **righteousness**.
If the **Spirit** of the one who **raised** Jesus from the dead **dwells**
    in you,
   the one who **raised** Christ from the dead
   will give life to your mortal bodies **also**,
   through his **Spirit** that **dwells** in you.
Consequently, brothers and sisters,
   we are not **debtors** to the flesh,
   to live **according** to the flesh.
For if you **live** according to the flesh, you will **die**,
   but if by the **Spirit** you put to **death** the deeds of the **body**,
   you will **live**.

For those who are **led** by the Spirit of God are **sons** of God.
For you did not receive a spirit of **slavery** to fall back into **fear**,
   but you received a spirit of **adoption**,
   through whom we cry, "**Abba, Father!**"

The authoritative tone of the first sentence is essential in order for what follows to make sense.

Shift tone to tell us what we truly are and what we have to do to retain our identity: allow God's Spirit to live in us!

Stress "is" not "in." Contrast "body"/ "dead" with "spirit"/"alive." These are "if/then" constructions; "then" is implied, not stated. Stress the "ifs" because they suggest the extent of our personal responsibility.

Speak with a sense of relief and peacefulness here.

"For if you live . . . you will die" should be inserted rather quickly but forcefully. Then return to the larger message of the text: "you will live."

This is the Good News of salvation. Pause between "Abba" and "Father." Since the one translates the other, give both equal emphasis.

In comparing the body of Christ to a human body, Paul says you can't rank the importance of the body's various parts, for the human body functions well only when all the parts work in harmony. The same is true of the body of Christ. Some do one kind of work and others do different work. Some enjoy one gift, others a different gift. But even these differences result from the work of the very same Spirit.

It's no accident that today's Gospel focuses on forgiveness. The only way the body will run smoothly is if its many members are able and willing to forgive the inevitable hurts they inflict on one another.

ROMANS. The incredible transformation initiated in us through Baptism claims us as children of the Spirit. We are no longer simply creatures of flesh, bound to the compulsions of the flesh. When we are of the flesh, we live our own lives, independent of God's will for us. But life in the Spirit means we gratefully embrace God's will as the path that leads to fullness of life. Paul's use of conditional language, even for the believer who has already been initiated ("If only the Spirit of God dwells in you . . . . If Christ is in you . . . if the Spirit dwells in you . . ."), indicates we still have an important role to play in our own salvation. We are given the gift, but we must accept it and live by it. If we don't, we "do not belong to Christ . . . [and] we will die." We must yield to the power of the Spirit already at work within us.

The reading ends with two significant assertions. The first, stated in a typical Pauline progression, asserts that we are "children of God," and therefore "heirs of

The Spirit **himself** bears witness with **our** spirit
    that we are **children** of God,
    and if **children**, then **heirs**,
    heirs of **God** and **joint** heirs with **Christ**,
    if only we **suffer** with him
    so that we may **also** be **glorified** with him.

Take us through Paul's nice progression: "children . . . heirs . . . co-heirs."

Contrast "suffer" and "glorified": the latter does not come without the former.

In John, Jesus' Resurrection, Ascension, and conferral of the Spirit all occur on one day. For more background, see the Gospel commentary of the Second Sunday of Easter.

Help the assembly hear each piece of information that John has packed into this sentence.

"His side," in this Gospel, was "pierced," while in Luke it says "feet."

Stress "Lord," not "saw," because they rejoiced not at the sight but at the *certainty* that it was Jesus.

Now that they perceive, Jesus offers peace a second time.

"Breathed" sounds like what it means.

Today Jesus' formula points more to initiation through baptismal faith than to penance.

GOSPEL   John 20:19–23

A reading from the holy Gospel according to John

On the evening of that **first** day of the week,
    when the doors were **locked**, where the **disciples** were,
    for fear of the **Jews**,
    Jesus came and **stood** in their midst
    and said to them, "**Peace** be with you."
When he had **said** this, he showed them his **hands** and his **side**.
The disciples **rejoiced** when they saw the Lord.
Jesus said to them **again**, "**Peace** be with you.
As the **Father** has sent **me**, so **I** send **you**."
And when he had said this, he **breathed** on them
    and said to them,
  "**Receive** the Holy **Spirit**.
Whose sins you **forgive** are **forgiven** them,
    and whose sins you **retain** are **retained**."

Or:

God"—no, more, we are "co-heirs with Christ." The second profound notion is found in the simple last sentence: we will be "glorified" with Christ, but only if we are first willing to "suffer" with him. There is no shortage of opportunities for such suffering in life. Our choice is whether we resist it or embrace it in the spirit of Christ. It seems that makes all the difference.

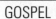 GOSPEL   JOHN 20. The opening sentence gives much significant information: it's the first day of the

week (Resurrection day), the disciples hide fearfully behind locked doors, yet, unexpectedly and miraculously, Jesus comes to them. Significantly, Jesus first offers "peace." The disciples will rejoice, but only after Jesus offers his pierced hands and side to persuade them of who he is. Clearly, it took some effort to convince the disciples that the one who stood before them was the same Lord who had taught and prayed with them the past three years. Even on this joyful day the Gospel reminds us that it is a crucified Lord who leads us.

After the disciples respond, Jesus repeats his peace greeting. His first greeting came before they understood it was really he, but perhaps he repeats it after they are convinced because peace is both hard to sustain and also the surest sign of the Spirit's presence.

"As the Father sent me" speaks comfort as much as commission. Jesus makes them apostles ("those sent"), but also seems to be saying, "As the Father empowered me to do my work, so will I empower you." "Breathed" is John's version of Pentecost, reminiscent of the imparting of

Make eye contact with the assembly.
Today, these words are addressed
directly to them.
"Another" and "always" are the key
words of this sentence.

Stress both what it means to love
(keeping commandments) and the
consequences (God dwells in us). Then,
just as forcefully, stress what it means to
disregard the commandments.

When you have two terms that mean
the same thing ("The Advocate . . . the
Holy Spirit"), build your energy from the
first to the second term. Sustain the
heightened energy all the way through
". . . in my name."
These words offer comfort and assurance.

GOSPEL John 14:15–16, 23b–26

A reading from the holy Gospel according to John

Jesus said to his disciples:
  "If you **love** me, you will **keep** my **commandments**.
and I will **ask** the Father,
  and he will give you another **Advocate** to be with you **always**.

"Whoever **loves** me will keep my **word**,
  and my **Father** will love **him**,
  and we will **come** to him and make our **dwelling** with him.
Those who do **not** love me do **not** keep my words;
  yet the word you **hear** is not **mine**
  but that of the **Father** who **sent** me.

"I have **told** you this while I am **with** you.
The **Advocate**, the Holy **Spirit** whom the Father
    will send in my **name**,
  will teach you **everything**
  and **remind** you of all that I **told** you."

life at creation; Jesus breathes *spiritual* life into his disciples and mandates them to forgive sins.

JOHN 14. Today's solemnity celebrates what Jesus promises in this part of the Last Supper discourse—the sending of "another Advocate," the Holy Spirit. That Spirit will be the ongoing assurance of the risen Christ's presence in his body, the Church. More than anything, the Advocate will be a teacher, helping us to comprehend fully the meaning of all that Jesus said and did in his earthly ministry. The Spirit testifies to

Jesus and convicts the world for rejecting the word of the Father that Jesus came to preach. Jesus, our first advocate, must return to the Father, but the Spirit will be sent to remain with us always.

Jesus makes clear what it means to be a true disciple: we prove our love for Christ by keeping his commandments. The first and greatest commandment, of course, is that we love one another. If we do that, we will be filled with the Father's love and God and Jesus will make a home in us. Much of the power of this text lies in Jesus' assertion that those who do not love him

are those who don't keep his commandment. It's a stark, hot-or-cold kind of contrast. Keeping the commandments is not an option for they are the words not of Jesus, but of God the Father.

MOST HOLY TRINITY

Lectionary #166

READING I Proverbs 8:22–31

A reading from the Book of Proverbs

Each idea is stated twice. Typically, you build intensity from the first to the second repetition of an idea. The speaker is Wisdom, a female persona in the original text.

Practice pacing and pauses. The text doesn't call for even pacing, but "bursts" of energy as new images are offered to elaborate further what was already stated. The reading will be deadly if everything is spoken with the same level of energy.

Each image adds to the declaration of how ancient Wisdom is. She is saying, "I was here before the oceans were dug out, and before the mountains—even before the earth was made, I was here!" There is excitement and energy in those assertions.

Renew your energy and speak this section with more reserve, but with great authority. "At every significant moment," Wisdom says, "I was there. And God delighted in me . . . and I delighted in the human race!"

This line summarizes the six preceding lines. When all those things occurred, it was *then* I stood beside God as confidant and helper.

Use *ritardando* (slowing toward the end) on the words ". . . in the human race."

Thus says the **wisdom** of **God**:
"The LORD **possessed** me, the **beginning** of his ways,
 the **forerunner** of his **prodigies** of long **ago**;
from of **old** I was poured **forth**,
 at the **first**, **before** the earth.
When there were no **depths** I was brought forth,
 when there were no **fountains** or springs of **water**;
before the **mountains** were settled into place,
 before the **hills**, I was brought forth;
while as yet the earth and **fields** were not **made**,
 nor the first **clods** of the **world**.

"When the Lord established the **heavens** I was **there**,
 when he marked out the **vault** over the face of the **deep**;
when he made **firm** the skies **above**,
 when he fixed **fast** the foundations of the **earth**;
when he set for the **sea** its **limit**,
 so that the **waters** should not transgress his **command**;
then was I **beside** him as his **craftsman**,
 and I was his **delight** day by day,
playing before him all the while,
 playing on the surface of his **earth**;
 and I found **delight** in the human **race**."

READING I In Christian tradition, Wisdom has been identified both with Christ and the Holy Spirit. Here, although not strictly speaking as a person, Wisdom is personified, that is, given the qualities of a human being who speaks of the creative work of God. The understanding of Wisdom as a manifestation of God's action and self-communication would develop over time. This text represents a step in the process. Later books assign her a more active role in creation; here she is more of a spectator relishing the beauty of God's work. Given later development and the Trinitarian context of today's solemnity, we can view Wisdom as a foreshadowing of both the Logos (Christ) through whom John tells us the world was created, and the Holy Spirit.

The harder task lies not in understanding the identity of Wisdom, but in dealing with the rich poetry of the text. Twenty-one lines say what could be said by one: Wisdom existed before the world began. Each idea is stated and immediately restated, but each line adds nuances of meaning that matter. Look for what's new in each line and stress that. Poetry communicates not only with the meaning of words but with their sound and rhythm as well. This is a song celebrating the privilege of being "possessed" by God and witnessing God's creation. Wisdom speaks with youthful exuberance of the genesis of earth and sky. She is "playing . . . playing!" in God's presence. "Craftsman" can also be interpreted as "confidant" and should suggest intimacy between Creator God and Wisdom, not an "apprentice." The reading climaxes in the last line where Wisdom reveals that her greatest delight is in humankind.

Make eye contact with the assembly.
Pause after "Therefore" to ensure
listeners are tuned in and ready to follow
the reasoning.

There is a joyful tone throughout. This is
not a courtroom argument, but a call to
rejoice in the gift of faith!

Stress "boast" so that the echo in the
next line will stand out.

It's easy to boast of "glory," but Christian
faith enables us to boast even of sorrows
and trials.

Avoid falling into a predictable cadence
by building (increasing energy) on the
new word in each line.

Don't rush the mention of the Holy Spirit.

READING II   Romans 5:1–5

A reading from the Letter of Saint Paul to the Romans

Brothers and sisters:
Therefore, since we have been **justified** by **faith**,
    we have **peace** with God through our Lord Jesus **Christ**,
    through whom we have gained **access** by faith
    to this **grace** in which we **stand**,
    and we **boast** in hope of the **glory** of God.
Not only that, but we even **boast** of our **afflictions**,
    knowing that **affliction** produces **endurance**,
    and **endurance**, proven **character**,
    and proven **character**, **hope**,
    and **hope** does not **disappoint**,
    because the love of **God** has been poured **out** into our **hearts**
    through the Holy **Spirit** that has been **given** to us.

READING II   If you look, you'll find the Trinitarian formula Paul uses to discuss redemption: God is the source of salvation, but it is Jesus who performed the saving act and the Spirit working in our hearts who enables us to experience its redeeming effects. In truth, the divine person is one, yet embodies three distinct persons who act distinctly but together. Such is the mystery of the Trinity. To make his points, Paul employs two four-step progressions that display his usual command of logic as each leads toward the same end point, hope. The first progression leads from "faith" to "peace" with God, from which we derive access to "grace," which in turn allows us to boast of our "hope." "We have peace" sets the confident tone of the entire passage. "Not only that . . ." introduces the second progression, and heightens the mood. Paul was never naïve. He understood affliction, but he also knew that God's love, which undergirds Christian hope, is great enough to help us stand even in the face of trials.

"Affliction" launches the second progression. From affliction comes "endurance;" endurance leads to "virtue," and virtue returns us to our earlier goal, "hope." For Paul, the journey through those stages is a joyful one, so speak in a joyful tone. After all, we have reason to walk in confident hope that never wonders if God has abandoned us. When we start with the premise that God justifies us through Christ, everything in life, even hardships, can confirm our hope; nothing can rob us of

This short text requires slow reading. Speak in a comforting tone.

Stress "he," not "comes," and then speak "Spirit of truth" as an elucidation of who "he" is.

Contrast "on his own" with "what he hears." What is "coming" is a greater comprehension of the mission of Jesus.

Each repetition of the word "you," together with eye contact, can remind the assembly that Jesus' words are meant also for them.

GOSPEL   John 16:12–15

A reading from the holy Gospel according to John

Jesus said to his **disciples**:
"I have much **more** to tell you, but you cannot **bear** it now.
But when he **comes**, the Spirit of **truth**,
    he will **guide** you to **all** truth.
He will not speak on his **own**,
    but he will speak what he **hears**,
    and will **declare** to you the things that are **coming**.
He will **glorify** me,
    because he will take from what is **mine** and **declare** it to you.
Everything that the **Father** has is **mine**;
    for this **reason** I told you that he will **take** from what is **mine**
    and **declare** it to you."

joy, unless we let it. Paul's reasoning is not based on logic but on faith—a faith that sees our hearts flooded with the Spirit-filled "love of God."

 GOSPEL This text imparts some helpful theology as we celebrate the solemnity of the Most Holy Trinity. Compared with other sections of Jesus' farewell discourse, it may feel a bit unemotional. In the verses immediately preceding today's selection Jesus promises the disciples, ". . . I tell you the truth"

(16:7). Here it is—unadorned, but not uncaring. Jesus' assertion that he has spoken as much as they can "bear," and his effort to prepare them for the future, hint at his affection. Promising that even more truth will be revealed with the arrival of the Spirit, he offers comfort and assurance. Speak his words in a tone that reflects the care implied, if not directly expressed, in the lines.

Cast in the future tense ("will" is repeated seven times), the passage engenders a sense of hopeful expectation. These words should comfort your assembly as

they did the disciples. The assurance that the Spirit is the way to "all truth" is meant for all believers, then and now. The closing sentences articulate implicit teaching on the Trinity: the Father, source of all truth, has revealed that truth to Jesus who imparts it to us through the Holy Spirit. That's the truth, and a great comfort, too.

MOST HOLY BODY AND BLOOD OF CHRIST

Lectionary #169

READING I   Genesis 14:18–20

Read slowly, using pause to full-advantage, or the reading may end before listeners are fully attuned to it. Often readers don't realize they're rushing. But remember that sentences frequently contain several thought units. Speak one thought at a time, not an entire sentence.

Melchizedek = mel-KIZ-ih-dek
Salem = SAY-luhm

King Melchizedek is also a priest of God.

In the blessing, note words marked for stress: first "Abram" then "God Most High."

Speak this line with a sense of gratitude.

A reading from the Book of Genesis

In those days, **Melchizedek**, king of **Salem**,
    brought out **bread** and **wine**,
    and being a **priest** of God Most **High**,
    he **blessed** Abram with these **words**:
"Blessed be **Abram** by God Most **High**,
    the **creator** of heaven and earth;
    and blessed be **God** Most **High**,
    who delivered your **foes** into your **hand**."
Then **Abram** gave him a **tenth** of **everything**.

READING II   1 Corinthians 11:23–26

It is Paul the teacher speaking today. Stress his assertion that what he tells us he got "from the Lord."

Although these words are very familiar, your sincerity will help us hear them anew.

Don't rush this line. Vary the stresses in the two "remembrance" directives.

A reading from the first Letter of Saint Paul to the Corinthians

Brothers and sisters:
I **received** from the **Lord** what I also handed on to **you**,
    that the Lord **Jesus**, on the night he was handed **over**,
    took **bread**, and, after he had given **thanks**,
    broke it and said, "This is my **body** that is for **you**.
Do this in **remembrance** of me."

READING I   Having won a decisive battle against great odds, Abram (who later will be called Abraham) returns to receive a hero's welcome from Melchizedek, priest and king of Salem. Then the two powerful figures gather around the simple elements of bread and wine and give thanks to God. As priest, Melchizedek speaks words of blessing extolling the power of the God who placed victory into the hands of his servant Abram. Abram responds by giving to Melchizedek one tenth of all his wealth. Christian Eucharist means "giving thanks"; as a liturgical community we give thanks around a table using the same simple elements used so long ago by Melchizedek. Clearly, the Church sees this ancient rite as a "type," that is, prefigurement, of the eucharistic meal that Jesus gave us as a memorial of him. We should leave this reading remembering two things: the bread and wine, and the blessings of Abram and of God. Remember that Melchizedek's blessing ended on a note of victory. Today's solemnity honors another victor, Jesus, who conquered the foes of sin and death, and who feeds multitudes by giving himself into their hands in the form of simple bread and simple wine.

READING II   Saint Paul writes to the Corinthians to correct certain abuses that had crept into their celebration of the eucharistic meal. To impress upon them the sacredness of what they were doing each time they gathered to bless the bread and wine, he repeats Jesus' words that so clearly express the *sacrificial* nature of Eucharist. Paul begins by naming the night of the Last Supper

Although you must stress "death of the Lord," end on a solemn, not a gloomy note.

In the same way also the **cup**, after supper, saying,
  "This **cup** is the new **covenant** in my **blood**.
Do this, as often as you **drink** it, in **remembrance** of me."
For as often as you **eat** this bread and **drink** the cup,
  you proclaim the **death** of the Lord until he **comes**.

GOSPEL   Luke 9:11b–17

A reading from the holy Gospel according to Luke

Stress the healings, for they too speak of God's abundance.

Jesus spoke to the crowds about the **kingdom** of **God**,
  and he **healed** those who needed to be **cured**.
As the day was drawing to a **close**,
  the **Twelve** approached him and said,
  "**Dismiss** the crowd
  so that they can go to the surrounding **villages** and **farms**
  and find **lodging** and **provisions**;
  for we are in a **deserted** place here."
He said to them, "Give them some food **yourselves**."
They replied, "Five **loaves** and two **fish** are all we **have**,
  unless we **ourselves** go and **buy** food for all these people."
Now the men there numbered about **five thousand**.
Then he said to his disciples,
  "Have them sit **down** in groups of about **fifty**."
They **did** so and made them all **sit** down.

Luke's theology is cloaked in familiar human details that give exciting energy to the story.

Given the healings, it seems ironic the disciples think Jesus has overlooked the crowd's need for supper. But their assumption makes for good drama. Contrast their concern and Jesus' confident nonchalance.

Jesus' actions are described in eucharistic language, but you must help them sound like a real human event, not an oft repeated liturgical ritual.

---

as the night Jesus "was handed over." Immediately the shadow of the cross looms over the eucharistic meal. Then, to ensure his readers have not missed the point, Paul drives it home saying that every time they eat and drink the meal they proclaim the *death* of the Lord. As we celebrate today's solemnity of the Body and Blood of Christ, Paul's words help us understand the ongoing significance of the Eucharist in the life of the Church.

As you read, you can do for your listeners what Paul did for his: remind them that what we commemorate is a supreme act of self-giving. The eucharistic formula Paul relates in this letter he claims to have received directly from the risen Lord himself. Because Paul's letters were written before the Gospels, this text to the Corinthians is the earliest written recounting of Jesus' Last Supper dialogue.

The pattern described by Paul (he took, gave thanks, and broke) is repeated in the Gospel feeding narrative where Jesus takes, blesses, breaks, and gives. These or similar verbs also appear in the Last Supper accounts of all three synoptic Gospel accounts. Accenting those verbs will not only connect us with today's Gospel, but will also help you read as slowly and as reverently as this text requires.

GOSPEL **Why have the compilers of the Lectionary chosen this** miracle story instead of the Last Supper narrative as the Gospel for today's solemnity? Perhaps because this text reveals a different aspect of Eucharist: the Second Reading stressed remembrance and sacrifice, but this story points to its superabundant nourishment. The disciples receive a

Stress "ate" and "satisfied." The ending is meant to be a surprise. Even for us who know it well, this tale can evoke wonder at the abundance of the kingdom.

Then taking the five **loaves** and the two **fish**,
   and looking up to **heaven**,
   he said the **blessing** over them, **broke** them,
   and gave them to the **disciples** to set before the **crowd**.
They all **ate** and were **satisfied**.
And when the leftover **fragments** were picked up,
   they filled **twelve** wicker **baskets**.

new directive: feed the reconstituted Israel with eucharistic bread. The most relevant aspects of the text are the need (the hunger of the crowd), the inability to meet that need with human means, the great numbers, and the overflowing abundance of the kingdom.

Many preachers will say this is a miracle of generosity: Jesus inspired the crowd to open their food sacks and share. If they are right, then this is a story about people already having all they need, if only they would contribute it all and thus create the abundance of God's kingdom. In that scenario, humans are the agents of the abundance.

But the opening sentence sets the mood: Jesus heals all who need healing—such is the reign of God. God does what we cannot. The multiplication story further illustrates that comforting truth. If we take the story at face value, we see that in fact it is God who creates abundance. We contribute but a puny amount, a few loaves and fish; God provides the rest. Of course, in most situations there is something we must contribute, but it's rarely enough on its own. God must give what we lack. The "sharing" interpretation of the story suggests we actually do have enough—there is no real lack but in generosity. In reality, we sometimes can't contribute even as little as a few loaves and fish. But if we offer our need, our trust, and our hunger to God, God will provide the rest.

11TH SUNDAY IN ORDINARY TIME

Lectionary #93

READING I   2 Samuel 12:7–10, 13

Nathan demands David's attention by announcing that he speaks for the Lord.

God's voice announces all the favors given David as if to say, "How could you?"

"Your lord" is a reference to Saul.

Speak the words "Why have you spurned the Lord . . . ?" with a tone of "How could you have done such a thing?" But do so quietly.

Uriah = yoo-RĪ-uh

Ammonites = AM-uh-nīts

Speak with authority here, not vindictiveness. This is an inevitable consequence of David's own choice.

You have few words to convey David's utter sincerity. Pause before you start and pause again after each of the first two words.

Announce God's forgiveness slowly. "You shall not die" should be spoken with sober authority.

A reading from the second Book of Samuel

Nathan said to **David**:
"Thus says the LORD God of **Israel**:
    'I **anointed** you **king** of Israel.
I **rescued** you from the hand of **Saul**.
I gave you your lord's **house** and your lord's **wives** for your **own**.
I gave you the house of **Israel** and of **Judah**.
And if this were not **enough**, I could count up for you still **more**.
Why have you **spurned** the LORD and done **evil** in his sight?
You have cut down **Uriah** the Hittite with the **sword**;
    you took his **wife** as your **own**,
    and him you **killed** with the sword of the **Ammonites**.
Now, therefore, the **sword** shall never **depart** from your house,
    because you have **despised** me
    and have taken the wife of **Uriah** to be **your** wife.'"
Then **David** said to **Nathan**,
    "I have **sinned** against the LORD."
Nathan answered David:
    "The LORD on **his** part has **forgiven** your sin:
    you shall not **die**."

READING I   Nathan goes to King David with a very unpleasant task: confront the King about his dual sins of adultery and murder. With all the women in the kingdom to choose from, David set his eyes on the wife of one of his most loyal soldiers, Uriah, who was away doing battle. David conceived a child with Bathsheba, then, to cover his misdeed, he arranged for Uriah to be killed "in the line of battle." God sends Nathan to convict the King of this unthinkable wrong. Look at all I did for you, says the Lord, enumerating favor upon favor. Then, in the starkest terms, God

names David's sins of lust and murder, and promises that, as a result, violence henceforth will be woven into the very DNA of David's family; the sword will never depart from his house. Generation after generation of David's line did, in fact, see the painful fulfillment of this prophecy.

The narrator's lines are brief but important for establishing mood. "Nathan said to David . . . " sets up the confrontation between prophet and king; both are powerful characters, but clearly it takes courage for Nathan to confront David.

When David repents, his words come without warning, but they are as sincere as they are brief. Signal his contrition in the way you say, "Then David said to Nathan . . . ." Don't rush this line, but anticipate the mercy Nathan is about to announce. Often more is communicated by the silence between words than by the words themselves.

The listing of the favors God bestowed on David should be spoken with increasing intensity. It all builds to the equivalent of "How could you?" God's actual question ("Why have you spurned . . .") is full of the

READING II   Galatians 2:16, 19–21

A reading from the Letter of Saint Paul to the Galatians

Brothers and sisters:
We who **know** that a person is not **justified** by works of the **law**
  but through **faith** in Jesus **Christ**,
  even **we** have believed in Christ Jesus
  that we may be justified by **faith** in Christ
  and not by **works** of the law,
  because by works of the law **no** one will be justified.
For through the law I **died** to the law,
  that I might **live** for **God**.
I have been **crucified** with Christ;
  yet I **live**, no longer **I**, but **Christ** lives in me;
  insofar as I now live in the **flesh**,
  I live by **faith** in the Son of **God**
  who has **loved** me and **given** himself up for me.
I do not nullify the **grace** of God;
  for if justification comes through the **law**,
  then Christ **died** for **nothing**.

Speak slowly and stress the contrasts throughout.

Salvation comes through faith in Jesus. Offer those words as comfort, not warning.

The law caused Christ's death, and that death made possible our salvation.

Paul is saying, "I have been *crucified* with Christ, and yet I still *live*. But the life I live is not really mine, for it is *Christ* who now lives in me!"
"Christ lives in me" is the highpoint of the reading and should sound like it.

It is grace, not our observance of law, that saves us. The final line must be spoken with great conviction.

frustration and disbelief you might direct at a loved one who has let you down. "Now, therefore, the sword shall never depart . . ." is full of regret, not anger. David was God's chosen; these consequences are his own doing, not a capricious punishment inflicted by God. What he finally realizes is not that he has done something wrong, but just how wrong his deed is. David is saying, "I have done a terrible thing!" His honest contrition is what sets him apart from King Saul, who, like Judas, despaired and took his own life.

The closing lines can be spoken with quiet intensity, Nathan assuring David: God has not abandoned you. You will survive this.

READING II This is not an easy text. In the early decades of Christianity when most Christians were converts from Judaism, some leaders insisted believers had to adhere to the Jewish law in addition to being baptized in Christ. Paul was the champion of letting go of the constraints of the old law, especially circumcision. He makes that argument here. It's our faith in Christ that justifies us, not clinging to the works of the law. No one, he insists, will be saved by slavish adherence to dietary rules or the practice of circumcision. Then Paul proclaims, "Through the law I died to the law." The various interpretations of that line differ only in how they get to the same point, which is this: the law has made itself obsolete, for salvation comes not from the law but from Christ. If it were the law that brought salvation, then Christ would have died in vain.

GOSPEL Luke 7:36—8:3

A reading from the holy Gospel according to Luke

A **Pharisee** invited Jesus to **dine** with him,
  and he entered the Pharisee's **house** and reclined at **table**.
Now there was a sinful **woman** in the city
  who **learned** that he was at table in the house of the Pharisee.
Bringing an **alabaster** flask of **ointment**,
  she stood behind him at his feet **weeping**
  and began to **bathe** his feet with her **tears**.
Then she **wiped** them with her **hair**,
  kissed them, and **anointed** them with the **ointment**.
When the Pharisee who had invited him **saw** this
    he said to himself,
  "If this man were a **prophet**,
  he would know **who** and what **sort** of woman this is
    who is **touching** him,
  that she is a **sinner**."
Jesus said to him in reply,
  "**Simon**, I have something to **say** to you."
"**Tell** me, teacher," he said.
"Two people were in **debt** to a certain **creditor**;
  one owed five **hundred** days' wages and the **other** owed **fifty**.
Since they were unable to **repay** the debt, he **forgave** it for **both**.
Which of them will love him **more**?"
Simon said in reply,
  "The **one**, I suppose, whose **larger** debt was forgiven."
He said to him, "You have judged **rightly**."

Narrate this story as a disciple, not as an objective narrator.

Pause slightly before the line "Now there was a sinful woman . . ." to indicate something important is about to happen. Describe the foot washing with tenderness and compassion.

Speak Simon's thoughts in a hushed tone as if not wanting to be overheard. Don't overstate his indignation.

The parable moves briskly until "Since they were unable . . . ." Read with awareness of your own inability to pay and gratitude at having your spiritual debt cancelled.

Simon is eager to offer the "right" answer.

Because the reading is short and Paul is laying down a theological argument, be careful not to rush. Note and stress the text's many contrasts: justification by faith, not legal observance; faith that justifies and law that does not; having died to the law to live for God. Yet more contrasts: "he was crucified with Christ, and yet he lives; he lives, yet it is no longer he who lives, but Christ who lives in him." He still lives in the "flesh," but it is a life of "faith" in the Son of God.

Although the technical language belies it, Paul is making a very personal statement about his faith. Make his bold declaration ("I live, no longer I, but Christ lives in me") a statement of your own faith. Paul concludes declaring his reliance on God's grace. Grace, of course, doesn't make law irrelevant (Jesus says we prove our love for him by keeping his commandments), but it's through Christ, not the law, that we are saved.

GOSPEL In this Gospel, Jesus reads both a mind and a heart. The mind belongs to Simon, a proud Pharisee who thinks he knows the heart of the woman who wipes the feet of Jesus with her tears. Simon, in fact, marvels that Jesus himself can't see this woman for who she obviously is. But Jesus has read the heart of the woman much better than the presumptuous Simon. So Jesus offers Simon and his guests a parable that bears directly on the scene unfolding before

The words "You did not give me water . . ." indicate that there is still hope that Simon's eyes might open. Jesus won't make his host defensive. Regret rather than admonishment colors the "little is forgiven" statement.

Then he turned to the **woman** and said to Simon,
  "Do you **see** this woman?
When I **entered** your house, **you** did not give me water for my **feet**,
  but **she** has bathed them with her **tears**
  and **wiped** them with her **hair**.
You did not give me a **kiss**,
  but she has not **ceased** kissing my feet since the time I **entered**.
You did not **anoint** my head with **oil**,
  but **she** anointed my **feet** with ointment.
So I **tell** you, her many **sins** have been **forgiven**
  because she has shown great **love**.
But the one to whom **little** is forgiven, **loves** little."

Jesus' words to the woman are gentle and hushed. Maintain a hushed tone for the puzzled reaction of the guests.

He said to her, "Your sins are **forgiven**."
The others at table said to themselves,
  "Who **is** this who even forgives **sins**?"
But he said to the **woman**,
  "Your **faith** has **saved** you; go in **peace**."

Afterward he journeyed from **one** town and village to **another**,
  preaching and proclaiming the **good news** of the kingdom
    of God.

Speak the list of names as an assertion that "all is well" as Jesus moves on to preach the Gospel.

Accompanying him were the **Twelve**
  and some **women** who had been cured of evil **spirits**
    and **infirmities**,
  Mary, called **Magdalene**, from whom seven **demons**
    had gone out,
  Joanna, the wife of Herod's steward **Chuza**,
  Susanna, and many **others** who **provided** for them out
    of their **resources**.

Simon's own table. Of two debtors forgiven different amounts, he asks, who will love the creditor more? The one forgiven more, says Simon.

Now Jesus sets the spotlight on the woman, noting how she, a sinner and an outcast, has shown him all the expected gestures of hospitality that Simon failed to provide. Her many sins have been forgiven and in response, she shows Jesus such great love. Note that the sequence is different from what we might expect: She does not show great love first and then as a

result receive forgiveness. Like the debtors of Jesus' parable, she is forgiven, and then she shows great love. Jesus has not only seen her "many sins," he has already forgiven them and the woman can't help but weep and perfume his feet in gratitude. Jesus' point is that those forgiven much will love much and those forgiven little will love but little. That's not an invitation to sin mightily, but to realize that no matter what our sins or state of life, we all have been forgiven much!

After publicly announcing that the woman's sins are forgiven and leaving controversy in his wake, Jesus sets out with the disciples and several women, including Magdalene, who, despite being misrepresented since the fifth century as a prostitute, is nonetheless one of several from whom Jesus drove out evil spirits. This Gospel focuses on the love and gratitude that result from having our debts cancelled and sins forgiven, and one does not need to be cured of evil spirits to understand that great joy.

12TH SUNDAY IN ORDINARY TIME

Lectionary #96

READING I   Zechariah 12:10–11, 13:1

Zechariah = zek-uh-RĪ-uh

God speaks a promise of grace and forgiveness. There is an exalted tone to these lines.

"And they . . . " is repeated three times. Each repetition is an opportunity to renew your energy. This is poetry. "See" the images as you describe them.

"On that day" is repeated twice. Poetry makes use of repetition to deepen the impact of the words. Use the repetition, don't gloss over it.

Hadadrimmon = hay-dad-RIM-uhn

Megiddo = meh-GID-doh

Christ will be the "fountain" that cleanses us from sin. Pause briefly after "Jerusalem" and before "to purify . . ." so you can set off "fountain."

A reading from the Book of the Prophet Zechariah

Thus says the LORD:
I will **pour out** on the house of **David**
and on the inhabitants of **Jerusalem**
a spirit of **grace** and **petition**;
and they shall **look** on him whom they have **pierced**,
and they shall **mourn** for him as one mourns
for an only **son**,
and they shall **grieve** over him as one **grieves**
over a **firstborn**.

On that **day** the mourning in **Jerusalem** shall be as great
as the mourning of **Hadadrimmon** in the plain
of **Megiddo**.

On that **day** there shall be **open** to the house of **David**
and to the inhabitants of **Jerusalem**,
a **fountain** to purify from **sin** and **uncleanness**.

READING I   Every Sunday celebrates the Resurrection and thus every Sunday reminds us of the necessary suffering and death that leads to the glory of Resurrection. With Lent and the Easter season behind us, you might think the liturgy would be on to other themes. But the paschal theme of death-Resurrection is so pervasive, so fundamental to our identity as followers of Christ that it cannot be limited to a season or two. It names who we are, a paschal people, committed to dying and rising in imitation of our Lord.

Was Zachariah speaking directly of Christ when he uttered these prophetic words? No, but the New Testament writers saw a very direct connection between Jesus and this prophecy spoken three to four hundred years before. Today's liturgy does the same. Christ, in a way the prophet could never have foreseen, fulfills the prophecy of Zachariah. But fulfillment is not the point of today's liturgy. Rather, it is the connection between repentance and redemption.

Zechariah sees the just one of God, the "Suffering Servant" in the words of

Isaiah, rejected and thrust through. But God intervenes by pouring out a new spirit on the evildoers who have committed the crime, a spirit of repentance for what they have done to God's chosen one. The very suffering they have inflicted on God's servant will be the source of purification and forgiveness. One has only to repent and "look on him whom they have pierced."

The looking is not intended to cause guilt, but to arouse in the one looking an overwhelming awareness of God's unlimited love. Recalling the forgiveness we

READING II   Galatians 3:26–29

A reading from the Letter of Saint Paul to the Galatians

Brothers and sisters:
Through **faith** you are all **children** of God in Christ **Jesus**.
For all of you who were **baptized** into Christ
    have **clothed** yourselves with Christ.
There is neither **Jew** nor **Greek**,
    there is neither **slave** nor **free** person,
    there is not **male** and **female**;
    for you are all **one** in Christ **Jesus**.
And if you **belong** to Christ,
    then you are Abraham's **descendant**,
    heirs according to the **promise**.

"Faith" is the key word in this line.

Balance "baptized" and "clothed." "Clothed" is a rich image.

The items on this list are not presented negatively. Speak them with an upbeat tone. What you are saying is that these things don't matter now, because we are one in Christ.

Make eye contact. This is good news and should sound like it: through Christ we inherit all the promises made to Abraham and his descendants.

GOSPEL   Luke 9:18–24

A reading from the holy Gospel according to Luke

Once when **Jesus** was praying in **solitude**,
    and the **disciples** were with him,
    he **asked** them, "Who do the **crowds** say that I **am**?"
They said in reply, "John the **Baptist**;
    others, **Elijah**;
    still **others**, 'One of the ancient **prophets** has arisen.'"
Then he said to them, "But who do **you** say that I am?"
Peter said in reply, "The **Christ** of **God**."

This scene opens in a quiet, secret place of prayer.

These responses can be offered eagerly, either as serious or preposterous speculation.

Jesus' second question is more pointed. Pause briefly after "you," and then finish the question. Peter's reply is a quiet act of courage, not a proclamation.

have received makes even sin a sign of victory and hope. It can make us supple, more gentle and humble—and perhaps, even willing to suffer for others as Jesus did.

READING II   Paul reminds us that, in Baptism, each of us has put on Christ. To be "clothed" in Christ is a radical concept. It means we are surrounded by Christ. We allow him to give us our identity, to transform us, to give us his face in place of our own. The effect is so powerful, Paul says, that our differences

are shed and what remains is our oneness in Christ. Jew and Greek, male and female become meaningless categories, for now all of us are one in Christ.

This putting on of Christ, of course, doesn't really wipe away our individuality. We remain unique and gifted individuals. But rank and status are removed. What remains is the flowering of our individuality within the body of Christ. No longer needing to compete or assert our egos, the best of who we are emerges as gift for all the members of the body.

When we accept Baptism and become incorporated into his body, we are united to who Christ is and also to what he does: his dying and rising become our dying and rising. We hear Jesus' challenge to take up our cross and follow him and we can answer, "Yes." The unexpected and often incomprehensible suffering that invades everyday life is no longer meaningless and random, but offers an opportunity to die with Christ that we might also rise with him. That's the greatest of the promises made to the descendants of Abraham, our father in faith.

"Rebuked them" will come as a surprise. Your tone can clarify that he's silencing rather than reprimanding them. Speak the prediction of suffering as a fact, not a lament.

He **rebuked** them
    and **directed** them not to **tell** this to **anyone**.

He said, "The Son of Man must **suffer greatly**
    and be **rejected** by the elders, the chief **priests**,
        and the **scribes**,
    and be **killed** and on the **third** day be **raised**."

Then he said to **all**,
    "If anyone wishes to come **after** me,
        he must **deny** himself
    and take up his cross **daily** and **follow** me.
For whoever wishes to **save** his life will **lose** it,
    but whoever **loses** his life for **my** sake will **save** it."

Make eye contact with the assembly. Today, this is spoken for them. Balance "save"/"lose" with "loses"/"save."

| GOSPEL | As at other significant moments in Jesus' ministry, Luke presents Jesus at prayer. Jesus waits for this time away from the crowds, to pose a key question to his disciples. It's hard to imagine he's looking for information in their responses. Surely he already knew something of what the crowds were saying about him. It seems more likely Jesus' original question ("Who do the *crowds* say that I am?") was but a prelude to the question that really mattered: "Who do *you* say that I am?" The crowd's speculation could have ranged from somber to silly, but Peter's reply comes like a sledgehammer on a six-penny nail. Jesus' way of signaling that Peter has hit the nail on the head is to order him and the others "not to tell this to anyone." In first century Palestine, "The Christ of God" suggested the long-awaited messiah—a soldier-king—who would drive the hated Roman enemy from Israel. But Luke's use of the title suggests the anointed one who comes to save all people, Jew and non-Jew alike.

How Jesus will become that source of salvation is bluntly stated in Jesus' own prediction of his suffering, death, and Resurrection. The transfiguration will follow on the heels of this first prediction of the Passion and will substantiate Jesus' claim that his suffering will lead to exaltation. But the disciples know none of that now. What they must somehow swallow is the promise that Jesus will suffer, and that anyone who wants to save his life must be willing to do the same.

13TH SUNDAY IN ORDINARY TIME

Lectionary #99

READING I   1 Kings 19:16b, 19–21

God's command is no sign of disfavor, but God's way of providing a helper and successor for Elijah. The names are challenging, so go slowly.

Elijah = ee-LĪ-juh

Elisha = ee-LĪ-shuh

Shaphat = SHAY-fat

Abel-meholah = AY-b*l-muh-HOH-lah

Practice pronouncing these names, and then speak them like those of familiar and respected ancestors.

The tone here is upbeat. The number of oxen is impressive.

Elijah's gesture is significant; don't rush it. Elisha's question is not demanding, but quite sincere.

Although it doesn't look positive, give Elijah's reply a positive tone.

Elisha's surrender and commitment to God's will is total. Speak with a sense of reverence.

A reading from the first Book of Kings

The LORD said to Elijah:
    "You shall anoint Elisha, son of Shaphat of Abel-meholah,
    as prophet to succeed you."

Elijah set out and came upon Elisha, son of Shaphat,
    as he was plowing with twelve yoke of oxen;
    he was following the twelfth.
Elijah went over to him and threw his cloak over him.
Elisha left the oxen, ran after Elijah, and said,
    "Please, let me kiss my father and mother goodbye,
    and I will follow you."
Elijah answered, "Go back!
Have I done anything to you?"
Elisha left him, and taking the yoke of oxen, slaughtered them;
    he used the plowing equipment for fuel to boil their flesh,
    and gave it to his people to eat.
Then Elisha left and followed Elijah as his attendant.

 READING I This text is about radical surrender to the will of God. Much as we would like to soften the demands of discipleship, ultimately we can hold nothing back from God. The prophet Elijah is a hero of the Old Testament who struggled to preserve the purity of Israel's worship against encroaching paganism. Because Elijah will need a successor, he is told to apprentice the young man, Elisha, who will eventually replace him. Owning "twelve yoke of oxen" was the mark of a wealthy family. Stressing that detail emphasizes just how much Elisha will be sacrificing by following Elijah. A cloak represented the personality and privileges of its owner, so placing Elijah's cloak on the shoulders of Elisha signifies the younger man's call and initiation into his prophetic mission. Elisha responds with exemplary eagerness, immediately leaving his oxen and running after Elijah. But his very reasonable request receives a puzzling response. Interpretations vary, but most commentators agree Elijah's answer is more indulgent than the one Jesus gives in today's Gospel. The Revised Standard Version Bible translates it as follows: "Go and return for I have done something important to you."

Elisha's total surrender to God's will is clearly demonstrated when he destroys his farming equipment and animals in order to offer sacrifice. Dignify those lines with the awareness that neither wealth nor family could deter Elisha from embracing God's call to be Elijah's helper and successor.

READING II   Galatians 5:1, 13–18

A reading from the Letter of Saint Paul to the Galatians

Brothers and sisters:
For **freedom** Christ set us **free**;
   so stand **firm** and do not submit **again** to the yoke of **slavery**.

For you were called for **freedom**, brothers and sisters.
But do not **use** this freedom
   as an opportunity for the **flesh**;
   rather, **serve** one another through **love**.
For the whole **law** is fulfilled in one **statement**,
   namely, *You shall **love** your **neighbor** as **yourself**.*
But if you go on **biting** and **devouring** one another,
   beware that you are not **consumed** by one another.

I say, then: **live** by the **Spirit**
   and you will certainly not **gratify** the desire of the **flesh**.
For the **flesh** has desires **against** the Spirit,
   and the **Spirit** against the **flesh**;
   these are **opposed** to each other,
   so that you may not **do** what you **want**.
But if you are guided by the **Spirit**, you are not under the **law**.

Begin with energy and strength. Contrast "freedom" with the "slavery" of the law and of excess.

Imagine being worried that a group you loved was squandering the progress they'd made. How would you use these words to advise them, especially knowing that "biting" and "devouring" behavior leads inevitably to being "consumed"?
Speak with authority, but not harshly. Energetically encourage the assembly to love one another.

Speak like a teacher clarifying matters. This is how we avoid consuming one another! The balance and rhythm of these lines is remarkable. Use somewhat less energy than in previous sentences, but start building to a new crescendo.

There should be no harshness here. Be firm but joyful.

READING II   Paul's Galatian converts have come under the influence of some meddlers who demand adherence to certain aspects of Mosaic law, including circumcision. Paul's rebuttal focuses on two aspects of freedom. First, Christ's death liberated us from reliance on the law; we are saved not by our works, but by his death. Second, freedom from the tyranny of law does not translate into licentiousness, that is, trading in one form of slavery to the flesh for another. Freedom in Christ means freedom to do what leads to salvation.

Paul's direct and spirited opening sets the tone for his admonitions about love. For Paul, "flesh" does not refer simply to sexual immorality, but to any form of selfishness. Love is the opposite of selfishness, and love is lived out in service. Like Jesus, Paul reduces the whole law to love, a love that proves itself in action. He warns his readers that the ways of the flesh—"biting and devouring"—lead only to destruction. The antidote to the poison of the flesh is the Spirit. But Paul's contrast of flesh and spirit is not a contrast of two aspects of human nature (our so-called "lower" and "higher" functions). "Flesh" represents all human opposition to God, but "Spirit" is a power from outside of ourselves; it is God's Spirit who helps us resist the allurements of the flesh—anger, envy, lust, pride, and so forth. The reason we embrace spirit over flesh is not out of fear of the law, but out of love, which, as he has told us, is the fulfillment of the law.

GOSPEL   Luke 9:51–62

A reading from the holy Gospel according to Luke

The first sentence announces the beginning of the end of Jesus' earthly ministry. Let your tone suggest its deeper meaning.

The Galilean ministry began with Jesus' rejection at Nazareth; here he's rejected by the Samaritans. Speak this narration in the voice of the hostile Samaritans.

When the days for Jesus' being taken **up** were **fulfilled**,
he resolutely determined to **journey** to **Jerusalem**,
and he sent **messengers** ahead of him.
On the **way** they entered a **Samaritan** village
to prepare for his **reception** there,
but they would not **welcome** him
because the **destination** of his journey was **Jerusalem**.

Contrast James' and John's quick anger with Jesus' resolve to move on.

When the disciples **James** and **John** saw this they **asked**,
"**Lord**, do you want us to call down fire from **heaven**
to **consume** them?"
Jesus **turned** and **rebuked** them, and they journeyed
to **another** village.

"I will follow . . ." should be spoken with great sincerity.

Jesus' tone asks, "Are you ready to embrace hardship for the kingdom?"

As they were **proceeding** on their journey someone **said** to him,
"I will follow you **wherever** you go."
Jesus **answered** him,
"**Foxes** have **dens** and birds of the **sky** have **nests**,
but the Son of **Man** has **nowhere** to rest his head."

Contrast Jesus' eager invitation with the hesitancy of the man invited.

And to **another** he said, "**Follow** me."
But **he** replied, "**Lord**, let me go **first** and bury my **father**."
But he **answered** him, "Let the **dead** bury their dead.
But **you**, **go** and proclaim the kingdom of **God**."
And **another** said, "**I** will follow you, Lord,
but first let me say **farewell** to my family at **home**."

Speak Jesus' last proverb very slowly. It's not a reproach, but a call to recognize the demands of the kingdom.

To **him** Jesus said, "No one who sets a **hand** to the plow
and looks to what was left **behind** is **fit** for the **kingdom**
of **God**."

GOSPEL Although seemingly disjointed, this Gospel's two episodes focus us on the cost of discipleship. The lesson started by Elisha is taken up by Jesus, and he does it by example. From this point on in Luke's Gospel account, Jesus journeys "resolutely" toward Jerusalem," knowing full well what awaits him there. This journey section of Luke's story begins as did the Galilean ministry, with Jesus being rejected. Despite the historical and political basis for the hostility of the Samaritans, James and John, proving how aptly they

were named ("sons of thunder") react with righteous anger. We don't hear Jesus' words of "reprimand," but perhaps they resembled his repudiation of Peter when *he* played the tempter. Unlike Elijah who *did* call down fire on opponents, Jesus eschews retaliation and sets off to meet his destiny.

If read in isolation, even Jesus' own resolve won't prepare us for the degree of challenge expressed in his three proverbs. The demands of discipleship are sometimes radical; at times we will need to live these words quite literally. But Jesus is

not as uncompromising as he appears. He speaks bluntly to shock his listeners into a new mindset. There are times when we can and should submit to the demands of filial piety—as did Elisha—but other rare times when everything must yield to the demands of the kingdom. "Let the dead . . ." forces his questioners (and us) to think about where the road we walk with him will lead. With his own hand fixed "to the plow," Jesus asks disciples to imitate his commitment. So rather than reproach, speak his last proverb like a call to heroic loyalty and dedication.

14TH SUNDAY IN ORDINARY TIME

Lectionary #102

READING I   Isaiah 66:10–14c

A reading from the Book of the Prophet Isaiah

Speak these images with comfort and delight and your assembly will hear "The word of the Lord" instead of embarrassed mumbling.

Thus says the LORD:
Rejoice with Jerusalem and be **glad** because of her,
    all you who **love** her;

The urgency increases steadily from "Rejoice" to "be glad" to the double "Exult."

exult, **exult** with her,
    all you who were **mourning** over her!
Oh, that you may suck **fully**

This tender image calls for a softer, gentler tone. The second set of couplets repeats the idea of the first one, so build energy.

    of the milk of her **comfort**,
that you may nurse with **delight**
    at her **abundant** breasts!
For **thus** says the LORD:

God is making a promise. Speak it with authority, but with the love with which a parent would promise an inheritance to a beloved child.

Lo, I will spread **prosperity** over Jerusalem like a **river**,
    and the wealth of the **nations** like an overflowing **torrent**.

Jerusalem as a nursing mother is a beautiful but rare biblical image.

As **nurslings**, you shall be carried in her **arms**,
    and **fondled** in her **lap**;

Now even God assumes the role of mother!

as a **mother** comforts her **child**,
    so will **I** comfort **you**;
    in **Jerusalem** you shall **find** your comfort.

"When you see this . . . " points to a future time, so pause slightly and then describe how heart and body will respond to God's power and mercy.

When you **see** this, your heart shall **rejoice**
    and your bodies **flourish** like the **grass**;
the LORD's **power** shall be **known** to his **servants**.

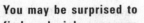

READING I You may be surprised to find such rich, sensuous imagery in the Lectionary, but scripture is not shy about celebrating God's creation, nor about using images that reveal God's bountiful goodness. As lector, you can make a real difference today both by communicating the exultant joy at Jerusalem's restoration and by expressing without embarrassment the profound motherly imagery that distinguishes this text.

Israel's children had languished in exile, longing for their home, mourning the destruction of the holy city, Jerusalem, and its temple. Now, in jubilant poetry, Isaiah sings of the end of exile and of Jerusalem's children returning to their cherished home. The city is depicted as a mother who welcomes her children and draws them close to her abundant breasts where they will be nurtured and comforted. The time of trial and sorrow is ended, the nation is returning to life and so they must "Rejoice! . . . and be glad . . . . Exult, exult!" Isaiah's imagery won't achieve its full impact unless the sound of your proclamation matches his joy. Speak from your aware-

ness that a new time has dawned when "prosperity" (better translated as "peace") flows "like a river" toward Jerusalem. A blend of similes follows: "Wealth . . . like an overflowing torrent" will be given. God and the city are both presented as a mother who nurses her children; those who see God's promise fulfilled will "flourish like grass" that receives life-giving moisture. God holds nothing back. Mercy and abundance will be showered upon God's beloved children. Because you are not sharing

READING II   Galatians 6:14–18

Paul writes this postscript as a summary of the whole letter.

Pause briefly after "boast," and then state forcefully in what one *can* boast—the cross of Christ!

Move quickly through the circumcision discussion, and then slow down for the point that really matters: "new creation."

He's winding down here. This prayer for peace is spoken gently and lovingly. This is what the assembly should remember!

This line, sandwiched between two blessings, is spoken with strength, not anger.

Speak this final blessing to your assembly. Sustain eye contact so that you can memorize the line.

A reading from the Letter of Saint Paul to the Galatians

Brothers and sisters:

May I never **boast** except in the **cross** of our Lord Jesus **Christ**,
    through which the world has been **crucified** to me,
        and **I** to the **world**.
For neither does **circumcision** mean **anything**,
        nor does **uncircumcision**,
    but only a **new creation**.
Peace and **mercy** be to all who **follow** this **rule**
    and to the **Israel** of **God**.

From now **on**, let no one make **troubles** for me;
    for I bear the **marks** of **Jesus** on my body.

The **grace** of our Lord Jesus **Christ** be with your **spirit**,
    brothers and sisters. **Amen**.

---

facts, but images, allow your listeners time to receive the images and to respond with their emotions and imagination. The entire text is a series of couplets in which the second line of the couplet repeats the idea stated in the first. That poetic device requires that you increase energy from the first to second line or else risk sounding redundant. This poetry offers comfort to anyone hoping for renewal and a fresh start. God's prophet doesn't hold back. Will you?

READING II Paul was a man of many talents and strong convictions; he never shied away from a fight. Throughout Galatians he has carried on a strong argument against opponents. Here at the end of the letter where he summarizes his chief points, that polemical tone is still evident. Paul has had to work hard to defend his status as "apostle" of Jesus, given that he was not one of the original twelve. But here, he asserts his *true* "boast," and it's not about status or rank, but about being a follower of the *crucified* Christ. Belonging to Christ makes

us a "new creation," yet some are still bickering over whether or not one needs to be circumcised. Toward that group that still has its priorities wrong, Paul sounds a final note of opposition. Circumcision is not an issue today, but other issues are, so every congregation can be reminded that through the cross of Jesus they, too, are new creations—and that nothing matters more than that. That is one of Paul's pervasive themes. Give it its due.

The Jerusalem Bible translates Paul's second-to-last sentence with pointed candor: "I want no more trouble from anybody

GOSPEL Luke 10:1–12, 17–20

A reading from the holy Gospel according to Luke

At **that** time the Lord appointed seventy-two **others**
    whom he sent **ahead** of him in **pairs**
    to every **town** and **place** he intended to **visit**.
He **said** to them,
    "The **harvest** is **abundant** but the **laborers** are **few**;
    so ask the **master** of the harvest
    to send out **laborers** for his harvest.
Go on your way;
    behold, I am sending you like **lambs** among **wolves**.
Carry no **money** bag, no **sack**, no **sandals**;
    and greet **no** one along the **way**.
Into whatever **house** you enter, **first** say,
    '**Peace** to this household.'
If a peaceful person **lives** there,
    your peace will **rest** on him;
    but if **not**, it will **return** to you.
Stay in the **same** house and **eat** and **drink** what is **offered** to you,
    for the laborer **deserves** his payment.
Do not move **about** from **one** house to **another**.

"Seventy-two" is symbolic of a mission to the nations (thought to number 72) as the mission of the Twelve was to the tribes of Israel.

Speak in an encouraging tone here.

The missionary must avoid all distractions from the work of the kingdom.

Speak the words "Peace to this household" in the way the post-Resurrection Jesus spoke it to his disciples. Those worthy will receive it; those unworthy will not!

---

after this." Paul has more than paid his dues and proven his allegiance to Christ. The "marks of Jesus"—the scars from the floggings and stoning that mark him as Christ's follower—are credentials enough to ensure he is never challenged again about his authority. But because Paul ends the letter with these words and then immediately follows them with a blessing, try speaking them as an expression of confident pride in his relationship with Christ, rather than as anger at his detractors. And don't just report that final benediction;

share it with the "brothers and sisters" who sit in your pews today.

GOSPEL Today's First Reading prepares us to read the Gospel with an awareness of the joy that comes to those who fulfill their task of proclaiming the kingdom. Without that awareness, embracing the work of the kingdom could seem overwhelming. But the end of the Gospel offers promise of the reward that awaits those who labor faithfully in

God's vineyard. Jesus knows these disciples he is sending on mission and offers them concrete advice that will focus them on their task and sustain them in their work. It's not all good news. They will go out like lambs among wolves, and there always will be fewer workers than the needs of the harvest, so they should raise up prayers to God for more willing servants like themselves. That he sends them out not alone, but "in pairs," immediately signals a mission that will be demanding and even perilous. As we saw last week, discipleship requires a single-mindedness that

Speak with the joyful tone of the missionary.

Whatever **town** you enter and they **welcome** you,
> **eat** what is set **before** you,
> **cure** the sick in it and **say** to them,
> 'The **kingdom** of **God** is at **hand** for you.'

Whatever town you enter and they do **not** receive you,
> go out into the **streets** and say,
> 'The **dust** of your town that clings to our **feet**,
> even **that** we **shake** off against you.'

Yet know **this**: the kingdom of **God** is at **hand**.

I **tell** you, it will be more tolerable for **Sodom** on that day
> than for **that** town."

The tone shifts here, becoming more sober. The announcement of the kingdom brings hope and salvation, but if it's rejected, God's judgment will be severe.

The seventy-two returned **rejoicing**, and said,
> "**Lord**, even the **demons** are subject to us because
> of your **name**."

Jesus said, "I have observed **Satan** fall like **lightning**
> from the **sky**.

Behold, I have given you the **power** to 'tread upon **serpents**'
> and **scorpions**
> and upon the full **force** of the **enemy**
> and **nothing** will **harm** you.

Nevertheless, do not rejoice because the **spirits** are subject to you,
> but **rejoice** because your **names** are written in **heaven**."

Joy is a constant theme in Luke. The disciples rejoice rightly in the success of their mission.

Stress the remarkable power Jesus has given them, and then contrast that with what he says *really* matters.

[Shorter: Luke 10:1–9]

---

is uncompromising—hence, no "money-bag," no "sandals," not even the customarily profuse and time-consuming greeting rituals common to that time and place.

But Jesus' missionaries are not without rights and powers. They may ignore dietary prohibitions and eat what's "set before" them, for each laborer "deserves his payment." And whether they are welcomed or rejected, they are to announce "the kingdom of God." Those who are open will hear the announcement as a sign of

peace and consolation, but for those who reject them, the same words, "the reign of God is near," will be an announcement of judgment. Jesus even commands that they shake the dust of such towns from their feet.

Luke brings the disciples home with trademark jubilation, marveling that demons were subject to them. Jesus asserts that the rise of the kingdom brings about the fall of Satan and assures them of the power he has entrusted to them. He then sobers their enthusiasm by claiming

that the greatest joy comes not from having spirits obey them, but in finding their names "written in heaven."

15TH SUNDAY IN ORDINARY TIME

Lectionary #105

READING I   Deuteronomy 30:10–14

A reading from the Book of Deuteronomy

Moses said to the **people**:
"If only you would **heed** the voice of the LORD, your **God**,
and keep his **commandments** and **statutes**
that are **written** in this book of the **law**,
when you **return** to the LORD, your God,
with all your **heart** and all your **soul**.

"For this **command** that I enjoin on you today
is not too **mysterious** and **remote** for you.
It is not up in the **sky**, that you should say,
'Who will go **up** in the sky to **get** it for us
and **tell** us of it, that we may carry it **out**?'
Nor is it across the **sea**, that you should say,
'Who will **cross** the sea to get it for us
and **tell** us of it, that we may carry it **out**?'
No, it is something very **near** to you,
already in your **mouths** and in your **hearts**;
you have **only** to carry it **out**."

Pause after "Moses" so that we know who is speaking.

Reading in your Bible the verses immediately preceding this passage will clarify the meaning.

The "command" is to love.

Shift from the voice of Moses to that of the apprehensive people.

Once again, it goes from Moses' voice to the voice of the people. Are these questions half-mocking or sincere?

Speak with conviction directly to the hearts of the assembly.

READING I   A basic principle of Catholic moral teaching asserts that within the human heart is a divine law that commands us to love. That is the message of this text; however the Lectionary passage begins in the middle of a sentence, so the meaning is difficult to understand. The thrust of the entire sentence is: The Lord will delight in you and your descendants "if only you would heed . . . and return to the Lord." (It may be helpful to consult an alternate translation of this passage.)

The text then mentions "this command" and makes much of the need to "carry it out." But we never hear the command. It doesn't appear until several verses after the conclusion of this excerpt where Moses addresses the people and says, "I have set before you life and death . . . . Choose life" (see Deuteronomy 31:19). The best way to choose life, of course, is to love—a command heard twice in today's Gospel and throughout Deuteronomy. Love of God and neighbor is the whole of the law. Moses assures the people that the law is not something outside of them, distant, inaccessible, and mysterious. The law is "very near," he tells them, as near,

as steady, and as necessary as the breath in your mouth and the beating of your hearts. Moses voices questions that express the people's fears that the law is more than they can handle. It's difficult to say whether he is half-mocking a people who are evading responsibility, or simply echoing their sincere self-doubt. Either way, Moses insists the law is already a part of them. Try to convey to your assembly the urgency Moses feels in this message: fidelity to God is possible; they can keep the law.

READING II   Colossians 1:15–20

A reading from the Letter of Saint Paul to the Colossians

Christ **Jesus** is the **image** of the invisible **God**,
  the **firstborn** of all **creation**.
For in **him** were created all things in **heaven** and on **earth**,
  the **visible** and the **invisible**,
  whether **thrones** or **dominions** or **principalities** or **powers**;
  all things were created **through** him and **for** him.
He is **before** all things,
  and in **him** all things hold **together**.
He is the **head** of the body, the **church**.
He is the **beginning**, the **firstborn** from the **dead**,
  that in **all** things he himself might be **preeminent**.
For in **him** all the **fullness** was pleased to **dwell**,
  and **through** him to **reconcile** all things for him,
  making **peace** by the **blood** of his **cross**
  through **him**, whether those on **earth** or those in **heaven**.

Begin with energy and authority. Christ makes visible the invisible God!

Thrones, dominations, principalities, and powers are ranks or categories of angels, all subordinate to Christ.

Speak joyfully and with conviction of how Christ sustains all things and holds them together.

The New Revised Standard Version reads: "For in him all the fullness of God was pleased to dwell, and through him God was pleased to reconcile to himself all things, whether on earth or in heaven, by making peace through the blood of his cross."

READING II This entire text is derived from an early Christian hymn that extols Christ as creator and redeemer. Like many hymns, it was written in part with a catechetical purpose. In Colossae, Christ's role in salvation was being subverted by certain teachers who had begun stressing the importance of angels in a way that undermined Christ's unique role. Paul cites this hymn to attack that error and to assert the preexistence of Christ who is the "first-born" of creation, the one through whom everything in heaven and on earth was made. And that includes every category of angels—thrones, dominations, and so on. The hymn proclaims that there is no other spiritual power that can compete with Christ, for all things visible and all things invisible were "created through him and for him." (Enjoy this rare opportunity to legitimately stress the prepositions.)

This Christ, who in the first half of the reading is extolled as the firstborn of all creation, is extolled in the second half as "the firstborn from the dead." Because he is the one who died and rose, he is the first of many who will likewise rise from the dead. Jesus now reigns as head over his body, the Church. But God has also made Jesus preeminent over "all things" in the universe. Besides glorifying Christ, that declaration reassures the Colossians that none of the spiritual beings proposed by the false teachers can take precedence over Jesus.

Despite being a magnificent hymn of praise, the song ends with a reminder of the means by which Christ brought peace and reconciliation to the world: the shedding of his blood. The translation of the

GOSPEL   Luke 10:25–37

A reading from the holy Gospel according to Luke

There was a scholar of the **law** who stood up to **test** him and said,
    "**Teacher**, what must I **do** to inherit eternal **life**?"
Jesus **said** to him, "What is written in the **law**?
How do you **read** it?"
He said in reply,
    "*You shall* **love** *the Lord, your God,*
    with all your **heart**,
    with all your **being**,
    with all your **strength**,
    and with all your **mind**,
    and your **neighbor** *as* **yourself**."
He **replied** to him, "You have answered **correctly**;
    do this and you will **live**."

But because he wished to **justify** himself, he said to Jesus,
    "And **who** is my neighbor?"
Jesus replied,
    "A **man** fell victim to **robbers**
    as he went down from **Jerusalem** to **Jericho**.
They **stripped** and **beat** him and went **off** leaving him half-**dead**.
A **priest** happened to be going down that road,
    but when he **saw** him, he **passed** by on the **opposite** side.
Likewise a **Levite** came to the place,
    and when **he** saw him, **he** passed by on the opposite side.

The lawyer, possibly a "scribe," need not be unsympathetic. He may be "testing" Jesus' sincerity or wisdom, not necessarily trying to trip him up.

Jesus has a positive attitude toward the law.

Read these lines sincerely, not like a rote classroom lesson.

Jesus affirms that right understanding and adherence to the law can lead to salvation.

Speak the question briskly, as if trying to keep Jesus from turning away.

Use the action verbs ("stripped," "beat," and so on) to create the drama of this scene.

Speak of the "priest" and the "Levite" without prejudice.

---

final verses of this text is somewhat confusing, and so the margin notes provide an alternate translation. Remember, this is a joyous hymn that celebrates Christ's unique role in the heavens and on the earth.

GOSPEL   The First Reading reminded us that keeping God's law is possible and that the essence of the law is written by God deep within our hearts. Jesus' story demonstrates that keeping the law of God is not so much a matter of how well tutored we might be, but of how well

we listen to the heart. Jesus' parable makes our understanding of the love of God concrete by demonstrating that we love God best when we love our neighbor. A lawyer asks an earnest question (only later we learn he "wished to justify himself"). Jesus points to the Mosaic law and asks for the man's understanding of it. As a scholar of the law, the lawyer gives a flawless response, synthesizing all of Jewish law as the love of God and neighbor. Jesus concurs with his response and gently dismisses him. But the lawyer asks a second question that, despite the exemplary reply

he's just given, reveals he lacks the depth of understanding that Jesus is about to impart. Avoid characterizing the lawyer as aloof or snobbish; despite the reference to seeking justification, there may be complexity to his character and, by the end of the episode, it's possible that both his eyes and heart have opened wider.

The lawyer wants to know who qualifies as neighbor, who can place love's demands on him. Jesus' reply will be surprising. This now classic story is quite simple. A man is victimized by robbers and

Samaritan = suh-MAYR-uh-tuhn

Set off the word "Samaritan" with a pause. Of course, it won't have the intended shock value it had for Jesus' audience.

Speak slowly here, so that you can convey the compassion with which the Samaritan treated the victim.

Jesus turns the question right back on the lawyer.

The lawyer stops to think before answering. Let his reply reveal the perhaps enthusiastic realization that "mercy" makes a neighbor.

Jesus' tone can suggest whether or not he senses the man's sincerity.

But a **Samaritan** traveler who came upon him
    was moved with **compassion** at the sight.
He **approached** the victim,
    poured **oil** and **wine** over his wounds and **bandaged** them.
Then he **lifted** him up on his own **animal**,
    took him to an **inn**, and **cared** for him.
The next **day** he took out two silver **coins**
    and gave them to the **innkeeper** with the instruction,
    'Take **care** of him.
If you spend **more** than what I have given you,
    I shall **repay** you on my way **back**.'
Which of these three, in **your** opinion,
    was **neighbor** to the robbers' victim?"
He answered, "The **one** who treated him with **mercy**."
Jesus said to him, "**Go** and do **likewise**."

left for dead on the roadside. We know nothing more about him but his desperate need. Similarly, we know nothing of the priest and Levite except that they passed him by. There is speculation about these religious men's concern for being rendered unclean by contact with the dying man. That assumption may indeed be built into Jesus' plotline, making the point that compassion always trumps the claims of legalism. That the Samaritan was a pariah in that culture hardly needs repeating. That

Jesus casts him as the hero after his recent rejection in Samaria is remarkable. Your tone can reflect the shock a contemporary would have felt at seeing such a hated enemy behave in so exemplary a fashion.

With his final question ("Which of these three . . . ?"), Jesus, without hostility, turns the tables on the scholar. Commentators point out the lawyer's "unwillingness" to answer "the Samaritan," opting instead to describe him as "the one who treated him with mercy." But does his response betray hostility toward Samaritans

or does it reveal deep conversion? He names the very quality that makes one neighbor, thus answering his own earlier question. Perhaps this teachable moment has convinced him that compassion is truly the heart of the law and disposed him to heed Jesus' instruction to "Go and do likewise."

16TH SUNDAY IN ORDINARY TIME

Lectionary #108

READING I — Genesis 18:1–10a

Make sure the assembly hears that it is the "Lord" who appeared.
Terebinth = TAYR-uh-binth
Mamre = MAHM-ray

Pause after "standing nearby" to give Abraham time to decide how he'll react.

His response is sudden, but slow the tempo when he actually speaks to the visitors. Stress the singular "Sir."

The line suggests his awareness that he's in the presence of the divine.

Abraham, like Martha in the Gospel, is rather anxious. He's preparing his very best for his visitors.

A reading from the Book of Genesis

The LORD appeared to **Abraham** by the terebinth of **Mamre**,
    as he sat in the entrance of his **tent**,
    while the day was growing **hot**.
Looking **up**, Abraham saw three **men** standing nearby.
When he **saw** them, he **ran** from the entrance of the tent
    to **greet** them;
    and **bowing** to the ground, he said:
    "**Sir**, if I may ask you this **favor**,
    please do not go on **past** your servant.
Let some **water** be brought, that you may bathe your **feet**,
    and then **rest** yourselves under the **tree**.
Now that you have come this **close** to your servant,
    let me bring you a little **food**, that you may **refresh** yourselves;
    and **afterward** you may go on your **way**."
The **men** replied, "Very **well**, do as you have **said**."

Abraham **hastened** into the tent and told **Sarah**,
    "**Quick**, three measures of fine **flour**! **Knead** it
    and make **rolls**."
He ran to the **herd**, picked out a tender, choice **steer**,
    and gave it to a **servant**, who quickly **prepared** it.
Then Abraham got some curds and **milk**,
    as well as the **steer** that had been prepared,

READING I   Two ancient stories are blended into one to create this delightful narrative. That explains the obvious ambiguity regarding the identity and number of Abraham's visitors. The opening states "the Lord appeared," but Abraham sees *three* men whom he addresses with the singular "Sir." Despite the singular/plural shifts, it's clear that Abraham realizes he is hosting God. It's possible the ancient editor retained the ambiguity to signal that God is both transcendent and mysterious but also a close and loving presence in the world. Exactly

when Abraham realizes he is entertaining the Lord is hard to pinpoint, but the details give clues. Abraham's response is excessive at every turn: he is an old man who "runs" to his guests, he offers "some water" and "a little food," but serves a royal feast, and he invites the men *urgently*, saying, "now that you have come this close" (as if realizing God has come down to humanity). Find the words that highlight his excess: "Quick," "three measures [half a bushel!] of fine flour," "a tender, choice steer," "he waited on them [not his servants]." In the

ancient world where travel was hazardous, hospitality was a vital part of the culture. But this exceeds expectations. His attitude reveals an understanding that besides good food and drink, hospitality means attentiveness to guests, a willingness to hear the word they speak.

The three visitor's only question concerns Sarah. Earlier, Abraham asked God to fulfill the promise of descendants through Ishmael, the son of Abraham and Hagaar, Sarah's servant. But God insists the promise will be kept through a son Sarah will bear. Stress the importance of

It is Abraham himself, not his servants, who waits on the guests.

and **set** these before the three men;
and he **waited** on them under the tree while they **ate**.

Your tone for this question should signal something important is about to occur.

They **asked** Abraham, "Where is your wife **Sarah**?"
He replied, "**There** in the **tent**."
One of them said, "I will surely **return** to you
　　about **this** time next **year**,
　and **Sarah** will then have a **son**."

Pause briefly after "Sarah," and then announce the good news.

READING II　Colossians 1:24–28

A reading from the Letter of Saint Paul to the Colossians

Although you speak of suffering, let your tone be joyful. Identify all the ideas in this long sentence, and then share them one at a time. Paul rejoices that in his flesh (take time with that powerful expression) he is mystically united with Christ's Passion.

As proclaimer, you, too, are a minister of the Church. Paul assigns himself three roles: sufferer, minister, and proclaimer.

The "mystery" is Christ who now lives in his body, the Church.

Brothers and sisters:
Now I **rejoice** in my sufferings for **your** sake,
　and in my **flesh** I am filling up
　　what is **lacking** in the afflictions of **Christ**
　on behalf of his **body**, which is the **church**,
　of which I am a **minister**
　　in accordance with God's **stewardship given** to me
　to bring to **completion** for you the **word** of **God**,
　the **mystery** hidden from **ages** and from generations **past**.
But **now** it has been **manifested** to his **holy** ones,
　to whom God chose to make **known** the riches of the **glory**
　　of this mystery among the **Gentiles**;
　it is **Christ** in you, the **hope** for **glory**.
It is **he** whom we proclaim,
　admonishing everyone and **teaching** everyone
　　with all **wisdom**,
　that we may present **everyone perfect** in **Christ**.

Paul's focus is on Christ. Make that clear.

---

this matriarch whose involvement in this drama fulfills God's joyful promise.

 Paul suffered much for the sake of the Gospel, including several imprisonments. He's jailed as he writes this letter, yet, remarkably, he rejoices in his suffering. The long opening sentence seems to suggest there was something lacking in Christ's suffering that Paul is now compensating for with his own. Nothing could be further from the truth. This much debated text implies no

deficiency in Christ's sacrifice. John Paul II wrote that because it was through suffering that Christ saved us, suffering itself has been redeemed and has somehow become salvific. That is, anyone who suffers can share in Christ's redemptive suffering. Although the "good" that Christ achieved in the redemption is "inexhaustible and infinite," and although no one can add to the redemption Christ achieved, at the same time, because the Church is his body, Christ has made it possible for all human suffering to unite with his own redemptive suffering. To the extent that we willingly

share in Christ's sufferings, to that extent we "help complete the suffering through which Christ redeemed the world." Because Christ continues to suffer in his body, the Church, his redemptive suffering continues unceasingly through us when we willingly offer up our sufferings to God (*Salvifici Dolores,* 23–24).

　The rest of the text outlines the gradual movement from "mystery" to revelation: the once hidden mystery (Christ lives in us) is now "manifested," "known," and something to preach, proclaim, and teach.

GOSPEL   Luke 10:38–42

A reading from the holy Gospel according to Luke

Jesus entered a **village**
  where a woman whose name was **Martha welcomed** him.
She had a **sister** named **Mary**
  who sat **beside** the Lord at his **feet** listening to him **speak**.
Martha, burdened with much **serving**, came to him and **said**,
  "**Lord**, do you not **care**
  that my sister has left me by **myself** to do the serving?
Tell her to **help** me."
The Lord said to her in **reply**,
  "**Martha**, **Martha**, you are **anxious** and **worried**
  about **many** things.
There is need of only **one** thing.
Mary has chosen the **better** part
  and it will not be **taken** from her."

All the details here are important:
A *woman* welcomed him; Mary *sat
at his feet*.

Martha is tired, frustrated, and feeling
rather neglected.

Her rapport with Jesus permits this
familiarity.

The double "Martha" suggests a playful,
coaxing tone.

The tone can be firm, but not harsh.

The same mature joy of Paul's opening
echoes through these lines.

 GOSPEL Luke rarely names those
who converse with Jesus,
yet here he names two women and Martha
is first. It is she who welcomed Jesus to
her home and she who engages him in
dialogue—and through her that a lesson
is taught. Mary is introduced almost par-
enthetically, but the simple language
describes a remarkable relationship. Mary
assumes a *disciple's* posture at Jesus' feet,

something women simply did not do. And
while we are only *told* that Martha welcomed Jesus, we are *shown* how Mary did
it—by *listening*. Luke's emphasis is clear:
true hospitality assumes the attitude of a
disciple and eagerly listens to the word of
the Lord. This is Luke's primary concern, not
a condemnation of Martha's culinary zeal.

So don't suggest a simplistic and mor-
alizing opposition between action and con-
templation. Jesus loves Martha as much as
Mary. Martha confidently approaches Jesus
the way a child sometimes approaches a
parent, complaining (she "has left me by

myself . . .") and demanding ("Tell her to
help me"). Jesus chastises Martha not for
what she does, but for how she does it:
"anxious and worried." His repetition of
her name signals affection and possible amusement at her consternation. His
tone must not condemn her behavior, but
invite her to remember why and for whom
she labors, so that she can listen even in
her busyness.

17TH SUNDAY IN ORDINARY TIME

Lectionary #111

READING I Genesis 18:20–32

Sodom = SOD-uhm

Gomorrah = guh-MOHR-ah

God's tone is strong and sober. The revelation that Sodom's sin demands punishment distresses Abraham and sparks his action on behalf of those who may be innocent. The tone of "outcry," "sin so grave," "cry," and the energy behind "I mean to find out" are what motivate Abraham to action.

"Visitors" refers to two of the three angelic/divine guests Abraham has just entertained. The third, representing God, remains to reveal God's intentions toward Sodom and Gomorrah.

Note the options for variety in delivery of Abraham's lines noted in the commentary. The author has made this a very human dialogue. Don't work against that.

Abraham is saying, "You'll ruin your reputation if you do this!"

God's tone can remain consistent throughout: patient and compassionate.

A reading from the Book of Genesis

In **those** days, the LORD said:

"The **outcry** against **Sodom** and **Gomorrah** is so **great**,
   and their **sin** so **grave**,
that I must **go** down and see whether or not their **actions**
   fully correspond to the **cry** against them that **comes** to me.
I mean to find **out**."

While **Abraham's visitors** walked on **farther** toward **Sodom**,
   the LORD remained **standing** before Abraham.
Then Abraham drew **nearer** and said:
   "Will you sweep away the **innocent** with the **guilty**?
Suppose there were fifty **innocent** people in the city;
   would you **wipe** out the place, rather than **spare** it
   for the sake of the **fifty** innocent people within it?
Far be it from **you** to do such a thing,
   to make the **innocent** die with the **guilty**
   so that the **innocent** and the **guilty** would be treated **alike**!
Should not the **judge** of all the **world** act with **justice**?"
The LORD **replied**,
   "If I find **fifty** innocent people in the city of Sodom,
   I will spare the whole **place** for **their** sake."

READING I Persistence in prayer is the theme of today's readings. There is an amazing contrast between the ominous opening monologue and the entertaining and colorful dialogue that follows. We learn that the sin of these cities cries to heaven for vengeance. That God allows Abraham to bargain and set ever-lower conditions for action against the cities makes their exchange all the more remarkable. It is no small matter over which God is willing to show mercy "if there are at least ten there."

This is a distinctively Semitic dialogue, folksy and somewhat comic. The style of bargaining depicted here can still be heard today between customers and vendors in the marketplaces of this part of the world. Abraham's familiar attitude with God is understandable given the lavish meal he earlier prepared for God and given the ancient Near Eastern belief that the servant of a god or king was also a friend. Try recalling someone you know whose ability to bargain is legendary. To sustain this lengthy text you'll need to borrow that

person's style. Although most will be familiar with the ending—it's not reported here—there is still suspense in the dialogue. But the focus is not on suspense, rather on God's patience and mercy.

The Semitic flavor is most evident in Abraham's insinuations that God's honor and reputation for justice are jeopardized if the innocent die with the guilty. Abraham's tone is not disrespectful; he speaks with confidence because of his solid relationship with God. God threatens in the beginning, but the balance of the text reveals calm, indulgent restraint. The

Abraham is a master of this game of bargaining.

Abraham spoke up **again**:
  "See how I am **presuming** to speak to my Lord,
    though I am but **dust** and **ashes**!
What if there are five **less** than fifty innocent people?
Will you destroy the whole **city** because of those **five**?"
He answered, "I will **not** destroy it, if I find **forty-five** there."

His energy builds, but without going too far.

But Abraham **persisted**, saying "What if only **forty** are
    found there?"
He replied, "I will **forbear** doing it for the sake of the **forty**."
Then Abraham said, "Let not my Lord grow **impatient** if I go on.
What if only **thirty** are found there?"
He replied, "I will forbear **doing** it if I can find but **thirty** there."
Still Abraham went **on**,
  "Since I have thus **dared** to speak to my Lord,
    what if there are no more than **twenty**?"

God seems not to tire of the process and indulges Abraham further.

The LORD answered, "I will not **destroy** it, for the sake
    of the **twenty**."
But he **still** persisted:
  "**Please**, let not my Lord grow **angry** if I speak up this **last** time.
What if there are at least **ten** there?"
He replied, "For the sake of those **ten**, I will **not destroy** it."

We don't hear how the story ends. The point here is how far God is willing to go to spare humanity of deserved punishment.

---

structure is cyclic: Abraham asks, God concedes, and Abraham asks again. God's refrain-like reassurance concludes each exchange before Abraham starts another salvo. Abraham's self-deprecation balances his relentless lobbying that almost (but never) transgresses the boundaries of propriety.

For variety, decide these questions: Does Abraham ever hesitate? Do you wonder if he's going too far? Speed up ("Whatifonlyfortyarefoundthere?")? Slow down ("What . . . if there are . . . at least . . . ten there?")? Decide, too, from

what point of view the narrator reports these proceedings: increasing amazement, disbelief, admiration, or detached neutrality?

God is given human qualities in this text: bargaining, indulgent, needing to "go see" despite being omniscient, and so forth. Don't minimize those features. And remember, the cities were destroyed! God is merciful, but God's justice is not cancelled. God answered Abraham's prayer, relenting over and over on the "number." For only "ten" God would have spared the city. But there were not ten.

READING II In this passage, Paul immediately states a powerful truth: through Baptism we were "buried" with Christ and also "raised with him" from the dead. The reason we have undergone this death and Resurrection with Christ is that we had "faith in the power of God." Of course that's more than just an explanation. Faith in God's power is also a formula for continuing in this new life in Christ, so give it proper stress. God forgave us when we were still "dead" in sin and living in

READING II   Colossians 2:12–14

A reading from the Letter of Saint Paul to the Colossians

This is a joyful announcement. Let your voice convey that.

Stress the importance of "faith."

"And even when . . . " suggests God's generosity and initiative. Contrast negative tone on "transgressions . . . flesh" with a positive tone on the good news ("forgiven us . . . obliterating the bond") that follows.

It's the cross that makes forgiveness possible!

Brothers and sisters:
You were **buried** with him in **baptism**,
   in which you were also **raised** with him
     through **faith** in the power of **God**,
     who **raised** him from the **dead**.
And even when you were **dead**
   in **transgressions** and the **uncircumcision** of your **flesh**,
   he brought you to **life** along with him,
   having **forgiven** us all our transgressions;
obliterating the bond against us, with its **legal** claims,
   which was **opposed** to us,
   he also **removed** it from our midst, **nailing** it to the **cross**.

GOSPEL   Luke 11:1–13

A reading from the holy Gospel according to Luke

Make sure the assembly hears that Jesus is in prayer.

This is not the version of the Lord's Prayer that the assembly is used to. Pause briefly after "Father."

Read the individual petitions as if Jesus were composing them on the spot.

Jesus was **praying** in a certain **place**, and when he had **finished**,
   one of his **disciples** said to him,
   "**Lord**, teach us to **pray** just as **John** taught **his** disciples."
He said to them, "When you **pray**, say:
   Father, **hallowed** be your **name**,
     your **kingdom come**.
     Give us each day our daily **bread**
     and **forgive** us our **sins**

"the uncircumcision" of the flesh. So forgiveness, Paul assures us, is ours as a pure, unmerited gift.

The Church in Colossae dealt with several errors; one was the belief that physical circumcision was required for Christian initiation. But Paul insists that God's gift was given without any such condition. The new risen life inaugurated by Christ's Resurrection is not something that awaits us in the next life, but a present reality we've already begun to live here and now.

That God has "forgiven us all our transgressions" is the Good News of salvation. Paul elaborates that point with an intriguing image. The "bond" (an IOU) that was held against us with all "its legal claims" has been cancelled. God put our debt of sin to death on the cross of Jesus—not because we deserved it and not because we earned it. It was a pure gift. Share that joyful message with strength and conviction.

GOSPEL   Jesus taught best by his example. Here he teaches prayer that way. The disciples *observe*

Jesus at prayer and ask him to teach them how to pray. It's important then that we *hear* what Jesus is doing in that first line. There are three units to this Gospel passage, and each could be proclaimed and discussed independently of the others. But there is also an artistic unity and interdependence that makes the three parts a necessary unit. "Father" is the bond that connects the first section to the third. The intervening parable humorously illustrates the primary message of today's readings: we should expect God to hear and answer prayer, but we must also persevere.

for we **ourselves** forgive **everyone** in **debt** to us,
and do not **subject** us to the final **test**."

Use more energy here. This is a colorful story. Remember that the exchange is between friends.

And he said to them, "Suppose one of you has a **friend**
to whom he goes at **midnight** and says,
'**Friend**, lend me three loaves of **bread**,
for a **friend** of mine has arrived at my **house** from a **journey**
and I have nothing to **offer** him,'
and he says in reply from **within**,
'Do not **bother** me; the door has already been **locked**
and my **children** and I are already in **bed**.

"I cannot" really means "I will not."

I cannot get **up** to give you **anything**.'
I **tell** you,
if he does not get up to give the visitor the loaves
because of their **friendship**,
he **will** get up to give him whatever he needs

The key word is saved for last: "persistence."
Jesus intensifies his teaching. These are matters of spiritual life and death.

because of his **persistence**.

"And I tell you, **ask** and you will **receive**;
seek and you will **find**;
knock and the door will be **opened** to you.
For everyone who **asks**, **receives**;
and the one who **seeks**, **finds**;
and to the one who **knocks**, the door will be **opened**.
What **father** among you would hand his son a **snake**
when he asks for a **fish**?

A scorpion could never be mistaken for an egg. Jesus employs intentional exaggeration to make his point.

Or hand him a **scorpion** when he asks for an **egg**?
If **you** then, who are **wicked**,

Don't emphasize the word "wicked." Keep your tone colloquial: God is not going to be outdone by you! Luke ends with a characteristic emphasis on the Spirit.

know how to give **good** gifts to your children,
how much **more** will the Father in **heaven**
give the Holy **Spirit** to those who **ask** him?"

Jesus responds immediately to the disciples' request for instruction in prayer. No single word in what he teaches them is more important than the tone-setting "Father." Vary your delivery from your usual recitation of the prayer by speaking one petition at a time, suggesting how Jesus might have spoken it if he were thinking it up on the spot when he taught his close friends.

Jesus' illustrative parable is as colorful as and even more animated than Abraham's dialogue with God in the First Reading. This is the story of a "persistent" (a better word is "shameless!") friend who gets what he wants because he won't accept no for an answer. Remember that the dialogue is between "friends," so the exchange exhibits no extremes of formality or anger. Jesus' point is clear: through persistence the friend receives "whatever he needs."

The narrator disappears in the last section as Jesus intensifies his teaching on prayer. In the Greek, the expression "I tell you" implies "I personally tell you . . . ."

The time spent and examples offered indicate this topic is of great importance to Jesus. Despite his definitive statements, Jesus is not endorsing a fundamentalist approach to prayer, nor suggesting we can magically control God with our intercessions. No. The words of the "Our Father" still echo in our ears reminding us that we must "seek" and "find" only those things that conform with God's will—glorification of God's name, the coming of the kingdom, forgiveness, and being spared the final test.

18TH SUNDAY IN ORDINARY TIME

Lectionary #114

READING I   Ecclesiastes 1:2; 2:21–23

A reading from the Book of Ecclesiastes

Vanity of **vanities**, says **Qoheleth**,
   vanity of **vanities**! **All** things are vanity!

Here is one who has labored with **wisdom** and **knowledge**
   and **skill**,
   and yet to **another** who has **not** labored over it,
   he must leave **property**.
This **also** is vanity and a great **misfortune**.
For what profit **comes** to man from all the **toil** and anxiety
   of **heart**
   with which he has **labored** under the **sun**?
All his days **sorrow** and **grief** are his occupation;
   even at **night** his mind is not at **rest**.
This **also** is **vanity**.

Qoheleth = koh-HEL-uhth

Qoheleth means "preacher." Don't exaggerate the lament, but speak with strong energy. The Gospel will make better sense in light of this.

This is not a tragic situation, but a frustrating reality many have to live with.

It all seems so futile!

Don't play this as the depths of depression; it is discouragement, even anger, at life's shifting fortunes.

READING I | Israel's Wisdom literature teaches about God and virtue and offers advice for everyday life. This passage represents a radical branch of that wisdom tradition. With stark, maybe shocking frankness, it speaks about the harsh realities and inconsistencies of life. If you find it upsetting, it's meant to be. Qoheleth wrote at a time when Israel did not yet believe in life after death, so if all one can hope for is the random fortune that life doles out, prospects may look bleak indeed.

Qoheleth is a preacher who likely is trying to provoke the reader. His "vanity" has nothing to do with bragging or egotism. It means folly, futility, senselessness, emptiness. "Vanity of vanities" is a Hebrew superlative meaning "greatest of vanities," that is, "total purposelessness!" It voices the frustration anyone might feel when prayers go unanswered, when the good suffer while the wicked flourish, when defeat waits around every corner and all you want to say is, "What's the use?" We

expect scripture to call us to joy and expectant faith, but this text tells us it's natural to sometimes feel discouraged and hollow. Using the ironic image of a person who labors hard his whole life only to leave his wealth to heirs who never lifted a finger, this somber text reinforces the Gospel's message that striving to amass material wealth is futile and pointless. Apart from God, life is meaningless! Eventually, belief in the life after death will transform this somber attitude, but your job is to share Qoheleth's sober outlook: injustice abounds

READING II   Colossians 3:1–5, 9–11

A reading from the Letter of Saint Paul to the Colossians

Brothers and sisters:

If you were **raised** with Christ, seek what is **above**,
     where Christ is **seated** at the **right** hand of **God**.
Think of what is **above**, not of what is on **earth**.
For you have **died**,
     and your life is **hidden** with Christ in **God**.
When Christ your life **appears**,
     then you **too** will appear with him in **glory**.

Put to **death**, then, the parts of you that are **earthly**:
     immorality, **impurity**, **passion**, evil **desire**,
     and the **greed** that is **idolatry**.
Stop **lying** to one another,
     since you have taken **off** the old self with its **practices**
     and have put on the **new** self,
     which is being **renewed**, for **knowledge**,
     in the **image** of its **creator**.
Here there is not **Greek** and **Jew**,
     circumcision and **uncircumcision**,
     barbarian, **Scythian**, **slave**, **free**;
     but **Christ** is **all** and **in** all.

---

*"Brothers and sisters" sets the tone.
"If you were raised" carries the sense of
"Because you were raised."*

*Utilize the contrasts: "above" and
"on earth."*

*Make eye contact and speak directly to
the assembly. Each word names a different
vice. Distinguish them and let your tone
convey how abhorrent they are to God.
Strong admonition requires strong
delivery! But the motivation is the good
and salvation of those who listen. Highlight
"taken off" and "put on".*

*The categories are "negative," but the
overall tone is positive for none of these
categories applies any longer. The last
line is rousing!*

Sythian = SITH-ee-uhn

---

and sorrow and grief are our constant companions. To help you prepare, you might want to listen to the evening news.

READING II — A constant theme in Paul is that in Christ we are new creations. In Baptism all have died and risen with Christ and already have begun to share in the new life of the kingdom. Here Paul provides the formula for maintaining that new life and it requires a transformation of what we value, what we do. His prescription rings with imperatives:

"seek what is above," "think," "put to death the parts . . . that are earthly," "stop lying." This is how we are to live as citizens of the heavenly kingdom, putting aside the ways of the world that are not consistent with our new identity. Impurity, passion, greed—all such things must now be set aside, for we are newly minted; we have shed our old self and have put on our new self, which is Christ.

Paul lists the things we must surrender for Christ and the things from which we are freed by Christ. The first list consists of strong words ("immorality, impurity . . .

idolatry") that make a strong impact. The second list also contains strong words, but its categories are not contemporary or familiar. Read it slowly so that the sound of even the unfamiliar words (uncircumcised, Scythian) conveys the message that categories and divisions do not apply in the Christian community. Life in the kingdom is characterized by freedom from divisive distinctions of race, gender, and class. And we achieve this state by yielding to Christ who is everything in everyone.

A reading from the holy Gospel according to Luke

Someone in the **crowd** said to **Jesus**,
    "**Teacher**, tell my **brother** to share the **inheritance** with me."
He **replied** to him,
    "**Friend**, who appointed **me** as your **judge** and **arbitrator**?"
Then he said to the **crowd**,
    "Take care to **guard** against all **greed**,
    for though one may be **rich**,
    one's **life** does not consist of **possessions**."

Then he told them a **parable**.
"There was a **rich** man whose land produced a bountiful **harvest**.
He **asked** himself, 'What shall I **do**,
    for I do not have **space** to **store** my harvest?'
And he said, '**This** is what I shall do:
    I shall **tear** down my barns and build **larger** ones.
There I shall **store** all my grain and **other** goods
    and I shall **say** to myself, "Now as for **you**,
    you have so **many** good things stored up for many **years**,
    rest, eat, drink, be **merry**!" '
But **God** said to him,
    '**You fool**, this **night** your **life** will be **demanded** of you;
    and the things you have **prepared**, to whom will they **belong**?'
Thus will it be for **all** who store up treasure for **themselves**
    but are **not** rich in what **matters** to **God**."

The questioner calls out from the crowd. Find an appropriate volume. Jesus' reply is not hostile or rude.

This comment is addressed to the crowd, so adjust your volume and intensity accordingly.
One does not live on bread alone.

Sharing the parable calls for a shift into a storyteller mode. Besides the narrator, you have the rich man and God to subtly differentiate from Jesus.

Enjoy sharing his well-crafted plan without slipping into an easy caricature of this rich "fool."

This is colorful language, especially the man's advice to himself. Use it.

This is strong language. God demands we find security only in God's bosom. What matters to God is the treasure we store up in heaven.

GOSPEL   Qoheleth lamented the unpredictable and transitory nature of all things. Jesus points to those that last. But he also echoes Ecclesiastes' message regarding the vanity of putting faith in earthly treasure, and he certainly knows the wisdom of living life expecting the unexpected. Someone in the crowd asks Jesus' help and appears to be rebuffed. But notice that while the questioner addresses Jesus as "Teacher," Jesus calls him "Friend." Jesus' reply may not be a rebuff at all, but an invitation to take a different attitude toward the disputed inheritance. "Guard against all greed" is as much directed at this brother as at the one holding the money. Jesus is inviting the cheated brother, as well as the crowd, to seek life elsewhere than in possessions.

The problem with the rich man of the parable is not the wealth he accumulates—that's done honestly enough. His mistake is in thinking that his security lies in those material possessions, that they will somehow guarantee him years of eating, drinking, and merry-making. Apparently the rich man has not read Qoheleth; we can imagine him losing sleep worrying even over his good fortune. His solution, in fact, follows Ecclesiastes perfectly: he labors with "wisdom, knowledge and skill," but only to amass more wealth that will be left to another. This realistic character who resembles us helps us recognize the folly of trying to ensure our own security. Jesus leaves no doubts about God's attitude toward efforts to store up human goods instead of what matters to God.

19TH SUNDAY IN ORDINARY TIME

Lectionary #117

READING I   Wisdom 18:6–9

A reading from the Book of Wisdom

The night of the **passover** was known **beforehand** to our **fathers**,
    that, with sure **knowledge** of the **oaths** in which they
        put their **faith**,
    they might have **courage**.
Your people **awaited** the **salvation** of the **just**
    and the **destruction** of their **foes**.
For when you **punished** our **adversaries**,
    in this you **glorified** us whom you had **summoned**.
For in **secret** the holy children of the **good**
    were offering **sacrifice**
    and putting into **effect** with one **accord** the **divine institution**.

READING II   Hebrews 11:1–2, 8–19

A reading from the Letter to the Hebrews

Brothers and sisters:
Faith is the **realization** of what is **hoped** for
    and **evidence** of things not **seen**.
Because of it the **ancients** were well **attested**.

By **faith** Abraham **obeyed** when he was called to go **out** to a place
    that he was to **receive** as an **inheritance**;
    he **went** out, not knowing **where** he was to go.

Read the first line slowly so that the context is clear. "Night," "known beforehand," "faith," and "awaited" will want special attention.

"Your people" signifies "God's people." The point is that they waited with great faith, trusting God would deliver them despite all the evidence to the contrary—and for this they were *glorified!*
Under the cover of night, they did what needed to be done to be ready.

This is a classic verse that summarizes all that will follow. Give it its due.

Stress "by faith" here and each time it recurs.

READING I   Although it is always helpful, this week, it is essential that you prepare by reading the Gospel first. Removed from the context of today's other readings this passage says little. Of course, your assembly won't have the advantage of having heard the Gospel before they hear your proclamation of Wisdom, but by highlighting key words in this passage you will till the soil for the sowing of the Gospel.

    Today, Wisdom and Luke focus on the need for preparedness, and their chief image is a long, faithful night watch, symbolizing readiness for the ultimate encounter with the Lord. Readiness is no accident, but results from doing what needs to be done. "The night" signifies the Passover when the angel of death bypassed the homes of the Israelites while bringing death to the firstborn of each Egyptian household. The text praises the faith of the "fathers" (the patriarchs of the Second Reading) who anticipated deliverance through the Exodus by putting their trust in the promises ("oaths") God had made to Abraham. So in a sense, they knew about the Passover "beforehand" (that is, before it occurred), and they acted on their faith by awaiting their salvation not blindly, but by preparing "in secret" for the moment of deliverance that they knew would come. (Contrast this with the slave of the Gospel who knew but did not prepare.) The final sentence describes the Passover night when the Israelites "fastened their belts" (compare with the Gospel) and, standing up, ate their meal awaiting the signal to flee Egypt. In the Gospel, Jesus promises

Abraham endured hardships willingly. Contrast "tents" with "city with foundations."

By **faith** he sojourned in the **promised** land as
    in a foreign **country**,
  dwelling in **tents** with **Isaac** and **Jacob**,
    heirs of the same **promise**;
for he was looking **forward** to the city with **foundations**,
  whose **architect** and **maker** is **God**.

Give strong emphasis to Abraham and Sarah's advanced age.

By **faith** he received power to **generate**,
  even though he was **past** the **normal** age
  —and Sarah herself was **sterile**—
for he thought that the one who had **made** the promise
    was **trustworthy**.

"As good as dead" is a colorful exaggeration.

So it was that there came **forth** from **one** man,
  himself as good as **dead**,
  descendants as **numerous** as the **stars** in the **sky**
  and as **countless** as the **sands** on the **seashore**.

"All these" refers to other heroes of faith left out of this excerpt.

All these **died** in faith.
They did not **receive** what had been promised
  but **saw** it and greeted it from **afar**
  and **acknowledged** themselves to be **strangers** and **aliens**
    on earth,
  for those who speak **thus** show that they are seeking
    a **homeland**.
If they had been thinking of the land from which they had **come**,
  they would have had opportunity to **return**.
But **now** they desire a **better** homeland, a **heavenly** one.

"God is not ashamed . . ." is a striking statement.

Therefore, God is not **ashamed** to be called their **God**,
  for he has **prepared** a **city** for them.

"The promise" that he would become a great nation was to be fulfilled through Isaac. But Abraham trusted that God could keep the promise even if Isaac were sacrificed.

By **faith** Abraham, when put to the **test**, offered up **Isaac**,
  and he who had **received** the promises was ready
    to **offer** his only **son**,
  of whom it was said,

reward for that kind of belt-fastened nocturnal vigilance. Because they observed the Passover ritual ("offering sacrifice"), God "glorified" the chosen ("summoned") Israelites. By stressing the references to faithful waiting and preparedness (especially in the first line and the last sentence), you'll connect this difficult text with today's other readings.

READING II Through repetition, not in spite of it, dance, music, and poetry achieve their impact. Repetition

draws us deeper into feelings and ideas. We may forget the rest of the piece, but the refrain lingers in memory. In lofty and exalted language, and with masterful use of repetition, the author of Hebrews presents a sublime teaching on faith, not by defining it theologically, but by using the great men and women of the Old Testament as models of a faith so firm that it withstands all the storms and trials of life.

Chapter 11 of Hebrews contains an extensive listing of heroes and heroines of faith. The brief sampling excerpted in this passage will likely be forgotten by your

assembly, but the simple refrain can be made unforgettable. The recurrence of "by faith" drives home the message that we are to be imitators of those whose faith has merited them God's promised reward.

Try reading the text stressing "by faith" each time it recurs. It may feel awkward, but don't emphasize the new idea in each new sentence; instead keep stressing the refrain. These ancestors in faith are remarkable because they believed without seeing. Abraham is the paragon: he left his home, lived in a foreign land, and trusted

"Through **Isaac** descendants shall bear your **name**."
He reasoned that **God** was able to **raise** even from the **dead**,
    and he received Isaac **back** as a **symbol**.

[Shorter: Hebrews 11:1–2, 8–12]

GOSPEL Luke 12:32–48

A reading from the holy Gospel according to Luke

Jesus said to his **disciples**:
    "Do not be **afraid** any longer, little **flock**,
    for your Father is **pleased** to give you the **kingdom**.
Sell your belongings and give **alms**.
Provide **money** bags for yourselves that do not wear **out**,
    an **inexhaustible** treasure in **heaven**
    that no **thief** can reach nor moth **destroy**.
For where your **treasure** is, there also will your **heart** be.

"**Gird** your **loins** and **light** your **lamps**
    and be like **servants** who await their master's return
        from a **wedding**,
    ready to open **immediately** when he comes and **knocks**.
Blessed are those servants
    whom the master finds **vigilant** on his arrival.
Amen, I say to you, he will **gird** himself,
    have them recline at **table**, and proceed to **wait** on **them**.
And should he come in the **second** or **third** watch
    and find them **prepared** in this way,
    blessed are those servants.
Be sure of **this**:
    if the master of the house had **known** the hour
    when the **thief** was coming,
    he would **not** have let his house be broken **into**.

Isaac is presented as a symbol of the risen Christ.

Make eye contact with the assembly. These lines should be spoken directly to the assembly.

"An inexhaustible treasure" is not a new idea; it's an elaboration of "money bags . . . that do not wear out." The paragraph ends with a classic line.

There is growing urgency in Jesus' use of his various images. A lack of preparedness can have dire consequences. He wants his disciples prepared.

This image is of a remarkable sight: the master waiting on the servants!

C. S. Lewis said the devil's greatest weapon is not convincing us there is no God, but that we have plenty of time.

---

that God could make him and Sarah parents at their advanced age (when he was "as good as dead"). The most extraordinary example of faith is saved for last—Abraham's willingness to sacrifice Isaac. The author suggests Abraham reasoned that even if he sacrificed his son, God could still fulfill the promise of making Abraham a great nation through Isaac by bringing the boy back from the dead. That's amazing faith! That closing is important, for in Isaac's escape from death, the author sees a symbol of Christ's own Resurrection.

GOSPEL Today's message of preparedness peaks in this Gospel. We should note that the readiness Luke proposes has a twin focus. First is the call to be ready, alert, on the job, prepared for the unexpected coming of the master. That aspect might push us toward a tone of moralistic warning, and the parables Jesus recounts certainly justify that tone. But there is also an element of hopeful expectancy in this Gospel, that is, an enthusiasm and eagerness for the coming of the Lord

that calls for encouragement, not warning. As you proclaim the seemingly stern admonitions, remember how the Gospel began—with gentle, caring words addressed to a "little flock." Jesus is speaking to friends whom he does not want to see caught unawares. The admonition to stop being afraid is a call for preparedness of a nontemporal nature, bracing not against storms that rattle buildings but winds that chill hearts. Like the heroes of faith of the text from Hebrews, Jesus' disciples must walk by faith, travel light, and know their only security lies in God's goodness. Let your

You **also** must be prepared, for at an **hour** you do not **expect**,
   the Son of **Man** will **come**."

Note that Jesus does not answer the question, but tells another story.

Then **Peter** said,
   "**Lord**, is this parable meant for **us** or for **everyone**?"
And the Lord **replied**,
   "**Who**, then, is the **faithful** and **prudent** steward
   whom the master will put in **charge** of his servants
   to distribute the **food** allowance at the proper **time**?
Blessed is that servant whom his **master** on **arrival** finds **doing** so.
Truly, I say to you, the master will put the servant
   in charge of **all** his property.

Keep the narration and dialogue animated. Jesus has drawn a very colorful example.

But if that servant says to himself,
   'My master is **delayed** in coming,'
   and begins to **beat** the menservants and the maidservants,
   to **eat** and **drink** and get **drunk**,
   then that servant's **master** will come
   on an unexpected **day** and at an unknown **hour**
   and will **punish** the servant **severely**
   and assign him a place with the **unfaithful**.

Clearly draw the contrast between the consequences for the servant who *knew* the master's will and those for the one who did not know.

That servant who **knew** his master's will
   but did not make **preparations** nor act in **accord** with his will
   shall be beaten **severely**;
   and the servant who was **ignorant** of his master's will
   but acted in a way **deserving** of a severe beating
   shall be beaten only **lightly**.

This is another classic and memorable line. Don't rush it.

Much will be **required** of the person **entrusted** with much,
   and still **more** will be demanded of the person **entrusted**
      with more."

[Shorter: Luke 12:35–40]

understanding of Jesus' motivation guide your tone.

In addition to four parables, this text contains two classic lines: one rings the bell of encouragement and inspiration ("Where your treasure is . . ."), while the other rings the warning bell ("much will be required . . ."). Jesus utilizes his parables to reveal the nature of Christian expectation. Each makes its own contribution and requires a tone appropriate to its distinctive image: the heavenly treasure protected

from "thief" and "moth," the "vigilant" servants whose watchfulness is rewarded with the extraordinary sight of their master girding himself with an apron, the "thief" who breaks in at an hour we "do not expect," and the colorfully juxtaposed faithful and abusive servants who merit reward and just punishment. Peter's question introduces a section with special ramifications for those in ministry. Jesus ignores the question, but your tone can suggest the answer is not meant for everyone. Knowing God's word and God's ways places great responsibility on those who

have been blessed with that knowledge. God expects more from those to whom God has given more; greater mercy awaits those who have not been so privileged. While the ominous quality of the final admonition should not be diluted, we are simultaneously reminded of God's goodness and generosity.

ASSUMPTION OF THE BLESSED VIRGIN MARY: VIGIL

Lectionary #621

READING I 1 Chronicles 15:3–4, 15–16; 16:1–2

A reading from the first Book of Chronicles

David assembled all **Israel** in **Jerusalem** to bring the **ark**
    of the LORD
    to the **place** that he had **prepared** for it.
David **also** called together the sons of **Aaron** and the **Levites**.

The **Levites** bore the ark of God on their **shoulders** with **poles**,
    as **Moses** had **ordained** according to the **word** of the LORD.

David commanded the **chiefs** of the **Levites**
    to appoint their **kinsmen** as **chanters**,
    to play on musical **instruments**, **harps**, **lyres**, and **cymbals**,
    to make a loud **sound** of **rejoicing**.

They **brought** in the ark of God and set it within the **tent**
    which David had **pitched** for it.
Then they offered up **burnt** offerings and **peace** offerings to God.
When David had **finished** offering up the burnt offerings
    and peace offerings,
    he **blessed** the people in the **name** of the LORD.

Stress the participation of all—people and religious leader alike.

Levites = LEE-vits

Suggest this was done out of great reverence for the ark.

You are describing a joyful festival full of music and singing. No detail was overlooked! Let the sound of your words convey their meaning.

This is a solemn moment. Use a quieter tone.

Speak with tenderness of David's blessing.

READING I Among the titles given Mary is "Ark of the New Covenant." Like Israel's ark, she was a sacred vessel who bore within her the word of God, only hers was not a word etched in stone, but the living and eternal Word. The joy we find in that truth gives us a sense of the joy experienced by Israel on this day when they enshrine their most sacred object. Despite major setbacks, which included capture by the Philistines, the ark of the covenant containing the tablets of the Ten Commandments finally reaches its resting place in the City of David.

For Israel, the ark represented God's very presence among them, so its safe return is a source of great joy.

Although the ark doesn't arrive until the last paragraph, the joyous anticipation is evident from the start. The unparalleled significance of this event for Israel is made clear by the extravagant preparations and the involvement of the whole people in the festivity. David swelled the celebration by assembling "all Israel" with her priests ("Sons of Aaron") and the lower ranking liturgical ministers ("Levites"). So sacred was the ark, that it could not be touched (doing so meant death!), so it was carried "with poles" as stipulated in Mosaic law.

The actual enshrinement is a holy and solemn moment. Because Israel as yet had no temple, the ark is enthroned within a "tent." But because the ark symbolizes God's presence, it is God whom the people welcome, not a mere object of wood and gold. Joy peaks in the final line where the word "blessed" suggests tenderness and provides a link to today's Gospel.

This short text requires a slow reading.	## READING II 1 Corinthians 15:54b–57
	A reading from the first Letter of Saint Paul to the Corinthians
"That" refers to our human bodies.	Brothers and sisters: When that which is **mortal** clothes itself with **immortality**, then the **word** that is **written** shall come **about**:
Don't fail to exploit this poetic device. Taunt death with confidence!	*Death is swallowed up in **victory**.* *Where, O death, is your **victory**?* *Where, O death, is your **sting**?*

This brief explanation precedes a final outburst of joy. Death is like a scorpion whose "sting" is "sin" (that gets its power from the law). Jesus has overcome sin, the poison that causes death. No sin means no death, so thanks be to God!	The **sting** of death is **sin**,
	  and the **power** of sin is the **law**.
	But thanks be to **God** who gives us the **victory**
	  through our **Lord** Jesus **Christ**.

READING II In her Assumption, Mary was the first to experience the bodily Resurrection that is promised to all who believe. That promise is what Paul is celebrating in this text. He describes a glorious consummation when death, the ultimate sign of defeat and the most destructive consequence of sin, will itself be destroyed. The text is brief and Paul's elegantly balanced reasoning might flow past your listeners too quickly for them to appreciate its beauty and power. So read slowly for two reasons: because short readings always require it, and because

progressive reasoning, if rushed, soon becomes progressive mush! Paul joyfully addresses matters of ultimate importance; your tone must convey that.

Paul's two "O death" taunts are a marvelous oratorical device that enables you to address death like a human person, to tell the vilest enemy, the ultimate symbol of defeat, that its power is at an end. Because we stand on the shoulders of the risen Jesus, we can muster the courage to confront this fearsome foe.

GOSPEL This Gospel is shorter than any other in the Lectionary. Be sure you don't finish reading before your people have begun to listen. To slow your pace and effectively employ each word without falling into a stilted delivery, envision the crowd in whose midst the woman calls out. To be heard, she had to speak slowly and distinctly. She probably speaks from experience of bearing and nursing her own children, yet her respect for Jesus makes her extol the one who was privileged to bear and nurse him. Jesus had demonstrated his power by driving out a

Avoid the possibility of your listeners tuning in too late by reading especially slowly.

Speak her line very deliberately. Is she possibly saying, "Would that I could have been that mother"?

Make eye contact. Speak to those in the assembly who hear and observe the word.

GOSPEL   Luke 11:27–28

A reading from the holy Gospel according to Luke

While Jesus was **speaking**,
   a **woman** from the crowd **called** out and **said** to him,
   "**Blessed** is the womb that **carried** you
   and the **breasts** at which you **nursed**."
He replied,
   "**Rather, blessed** are those
   who **hear** the word of **God** and **observe** it."

demon and some questioned if he did it by the power of Satan. Her spontaneous outburst affirms he is a man of God.

   Jesus' reply carries no disrespect for Mary. Nor does he deny the value of the biological relationship. Rather, he announces an even greater privilege: Hearing the word of God and observing it. Mary was the model of such discipleship!

ASSUMPTION OF THE BLESSED VIRGIN MARY: DAY

Lectionary #622

READING I   Revelation 11:19a; 12:1–6a, 10ab

A reading from the Book of Revelation

God's **temple** in heaven was **opened**,
  and the **ark** of his **covenant** could be seen in the temple.

A great **sign** appeared in the sky, a **woman** clothed with the **sun**,
  with the **moon** beneath her **feet**,
  and on her **head** a **crown** of twelve **stars**.
She was with **child** and wailed **aloud** in **pain** as she **labored**
    to give **birth**.
Then **another** sign appeared in the sky;
  it was a huge red **dragon**, with seven **heads** and ten **horns**,
  and on its heads were seven **diadems**.
Its **tail** swept away a **third** of the **stars** in the **sky**
  and **hurled** them down to the **earth**.
Then the dragon stood before the **woman** about to give birth,
  to **devour** her **child** when she gave birth.
She gave birth to a **son**, a **male** child,
  destined to **rule** all the **nations** with an iron **rod**.
Her child was caught up to **God** and his **throne**.
The woman herself **fled** into the **desert**
  where she had a place **prepared** by God.

The sound of the opening lines sets the tone for all that follows.

Read slowly so the images can register. The woman is an awesome figure; your tone must convey her grandeur despite the graphic labor pains.

"Red" evokes blood and murder.
Diadems = DI-uh-demz
Diadems are crowns.

The dragon is Satan who rebelled against heaven and battled Michael the archangel.

Use a slower, calmer tone here. Stress God's initiative in rescuing both the child and the mother.

READING I John's grand, apocalyptic vision presents a "woman" whose identity is debated. Very likely, she symbolizes Israel and the Church, but within the context of today's solemnity we can discern Mary within the elaborate imagery of this cosmic vision, and the child she bears is the Messiah, the "Anointed One" who brings "salvation." The choice of this reading underscores the importance of Mary's role in God's plan of salvation. You must make sure that as you describe this dramatic scene of clashing cosmic forces you give prominence to the woman who is at the center of the drama. Her dignity and greatness, the overpowering threat that menaces her, and the ultimate rescue of mother and child are what you must help the assembly hear.

The tone of the opening lines should suggest the grand scope of what will follow. The deleted half of verse 19 describes the holiest part of the temple opening amid roaring thunder and lightening flashes revealing the ark of the covenant. This sacred box, that held the tablets on which were written the Ten Commandments, symbolized God's presence amongst people. By skipping verses, our excerpt connects "the ark" with the "woman." Christian tradition, in fact, has long made this link, naming Mary the ark of the new covenant.

The red dragon clearly represents the devil and all the forces of evil. Its "seven heads" suggest pagan Rome, the city built on seven hills. All the descriptive words add up to a destructive and terrifying scene and the overriding mood is one of menace, especially as the dragon waits to devour the newborn. But God rescues mother and

Then I heard a loud **voice** in heaven say:
   "**Now** have **salvation** and **power** come,
      and the **Kingdom** of our **God**
      and the **authority** of his **Anointed One**."

> **READING II** 1 Corinthians 15:20–27

A reading from the first Letter of Saint Paul to the Corinthians

Brothers and sisters:
Christ has been **raised** from the dead,
   the **firstfruits** of those who have fallen **asleep**.
For since **death** came through **man**,
   the **resurrection** of the dead came **also** through man.
For just as in **Adam** all **die**,
   so too in **Christ** shall all be brought to **life**,
   but each one in proper **order**:
   Christ the **firstfruits**;
   then, at his **coming**, those who **belong** to Christ;
   then comes the **end**,
   when he hands over the **Kingdom** to his **God** and **Father**,
   when he has **destroyed** every **sovereignty**
   and every **authority** and **power**.
For he must **reign** until he has put all his **enemies** under his **feet**.
The **last** enemy to be destroyed is **death**,
   for "he subjected **everything** under his **feet**."

Sidebar margin notes (left column):

Announce this joyous news with great authority.

Start strong, as if there were an exclamation point at the end of ". . . raised from the dead."

Lead your listeners through Paul's presentation one idea at a time.

In a persuasive tone, balance and contrast Adam and Christ.

Describe "the end" with a sense of Christ's sovereignty over all things.

Set off "death" by pausing before the word. "Reign" and "under his feet" extend Paul's royal and military imagery, giving us a sense of the dignity with which to conclude his spirited reflection. Use ritardando (slowing toward the end) on the words "he subjected . . . feet."

Bottom section:

child. Ironically, the child is destined to "shepherd" (an alternative translation of "rule" and a gentle word) but with "an iron rod." Heaven has the final word, announcing salvation and security in the kingdom of God and under the authority of the Anointed One.

READING II Some readings warm up slowly, but this one takes off immediately. The entire passage is built on the victorious announcement of the first line. Having shared the great truth of

Christ's Resurrection, Paul begins to elaborate on the consequences of that singular event. Yes, Christ is raised, but he is only the "first fruits" of those who have died. Through God's mercy, the singular event of Christ's rising is made plural; now all who believe in him can share in his victory over death. Paul is a master at balance and organization. Often, however, his constructions are overly complex and confusing. Here the simplicity is both beautiful and persuasive. He deftly contrasts Adam and Christ. Since "Death" came through "man" (the sin of Adam), so also "resurrection"

came through "man" (the self-sacrifice of Christ). Those who are "in Adam" are destined to die; those who are "in Christ," of whom Mary ranks first, "shall be brought to life." The Church's conviction that Mary has already experienced the fullness of Resurrection and dwells with Jesus in the heavenly kingdom is the reason this text was chosen for this solemnity.

Besides balancing Paul's ideas, be sure you also provide contrast by giving negative and positive values to the death-life images. For Paul everything, even the

See the Gospel commentary for the Fourth Sunday of Advent for further background on this passage.

Speak the names and places with a familiar fondness and reverence.

Zechariah = zek-uh-R -uh

Stress that Elizabeth's prompting is from the Holy Spirit.

Be sure this doesn't sound like a rote recitation of the Hail Mary.

Elizabeth, already awed by her own late-in-life pregnancy, is overawed by Mary's situation and all it bodes for her and Israel.
Deliver these lines slowly and with extra care.

Take a breath and proclaim these lines with exuberance.

Mary's words are filled with gratitude and humility. How could God have done so much for me? Praise the mighty God who does not forget the needy!
Note the shift to the plural. Direct these lines to the assembly.

GOSPEL   Luke 1:39—56

A reading from the holy Gospel according to Luke

Mary set **out**
and traveled to the **hill** country in **haste**
to a town of **Judah**,
where she entered the house of **Zechariah**
and greeted **Elizabeth**.
When Elizabeth **heard** Mary's **greeting**,
the **infant leaped** in her **womb**,
and **Elizabeth**, filled with the Holy **Spirit**,
cried out in a loud **voice** and said,
"**Blessed** are you among women,
and blessed is the **fruit** of your **womb**.
And how does this **happen** to me,
that the mother of my **Lord** should **come** to me?
For at the moment the sound of your **greeting** reached my **ears**,
the **infant** in my womb **leaped** for **joy**.
Blessed are you who **believed**
that what was **spoken** to you by the **Lord**
would be **fulfilled**."

And Mary said:
"My **soul** proclaims the **greatness** of the Lord;
my **spirit rejoices** in God my **Savior**
for he has **looked** with favor on his lowly **servant**.
From this **day** all **generations** will call me **blessed**:
the **Almighty** has done great **things** for me,
and **holy** is his **Name**.
He has **mercy** on those who **fear** him
in **every** generation.

Resurrection, follows a proper order: first "Christ," "then . . . those who belong to Christ." With royal and military language, he describes what precedes and accompanies the "end": first, all demonic forces ("every sovereignty, authority and power") will be destroyed, and then the kingdom will be entrusted to God. In the end, even death will die for death is the result of sin and in the kingdom, sin will be no more.

GOSPEL The first line of Mary's song-poem ("My soul proclaims . . .") sets the tone of joy that pervades this text and this ancient Marian solemnity as well. We last heard this Gospel in Advent. But then our focus was on the infancy narrative; today, it is on Mary as an exemplary woman of faith and an instrument of God's plan of salvation.

Mary left Nazareth in haste and hurries to the side of her pregnant, though aging, cousin. Mary's greeting causes Elizabeth's child to stir within her; this child, too, is destined for greatness and his

spirit responds with joy to the presence of the child in Mary's womb. The Spirit, a constant theme in Luke, moves Elizabeth to play prophetess; she lauds Mary for trusting that the impossible could happen, that God's word would not fail her, that the promise would become reality. The elder cousin, herself highly favored in her old age, defers to Mary calling her "blessed" and "mother of my Lord." There is a sense of wonder in those lines, of realities far greater than the players involved. There is also a sense of surrender to those realties

Emphasize the reversal of fortunes celebrated in these lines.

He has shown the **strength** of his arm,
and has **scattered** the proud in their **conceit**.
He has cast down the **mighty** from their **thrones**,
and has **lifted** up the **lowly**.
He has filled the **hungry** with **good** things,
and the **rich** he has sent away **empty**.

In sending the Messiah, God has kept the promises made to all the ancestors. Pause at the end of the song.

He has come to the **help** of his servant **Israel**
for he has **remembered** his promise of **mercy**,
the promise he made to our **fathers**,
to **Abraham** and his **children** for ever."

Use a quieter tone here. Mary returns home after the birth of John.

Mary **remained** with her about three **months**
and then **returned** to her **home**.

and it is for that surrender that Mary is most praised.

Mary's song continues the theme. The message of the song lauds the upending of the status quo, the reversal of fortune and reversal of roles between the mighty and the lowly. The poetry conveys a strong sense of being swept up by benevolent but mighty forces that bring right order to the world. Many of Luke's typical emphases resound in these lines: joy and exultation ("My soul proclaims . . . my spirit rejoices), the elevation of the lowly (". . . all generations will call me blessed," "has lifted up the lowly," "filled the hungry with good things"), the overthrow of the mighty ("scattered the proud," "cast down the mighty," "the rich he has sent away empty"), and the fulfillment of old testament prophecy ("he has remembered his promise . . . to Abraham and his children"). Midway through the song, there is a shift from first to third person plural ("He has mercy on those who fear him"). Mary is no longer speaking only of herself; she becomes spokesperson for all the Anawim, those "poor ones" who rejoice in their neediness and their dependence on God. Mary personifies Israel, old and new, rejoicing at the coming of Messiah. Appropriately, the word "promise" appears twice at the end of the song. Mary is the paragon of the Christian life of promise and fulfillment. Christian faith demands that we all do what Mary did: believe that God's promises to us will be fulfilled.

21st SUNDAY IN ORDINARY TIME

Lectionary #123

READING II   Isaiah 66:18–21

A reading from the Book of the Prophet Isaiah

Thus says the LORD:
I know their **works** and their **thoughts**,
and I come to gather **nations** of every **language**;
    they shall **come** and see my **glory**.
I will set a **sign** among them;
    from them I will send **fugitives** to the nations:
        to **Tarshish**, **Put** and **Lud**, **Mosoch**, **Tubal** and **Javan**,
        to the distant **coastlands**
        that have never **heard** of my fame, or **seen** my **glory**;
    and they shall **proclaim** my glory among the nations.
They shall bring all your **brothers** and **sisters** from all the nations
    as an **offering** to the LORD,
        on **horses** and in **chariots**, in **carts**, upon **mules**
            and **dromedaries**,
        to **Jerusalem**, my holy **mountain**, says the LORD,
    just as the **Israelites** bring **their** offering
        to the **house** of the LORD in **clean vessels**.
Some of these I will take as **priests** and **Levites**, says the LORD.

"I come to gather . . . " must be spoken with great dignity and authority.

The "sign" refers to Jewish refugees who will speak of God in foreign lands.

Tarshish = TAHR-shish

Put = poot

Lud = LUHD

Mosoch = MAH-sock

Tubal = TOO-bahl

Javan = JAY-vuhn

You are describing a marvelous sight: foreigners returning Jewish refugees to their homeland. Enjoy reading the exhaustive list of means of transport. Israelites and foreigners will offer sacrifice together.

This was a shocking message to the original readers. Speak it with joy.

READING I   In today's readings, the whole world is invited to feast in the kingdom. The voice of God heralds that message in the opening sentence, so take plenty of time to proclaim the line with authority. Beginnings are always important, but they are also times when people are most distracted. Make sure your assembly is settled and listening before you speak that critical sentence.

God has a plan to send to every nation "fugitives" from Jerusalem who will "proclaim" God's glory. Upon hearing of the one true God, the citizens of these foreign lands will become God's servants and then spread the message even further among the Gentiles. The "sign" God plans to set among the nations is these "missionary" refugees.

The ancient nations listed were found in areas of Spain, Africa, near the Black Sea, and Greece. Practice their pronunciation so you won't stumble, but the idea is not to speak of them with familiarity but with the insinuation that they are far and foreign places that nonetheless will "see" the glory of God.

"They shall bring" refers to the foreigners who, responding to God's good-ness, bring "all your brethren" (that is, Jews scattered throughout the nations) back to Jerusalem, and every available means of transport—horses, chariots, carts—will be utilized to achieve this goal. The last sentence makes a radical and startling announcement: God will actually give the special roles of priest and Levite to some of the foreigners, revealing an awareness that grows steadily throughout the Old Testament that salvation is meant for all.

READING II   Hebrews 12:5–7, 11–13

A reading from the Letter to the Hebrews

Brothers and sisters,
You have **forgotten** the **exhortation** addressed to you as **children:**
"My **son,** do not disdain the **discipline** of the Lord
    or lose **heart** when **reproved** by him;
   for whom the Lord **loves,** he **disciplines;**
    he **scourges** every son he **acknowledges.**"
Endure your trials as "**discipline**";
   God treats you as **sons.**
For what "**son**" is there whom his father does **not** discipline?
At the time,
   all discipline seems a cause not for **joy** but for **pain,**
   yet **later** it brings the **peaceful** fruit of **righteousness**
   to those who are **trained** by it.

So **strengthen** your drooping **hands** and your weak **knees.**
Make straight **paths** for your feet,
   that what is **lame** may not be **disjointed** but **healed.**

This quoted proverb contains a "chiasmus," a reversal of expected word order in two otherwise parallel phrases. The first couplet follows the expected format: (A) "do not disdain" (B) "discipline" (A) "or lose heart" (B) "when reproved." The second couplet starts with the expected pattern: (A) "Whom the Lord loves" (B) "he disciplines" but then reverses it: (B) "he scourges" (A) "every son." The word "scourges" surprises, and because of its unexpected position, should receive added emphasis.

The author calls for a new way of seeing the trials that enter our lives.

Don't make this sound too easy. It's a truth that takes much effort to live.

Make eye contact with the assembly. Speak like a loving parent or wise teacher.

READING II | The letter to the Hebrews was written to offer encouragement to believers who faced the very real danger of abandoning their faith in Christ. Alternating instruction and encouragement, the author seeks to protect his readers from themselves. These Christians have already suffered for their faith, but it is not persecution or martyrdom that threatens them now. They have lost their fervor and grown lukewarm in their faith. It's not always easy to run the race and keep our eyes on the goal. As we face life's challenges, we grow weary and lax. So the author quotes the Book of Proverbs to remind the reader that trials are a sign of God's love, God's way of tilling soil to bring forth "the peaceful fruit of righteousness." The father–son analogy is helpful, but the verses deleted from this passage add clarity: "If you are without discipline . . . you are not sons but bastards." The author suggests that discipline is real proof of filial relationship, presumably because fathers might not love illegitimate children enough to invest time and effort in their upbringing.

Mainly, the author seeks to clarify our blurred vision. Things are not always as they seem; what brings pain today may later bring joy. Christ is our model. He was God's only Son, yet he endured the discipline of the cross. The trite expression is "No pain no gain." If we suffer without understanding, pain is meaningless. But when we see God's hand in the discipline, we can endure. Then our gain is inestimable, and we can even rejoice in what others see as sorrow.

GOSPEL Luke 13:22–30

A reading from the holy Gospel according to Luke

Jesus passed through **towns** and **villages**,
    teaching as he went and making his way to **Jerusalem**.
Someone **asked** him,
    "**Lord**, will only a **few** people be **saved**?"
He **answered** them,
"**Strive** to enter through the **narrow** gate,
    for **many**, I tell you, will **attempt** to enter
    but will not be **strong** enough.
After the **master** of the house has **arisen** and **locked** the door,
    then will you stand **outside knocking** and **saying**,
    '**Lord**, open the **door** for us.'
He will say to you in reply,
    'I do not **know** where you are **from**.'
And **you** will say,
    'We ate and drank in your **company** and you taught
        in our **streets**.'
Then **he** will say to you,
    'I do not **know** where you are **from**.
Depart from me, all you **evildoers**!'
And there will be **wailing** and grinding of **teeth**
    when you see **Abraham**, **Isaac**, and **Jacob**
    and all the **prophets** in the kingdom of **God**
    and you **yourselves** cast **out**.
And people will come from the **east** and the **west**
    and from the **north** and the **south**
    and will recline at **table** in the kingdom of **God**.
For **behold**, some are **last** who will be **first**,
    and some are **first** who will be **last**."

Stress the word "teaching," for the balance of the text contains an important lesson.

Imagine the questioner calling out from the crowd.

"Strive" suggests a real effort and struggle to enter.

Speak with the urgency of those who are excluded.

They're protesting: be reasonable— we even dined with you! The reply is unforgiving.

Contrast the tone of "wailing" and "grinding" with the feasting of the patriarchs and prophets.

Today, this is the heart of the message: salvation is open to all who open their hearts to Christ.

Make eye contact with the assembly. Don't soften the somber tone.

GOSPEL Were not this passage placed in context with the First Reading it would be natural and correct to stress the parable of the narrow door. But today's liturgy focuses us on universalism, not the struggle, straining, and striving required to enter the kingdom. Without denying the difficulty of entering, the liturgy focuses us on the final sentences of this text. The earlier part of the pericope sets up the stunning reversal proclaimed there.

The opening raises the specter of the cross, for Jesus is making his way to Jerusalem, Luke's codeword for Jesus' Passion and death. We would probably like a different answer to the question of how many will be saved, but Jesus' reply stresses only the difficulty involved and the foolishness of taking salvation for granted. Jesus is no soft and easy messiah here. His words suggest urgency, for the narrow door will not remain open forever. The master rises unexpectedly to lock it. The dialogue between master and those barred grows increasingly urgent as those who presumed inclusion find themselves left out, and no appeal will save them. Contrast their claim to having eaten and drunk with him, with the master's blunt reply: "I do not know where you are from."

The reading ends with a litany of inclusion (east, west, north, and south) that announces the paradox of the last-called (Gentiles) preceding the first-called (Israel) at the eschatological banquet. This is a warning to all of us regarding complacency, and a reminder of how easily the tables can turn.

22ND SUNDAY IN ORDINARY TIME

Lectionary #126

READING I   Sirach 3:17–18, 20, 28–29

Sirach = SEER-ak

Each pair of lines is either an "if/then" proposition or a construct where the second line completes a thought or analogy begun in the first. For example, "My son, [if you] conduct your affairs with humility, [then] you will be loved." Again: "[If you] humble yourself [then] you will find favor." Or the simile of the last two lines: "[As] water quenches a flaming fire . . . alms atone for sins."

To avoid falling into the same intonation pattern for each couplet, build energy from the first to second couplet as you tell us what we ought to do. Keep the intensity but lower the volume on the third couplet where you teach what not to do. Then build again on the last two couplets ending with an upward inflection on the good news of the last line.

The basic idea is this: you did not do this, but you did do that. "That which could be touched" means that you have not approached something tangible, that is, the site of the first covenant where God spoke to Moses. No, you have approached an intangible, spiritual reality, the heavenly Jerusalem. Use a faster pace here. You're saying: you didn't do this, or this, or this!

A reading from the Book of Sirach

My **child**, conduct your affairs with **humility**,
  and you will be loved **more** than a giver of **gifts**.
Humble yourself the **more**, the **greater** you are,
  and you will find **favor** with God.
What is too **sublime** for you, **seek** not,
  into things beyond your **strength search** not.
The mind of a **sage** appreciates **proverbs**,
  and an **attentive** ear is the joy of the **wise**.
Water quenches a flaming **fire**,
  and **alms** atone for **sins**.

READING II   Hebrews 12:18–19, 22–24a

A reading from the Letter to the Hebrews

Brothers and sisters:
You have not **approached** that which could be **touched**
  and a blazing **fire** and gloomy **darkness**
  and **storm** and a **trumpet** blast
  and a **voice** speaking words such that those who **heard**
  begged that **no** message be further **addressed** to them.

READING I   The book of Sirach is a collection of epigrams or wise sayings. Written about 200 years before Christ, it offers advice on various areas of life, including right relationship with God. Its wide ranging subject matter makes it a frequent choice for liturgical reading. Maxims selected for today cluster around the theme of humility, but note the variety with which they address that concept. In the same way that "A stitch in time saves nine" echoes the message of "Don't put off until tomorrow what you can do today,"

these maxims avoid redundancy through variety of expression. Proverbs are designed to take center stage alone since they don't depend on what went before or after to make their point. So allow each to "exit" before the next is introduced, but remember you are speaking on a theme.

These verses alternate between worldly shrewdness and more spiritual advice. Sirach recommends humility both for the "conduct [of worldly] affairs" and in order to "find favor with God." Then he endorses a prudent sense of one's own limitations (don't grasp beyond your reach!)

and the appreciation of wisdom (". . . a sage appreciates proverbs"). The spiritual dimension returns in the final observation that "alms" can quench the fire of "sins." There is a possible pitfall: because the proverbs are short and have similar structure and cadence, you could fall into an identical intonation pattern for each one. See the margin notes suggestion for how to avoid that. A selection addressed to "my son" likely calls for the tone of a parent or teacher.

Use a more positive and hopeful tone here. This is what you have approached through your Baptism: the new Jerusalem. And you have entered into the company of angels and holy souls and, most importantly, of Jesus himself who intercedes for you and has sealed a new covenant with his blood! Slower pace for this section, and much joy!

No, you have approached Mount **Zion**
and the city of the living **God**, the heavenly **Jerusalem**,
and countless **angels** in festal **gathering**,
and the assembly of the **firstborn** enrolled in **heaven**,
and **God** the judge of **all**,
and the spirits of the **just** made **perfect**,
and **Jesus**, the **mediator** of a new **covenant**,
and the sprinkled **blood** that speaks more **eloquently**
than that of **Abel**.

GOSPEL   Luke 14:1, 7–14

A reading from the holy Gospel according to Luke

Jesus is being carefully observed, and he knows it.

These banquet guests are the characters of Jesus' parable. He doesn't mask that. Decide on your tone. Is Jesus angry and how much? Does he speak loudly or whisper? Whether he is philosophical and reasonable or impassioned and scolding will depend on your sense of what's appropriate under such circumstances and how mindful of propriety Jesus might have been.

On a **sabbath Jesus** went to dine
at the home of one of the leading **Pharisees**,
and the people there were **observing** him **carefully**.

He told a **parable** to those who had been invited,
noticing how they were choosing the places of **honor**
at the table.
"When you are **invited** by someone to a **wedding** banquet,
do not recline at table in the place of **honor**.
A more **distinguished** guest than you may have been
invited by him,
and the host who invited **both** of you may approach **you**
and say,
'Give your place to **this** man,'
and then you would proceed with **embarrassment**
to take the **lowest** place.

READING II   These lines from Hebrews are among the most beautiful in the New Testament. The author is simultaneously looking backward and forward in time. He contrasts two large assemblies. The first one is gathered with Moses on Mount Sinai as God and the people consummate the covenant amid awe-inspiring manifestations of God's presence and power (the Exodus reading from the Pentecost Vigil describes that terrifying encounter where even Moses trembled). The other is an entirely different gathering in the "heavenly Jerusalem" where the just approach "the living God" not with fear but festive joy. In this vision, humans and "angels" intermingle. The God who is "judge of all" can be approached freely, in stark contrast with the first assembly where God's "voice" was so intimidating that the people begged that God's words not be "addressed to them."

The hinge on which the reading swings is the word "No" in the middle of the text. Like the flipping of a switch, that word changes the tone of the reading. You have rich language with which to paint two canvases. The first is done in dark and somber hues: "untouchable mountain," "blazing fire," "gloomy darkness," "storm and trumpet blast." Take adequate time and expend the necessary energy to give these images life. The second canvas contains brighter and lighter tones. Great joy fills the city ruled by an accessible God whom all can approach (only Moses drew near to God on Mount Sinai). A vast assembly inhabits the heavenly Jerusalem; they stand before God unafraid in the company of angels and with Jesus the Lord who, through the shedding of his innocent blood,

Make it clear this is not just a strategy to get to the highest place by "seeming" humble.

This maxim is the theme of today's First Reading and Gospel.

Jesus tells the host to do the opposite of what he's done: invited friends and dignitaries like Jesus who, even if they can't reciprocate with dinner, can at least lend the prestige of their presence. The advice is illogical, but Jesus' conviction that it will make the host more like God gives him courage to advance it.

Rather, when you are invited,
   go and take the **lowest** place
   so that when the host **comes** to you he may say,
   'My **friend**, move up to a **higher** position.'
Then you will enjoy the **esteem** of your companions at the table.
For every one who **exalts** himself will be **humbled**,
   but the one who **humbles** himself will be **exalted**."
Then he said to the **host** who invited him,
   "When you hold a **lunch** or a **dinner**,
   do not invite your **friends** or your **brothers**
   or your **relatives** or your wealthy **neighbors**,
   in case they may invite you **back** and you have **repayment**.
Rather, when you hold a banquet,
   invite the **poor**, the **crippled**, the **lame**, the **blind**;
   blessed **indeed** will you be because of their **inability**
      to repay you.
For you will be **repaid** at the **resurrection** of the **righteous**."

has inaugurated a new covenant that brings salvation to all.

GOSPEL | The meal context of this episode is a major clue to Jesus' tone as he offers advice to guests and host. The other evidence might justify a knee-jerk conclusion: among the "Pharisees" who observed "him carefully," Jesus admonishes the guests who jockey for the best positions at table. The conclusion is that a group of hypocrites is about to receive their comeuppance. But consider that Jesus is a guest, too; presumably

he desires the instruction and salvation of the Pharisees as much as anyone else's. Scolding guests and embarrassing a host prior to a meal makes for sweaty palms and poor digestion. Yet Luke gives us challenging teaching in the context of an elaborate Sabbath banquet.

In concert with the First Reading, Jesus teaches about humility, and it's not a backdoor strategy for getting the highest place in the end. We're not to feign humility by taking the lowest place in expectation of later being invited higher; we are to assume the place of the lowly, walk in

their shoes and sit in their seat and know life from their perspective. When we have learned what they have to teach us, we may indeed be invited to take a higher place. And when we give a feast and invite guests, we are to invite those who have nothing to give in return, for that is how God gives. When we give like that, when we've made the outcast our neighbor, we will have lived the Gospel and our reward will be eternal life.

23RD SUNDAY IN ORDINARY TIME

Lectionary #129

READING I   Wisdom 9:13–18b

A reading from the Book of Wisdom

Who can **know** God's **counsel**,
  or who can **conceive** what the LORD **intends**?
For the deliberations of **mortals** are **timid**,
  and **unsure** are our **plans**.
For the corruptible **body burdens** the **soul**
  and the earthen **shelter** weighs down the **mind**
    that has many **concerns**.
And **scarce** do we guess the things on **earth**,
  and what is within our **grasp** we find with **difficulty**;
    but when things are in **heaven**, **who** can search them out?
Or who ever knew your **counsel**, except you had given **wisdom**
  and sent your holy **spirit** from on **high**?
And thus were the **paths** of those on **earth** made **straight**.

These are xaggerated rhetorical questions. The expected answer, of course, is "No one!"
The expected word order is reversed, putting focus on the word "unsure."

Both lines state the same idea, so build from the first to the second line.

"And what is . . . grasp" is another chiasmus. We struggle to understand the meaning of our lives.

"Except you had given . . . " means "unless you had given wisdom." Wisdom is our only hope of finding God's will for our lives.

READING I Christian discipleship is a serious matter: the Gospel tells us it is not easy to pursue; Wisdom tells us it is even difficult to understand. Hence, this poetic prayer for wisdom is placed on the lips of King Solomon.

You already know poetry follows its own rules: it repeats ideas without embarrassment; it uses words like musical notes giving each value and color that enables their sound to say as much as their meaning; it uses literary devices to add variety and interest. Here, the first three couplets employ parallelism, a device that repeats in the second line an idea that was already stated in the first. "Who can conceive what the Lord intends" asks the same question as "Who can know God's counsel." Verse two uses a chiasmus (a reversal of the expected word order) to flip the balance. The expected word order would be AB/AB: (A) "deliberations" . . . are (B) "timid," (A) "Plans" are (B) "unsure." But by reversing the expected order, (B) "unsure are our (A) plans," "unsure" receives the stress and better makes the author's point that confusion is our lot.

The third verse, like the Gospel, stresses the need to be freed of the burdens of earthly concerns in order to know God's will. The fourth verse expresses the futility of seeking to know God's ways when our own cause us such confusion. But the important word "except" (which means "unless") switches on the light of hope, pointing to "Wisdom" and the "spirit" as sources of truth that keep us from stumbling in the dark.

Philemon = fi-LEE-muhn

Paul is not above using his age to secure a favor, and on top of it, he's a prisoner!

Onesimus = oh-NES-ih-muhs

Pause slightly after "become," and then stress "imprisonment" to help clarify that Paul is a spiritual—not biological—father. He speaks with great emotion.

Paul wanted to keep Onesimus with him, but wouldn't do it without Philemon's permission. Contrast "forced" and "voluntary." Of course, he's hinting Philemon should send Onesimus back.

Paul is earnestly entreating that Philemon free Onesimus and treat him as he would treat Paul himself.

READING II   Philemon 9–10, 12–17

A reading from the Letter of Saint Paul to Philemon

I, **Paul**, an **old** man,
    and now also a **prisoner** for Christ **Jesus**,
    urge you on behalf of my child **Onesimus**,
    whose **father** I have become in my **imprisonment**;
    I am **sending** him, that is, my own **heart**, **back** to you.
I should have liked to **retain** him for myself,
    so that he might **serve** me on your **behalf**
    in my **imprisonment** for the **gospel**,
    but I did not want to do **anything** without your **consent**,
    so that the **good** you do might not be **forced** but **voluntary**.
Perhaps this is why he was **away** from you for a while,
    that you might have him **back forever**,
    no longer as a **slave**
    but more than a slave, a **brother**,
    beloved especially to **me**, but even more so to **you**,
    as a **man** and in the **Lord**.
So if you regard me as a **partner**, welcome **him** as you would **me**.

READING II Paul usually writes letters meant to instruct all the members of a community. This very short letter is addressed to an individual. Yet its place in the canon of New Testament writings tells us its message is more than personal. While Paul does not directly challenge the institution of slavery, he models an attitude that will eventually guide Christianity to abhor that system. So the letter turns out to be an apostolic, community oriented appeal after all.

As an aging servant of the Gospel, Paul meets Philemon's runaway slave Onesimus in prison. Paul not only converts him to Christ, but he becomes quite fond of the young man. Paul, however, sends him back to his master, this letter in hand, pleading Onesimus be received not as a slave but as a brother in the Lord. Paul also hints that he would like to have Onesimus back as a coworker in preaching the Gospel. He's so eager, in fact, that he doesn't shy from appealing to sentiment: this "old man" and "prisoner," he says, seeks a favor on behalf of a beloved "child" whom he has brought to life in Christ. Then, with obvious emotion, he adds, "I am sending my heart."

Paul could order Philemon, but he wants any favor he receives to be "voluntary."

By challenging Philemon to freely love and respect Onesimus and treat him as a brother, Paul transforms the relationship between master and slave, and in that culture, that was a revolutionary challenge indeed.

GOSPEL In the end, Christ expects everything of us. Anyone who doesn't know that hasn't read this passage. It's remarkable that Jesus makes

GOSPEL   Luke 14:25–33

A reading from the holy Gospel according to Luke

Great **crowds** were traveling with **Jesus**,
and he turned and **addressed** them,
"If anyone comes to me without **hating** his **father** and **mother**,
wife and **children**, **brothers** and **sisters**,
and even his own **life**,
he **cannot** be my **disciple**.
Whoever does not carry his own **cross** and come **after** me
cannot be my **disciple**.
Which of you wishing to construct a **tower**
does not **first** sit down and calculate the **cost**
to see if there is **enough** for its **completion**?
Otherwise, after laying the **foundation**
and finding himself unable to **finish** the work
the onlookers should **laugh** at him and say,
'This one **began** to build but did not have the **resources**
to **finish**.'
Or what **king** marching into **battle** would not first **sit** down
and decide whether with **ten** thousand troops
he can **successfully** oppose **another** king
advancing upon him with **twenty** thousand troops?
But if **not**, while he is still far **away**,
he will send a **delegation** to ask for **peace** terms.
In the same **way**,
anyone of you who does not **renounce** all his **possessions**
cannot be my **disciple**."

The great crowds may be the motivator for this hard saying. He wants disciples, not curiosity seekers.

Stress "his own life" more than the other items in the list.

It's this willingness to carry one's cross that Jesus is demanding.

Speak the parables in a more reasonable, conversational tone, as if you were saying, "You would make these preparations, wouldn't you? Don't do any less for me."

Contrast "ten thousand" with "twenty thousand."

Jesus goes back to the beginning. He says you must let go of everything if you want to be his disciple. Speak with authority.

---

the cost of discipleship so plain up front. Who would follow such an uncompromising leader? Could anyone turn away from parents, children, spouse and even one's own self? Clearly there are two things at work here: Jesus is speaking figuratively and he is telling his disciples that following him may cost their very lives. Using hyperbole doesn't mean the message isn't true, but it doesn't mean it's meant literally either. Discipleship doesn't come cheaply. Surrendering relationships may be necessary. Jesus is not asking that we abandon

spouse and kids, but that nothing be more important to us than our commitment to him. No person or possession can ever claim us as he does! Speak this hard saying in a way that neither compromises it nor renders it brutally harsh.

Luke hints at what occasioned this teaching: "Great crowds" followed Jesus, and radical demands soon turn idealistic romantics into former followers. Jesus warns them that only those prepared to give all can persevere. So he lists the most compelling attachments that disciples must surrender. Without softening the

requirements, Jesus' parables render them more reasonable. Look, he says, in so many areas you struggle, sacrifice, prepare, and it seems quite reasonable. No less is expected of those who follow me. The last sentence is uncompromising and stark. To avoid the fate of the "king" who must negotiate in weakness, Jesus counsels renouncing all distracting "possessions," as the surest way to strength, and to oneness with him.

24TH SUNDAY IN ORDINARY TIME

Lectionary #132

READING I   Exodus 32:7–11, 13–14

A reading from the Book of Exodus

The LORD said to **Moses**,
"Go down at **once** to your **people**,
    whom you brought **out** of the land of **Egypt**,
    for they have become **depraved**.
They have soon turned **aside** from the way I pointed **out** to them,
    making for themselves a molten **calf** and **worshiping** it,
    sacrificing to it and crying out,
    '**This** is your God, O **Israel**,
    who brought you **out** of the land of **Egypt**!'
I see how **stiff-necked** this people is," continued the LORD
        to Moses.
"Let me **alone**, then,
    that my **wrath** may blaze up **against** them to **consume** them.
Then I will make of you a **great nation**."

But Moses **implored** the LORD, his God, saying,
"**Why**, O LORD, should your **wrath** blaze up
        against your own **people**,
    whom **you** brought out of the land of Egypt
    with such **great** power and with so strong a **hand**?
Remember your **servants Abraham**, **Isaac**, and **Israel**,
    and how you **swore** to them by your own **self**, saying,
    'I will make your **descendants** as numerous as the **stars**
        in the **sky**;

Make sure you stress that it's the "Lord" who is speaking.

Without overdoing it, make sure God's anger is clearly communicated.

This is the source of God's wrath: they've turned (once again!) to idolatry. God mockingly quotes the people's arrogant claim: "This is your God."

God's anger is righteous. God is saying, "Let me do this, and then I will keep my promises."

Shift to a slower tone here. Moses is the protective parent trying to calm the angry parent.

Don't let this sound disingenuous; speak with great sincerity.

READING I   Israel had a wonderfully anthropomorphic understanding of God. They depicted God as capable of volatile human emotions like the passionate wrath demonstrated here; they also presented God as someone who worried about such matters as reputation and honor. To do justice to this passage, take it at face value giving God a vocabulary of anger and vengeance and Moses the same negotiating savvy demonstrated by Abraham when he bargained for Sodom and Gomorrah.

God's fury is sparked by the sin of idolatry, the most consistent of Israel's sins, made even more shameful now because Israel has so recently received the Ten Commandments. The author puts into the mouth of God language that pulls no punches in naming Israel's offenses and in expressing God's righteous anger. Of course, it's all a set up for the end of the story where God relents and shows this stiff-necked people undeserved mercy. The greater the people's guilt, the less deserving they are of mercy, the better the quality of God's love is revealed. Obviously,

you must not hold back then when narrating how the people "have become depraved" or when expressing God's desire to let divine anger "blaze up . . . [and] consume them." Good proclamation requires communicating a piece of scripture (which is literature before it is anything else) in its artistic, intellectual, and emotional totality. The emotions given God here are no exception.

God and Moses talk about the people the way parents sometimes talk about their children. God refers to them as "your people whom you brought" out of Egypt. Moses

and all this **land** that I promised,
I will give your **descendants** as their **perpetual heritage.'"**
So the LORD **relented** in the punishment
he had threatened to **inflict** on his **people**.

Pause after Moses speaks. Make eye contact with the assembly, and then announce the good news of God's mercy.

READING II   1 Timothy 1:12–17

A reading from the first Letter of Saint Paul to Timothy

Beloved:
I am **grateful** to him who has **strengthened** me, Christ **Jesus**
    our **Lord**,
    because he considered me **trustworthy**
    in **appointing** me to the **ministry**.
I was once a **blasphemer** and a **persecutor** and **arrogant**,
    but I have been **mercifully** treated
    because I acted out of **ignorance** in my unbelief.
Indeed, the **grace** of our Lord has been **abundant**,
    along with the **faith** and **love** that are in Christ **Jesus**.
This saying is **trustworthy** and deserves full **acceptance**:
    Christ **Jesus** came into the **world** to save **sinners**.
Of these I am the **foremost**.
But for that **reason** I was **mercifully** treated,
    so that in **me**, as the **foremost**,
    Christ Jesus might display all his **patience** as an **example**
    for those who would come to **believe** in him for everlasting **life**.
To the king of **ages**, **incorruptible**, **invisible**, the **only** God,
    honor and **glory forever** and **ever**. **Amen**.

The first word sets the tone.

"Grateful" is the mood of the entire reading. Even as he critiques himself, Paul is aware that he was and remains forgiven for all his mistakes and transgressions.

After quickly reciting the litany of Paul's sins, take more time with this declaration of God's bountiful mercy.
Speak slowly here, with authority and power.

Paul is saying, "I'm an example of what God can do in anyone's life!"

Slowly build intensity up to the end. This is a sincere prayer of praise and gratitude.

returns the favor, repeating God's own words to persuade God not to destroy "your people whom you brought . . . ." This is an important point in Moses' case for sparing the people; it would be contradictory for God to save a people so miraculously only to destroy them. But his second argument is more critical and the one that connects us with the Gospel. Moses carefully reviews the promises God made to the patriarchs, Israel's beloved ancestors. It's as if Moses is reminding a father of the promises he made to his own children. "Remember your servants," he says, you "swore" to them. In scripture, it is usually God who reminds the people of the covenant. But Moses makes bold to switch roles, and effectively reminds God. The last line is more conversion than announcement. With grateful awareness that God's most basic posture is forgiveness, slowly reveal God's change of heart.

READING II In the first-person testimony of this text, a very candid Paul confesses aspects of his life with honest and humble emotion. It was no secret during his lifetime that Paul started out as an enemy of the Christian community. In his ignorance of Christ, he persecuted Christians with all his might. Then a dramatic and mystical encounter with the risen Christ changed everything. This enemy turned apostle and helped spread the Gospel throughout the known world. Here, Paul is held up as an "example" for more than Timothy: all Christians were interested in his past and present status.

GOSPEL Luke 15:1–32

A reading from the holy Gospel according to Luke

Tax collectors and **sinners** were all drawing **near** to **listen**
    to **Jesus**,
  but the **Pharisees** and **scribes** began to **complain**, saying,
  "This man welcomes **sinners** and **eats** with them."
So to **them** he addressed this **parable**.
"What **man** among you having a **hundred** sheep
    and losing **one** of them
  would not **leave** the ninety-nine in the desert
  and go after the **lost** one until he **finds** it?
And when he **does** find it,
  he sets it on his **shoulders** with great **joy**
  and, upon his arrival **home**,
  he calls together his **friends** and **neighbors** and says to them,
  '**Rejoice** with me because I have **found** my lost sheep.'
I **tell** you, in just the **same** way
  there will be more **joy** in **heaven** over one **sinner** who **repents**
  than over ninety-nine **righteous** people
  who have no **need** of repentance.

"Or what **woman** having **ten** coins and losing **one**
  would not light a **lamp** and sweep the **house**,
  searching **carefully** until she **finds** it?
And when she **does** find it,
  she calls together her **friends** and **neighbors**
  and **says** to them,
  '**Rejoice** with me because I have **found** the coin that I **lost**.'

Composition of Jesus' audience is a significant detail. Stress it as well as their disdain for the company he keeps.

Stress the word "them."

"Lost" becomes a refrain in these three stories.

God's joy in dispensing salvation is a major motif in Luke.

Luke presents God's love for sinners through male and female images.

Here, too, stress the rejoicing.

He acknowledges his failings with obvious regret but also with a bit of flamboyance, even calling himself "the foremost" of sinners. Paul is indeed using himself as an example. He does this to prove that if Christ could overwhelm the darkness in him, who was such an extreme case, then the light of Christ's grace could do the same for anyone. Notice that his gratitude is as generous as his self-abasement: "I have been mercifully treated" (repeated twice) and "The grace of our Lord has been abundant" are sincere and poetic expressions of God's mercy.

Gratitude underlies the entire text. Christ came to save sinners; he came to heal the sick, not the healthy. Christ loved Paul and chose him while Paul was still Christ's enemy. That's what Paul—and every Christian—celebrates. Who among us is not a sinner? Who has not received God's mercy in abundance? But how do we read such rich self-disclosure? If you've ever witnessed someone recall a traumatic event—rape, near-fatal crash, war memories—you've probably noticed the

story was told with little inflection; the speaker probably "relived" the events but without reenacting them. Very often, the more serious or tragic the event, the more internalized the retelling. If you display too much emotion you will rob the assembly of the opportunity to experience those emotions themselves. This testimony is already overstated, so an understated delivery will convey more sincerity. You don't have to be Paul as you read, but you must know him and understand his emotions—even feel them. That shouldn't be hard if you recall your own sinfulness

Make good eye contact for this line.	In just the **same way**, I **tell** you,
	    there will be **rejoicing** among the **angels** of **God**
	    over one **sinner** who **repents**."

Pause and start with renewed energy.	Then he said,
	    "A man had **two sons**, and the **younger** son said to his father,
	    '**Father** give me the **share** of your **estate** that should **come**
	        to me.'
	So the father **divided** the property between them.
	After a few **days**, the younger son **collected** all his belongings
	    and **set** off to a **distant** country
	    where he **squandered** his inheritance on a life of **dissipation**.

"Squandered" and "dissipation" are expressive words. Use them well.	When he had freely spent **everything**,
	    a severe **famine** struck that country,
	    and he found himself in dire **need**.

This is the ultimate indignity: a Jew feeding a Gentile's swine.	So he **hired** himself out to one of the local **citizens**
	    who sent him to his **farm** to tend the **swine**.
	And he **longed** to eat his fill of the **pods** on which the **swine** fed,
	    but nobody **gave** him any.

He comes to his senses, not to repentance. His self-inflicted degradation motivates his return.	Coming to his **senses** he thought,
	    'How many of my father's hired **workers**
	    have **more** than enough food to eat,
	    but here am **I**, **dying** from **hunger**.
	I shall **get** up and **go** to my father and I shall **say** to him,
	    "**Father**, I have **sinned** against **heaven** and against **you**.

This rehearsal of his apology should lack real sincerity. Save that for later.	I no longer **deserve** to be called your **son**; treat **me** as you would treat one of your **hired workers**."'

and how often God has forgiven you. "This saying is trustworthy . . ." is the writer's sincerest moment, so give it the time it requires. The last sentence is a sincere prayer of gratitude and praise directed at a God whose greatness is experienced through mercy.

GOSPEL When last we encountered the prodigal it was Lent and his story stood alone. Today his tale is prefaced by two other parables that focus us on elements different from those stressed in Lent. Then the accent was on the son who, appropriate to that season, modeled baptismal conversion. Today the Father rises to prominence. The two brief parables suggest a proactive God who spares no effort in seeking and saving those who are lost. In the light of those stories the behavior of the father comes to prominence and his remarkable initiative becomes our focus.

Luke spends little time on setting, but what he gives is always important. Without saying so, he hints that Jesus shares these stories in response to the murmurs of the religious leaders who are scandalized that Jesus draws sinners like garbage draws flies. Jesus' proactive stance (he even "welcomes sinners and eats with them") troubles them deeply. To demonstrate that the Son of Man comes to seek and save the lost, Jesus tells parables of a lost sheep, a lost coin and a lost son.

Using both male and female images, Luke presents stories that express God's joy in dispensing salvation. It is important to stress the great effort expended by shepherd and woman to retrieve what they

Pause after "Went back . . . father." Then start steadily building energy with the next line. Emphasize the father's initiative: He "ran . . . embraced. . . kissed."

Now the lines can be delivered sincerely.

This is the third emphasis on rejoicing. The son is restored to his full status. The ring is a sign of household authority.

Pause briefly as the mood changes. Your tone can signal the trouble ahead.

Speak this narration ("He called . . . might mean") in the voice of the elder son.

Here, too, speak the narration in the son's angry voice.

Again, the father initiates.

So he got up and went **back** to his father.
While he was still a **long** way off,
 his father caught **sight** of him,
 and was filled with **compassion**.
He **ran** to his son, **embraced** him and **kissed** him.
His son **said** to him,
 'Father, I have **sinned** against **heaven** and against **you**;
 I no longer **deserve** to be called your **son**.'
But his **father** ordered his **servants**,
 '**Quickly** bring the finest **robe** and put it **on** him;
 put a **ring** on his **finger** and **sandals** on his **feet**.
Take the fattened **calf** and **slaughter** it.
Then let us **celebrate** with a **feast**,
 because this **son** of mine was **dead**, and has come to **life** again;
 he was **lost**, and has been **found**.'
Then the **celebration began**.
Now the **older** son had been out in the **field**
 and, on his way **back**, as he **neared** the house,
 he heard the sound of **music** and **dancing**.
He called one of the **servants** and asked what this might **mean**.
The servant said to him,
 'Your **brother** has returned
 and your **father** has slaughtered the fattened **calf**
 because he has him **back** safe and **sound**.'
He became **angry**,
 and when he **refused** to enter the house,
 his **father** came **out** and **pleaded** with him.

lost, for both characters represent the proactive God who is always working for our good. The shepherd leaves the "ninety-nine" in the desert, risking peril for the sake of the one lost sheep. The woman lights and sweeps and searches "carefully," not stopping until she has found her coin. The other point of focus is the jubilation expressed in each parable that echoes the joy of the angels in heaven over a sinner's repentance. Prefaced by these two parables, the prodigal narrative becomes even more clearly an illustration of God's overabundant mercy and forgiveness.

This classic story has so penetrated our imaginations that it has become the archetype of forgiveness. It is well worth telling twice in one year, especially if the telling presents a clearer image of the God of mercy. (A detailed discussion of this parable is found in the commentary for the Fourth Sunday of Lent.) Today, notice especially that the boy's motives for returning home are just as selfish as those that sent him to the far country: he's still thinking about himself. It is his self—induced suffering that brings him to his senses. He knows

where home is and where safety and forgiveness await. The father's running "while he was still a long way off" is spontaneous, and wholly independent of the son's pure or impure motives. It's this initiative and the lavish and unmerited mercy he dispenses that make the father so apt an image of the heavenly Father. In typical fashion, Luke offers great detail regarding the joyous celebration that welcomes the boy home.

In today's context, the elder son also receives greater prominence. His narrow understanding of justice and love serves

The son is convinced he has a legitimate grievance.

His resentment bubbles over here.

Speak slowly and with compassion. The father loves this son as much as the prodigal.

Stress the need to rejoice.

He said to his father in reply,
    '**Look**, all these years I **served** you
    and not **once** did I disobey your **orders**;
    yet you never gave me even a young **goat** to feast on
        with my friends.
But when your son **returns**,
    who **swallowed** up your property with **prostitutes**,
    for **him** you slaughter the fattened **calf**.'
He **said** to him,
    '**My son**, you are here with me **always**;
    everything I have is **yours**.
But now we must **celebrate** and **rejoice**,
    because your brother was **dead** and has come to **life** again;
    he was **lost** and has been **found**.'"

[Shorter: Luke 15:1–10]

as a foil for the father's magnanimity. The elder brother feels his behavior entitles him to be treated like a son, while his younger brother has lost that privilege. He deeply resents the father's freely given love. But the father proves himself a good parent even to this child. He reminds him that he always will have a place in the father's home and the father's heart. But he won't accept the elder's quid pro quo understanding of love; instead, he insists on the need for rejoicing ("we must cele-brate") over a dead son who has returned to life.

25TH SUNDAY IN ORDINARY TIME

Lectionary #135

READING I   Amos 8:4–7

A reading from the Book of the Prophet Amos

Hear this, you who **trample** upon the **needy**
    and destroy the **poor** of the land!
"When will the **new** moon be **over**," you ask,
    "that we may **sell** our grain,
    and the **sabbath**, that we may **display** the **wheat**?
We will **diminish** the **ephah**,
    add to the **shekel**,
    and fix our **scales** for **cheating**!
We will buy the **lowly** for **silver**,
    and the **poor** for a pair of **sandals**;
    even the **refuse** of the wheat we will **sell**!"
The **LORD** has sworn by the **pride** of **Jacob**:
    Never will I forget a **thing** they have **done**!

We read from Amos next week as well.

The opening should sound like the threat it is!

These cheaters can't wait to resume their exploitation. Make sure the sinister motives are heard in your tone.

"New moon" and "Sabbath" are times when work is not permitted.

ephah = EE-fah

shekel = SHEK-*l

An ephah is a unit of measure, while a shekel is a unit of weight.

Amos exaggerates their callous disregard for the poor. They will sell debtors into slavery.

This is an even greater threat than in the opening line.

 Amos' strong words address two serious sins: greed and hypocrisy. The threat embedded in the opening statement is addressed to merchants whose plundering greed has caused them to "trample" and "destroy" the poor and needy. Often called the prophet of social justice, Amos spoke his prophecies in the northern kingdom at a time of great political success that saw the rich growing richer while the poor grew poorer. He openly challenged a brazenly legalistic and hypocritical system that reeked of the insincere religiosity depicted here.

Be especially attentive to tone in the lines where Amos parodies the merchants' scheming. At first, we might wonder where their evil lies, for without proper tone the trickery could sound as innocent as a nursery rhyme. Only the word "cheated" exposes these merchants as predators who dig claws into the helpless poor. Your characterization, without exaggeration, must reveal their true colors. Your tone must also suggest why these merchants can't wait for the "new moon" festival and "Sabbath" to be over: both are holy times when no business could be transacted. But

instead of using the time for worship and genuine piety, these merchants use the time off to conspire to defraud the poor by altering the common units of measure ("the ehpah" and "the shekel") to their own advantage. These affluent plotters won't stop at defrauding however: For as little as "a pair of sandals" they will eagerly buy and sell into slavery paupers who cannot pay their debts. Gleefully, they sell bad grain that should be thrown away like garbage. Amos' outcry is made in the name of God who promises "never [to] forget" the evil done by these hypocrites who lack

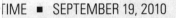

READING II   1 Timothy 2:1–8

A reading from the first Letter of Saint Paul to Timothy

Beloved:
First of all, I ask that **supplications**, **prayers**,
    petitions, and **thanksgivings** be offered for **everyone**,
    for **kings** and for all in **authority**,
    that we may lead a **quiet** and **tranquil** life
    in all **devotion** and **dignity**.
This is **good** and **pleasing** to God our **savior**,
    who wills **everyone** to be **saved**
    and to come to **knowledge** of the **truth**.
        For there is **one** God.
        There is also one **mediator** between God and men,
        the **man** Christ **Jesus**,
        who **gave** himself as **ransom** for **all**.
This was the **testimony** at the proper **time**.
For **this** I was appointed **preacher** and **apostle**
    —I am speaking the **truth**, I am not **lying**—,
    teacher of the **Gentiles** in **faith** and **truth**.

It is my **wish**, then, that in **every** place the men should **pray**,
    lifting up holy **hands**, without **anger** or **argument**.

Look at the assembly when you speak "Beloved."

The redundancy of the list creates emphasis. Speak with urgency.

Stress God's desire for all to know truth and salvation.

Speak these lines as both a prayer and a declaration of faith in Jesus.

Paul's legitimate claim to his ministry to the Gentiles should be asserted with conviction.

End on a softer note, calling for pure and humble prayer from all and for all.

---

true morality. His words were meant to shock the wicked among his listeners. Without melodrama, find a way to let these words have that power today.

READING II Each of today's readings focuses on some aspect of social responsibility. This one centers on the need to pray for the political system. Since the time of Cyrus, the Persian king who permitted the Israelites to return from exile, the Jews prayed even for pagan rulers. This letter affirms that practice,

asserting that a stable social order is the very basis for tranquil living that leads to "devotion" and "dignity." The nightly news regularly makes us aware of the precarious stability of global political situations and the wide-ranging influence of decisions made by political leaders. We hardly need this text to convince us that prayer for leaders is necessary, but that it is "good and pleasing to God" is welcome reassurance. So speak those words with conviction that prayer for leaders otherwise removed from our direct influence can make a real difference.

The liturgical practice of the early Church included intercessions like those seen here. The Church is to be a people of prayer that intercedes "for everyone, for kings and for all in authority . . . that we may be able to lead a . . . tranquil life." What we see here is an early form of the intercessory formula we still use today: Let us pray for such and such, that such and such may follow. The list found in the first sentence does not name four different kinds of prayer; the repetition is an intentional redundancy that adds to the sense of

GOSPEL   Luke 16:1–13

A reading from the holy Gospel according to Luke

Jesus said to his **disciples**,
"A **rich** man had a **steward**
who was **reported** to him for **squandering** his property.
He **summoned** him and said,
'What is this I **hear** about you?
Prepare a full **account** of your **stewardship**,
because you can no **longer** be my steward.'
The steward said to himself, 'What shall I **do**,
now that my **master** is taking the position of steward
away from me?
I am not **strong** enough to **dig** and I am **ashamed** to **beg**.
I **know** what I shall do so that,
when I am **removed** from the stewardship,
they may **welcome** me into their **homes**.'
He called in his master's **debtors** one by **one**.
To the **first** he said,
'How much do you **owe** my master?'
He replied, 'One **hundred** measures of **olive** oil.'
He said to him, 'Here is your **promissory** note.
Sit down and quickly write one for **fifty**.'
Then to **another** the steward said, 'And **you**,
how much do **you** owe?'
He replied, 'One **hundred** kors of **wheat**.'
The steward **said** to him, 'Here is **your** promissory note;
write one for **eighty**.'

Throughout this text Jesus is teaching the disciples.

The rich man is harsh and demanding.

Although dishonest, the manger is not unappealing.

He suddenly knows what to do!

Let him speak kindly to the debtors. He's putting goodwill in the bank.

A kor is a unit of measure equaling 10 ephahs or 10 bushels.

urgency. Take extra care with the declaration that all prayer is mediated through Jesus because it is both a prayer and a statement of faith. The legitimacy of Paul's role as "preacher and apostle" is strongly asserted, for it is a ministry Paul received directly from the one mediator, Christ Jesus. Since Paul was not one of "the Twelve," this assertion of apostolic authority ("I am not lying") is important to all those who received the truth of the Gospel from him. The text ends with a final plea that all pray with pure intentions "lifting up holy hands"—another glimpse into early liturgical practice.

GOSPEL It is hard to be comfortable with this parable. Its message is confusing, its main character hardly exemplary, and yet Jesus makes him an example. The enigmatic and shocking character of the parable may motivate some to shorten the Gospel reading and avoid having to deal with what seems poor judgment on Jesus' part. But among the riches of scripture is its ability to shock; don't deprive your assembly of the potential jolt. The most attractive interpretation of this parable maintains that the owner praises the industrious manager because he himself has been robbed of nothing, for the steward merely waives the commission that would have been his for negotiating his master's business. Others contend no evidence exists that the steward had any personal claim to the commission. The master, they say, who was himself an unjust and usurious absentee landlord,

Speak with strong emphasis about both the master's commendation and Jesus' rationale for the praise.

And the master **commended** that dishonest steward
    for acting **prudently**.

"For the children of **this** world
    are more **prudent** in dealing with their own **generation**
    than are the children of **light**.

These verses probably were not part of the original parable. Speak them as the advice of one friend to another over matters of life and death.

I **tell** you, make **friends** for yourselves with dishonest wealth,
    so that when it **fails**, you will be welcomed
        into **eternal** dwellings.
The person who is **trustworthy** in very **small** matters
    is also trustworthy in **great** ones;
    and the person who is **dishonest** in very small matters
    is also **dishonest** in great ones.

"Dishonest wealth" is the riches of the world. "True wealth" is the riches of the kingdom of God.

If, therefore, you are not trustworthy with **dishonest** wealth,
    who will trust you with **true** wealth?
If you are **not** trustworthy with what belongs to **another**,
    who will give you what is **yours**?
No servant can serve **two** masters.

All the preceding adds up to this: God must be the priority; worldly pursuits must never compromise our commitment to God.

He will either **hate** one and love the **other**,
    or be **devoted** to one and **despise** the other.
You cannot serve both **God** and **mammon**."

[Shorter: Luke 16:10–13]

admires the resourcefulness of a subordinate who manages to out-con him. Clever, decisive, and lacking self pity, the steward sets about to turn debtors into allies. His soliloquy reveals him to be rather likable, or at least someone we can identify with: "What shall I do . . . dig ditches . . . go begging . . . ?" Of course not! And when he finds an answer, I know what I'll do!

Take care to note that Jesus praises the steward's shrewdness, not his dishonesty. Jesus wants disciples to pursue the kingdom with as much initiative and decisiveness as the steward pursued his own selfish interests. Just imagine how the work of the Gospel would flourish if those doing the work were as inventive and resourceful as this clever manager. Three moralizations about the proper use of money follow the parable. "Make friends . . . with dishonest wealth": all the world's treasures seem to be included in this category. Worldly wealth is not being judged negatively, but we are told to use it wisely and to share it (give alms) to win heavenly allies who can intercede for us when that wealth eventually fails us. "If you are not trustworthy with dishonest wealth" tells us that one who does not share paltry material wealth will not receive heavenly ("true") treasure. "God and mammon" reminds us that enslavement to money (a form of idolatry) can be avoided only if we hold it lightly and share it, giving God priority in our lives.

26TH SUNDAY IN ORDINARY TIME

Lectionary #138

READING I   Amos 6:1a, 4–7

A reading from the Book of the Prophet Amos

Amos attacks the attitude that motivates the behavior of the rich more than their specific actions.

Thus says the LORD, the God of **hosts**:
Woe to the **complacent** in **Zion**!
Lying upon beds of **ivory**,
   stretched **comfortably** on their **couches**,
they eat **lambs** taken from the **flock**,
   and **calves** from the **stall**!
Improvising to the music of the **harp**,
   like **David**, they devise their own **accompaniment**.
They drink wine from **bowls**
   and **anoint** themselves with the best **oils**;
   yet they are not made **ill** by the collapse of **Joseph**!
Therefore, now they shall be the **first** to go into **exile**,
   and their wanton **revelry** shall be done **away** with.

Let your tone tell the assembly that this behavior is self-indulgent and hypocritical.

Calves that fed on milk rather than grazed on grass were to be reserved for sacrifice to God.

To "drink wine from bowls" is sign of their excess. They have nothing better to do!

"Joseph" represents the entire nation. The impending "collapse" is the result of their self-indulgence at the expense of the poor.

Speak these final lines with regret. He would much rather see them repent than go into exile.

READING II   1 Timothy 6:11–16

A reading from the first Letter of Saint Paul to Timothy

"Man of God" should be spoken with reverence and respect. To slow your delivery of the opening list and to give each virtue its own unique quality, think of someone who embodies that virtue and "see" that person as you name the quality.

But **you**, man of God, pursue **righteousness**,
   devotion, **faith**, **love**, **patience** and **gentleness**.
Compete **well** for the **faith**.

READING I The prosperous northern kingdom of Israel is rotting from within. Its wealthy citizens have grown "complacent"; they neglect the needs of the poor and indulge in excesses that reveal hearts unacquainted with justice. Amos threatens that the nation may soon crumble ("the collapse of Joseph" is a metaphor for the whole people), but the idle rich continue to indulge in the very pleasures that are precipitating their downfall. Because some of the allusions are ambiguous (what's wrong with eating "lambs from the flock" or "calves from the stall"?), your tone will have to suggest that these are lavish excesses embraced by a people who go through the motions of observing the covenant while neglecting the disadvantaged among them. Amos rails against such hypocrisy that divorces love of God from love of neighbor. But Amos is more concerned with asserting the rights of the needy than he is with condemning the corrupt.

Amos mocks the indulgent attitude of the pampered rich. Let the sound of the words suggest the full meaning of his sarcastic critique: the leaders sleep in beds inlaid with expensive "ivory," eat only the choicest young "lambs" and tender milk-fed rather than grass-grazed calves, both of which are to be reserved for the Lord, not for their own bellies. They drink wine by the "bowl" and improvise dances and music, not piously as did David, but to numb themselves to the decay that surrounds them. The three most important words are "Woe" that introduces the indictments, "yet" that contrasts what they do with what they should be doing, and "therefore" that announces the painful consequences.

Make eye contact and speak this admonition to the assembly.

These 12 lines all comprise one sentence. Share one thought at a time. There is a sense of prayer throughout this entire section.

Lay hold of **eternal** life, to which you were **called**
> when you made the noble **confession** in the presence
> > of many **witnesses**.
I **charge** you before God, who gives life to **all** things,
> and before Christ **Jesus**,
> who gave testimony under Pontius **Pilate**
> > for the noble **confession**,
> to keep the **commandment** without **stain** or **reproach**
> until the **appearance** of our **Lord** Jesus **Christ**
> that the **blessed** and **only** ruler
> will make **manifest** at the **proper** time,
> the **King** of **kings** and **Lord** of **lords**,
> who alone has **immortality**, who dwells
> > in unapproachable **light**,
> and whom no human being has **seen** or **can** see.
To **him** be **honor** and eternal **power**. **Amen**.

Here the prayer is explicit. Speak it slowly and reverently.

GOSPEL Luke 16:19–31

A reading from the holy Gospel according to Luke

Jesus said to the **Pharisees**:
"There was a **rich** man who dressed in purple **garments**
> and fine **linen**
> and dined **sumptuously** each day.
And lying at his door was a **poor** man named **Lazarus**,
> covered with **sores**,
> who would **gladly** have eaten his fill of the **scraps**
> that **fell** from the rich man's **table**.
Dogs even used to come and lick his **sores**.

Only Luke records this parable. Luke often presents Jesus' position on money and the relationship of rich and poor. Addressed to the Pharisees, the parable's chief message is the need for all to listen, hear, and repent while there is time.

Contrast the words of sumptuous over-abundance ("purple garments and fine linen" and "dined sumptuously") with words that cause immediate discomfort ("sores," "scraps," "dogs," and "licked") Positive and negative coloring also characterizes the afterlife descriptions ("bosom of Abraham" and "torment").

READING II Those who advance in the spiritual life come to understand the necessity of valuing God above all things. The world offers many distractions and temptations, but those who would lead the Christian community must not be seduced by wealth or worldly vices. Although this letter is addressed to Church leaders, the liturgy applies these words to each of us. "Man of God," a title used for Moses and Old Testament prophets, signifies the great spiritual power attributed to leaders, and hence the great responsibility

they bear, but today you apply that honorific to each member of the assembly.

The reading begins with imperatives: "Pursue," "Compete," "Lay hold of," "I charge you . . . keep the commandment." Imperatives must be spoken with authority and conviction. "Compete well for the faith" is an admonition to continue fighting the good fight despite opposition or setbacks. "In the presence of witnesses" refers to Timothy's Baptism through which he publicly professed his faith and echoed Jesus' own confession before Pilate. The confusing phrase "Keep the command-

ment" doesn't charge Timothy to observe any single "commandment," but all that God has revealed through Jesus. Because this letter is sent from one elder to another, the admonitions are somewhat softened, but because the issues are so important and the example of a leader so influential, you must speak them with urgency. The text ends with a simple but sincere prayer of praise.

GOSPEL Jesus' parable is a cautionary tale about missed opportunity and the danger of assuming we

Let your tone contrast the fate of Lazarus with the torment of the rich man.

When the poor man **died**,
 he was carried away by **angels** to the bosom of **Abraham**.
The **rich** man **also** died and was **buried**,
 and from the **netherworld**, where he was in **torment**,
 he raised his **eyes** and saw **Abraham** far **off**
 and **Lazarus** at his **side**.

He rather arrogantly expects Abraham and Lazarus to comply.

And he **cried** out, 'Father **Abraham**, have **pity** on me.
Send **Lazarus** to dip the tip of his **finger** in **water** and cool
 my **tongue**,
 for I am suffering **torment** in these **flames**.'

Note that Abraham calls him "Child." Abraham's subtle and nonjudgmental tone will add horror to the irreversibility of the situation.

Abraham replied,
 'My **child**, remember that you received
 what was **good** during your lifetime
 while **Lazarus** likewise received what was **bad**;
 but now **he** is **comforted** here, whereas **you** are **tormented**.
Moreover, between **us** and **you** a great **chasm** is established
 to prevent anyone from **crossing** who might wish to go
 from **our** side to **yours** or from **your** side to **ours**.'

His urgency grows; his concern is genuine, but limited to his family.

He said, 'Then I **beg** you, father,
 send him to my **father's** house, for I have five **brothers**,
 so that he may **warn** them,
 lest they **too** come to this place of **torment**.'

Abraham's reply is not a rebuke, but your tone can suggest "Moses and prophets" are necessary and sufficient.

But Abraham **replied**, 'They have **Moses** and the **prophets**.
Let them **listen** to them.'

The rich man sets up a profound irony.

He said, 'Oh **no**, father Abraham,
 but if someone from the **dead** goes to them, they will **repent**.'
Then **Abraham** said, 'If they will not listen to **Moses**
 and the **prophets**,
 neither will they be persuaded if someone should **rise**
 from the **dead**.'"

Because this is of ultimate importance, Abraham pulls no punches. Deliver the line starkly and firmly.

have plenty of time for ultimate matters like salvation. The hard and sobering truth taught by the story is that some opportunities can be lost forever and some decisions never can be reversed.

Why has the rich man merited the torment that is his fate? The fact that he recognizes Lazarus in the afterlife suggests that in this life he knew of the man's need but ignored his moral responsibility. In fact, the rich man is so accustomed to thinking of Lazarus as subservient that he doesn't hesitate to ask him to leave Abraham's

bosom to come wait on him. Think carefully about your characterization of the rich man. He is not entirely unsympathetic. On the plus side is a surprising lack of bitterness about his tragic fate and his genuine, although belated, concern for his "brothers." The rich man's naive argument that someone from the dead can surely lead his brothers to repentance spotlights the sad reality that even the miracle of the Resurrection cannot compel faith, nor turn faith into just action.

If Jesus' parable is meant to speak to us, must we not recognize the rich man in

ourselves? If he is too darkly drawn, we will identify only with poor Lazarus and miss the story's point. The more sincere the rich man, the more genuine his concern for his brothers, and the more temperate Abraham's explanations and denials, the more powerfully the message and warning of this parable will be heard.

27TH SUNDAY IN ORDINARY TIME

Lectionary #141

READING I — Habakkuk 1:2–3; 2:2–4

Habakkuk = huh-BAK-kuhk or
HAB-uh-kuhk

What emotion do you hear in the intense and repeated questions? Is he despairing, expressing anger, or begging God to take action and show mercy?

Think of a real-life situation that seems hopeless, perhaps a loved one dying of cancer, and let that struggle inform how you speak these lines.

Pause before starting this section. Habakkuk quotes God, so speak with solemn authority.

The same idea is stated six times: the vision of deliverance will be fulfilled! Speak with loving assurance.

It's faith that makes the difference between those who lose heart and those who persevere.

A reading from the Book of the Prophet Habakkuk

How **long**, O LORD? I cry for **help**
　　but you do not **listen**!
I cry out to you, "**Violence!**"
　　but you do not **intervene**.
Why do you let me see **ruin**;
　　why must I look at **misery**?
Destruction and **violence** are before me;
　　there is **strife**, and clamorous **discord**.
Then the LORD **answered** me and said:
　　Write down the vision **clearly** upon the **tablets**,
　　so that one can read it **readily**.
For the **vision** still has its **time**,
　　presses on to **fulfillment**, and will not **disappoint**;
if it **delays**, **wait** for it,
　　it will surely **come**, it will **not** be **late**.
The **rash** one has no **integrity**;
　　but the **just** one, because of his **faith**, shall **live**.

READING I — The silence of God in the face of evil is one of the perennial human enigmas. Scripture is unafraid to articulate human struggle, confusion, even anger at what looks like divine indifference. The book of Job and some of the psalms later developed into an art from the human questioning of the ways of God first articulated by Habakkuk. Writing at a desperate time of faithlessness and political peril in the southern kingdom of Judah, the prophet makes bold to complain about the circumstances, and even questions

God's handling of the world. Everywhere the prophet sees violence, misery, and injustice, not to mention impending invasion from Babylonia. Yet God seems to be doing nothing. Imagine living through the Holocaust, praying day after day, and seeing nothing change. That's the feeling of these lines. If you will do nothing to intervene, the disheartened prophet tells God, can't I at least be spared the sight of ruin and discord?

The second half of the text presents God's response and the mood changes dramatically. In words calm and reassuring,

God instructs Habakkuk to record the vision of deliverance he has been shown. It was believed in that time that writing something down somehow helped it come true. God's instruction is then also assurance that help will come, but it must be awaited with faith. God asserts six times that the vision will not disappoint. The repetitions offer comfort while calling for patience, that is, the faith-filled perseverance and trust in the face of adversity that distinguishes the "rash" from the "just."

READING II   2 Timothy 1:6–8, 13–14

A reading from the second Letter of Saint Paul to Timothy

Beloved:
I **remind** you to stir into **flame**
    the **gift** of God that you have through the **imposition**
        of my **hands**.
For God did not give us a spirit of **cowardice**
    but rather of **power** and **love** and **self-control**.
So do not be **ashamed** of your **testimony** to our **Lord**,
    nor of me, a **prisoner** for his **sake**;
    but **bear** your share of **hardship** for the **gospel**
    with the **strength** that comes from **God**.

Take as your **norm** the sound **words** that you heard from **me**,
    in the **faith** and **love** that are in Christ **Jesus**.
Guard this rich **trust** with the help of the Holy **Spirit**
    that dwells **within** us.

The text summons believers to action: "Stir into flame . . . do not be ashamed . . . bear your share of hardship."

Be sure to differentiate the three qualities: "power," "love," and "self-control."

Even today, many suffer heroically for the Gospel, sometimes in dramatic ways, sometimes in everyday, ordinary ways.

How would someone suffering for the faith speak this command to guard it?

READING II   The theme of faith runs through today's readings. Like Habakkuk, the letter to Timothy endorses faith in the face of adversity. Such faith requires strength and the words of this text—"stir," "power," "strength," "bear," "hardship," "guard"—all connote the effort required to live a righteous Christian life. Although addressed to an elder ordained by Paul ("through the imposition of my hands"), today we hear in these words a general call to rekindle the fire of faith we demonstrated when we first embraced the faith. These words are attributed to the imprisoned Paul who understands well the wearying effects of discipleship and who knows that faith can never be put on autopilot: circumstances ("hardships") conspire to rob us of faith and require that we constantly revive it ("stir [it] into flame"). Only one who has borne hardship can ask the same of others. Perhaps your own experience of life's pain can undergird your sharing of these lines.

Where are we to derive the daily doses of strength we need to endure life's setbacks and continue walking the path of faith? The answer is clear: "From God . . . with the help of the Holy Spirit that dwells within us." Our help is from above; there is no other reliable source of strength. By the time of this writing, the unadorned Good News of Jesus has become a "rich trust" to be cherished and protected. So well has it been guarded that we can say with certainty the faith we share today is the faith of the apostles.

GOSPEL Luke 17:5–10

A reading from the holy Gospel according to Luke

Speak their request sincerely.

The **apostles** said to the **Lord**, "**Increase** our faith."
The Lord **replied**,
   "If you have **faith** the size of a **mustard** seed,
   you would say to this **mulberry** tree,
   'Be **uprooted** and planted in the **sea**,' and it would **obey** you.

Don't let this sound like a reproach.
Jesus is teaching them the power of faith.

These sayings are found only in Luke.

"**Who** among you would say to your **servant**
   who has just come in from **plowing** or tending **sheep**
      in the field,
   'Come here **immediately** and take your place at **table**'?
Would he not **rather** say to him,
   '**Prepare** something for me to **eat**.

Contrast "Come here immediately . . ."
with "Prepare something for me . . . ."
The focus is not the master, but the
expectations of the servants. Even when
they are tired from working long on one
aspect of their job, they can't expect to be
able to ignore another equally important
aspect of their work.

Put on your **apron** and **wait** on me while I **eat** and **drink**.
You may eat and drink when I am **finished**'?
Is he **grateful** to that servant because he did what
      was **commanded**?
So should it be with **you**.
When you have done **all** you have been **commanded**,
   say, 'We are **unprofitable** servants;
   we have **done** what we were **obliged** to do.'"

The parable is not about working until
we drop, but about living all the
demands of the Gospel: love, purity, and
forgiveness—without compromise.

GOSPEL All the synoptics recount the parable of the mustard seed and in all three gospels it is told in a context where the disciples express a desire to be like Jesus. But in Matthew and Mark the disciples want to emulate Jesus' ability to work miracles and drive out demons while here in Luke the request for increased faith seems genuinely motivated by a desire to better love and follow Jesus. In response to Jesus' warning that though scandals will inevitably come they do not want to be the ones through whom

such evils occur, the disciples ask for increased faith. Jesus answers with an obvious exaggeration, stating that disproportionately profound results can be achieved by imperceptible causes. A steady drip that has gouged its way through solid stone is a less exaggerated parallel. In Matthew, Jesus shares the parable out of frustration at the disciples' lack of faith, but here it is a teaching, not a rebuke.

Jesus implies no unworthiness in the disciples, only that faithful discipleship is no claim check for rewards. The unsettling truth is that faith is its own reward and we

should expect no laurels for simply doing our duty. The master in the parable is not rude or insensitive; he asks only just service from his servants. Jesus alerts his disciples that faith makes claims on us. When we embrace faith, we must willingly do all it requires of us—love, forgive, challenge, and repent. The closing lines state the challenge starkly: in serving the Gospel and the kingdom it heralds, there is no such thing as going beyond the call of duty.

28TH SUNDAY IN ORDINARY TIME

Lectionary #144

READING I 2 Kings 5:14–17

A reading from the second Book of Kings

Naaman = NAY-uh-muhn

Elisha = ee-LĪ-shuh

Naaman's newfound faith will be too surprising if the transforming impact of the healing (communicated by reading slowly and "seeing" the images you describe) is not suggested.

Let even this narration suggest the gratitude with which Naaman now approaches Elisha.

Elisha is not being rude, although he's clearly forceful in his refusal. He's done his duty and expects no reward.

This is a humble request. He will build an altar on the soil and there worship only the God of Israel.

Naaman went down and plunged into the **Jordan seven times**
  at the word of **Elisha**, the man of **God**.
His **flesh** became again like the flesh of a little **child**,
  and he was **clean** of his **leprosy**.

Naaman returned with his whole **retinue** to the man of **God**.
On his **arrival** he **stood** before Elisha and **said**,
  "Now I **know** that there is no **God** in all the **earth**,
    except in **Israel**.
Please accept a **gift** from your servant."

Elisha replied, "As the LORD **lives** whom I **serve**, I will not
    take it,"
  and despite Naaman's **urging**, he still **refused**.
Naaman said: "If you will not **accept**,
  please let **me**, your **servant**, have two mule-loads of **earth**,
  for I will no **longer** offer holocaust or sacrifice
  to any **other** god except to the LORD."

READING I   We enter this scene in the middle of things. Naaman, an army commander and adjutant to a foreign king, comes to Israel seeking a cure for his leprosy. Initially, he resents Elisha's command to wash seven times in the Jordan, thinking a high ranking dignitary like himself would be cured by spectacular means, not by bathing in a puny Israelite river. But his servants help him see reason and he finally yields.

Then two miracles occur: Naaman is healed and he experiences a profound conversion. "Plunged," "seven times," and "little child" help to create a sense of the amazing miracle. His physical healing sets the stage for the conversion that immediately follows. The focus of the reading is less on the miracle than on the gratitude of this foreigner whose cure leads to his confession of faith. When this foreign dignitary returns home, he will be duty bound to regularly appear in the temple of his nation's god, yet remarkably he proclaims that there is no God "except in Israel." It's a bold and risky assertion reflecting the depth of his new-found faith. He asks for Israelite soil because of the belief that a god could not be worshipped in a foreign land. If Israel's God can only be worshipped in Israel, Naaman needs to bring home Israel's soil so he can set up upon it an altar to Israel's God. Henceforth he will worship no other god! Another bold and risky commitment! When Elisha refuses a reward, it's not out of arrogance or anger, but because in being God's instrument he has done no more than his duty.

READING II   2 Timothy 2:8–13

A reading from the second Letter of Saint Paul to Timothy

Beloved:
Remember Jesus **Christ**, raised from the **dead**,
   a descendant of **David**:
   such is my **gospel**, for which I am **suffering**,
   even to the point of **chains**, like a **criminal**.
But the word of **God** is **not** chained.
Therefore, I bear with **everything** for the sake of those
   who are **chosen**,
   so that they **too** may obtain the **salvation** that is
   in Christ **Jesus**,
   together with eternal **glory**.
This saying is **trustworthy**:
   If we have **died** with him
   we shall also **live** with him;
   if we **persevere**
   we shall also **reign** with him.
   But if we **deny** him
   he will deny **us**.
   If **we** are **unfaithful**
   he remains **faithful**,
   for he **cannot** deny **himself**.

READING II In Catholic liturgy, remembering isn't simply the recalling of a past event. It's a great mystery, but our conviction is that remembering makes the saving events of the past present in the now. So, what the author of Timothy asks is what we do every time we gather: remember Jesus and his death and Resurrection and experience anew his saving power. There is an extremely personal tone to this writing: Paul preaches the Gospel of Jesus, suffers for it, and does so willingly because though his hands are chained, his heart and the word of God are not. This is an uplifting and encouraging message. Paul suffers gladly because he knows his suffering is not useless, but benefits others—those "who are chosen"—and helps bring them to eternal life.

A poetic series of contrasts (probably excerpted from an early baptismal hymn) concludes the passage. These "trustworthy" sayings reassure us of what will be our destiny "if" we conform our lives to Christ. Speak these lines with confidence. There are obvious contrasts ("if we have died . . . we shall also live," "If we persevere . . . we shall also reign"), but through their triple repetition of "with him," the lines also suggest a deep union with Christ. That intimacy is reinforced, not contradicted, by the sobering "if we deny . . . he will deny" statement. Christ remains consistent, so that even if we are unfaithful he will remain faithful to God and the promises (dire or comforting) he has made.

GOSPEL Luke 17:11–19

A reading from the holy Gospel according to Luke

As **Jesus** continued his journey to **Jerusalem**,
    he traveled through **Samaria** and **Galilee**.
As he was entering a **village**, ten **lepers** met him.
They stood at a **distance** from him and raised their **voices**, saying,
    "**Jesus**, **Master**! Have **pity** on us!"
And when he **saw** them, he said,
    "Go **show** yourselves to the **priests**."
As they were **going** they were **cleansed**.
And **one** of them, **realizing** he had been **healed**,
    returned, glorifying **God** in a loud **voice**;
    and he fell at the **feet** of Jesus and **thanked** him.
He was a **Samaritan**.
Jesus said in **reply**,
    "**Ten** were cleansed, were they **not**?
Where are the other **nine**?
Has none but this **foreigner** returned to give thanks to **God**?"
Then he **said** to him, "**Stand** up and **go**;
    your **faith** has **saved** you."

"Journey" refers to his Passion.

Samaria = suh-MAYR-ee-uh
Galilee = GAL-ih-lee
Lepers stood apart and rang bells to alert others of their contagious disease.

How you read "When he saw them . . ." can communicate a loving response.

Cures of leprosy had to be authenticated by priests.

Your surprised and joyful delivery of "As they were going . . ." can hint at the lepers' own joy over their healing. Don't hold back on the Samaritan's expression of gratitude.

Let real regret register in Jesus' voice. "Has none . . ." is meant to extol the Samaritan.
Here is the greatest healing!

GOSPEL The opening line may account for the no frills tone of this healing story. Jesus continues his unflinching journey toward his destiny. Unlike Naaman, these lepers don't need a cure to start believing; for them faith comes first. Their double salutation ("Jesus" and "master") reveals this. Keeping their distance as required by law, they cry for pity as Jesus passes. We don't see overt compassion from Jesus and Luke shares no conversation, only the instructions Jesus gives. Let your tone suggest underlying compassion, but the absence of overt

tenderness suggests a different agenda and spotlights the severity of the test to which these lepers are subjected. Already believing, Jesus tests their faith further ("Go show yourselves . . .") and they immediately respond. Because Luke spends no time describing it, it's clear his interest is not in the miracle itself. The focus is meant to rest on the faith and gratitude demonstrated by the unexpected hero—the Samaritan. The announcement of his identity should come as a surprise. His contemporaries surely would have expected him to be the last to return!

Some commentators make excuses for the nine who didn't return. But Jesus is clearly disappointed. You must ask, "Has none but this foreigner returned . . . ?" in a way that does not devalue the Samaritan's dignity. Like Naaman, he's a foreigner who is being held up as a role model. The miracle will not be undone, yet Jesus laments not because he isn't properly thanked, but because he cannot assure the other nine of the more profound healing he promises the Samaritan: salvation.

29TH SUNDAY IN ORDINARY TIME

Lectionary #147

READING I   Exodus 17:8–13

A reading from the Book of Exodus

In those days, **Amalek** came and waged **war** against **Israel**.
Moses, therefore, said to **Joshua**,
    "Pick out certain **men**,
    and **tomorrow** go out and **engage** Amalek in **battle**.
I will be standing on top of the **hill**
    with the staff of **God** in my hand."
So Joshua **did** as Moses **told** him:
    he **engaged** Amalek in battle
    after Moses had **climbed** to the top of the hill
        with **Aaron** and **Hur**.
As long as Moses kept his **hands** raised **up**,
    Israel had the **better** of the fight,
    but when he let his hands **rest**,
    Amalek had the better of the fight.
Moses' **hands**, however, grew **tired**;
    so they put a **rock** in place for him to **sit** on.
Meanwhile Aaron and **Hur supported** his hands,
    one on **one** side and one on the **other**,
    so that his hands remained **steady** till **sunset**.
And Joshua **mowed** down Amalek and his **people**
    with the **edge** of the **sword**.

Margin notes

Amalek = AM-uh-lek
Amalek is the aggressor.
Moses makes the decision to fight off the attack. Let him speak decisively.

The "staff of God" has become a sign of God's protective presence.

Don't rush here. Suggest the passage of time and the struggle of war.
Aaron = AYR-uhn
Hur = her

Use contrasting tone color to distinguish the effect on the battle of upraised and resting hands.

Adjust your pace to suggest the weariness.

Speak slowly here.

Do not downplay the brutality. The homilist can explain the context.

READING I Today's liturgy presents Moses in a posture of intense prayer. What he did with the help of Aaron and Hur is not some kind of magic that cast a spell on God, but an act of persevering faith expressed through his physical posture. More importantly, the iconic posture—arms extended and staff outstretched—visibly represents God's protective presence among the people.

The description of war is done in stark and weighty language that complements the image of Moses unable to hold up his arms. Phrases like "Waged war," "engaged Amalek in battle," "after Moses had climbed," and "As long as Moses kept his hands . . ." require you to slow your delivery and suggest what weighty business war is. Note that the "staff of God" Moses will be holding during the battle is the same staff he used unflinchingly to call the waters of the sea back down on Pharaoh's army. The impact made on the battle by the position of Moses' hands, especially the words that convey persistent effort ("his hands remained steady till sunset"), need to be emphasized because they link this text to the Gospel message about the need for constant prayer.

The brutality of the final sentence expresses a different culture's understanding of the ways of God—an understanding that is not rare in the Old Testament. As at the Red Sea, God acts decisively on behalf of Israel. Don't shrink from the bloody imagery: "mowed down" is intentionally startling. The homilist can explain that the author sees this victory as just punishment for an army that tried to deprive Israel of its God-given inheritance: the Promised Land.

READING II 2 Timothy 3:14—4:2

A reading from the second Letter of Saint Paul to Timothy

Beloved:
Remain **faithful** to what you have **learned** and **believed**,
    because you know from **whom** you learned it,
    and that from **infancy** you have known the sacred **Scriptures**,
    which are capable of giving you **wisdom** for **salvation**
    through **faith** in Christ **Jesus**.
All Scripture is **inspired** by **God**
    and is useful for **teaching**, for **refutation**, for **correction**,
    and for **training** in righteousness,
    so that one who **belongs** to God may be **competent**,
    equipped for every good **work**.

I **charge** you in the presence of **God** and of Christ **Jesus**,
    who will judge the **living** and the **dead**,
    and by his **appearing** and his kingly **power**:
    proclaim the **word**;
    be **persistent** whether it is **convenient** or **inconvenient**;
    convince, reprimand, encourage through all **patience**
        and **teaching**.

Speak these lines as if they were your last opportunity to advise someone you cherish about how to survive future trials.

Speak with reverence of "the sacred scriptures."

Don't rush, but highlight each of scripture's characteristics.

"I charge you" is a strong admonition, made stronger by invoking God and Jesus.

So much is said in this sentence that nearly every word requires emphasis. You can do that well only if you have the patience to speak slowly and to teach with every word.

READING II In this letter, a wise older teacher, Paul, offers important advice to a young disciple he had ordained. The urgency in the admonitions springs from the fact that Paul is in prison facing death. So the words take on not only the feel of an elder's final entreaty to his beloved pupil but also the resonance of a last will and testament. Although addressed to Timothy, the message applies to all, then and now. In earlier verses, Paul cautions Timothy against false teachers. Here he urges him to "remain faithful" to the authentic faith he received from known, orthodox teachers (that is, Paul). The importance of scripture as a source of wisdom that leads to salvation is highly stressed. All the reasons why we value and immerse ourselves in scripture are listed here: it's inspired; it's useful for teaching, refutation, correction, and holiness. If you race through that listing, you'll overwhelm rather than reveal the message. So read slowly and distinguish one quality from another.

An urgent and serious charge is laid on Timothy in the second paragraph. This is discipleship 101. Whether "convenient or inconvenient," we are to do the hard stuff: convince those who need convincing, reprimand those who need to be reprimanded, encourage the downhearted, and teach always with patience. Whether parent, spouse, boss, bishop, or teacher, those are words to live by.

GOSPEL   Luke 18:1–8

A reading from the holy Gospel according to Luke

Jesus told his **disciples** a **parable**
about the **necessity** for them to pray **always**
without becoming **weary**.
He **said**, "There was a **judge** in a certain **town**
who neither **feared God** nor **respected** any human **being**.
And a **widow** in that town used to **come** to him and say,
'Render a just **decision** for me against my **adversary**.'
For a **long** time the judge was **unwilling**, but **eventually**
he thought,
'While it is **true** that I neither fear **God** nor respect
any human **being**,
because this **widow** keeps **bothering** me
I shall deliver a just **decision** for her
lest she finally come and **strike** me.'"
The **Lord** said, "Pay **attention** to what the dishonest judge **says**.
Will not **God** then secure the rights of his **chosen** ones
who **call** out to him **day** and **night**?
Will he be **slow** to answer them?
I **tell** you, he will **see** to it that justice is done for them **speedily**.
But when the Son of Man **comes**, will he find **faith** on earth?"

Stress what the parable is about to teach us: be constant in prayer.

Jesus speaks of a judge without judgment.

Widows were among the disadvantaged on whose behalf the prophets often spoke.

Don't shy from characterizing the judge as a selfish conniver who knows how to survive. Use of this unsympathetic judge to illustrate an aspect of God is ironic, even humorous.

"Pay attention" means to understand.

Make sure Jesus' rhetorical questions are heard as questions. Pause between them to give the assembly time to think. Make eye contact on the final question.

GOSPEL This uniquely Lucan parable makes explicit what today's other readings said less plainly: perseverance is a necessary component of prayer. Luke's introduction points to the identity of the parable's main character. Certainly, the unjust judge holds the stage longer, but if this is a parable on the necessity of praying always, then the woman shares, or outright steals, the spotlight. The corrupt nature of the judge, who neither fears God nor respects human beings, is important because Luke compares him

to God by highlighting the differences. If so unjust a man finally responds justly to persistence, how much more will the loving God answer the faithful prayers of believers? Make the character distinctive and believable, even unlikable, since only one aspect of his behavior is held up for imitation, not his whole personality. The woman also needs her own "voice" for her brief line. As he does elsewhere, Jesus encourages disciples to be as shrewd and persistent in pursuing the things of the kingdom as others are at worldly pursuits. Even in prayer, their diligence instructs us!

Luke wrote for a community that faced persecution as they eagerly awaited the parousia. The parable tells them that, despite evidence to the contrary, God does hear and will respond to earnest prayer. Jesus' rhetorical questions in the closing lines are meant to reassure, not discourage, so give them a positive tone. But, after he reassures us of God's fidelity, Jesus poses a stark and challenging final question that very pointedly asks about the reliability of our own faith.

30TH SUNDAY IN ORDINARY TIME

Lectionary #150

READING I   Sirach 35:12–14, 16–18

A reading from the Book of Sirach

Establish eye contact, and then confidently assert this truth.

Speak in a compassionate tone, expressing concern not condescension, for the oppressed.

The first paragraph describes God and how God works; the second one describes those who pray and why they are heard.

As with "The Lord is not deaf" above, speak "prayer . . . pierces the clouds" with bold conviction.

God's mercy never comes too late.

> The LORD is a God of **justice**,
>   who knows no **favorites**.
> Though not **unduly** partial toward the **weak**,
>   yet he **hears** the cry of the **oppressed**.
> The LORD is not **deaf** to the wail of the **orphan**,
>   nor to the **widow** when she pours out her **complaint**.
> The one who serves God **willingly** is **heard**;
>   his **petition** reaches the **heavens**.
> The prayer of the **lowly** pierces the **clouds**;
>   it does not **rest** till it reaches its **goal**,
> nor will it **withdraw** till the Most High **responds**,
>   judges **justly** and affirms the **right**,
> and the LORD will not **delay**.

READING I   Last week's readings focused on the need for persistence in prayer; this week's examine the attitude with which one ought to pray. God is just and plays "no favorites" between rich and poor. But though God is not "unduly partial" to the weak, it is "the oppressed," "the orphan," and "the widow" who are cited here. These "oppressed" resemble the widow of last week's Gospel, and their prayer, like her perseverance, "does not rest till it reaches its goal." But

more important today is the character of those to whom "the Most High responds."

Sirach reasserts God's impartiality and clarifies whose prayers are most efficacious by explaining that anyone who "serves God willingly" and who is "lowly" is heard by God. Here we have found the heart of this text—it is the interior attitude of humility, not the external circumstances of poverty, which makes prayer pleasing to God. Today's Gospel will illustrate that point with striking clarity. Use the second half of the reading to speak directly to your

assembly and to convince them that the "willing" and "lowly" are not to be found only in destitute, faraway locations but are sitting in the pews right beside them, and, in fact, could include many of them. In the verbs of the last sentence you have your best tools for communicating Sirach's message. "Pierces," "reaches," and "withdraw" lead to the most important verbs: "responds," "judges," and "affirms," which promise God's timely and loving response.

READING II 2 Timothy 4:6–8, 16–18

A reading from the second Letter of Saint Paul to Timothy

Beloved:
I am **already** being **poured** out like a **libation**,
 and the time of my **departure** is at **hand**.
I have competed **well**; I have **finished** the **race**;
 I have **kept** the **faith**.
From now on the crown of **righteousness** awaits me,
 which the **Lord**, the just **judge**,
 will **award** to me on that day, and not only to **me**,
 but to **all** who have **longed** for his **appearance**.

At my **first** defense no one **appeared** on my **behalf**,
 but everyone **deserted** me.
May it not be held **against** them!
But the **Lord** stood by me and gave me **strength**,
 so that **through** me the **proclamation** might be **completed**
 and all the **Gentiles** might **hear** it.
And I was **rescued** from the **lion's** mouth.
The Lord will **rescue** me from every evil **threat**
 and will bring me **safe** to his heavenly **kingdom**.
To him be **glory forever** and **ever**. **Amen**.

Sidebar notes (left column):

"Libation" is the wine poured out as a sacrifice. "Departure" refers to death. Speak with the confidence of one who knows he has done all he could.

Speak with gratitude, not pride. There is great energy in these short phrases.

This is a painful memory spoken with regret, not resentment.

He expresses abiding trust in God.

Paul will not be rescued from prison, but for the "heavenly kingdom."

 This letter presents Paul writing in his most intensely personal and emotional way. It is the closing portion of a farewell letter of a man who expects soon to die written to a young protégé who is also a colleague. What a true privilege it is to proclaim such a text that reveals the sacrifices and the depth of commitment of our ancestors in faith. Employ the rich language and take the time needed to move from one image to another.

In poetic words, Paul presents his imminent death ("departure") as an act of worship ("libation") offered to God. He uses athletic imagery, phrased in appropriately short and fast-paced lines, to give a self-assessment of his ministry as an apostle: "I have competed well . . . finished the race . . . kept the faith [and] now the crown of righteousness [the laurel wreath awarded winning athletes] awaits me."

Although the second paragraph is weaker than the first, be careful not to lapse into a tone of whining self-pity. That's not Paul's character. Forgiveness ("May it not be held against them!") and trust in God ("the Lord stood by me . . . . The Lord will rescue me . . .") are the qualities that distinguish Paul and invite our emulation. Read the lines several times imagining what it would feel like to be making a case for your life as you draw near its end. That will help you decide on Paul's tone and the pace with which you'll express it. The phrases are longer and more fluid in this paragraph; appropriate since they lead to a climactic prayer of praise.

GOSPEL Luke 18:9–14

A reading from the holy Gospel according to Luke

Jesus addressed this **parable**
    to those who were convinced of their own **righteousness**
    and **despised** everyone **else**.
"Two **people** went up to the **temple** area to **pray**;
    one was a **Pharisee** and the **other** was a **tax** collector.
The **Pharisee** took up his position and spoke this prayer
    to himself,
    'O **God**, I **thank** you that I am **not** like the **rest** of humanity—
    greedy, **dishonest**, **adulterous**—or even like this **tax** collector.
I fast **twice** a week, and I pay **tithes** on my whole **income**.'
But the **tax** collector stood off at a **distance**
    and would not even raise his **eyes** to **heaven**
    but beat his **breast** and **prayed**,
    'O **God**, be **merciful** to me a **sinner**.'
I **tell** you, the **latter** went home **justified**, **not** the **former**;
    for whoever **exalts** himself will be **humbled**,
    and the one who **humbles** himself will be **exalted**."

Speak the introduction with regret, not condemnation.

Introduce the two characters without partiality.

Don't make the Pharisee sound sinister. He really does all these things. Pause at end of the dialogue.

Use a slower pace and softer volume. Speak "Be merciful . . . " simply and sincerely.

Jesus' strong voice reemerges. He's subverting expectations. How might that affect his tone?

GOSPEL | Luke begins with an editorial comment that gives away the lesson of this parable. His introduction even describes the character of the righteous Pharisee who despises the tax collector. That's almost too much information at the start, for it tempts us to caricature the man as a condescending snob. But what if the Pharisee spoke sincerely, believing all he says about himself and seeing nothing wrong with his self-preening? An underplayed Pharisee better respects the integrity of the story and better speaks to us about ourselves. After all, most of those who will hear this parable today, at least outwardly, resemble the Pharisee more than the tax collector. The Pharisee's words will do enough to convict him without you having to manipulate his tone; his sin is not his arrogance but his self-reliant attitude regarding justification.

The Pharisee defines himself by what he is not, and then by what he does ("fast" and "pray"). Remember, it's not their roles as tax collector or Pharisee that makes one and not the other "justified." As with many parables, this one reverses expectations. God justifies the tax collector because he is humble enough to believe he can be forgiven what are likely very real sins. The Pharisee may indeed sin less, but he thinks that merits him reward; he hasn't learned that salvation is God's free gift. Luke's summary repeats the saying about the exalted and humbled that capped the parable of where to sit at a feast (14:11), which itself echoes the assertion in Mary's Magnificat that God has deposed the mighty and raised up the lowly.

31ST SUNDAY IN ORDINARY TIME

Lectionary #153

READING I   Wisdom 11:22—12:2

A reading from the Book of Wisdom

Speak of God's grandeur with wonder and of God's mercy with gratitude.

Before the LORD the whole **universe** is as a **grain**
   from a **balance**
      or a drop of morning **dew** come down upon the **earth**.

The couplets of this text state an idea and then restate it in a slightly different way. Don't think the second line is a redundancy that can be underplayed. It requires the same energy and enthusiasm as the first.

But you have **mercy** on **all**, because you can **do** all things;
   and you **overlook** people's **sins** that they may **repent**.
For you **love** all things that **are**

Existence connotes goodness. All things have been made good by a loving God. Don't speak this like a courtroom argument, but marveling at the generosity of God.

   and loathe **nothing** that you have **made**;
      for what you **hated**, you would not have **fashioned**.
And how could a thing **remain**, unless you **willed** it;
   or be **preserved**, had it not been called **forth** by you?

The writer is not telling God something God doesn't know; he is rejoicing and praising God! "Lover of souls" is a gorgeous expression.

But you **spare** all things, because they are **yours**,
   O LORD and **lover** of **souls**,
      for your imperishable **spirit** is in all things!

Here, too, you are rejoicing because even God's "rebuke" is offered for our salvation!

Therefore you **rebuke offenders little** by **little**,
   warn them and **remind** them of the **sins**
      they are committing,
         that they may **abandon** their wickedness and **believe**
            in you, O LORD!

READING I A feature that sets the stories of the Old Testament apart from the literature of Israel's ancient neighbors is the characterization of God as a good and loving creator who is intimately involved with creation and who created all things and made them good. While other cultures imagined gods creating both good and evil, Genesis boldly claims that God created only "good." The colloquial maxim "God does not make junk!" may have been inspired by these lines, for the text declares that existence is goodness, that is, we "are" and therefore God loves us.

Written in the century before the birth of Jesus, the book of Wisdom demonstrates how God's "imperishable spirit" had been at work tilling the soil for the seed of the Gospel that Christ would bring. With beautiful imagery, the passage paints a portrait of a powerful, transcendent God who is also concerned and caring, overflowing with mercy and forgiveness. More complex than the gods of other ancient cultures, Israel's God is Lord of the universe and a "lover of souls," as far from us as the heavens are from the earth and as near as our own breathing. By revealing even more fully the loving nature of God, Jesus demonstrated that the New Testament is in continuity with the Old. A statement like "you loathe nothing that you have made" anticipates in spirit the saving work of Jesus.

The final paragraph movingly describes God's patience and tender mercy which, little by little, warns us of our sins so we might repent. Today's Gospel story will powerfully illustrate the healing power of such merciful love.

READING II   2 Thessalonians 1:11—2:2

A reading from the second Letter of Saint Paul to the Thessalonians

Note that the letter begins with a prayer. That must color your tone.

Speak with energy and sincerity. Paul is asking that God glorify Christ through the lives of the Thessalonian believer.

There is a major mood shift here: Paul forcefully admonishes them not to let themselves be fooled or to become hysterical over false teachings.
"Oral revelation" tells us not to be alarmed by any purported spirit-inspired revelation.
"Or by a letter" indicates the possibility a forged letter being circulated.

Brothers and sisters:
We always **pray** for you,
that our God may make you **worthy** of his calling
and powerfully bring to **fulfillment** every good **purpose**
and every **effort** of **faith**,
that the **name** of our Lord **Jesus** may be **glorified** in you,
and **you** in **him**,
in accord with the **grace** of our God and **Lord** Jesus **Christ**.

We **ask** you, brothers and sisters,
with regard to the **coming** of our Lord Jesus Christ
and our **assembling** with him,
not to be **shaken** out of your **minds** suddenly, or to be **alarmed**
either by a "**spirit**," or by an oral **statement**,
or by a **letter** allegedly from **us**
to the **effect** that the day of the **Lord** is at **hand**.

READING II Paul prays "that the name of the Lord Jesus may be glorified in [us]." But how is that to be accomplished? The answer is simple: by doing all the good we can do, allowing God to fulfill "every good purpose and every effort of faith" in us. That means surrendering our lives to God, letting God have sway over our decisions, living in a way that says, "I belong to God." Yes, it's true that the Church is a human institution that is prone to the same failings and imperfections that afflict the rest of the world. But

we must not forget that the Church is also a sign of the glory of Christ. The Church, in its members, must never fail to be a sacrament, a living, unmistakable sign of the presence of Christ in the world.

Written at a time when the second coming of Christ was both eagerly anticipated and expected soon, Paul writes to caution the Thessalonians that Christ has not yet returned as some alleged. He wants them to downplay this anticipation of Christ's return so they can focus, instead, on living the Gospel until whatever day Jesus does come back. He's calling for

calm, for reason, and for patient endurance. Speak in a reassuring tone.

 GOSPEL The First Reading says God rebukes offenders and reminds them of their sins so that they abandon their wickedness. But here, Jesus never speaks of sin nor offers even a mild rebuke. Instead, he invites himself to dinner. That turns out to be the most convicting act of all. It's Jesus' acceptance that catches Zacchaeus off guard and flips his

GOSPEL Luke 19:1–10

A reading from the holy Gospel according to Luke

At that **time**, **Jesus** came to **Jericho** and intended
    to pass **through** the town.
Now a **man** there named **Zacchaeus**,
    who was a chief **tax** collector and also a **wealthy** man,
    was seeking to **see** who Jesus **was**;
    but he could **not** see him because of the **crowd**,
    for he was **short** in **stature**.
So he **ran** ahead and climbed a **sycamore** tree in order to see Jesus,
    who was about to **pass** that **way**.
When he **reached** the place, Jesus **looked** up and said,
    "**Zacchaeus**, come down **quickly**,
    for **today** I must **stay** at your **house**."
And he **came** down quickly and received him with **joy**.
When they all **saw** this, they began to **grumble**, saying,
    "He has gone to stay at the house of a **sinner**."
But Zacchaeus **stood** there and said to the Lord,
    "**Behold**, **half** of my possessions, Lord, I shall **give** to the **poor**,
    and if I have **extorted** anything from **anyone**
    I shall **repay** it **four** times **over**."
And **Jesus** said to him,
    "**Today salvation** has come to this house
    because this man **too** is a **descendant** of **Abraham**.
For the Son of **Man** has come to **seek**
    and to **save** what was **lost**."

Jericho = JAYR-ih-koh

Zacchaeus = zuh-KEE-uhs (not-KAY-)

Don't rush details that he is "chief tax collector" and "wealthy."

Stress the words "he was seeking."

You should marvel at the lengths to which this man goes to see Jesus.

Let Jesus speak loud enough for the crowd to hear!

Deliver these lines with the dismay with which Zacchaeus might have heard the grumbling.

Suddenly, Zacchaeus knows what he must do!

Imagine Jesus announcing this to the crowd as well as to Zacchaeus. Speak the final line directly to the assembly.

world upside down. Accustomed to rejection and contempt, this tax collector is suddenly confronted with a celebrity who wants to make a home at his house. And Zacchaeus' transformation is instantaneous and complete. We know this not because of what Zacchaeus says, anyone can swear to change and promise restitution without following up, or make initial changes that fade with the next morning's dew. But Jesus, the great reader of hearts, makes a solemn pronouncement: "Today, salvation has come to this house."

Zacchaeus is saved. He, too, is a son of Abraham. The Good Shepherd has found another lost sheep.

One gets the feeling that Zacchaeus may not have known he was lost until he was found. Or did he? At the end, Jesus says the Son of Man came to seek the lost. But at the start, Luke says Zacchaeus was seeking to see Jesus. Something in this tax collector sought out the seeker of souls. Note that it's the moment immediately after Zacchaeus sees Jesus join the ranks of the outcast ("They began to grumble . . . 'He has gone to stay at the house of a sinner' ")

that he announces his decision to reform. This teacher has not judged or disdained him, but reached out to him at the risk of his own reputation. If Zacchaeus needed a sacrament of God's love, he certainly finds one in Jesus. Perhaps the most dramatic thing Jesus teaches in this episode is that the best way to help someone recognize their sin is to show them pure love.

COMMEMORATION OF ALL THE FAITHFUL DEPARTED

Lectionary #668

READING I   Wisdom 3:1–9

A reading from the Book of Wisdom

The melodic opening line is the foundation for all that follows. Speak with joyful confidence.
Let your tone convey that here appearances don't match the reality.

This is another line to be delivered with utter conviction.

The purification that may come after death is not to be feared but welcomed as God's gift that prepares one for final judgment. Speak with authority.

The energy builds and the tempo quickens a bit as you offer the lovely image of souls shining like sparks.

The final sentence can be delivered at a slower pace, emphasizing the "grace," "mercy," and "care" that await God's elect.

The souls of the **just** are in the hand of **God**,
    and no **torment** shall touch them.
They **seemed**, in the view of the **foolish**, to be **dead**;
    and their passing **away** was thought an **affliction**
    and their going **forth** from us, utter **destruction**.
But **they** are in **peace**.
For if before **men**, indeed, they be **punished**,
    yet is their **hope** full of **immortality**;
chastised a **little**, they shall be greatly **blessed**,
    because God **tried** them
    and found them **worthy** of himself.
As **gold** in the **furnace**, he **proved** them,
    and as sacrificial **offerings** he took them to **himself**.
In the time of their **visitation** they shall **shine**,
    and shall **dart** about as **sparks** through **stubble**;
they shall **judge nations** and **rule** over **peoples**,
    and the LORD shall be their **King forever**.
Those who **trust** in him shall understand **truth**,
    and the **faithful** shall **abide** with him in **love**:
because **grace** and **mercy** are with his **holy** ones,
    and his **care** is with his **elect**.

The readings given here are suggestions. Any reading from the Lectionary for the Commemoration of All the Faithful Departed (#668) or the Masses for the Dead (#1011–1015) may be used.

READING I   Context always sets the tone and today's context—remembering those (loved ones) who, in faith, have gone home to the Lord—requires that this text be proclaimed with conviction and joy. The opening sentence offers profound comfort to anyone experiencing loss and grief. The foolish believe death is the final word; that those who have died are in oblivion. But, in fact, the souls of the just are with God, living in peace. The wisdom that comes with faith enables us to see that even if "they are chastised a little" (some understand that as a suggestion of purgatory), their ultimate reward is assured, for having purified them like "gold in the furnace," God will make them shine like sparks from a raging fire.

The reading moves through a three-part progression: 1) the just are safe with God; 2) they may experience purification, but that cleansing is a sign of God's compassion and love for it prepares the just for "their time of visitation" (that is, judgment); and 3) after their judgment, the just will judge and rule nations, understand truth, and receive grace and mercy in abundance. It's no wonder this comforting text is read so often at funerals. It offers "hope full of immortality," promising us who are left behind that the loved ones we've lost await us in glory and assuring us that, if we remain just and holy, we too will be among the elect who inherit that same hope of immortality.

READING II   Romans 5:5–11

A reading from the Letter of Saint Paul to the Romans

Brothers and sisters:
Hope does not **disappoint**,
   because the **love** of God has been **poured** out into our **hearts**
   through the Holy **Spirit** that has been **given** to us.
For **Christ**, while we were still **helpless**,
   died at the appointed time for the **ungodly**.
Indeed, only with **difficulty** does one die for a **just** person,
   though perhaps for a **good** person
   one might even **find** courage to die.
But God **proves** his love for us
   in that while we were **still sinners** Christ **died** for us.
How much **more** then, since we are now **justified** by his **Blood**,
   will we be **saved** through **him** from the **wrath**.
Indeed, if, while we were **enemies**,
   we were **reconciled** to God through the **death** of his **Son**,
   how much **more**, once **reconciled**,
   will we be **saved** by his **life**.
Not only **that**,
   but we also **boast** of God through our **Lord** Jesus **Christ**,
   through **whom** we have now **received reconciliation**.

Or:

Look right at the assembly and speak with confidence and joy. You'll be more convincing if you get in touch with the love of God in your own heart.

Marvel at the generosity of God.

The comparison serves to highlight God's mercy all the more and climaxes at the words ". . . Christ died for us."

Renew your energy here and build on the previous point. If God loved us enough to save us while we were alienated, how much more will God bestow on us now that we have been reconciled through Christ?

Let your voice swell with boasting of the goodness of God!

READING II **ROMANS 5.** Ask someone what words dominated their childhood, and chances are that among them you'll find the word "if." If you're good, if you do your homework, if you pick up you clothes . . . . So much of what was fun and exciting and good in childhood happened only if. With God it's not that way. While we were still sinners, Paul tells us, the love of God was poured out in our hearts. We didn't earn or deserve it. God became one of us, lived and died for us, and did it out of pure love. God didn't wait for us to "clean up our act," or "get it all together." No, God took the initiative. God's love has completely transformed us. We have been justified by faith and brought to peace with God because of what Jesus did for us. God reached right into our unworthiness and made us worthy.

Paul wants to make sure we understand how remarkable this is. Even the most altruistic of human actions cannot compare with what God has done. Yes, on occasion someone may be willing to die for the sake of another really good human being. Friends do sacrifice themselves for friends and parents for children. But Christ gave his life for us even though we in no way deserved such extravagant love.

And if God did all that before we were "justified," imagine, Paul says, how much more God will do for us now that we live in grace and in the reconciliation Christ won for us through his death!

READING II   Romans 6:3–9

A reading from the Letter of Saint Paul to the Romans

Brothers and sisters:
Are you **unaware** that we who were **baptized** into Christ Jesus
    were baptized into his **death**?
We were indeed **buried** with him through **baptism** into **death**,
    so **that**, just as **Christ** was **raised** from the dead
    by the **glory** of the **Father**,
    we **too** might live in **newness** of life.

For if we have grown into **union** with him through a **death**
    like his,
    we shall also be **united** with him in the **resurrection**.
We know that our **old** self was **crucified** with him,
    so that our sinful **body** might be done **away** with,
    that we might no **longer** be in **slavery** to **sin**.
For a **dead** person has been **absolved** from sin.
If, then, we have **died** with Christ,
    we believe that we shall also **live** with him.
We know that **Christ**, **raised** from the **dead**, dies no **more**;
    death no longer has **power** over **him**.

Paul's literary device is a rhetorical question. Let it sound like a question. Make eye contact and speak as directly as Paul writes.

Take the time to understand Paul's point: what happened to Christ will happen to us. He died and was buried, then rose. We die and are buried in Baptism; we, too, will rise to new life.

Paul develops the idea: we were made one with Christ by sharing a death (Baptism) like his; so we also will be made one with him in experiencing Resurrection.

Don't let this sound repetitive. Sustain the energy. Contrast the words "died" and "live."

"We know" means that we are convinced! "Dies no more . . . death no longer has power . . ." is the same idea stated twice. The greater stress goes to the second statement.

ROMANS 6. Also read at the Easter Vigil in the context of other readings that speak of salvation history, with this text Paul projects us into our future, reflecting on the implications of Christ's death and Resurrection for all people and for all time.

At the Easter Vigil we viewed these words symbolically, seeing in our Baptism a parallel to Christ's death and Resurrection. In baptismal theology, "death" and "burial" in the waters of Baptism are a pathway to "new life" in Christ. Inauguration into that new life begins here on earth, but here we only taste the fullness that won't be fully ours until after death. Today, however, Paul's words remind us that those who have gone before us in faith are on the very threshold (if not already through the door) of the fullness of the kingdom that Christ shares with his saints and angels.

"Are you not aware . . . ?" he asks, that our old self died and was buried with Christ? He expects us to know the answer and to believe that "death" is good news, not bad, for it leads to glory with Christ. For those claimed in death by Christ, Resurrection is no longer future hope but a present reality. Though fullness of glory is assured only for the saints we celebrated in yesterday's solemnity, All Saints, today we rejoice in the belief that whatever purgation comes after death will eventually lead the faithful to living with Christ in full and endless glory.

Because "death" and "burial" in Christ lead to life, speak in an upbeat tone as you proclaim Paul's series of balanced ideas: "If we have grown . . . through a death like his, we shall also be united . . . in the Resurrection." Paul proclaims joyously

Pause at end of line to shift into the attitude of Jesus. Although he's addressing the crowds, keep the tone personal and intimate.

Stress the word "this." Repetition of the previous line places extra focus on what will follow: "That I should not lose anything . . . ."

Again, stress the word "this." God longs for our salvation more than we do.
Stress the verbs "sees" and "believes." Make eye contact as you deliver this comforting final line.

GOSPEL   John 6:37–40

A reading from the holy Gospel according to John

Jesus said to the **crowds**:
"**Everything** that the Father **gives** me will **come** to me,
    and I will not **reject** anyone who comes to me,
        because I came down from **heaven** not to do my **own** will
        but the **will** of the one who **sent** me.
And **this** is the will of the one who sent me,
    that I should not **lose anything** of what he gave me,
    but that I should **raise** it on the last **day**.
For this **is** the will of my **Father**,
    that **everyone** who **sees** the **Son** and **believes** in him
    may have **eternal life**,
    and I shall **raise** him on the **last day**."

---

what "we know": that freedom and life are available to all who believe. Good news even for us who have not yet gone to the Lord.

GOSPEL | Many rejected Jesus during his life and many still reject him now. But his mission was to embrace all and reject no one who comes to him with an open heart. So often we think of what might exclude us from the kingdom and we think Christ came to make sure we knew what choices and behaviors

would remove our names from the roll of the elect. But Jesus' mission, he asserts, was just the opposite. He came to win our hearts, to shelter us under his arms like a mother hen shelters her young. He came to ensure that none was lost, for he is the good shepherd whose very job description it is not to lose anything of what God gave him. Only our own will, our pride, our desire for autonomy apart from God and Christ can separate us from our hope and our true home.

On this observance, these words are especially reassuring to those who have

lost loved ones. All Souls differs from All Saints in one key aspect: we lack assurance that the souls we loved in life have entered into the fullness of glory with Christ. Some have, others surely will, and some perhaps will not. We do not know for sure. But to anyone concerned about the fate of their dearly departed, these words of Jesus resound with hope. It is the will of the Father that everyone who set their eyes on Jesus and believed, Christ will raise to life.

32ND SUNDAY IN ORDINARY TIME

Lectionary #156

READING I   2 Maccabees 7:1–2, 9–14

A reading from the second Book of Maccabees

It **happened** that seven **brothers** with their **mother** were **arrested**
and **tortured** with **whips** and **scourges** by the **king**,
to force them to eat **pork** in **violation** of God's **law**.
One of the brothers, speaking for the **others**, said:
"What do you expect to **achieve** by **questioning** us?
We are ready to **die** rather than **transgress** the laws
of our **ancestors**."

At the point of **death** he said:
"You accursed **fiend**, you are depriving us of this **present** life,
but the **King** of the **world** will **raise** us up to live **again forever**.
It is for **his** laws that we are **dying**."

After him the **third** suffered their cruel **sport**.
He put out his tongue at **once** when told to do so,
and **bravely** held out his **hands**, as he spoke these noble **words**:
"It was from **Heaven** that I received these;
for the sake of his **laws** I **disdain** them;
from **him** I hope to receive them **again**."
Even the **king** and his **attendants** marveled
at the young man's **courage**,
because he regarded his **sufferings** as **nothing**.

After he had **died**,
they **tortured** and **maltreated** the **fourth** brother
in the **same** way.

Don't shy away from this violent language.

"We are ready . . . " suggests they have pondered their fate and embrace it with open eyes.

"He" refers to the second brother. Let him mock his persecutors with his conviction that he will rise again.

"Cruel sport" is an ironic image. Give him a "noble" and confident tone.

His confidence makes them marvel.

Contrast "sufferings" and "nothing."

READING I As the liturgical year draws to a close, the readings invite us to reflect on the transitory nature of human life and the destiny of eternal life that awaits us. We call this concern with the "end times" and life after death "eschatology." Belief in life after death came gradually to the Hebrew people and was not universally accepted even in Jesus' day. Belief in resurrection from the dead is not clearly expressed in the Old Testament until about 150 years before the birth of Jesus when it surfaces in the book of Daniel and in the second book of Maccabees, from which today's text is taken. It's affirmation of belief in life after death makes today's text very significant.

The story recounts the martyrdom of seven Jewish brothers and their mother at the hands of the occupying Seleucid Greeks near the end of the second century before Christ. Today's passage, from which the graphic and gory details have been deleted, tells only part of the story. This reading was chosen for today's liturgy less to extol the brothers' heroic determination to faithfully follow God's law and more to proclaim the brothers' belief that they will "live again forever." That's what connects this reading to the Gospel. However, the brothers' conviction that they will live again is demonstrated through their willingness to suffer and die, therefore the powerful descriptions of the young men's valor and their edifying speeches must be proclaimed with nobility and conviction.

In paragraph one violent words abound: "tortured," "whips," "scourges," "force," and "violation." In contrast, the first brother "speak[s] for the others" with

He chooses to die because of his hope of restoration.

When **he** was near death, he said,
"It is my **choice** to die at the hands of **men**
with the hope **God** gives of being **raised** up by him;
but for **you**, there will be **no** resurrection to life."

He reflects the belief that only the good would rise from the dead. For evildoers, there was no life after death.

READING II   2 Thessalonians 2:16—3:5

A reading from the second Letter of Saint Paul to the Thessalonians

Read one phrase (that is, one thought) at a time. The tone is upbeat and hopeful.

Brothers and sisters:
May our Lord Jesus Christ **himself** and God our **Father**,
who has **loved** us and given us everlasting **encouragement**
and good **hope** through his **grace**,
encourage your **hearts** and **strengthen** them
in every good **deed** and **word**.

This is a genuine request for prayer, not for Paul himself, but for the spread of the Gospel.

There are those who work actively against the Gospel. "Perverse" and "wicked" are two different attributes.

Stress God's faithfulness in contrast with those who do not have faith.

These words are encouraging and motivating.

Note that this is another prayer. Make eye contact with the assembly.

Finally, brothers and sisters, **pray** for us,
so that the **word** of the Lord may speed **forward** and be **glorified**,
as it did among **you**,
and that we may be **delivered** from **perverse** and wicked **people**,
for not **all** have **faith**.
But the **Lord** is faithful;
he will **strengthen** you and guard you from the **evil** one.
We are **confident** of you in the Lord that what we **instruct** you,
you are **doing** and will **continue** to do.
May the Lord **direct** your hearts to the love of **God**
and to the **endurance** of **Christ**.

---

apparent calm. The text offers clues to each brother's tone that, if noted, will enable you to describe four distinct individuals, each with his own message. The first is defined as confident spokesman for the rest; the second brother, who knows well why he is dying, mockingly asserts that what his tormentors take from him God will restore; the third spoke with "noble words," which suggests tone as well as content; the fourth, who has seen three brothers die, is himself "near death," yet

he affirms his faith in God's power to raise him back to life.

READING II — The Thessalonians had expected Christ's second coming within their lifetimes. But the parousia was obviously delayed and so the early Christians had to figure out how to live as Christians until Jesus did return. A series of exhortations about how to live faithfully in the present constitutes the second part of Thessalonians. The bulk of today's reading introduces that exhorta-

tory section with a request for prayers and with an expression of confidence that God will continue to strengthen the community to live a life of faith. We will read more of this section next week.

Today we are offered encouragement that though we will most certainly meet opposition, though people of narrow vision and evil intent will work against us, we need not worry about getting the job done, because the job is really not our doing in the first place. It is the "word of the Lord" that must make progress, not us. Our chief

GOSPEL   Luke 20:27–38

A reading from the holy Gospel according to Luke

Some **Sadducees**, those who **deny** that there is a **resurrection**,
    came **forward** and put this **question** to Jesus, saying,
    "**Teacher**, **Moses** wrote for us,
    If someone's **brother** *dies leaving a* **wife** *but no* **child**,
    his **brother** *must* **take** *the wife*
    and raise up **descendants** *for his brother.*
Now there were **seven** brothers;
    the **first** married a woman but died **childless**.
Then the **second** and the **third** married her,
    and likewise all the **seven** died childless.
Finally the **woman** also died.
Now at the **resurrection** whose **wife** will that woman **be**?
For all **seven** had been married to her."
Jesus said to them,
    "The children of **this** age **marry** and **remarry**;
    but those who are deemed **worthy** to attain to the **coming** age
    and to the **resurrection** of the **dead**
    neither **marry** nor are **given** in marriage.
They can no longer **die**,
    for they are like **angels**;
    and they are the **children** of **God**
    because **they** are the ones who will **rise**.

Sadducees = SAD-yoo-seez

Your tone should signal the coming confrontation.

The Sadducees are citing the law of levirate marriage (see Deuteronomy 25:5–10) that required a surviving brother to marry the widow of a brother who died without a son, so the deceased's lineage would not die out.

Speak sincerely here, without exaggeration.

Your tone should ask, "Can you believe it?"

They think they've set the perfect trap.

Allow Jesus a moment to "think" before you begin. Contrast "this age" with the "coming age."

Speak joyfully here. You are describing the bliss of heaven.

---

task is to remain faithful, to believe and do what we can, trusting that God will somehow bring about the kingdom despite what we are unable to do.

The writer longs for the Gospel to spread and root in other areas as well as it did among the Thessalonians. They are to trust that God will provide the strength they need and shield them from Satan's wiles. Having begun with a prayer and having asked for prayer, the author ends with a prayer that the Lord govern his readers' hearts with the love of God and the constancy of Christ.

Proclaim with confidence that our task is to be faithful and to work out of that faith as hard as we are able. When our efforts seem inadequate, we can remain peaceful because the work of salvation is being accomplished at every moment in Christ, and in ways we could never imagine or control.

GOSPEL The religious leaders never tired of setting traps for him and Jesus never failed to elude them. Probably frustrated, they come to try again

and if ever their motives are transparent it is here. Whose wife will she be? It's a good scheme guaranteed to engage the imagination of the crowd and to force Jesus into a corner where he'll have to offend some faction. But though the story is contrived and farfetched, the leaders are seeking to do more than just entrap and ridicule Jesus. The Sadducees are very interested in their question because they think it illustrates the absurdity of belief in an afterlife. So don't characterize them as overly sinister; doing so would render Jesus' opponents as caricatures and the

Speak the last line with conviction and great reverence.

That the dead **will** rise
  even **Moses** made known in the passage about the **bush**,
  when he called out '**Lord**,'
  the God of **Abraham**, the God of **Isaac**, and the God of **Jacob**;
  and he is not God of the **dead**, but of the **living**,
  for to **him all** are alive."

[Shorter: Luke 20:27, 34–38]

important theological question being debated would seem less significant. Unlike the Pharisees who believed in Resurrection, the Sadducees rejected that notion. They want this obviously fictitious story to sound credible so it will engage Jesus and the crowd. Imagine yourself preparing to debate an issue and designing a fool-proof argument that will annihilate your opponent. That's what the leaders think they've done. Tell the story simply, without any sense of grief over the deaths

(in fact, there's humor in the words "Finally the woman . . . died").

Jesus responds, instructing the crowd as well as the Pharisees. He turns their use of scripture against them by referring to Moses and the bush. If Moses calls the Lord the "God of Abraham, Isaac and Jacob," then these patriarchs must somehow be alive. Jesus asserts two teachings: death alters life so radically that old categories no longer apply, and God is Lord of the living, not the dead. His well developed contrasts indicate Jesus' investment in the debate. When you speak the last line, pause briefly

after the word "All" to recall those from your parish you buried in the past year. Then remind their neighbors sitting before you that they are still "alive"—a fitting reminder in this the month of November.

33RD SUNDAY IN ORDINARY TIME

Lectionary #159

READING I   Malachi 3:19–20a

A reading from the Book of the Prophet Malachi

Lo, the day is **coming**, **blazing** like an **oven**,
    when all the **proud** and all **evildoers** will be **stubble**,
and the **day** that is coming will set them on **fire**,
    leaving them neither **root** nor **branch**,
    says the LORD of **hosts**.
But for **you** who **fear** my **name**, there will arise
    the **sun** of **justice** with its **healing rays**.

Malachi = MAL-uh-kī

This short text requires a slow reading. Start strong. This is meant to be unsettling.

This is a threat and a promise. Don't dilute it.

Pause before the last sentence. Shift the mood by emphasizing the words "But . . . ." Make eye contact with the assembly. Note how the text uses fire imagery to suggest both cataclysmic purgation and healing warmth.

READING II   2 Thessalonians 3:7–12

A reading from the second Letter of Saint Paul to the Thessalonians

Brothers and sisters:
You **know** how one must **imitate** us.
For we did not act in a **disorderly** way among you,
    nor did we eat **food** received **free** from anyone.
On the **contrary**, in **toil** and **drudgery**, **night** and **day**
    we **worked**, so as not to **burden** any of you.

Thessalonians = thes-uh-LOH-nee-uhnz

As teacher, Paul had every right to demand support, but he depended on no one and worked tirelessly. Paul doesn't cite his own conduct as self-aggrandizement but as model behavior to imitate.

READING I   Today the liturgy presents a text that reads like a trumpet blast: "Lo, the day is coming, blazing like an oven . . . ." Malachi has our attention, and it doesn't sound like it's going to be good news: "when all the proud and all evildoers will be stubble." If you've imagined final judgment as a fearful, awesome event, Malachi fuels the fire with his image of cataclysmic purgation: nothing will be left in the wake of the vaporizing heat of God's judgment. If that sounds frightening, it's supposed to. But not so that we lose hope; we simply need to know the seriousness of what lies ahead, at some point, for each of us.

Addressed to a post-exilic community that despite rebuilding the temple is plagued with disillusionment, political insecurity, and religious laxity, this prophecy seeks to rouse the people to courageous watchfulness for the coming day of the Lord. That day will bring both destruction and healing—and the source of each will be fire. The long first sentence is full of threat directed at arrogant "evildoers." Speak forcefully the images of a consuming flame that will destroy all evil in its path. Short, sharp words like "fire," "root," and "branch" add to the tone of uncompromising judgment. In contrast, the warming "sun" will rise in defense of the humble, the poor, and the faithful to protect them with "its healing rays." With a tone that's either gentle or powerful, use those words to arouse vigilance and inspire hope.

Not that we do not have the **right**.
Rather, we wanted to **present** ourselves as a **model** for you,
    so that you might **imitate** us.
In **fact**, when we were **with** you,
    we **instructed** you that if anyone was **unwilling** to work,
    neither should that one **eat**.
We hear that some **are** conducting themselves among you
        in a **disorderly** way,
    by not keeping **busy** but minding the business of **others**.
Such people we **instruct** and **urge** in the Lord Jesus **Christ**
        to work **quietly**
    and to eat their **own** food.

The tone is insistent because the disruption caused by the "sponges" in the community is great.

The tone grows even more direct in the second paragraph.

GOSPEL Luke 21:5–19

A reading from the holy Gospel according to Luke

While **some** people were speaking about
    how the **temple** was adorned with costly **stones**
        and votive **offerings**,
    Jesus said, "**All** that you see here—
    the days will **come** when there will not be left
    a **stone** upon **another** stone that will not be thrown **down**."

Then they **asked** him,
"**Teacher**, **when** will this happen?
And what **sign** will there be when all these things
        are **about** to happen?"

Start in a tone that suggests something momentous is going to be shared.

Jesus cannot be happy about the fate of the temple.

They are obviously distressed by his announcement.

READING II Being alert and watchful for the coming day of the Lord is good and necessary. But it is possible to go too far! It seems the Christians in Thessalonica did just that. They were so convinced that Jesus was returning soon, that they stopped working and sat around idly waiting and watching for the parousia.

Paul has no patience for that nonsense. He gives orders, not suggestions, about what should be done. Get to work, he says, and let me be the model for how hard you should be working. He labored "day and night . . . to the point of exhaustion." Paul is not talking about the work of salvation, but about physical labor—the kind of gainful employment that keeps one from becoming a burden on the community. His goal is to make these misguided believers stop sponging off the rest of the community and start contributing their fair share.

Besides burdening others, freeloaders can quickly turn into busybodies. They disrupt the peace of the community by poking their noses in places they don't belong. Such activity usually results from having too little to do. When you have business of your own, you don't have time to try and run everyone else's.

Paul's concern for the peace of the community results in his laying down a clear "instruction": you don't work, you don't eat. Is that contrary to Christian charity? Hardly. Refusing food to those who can't provide for themselves is lack of charity. But refusing to feed those who can care for themselves but won't is a favor and an act of true love.

These comments and what follows reflect Jesus' concern for his followers. They must hear so they won't be deceived.

"Do not be terrified" means "don't overreact," but the news is still dire. Find a tonal balance between the poles of sounding-the-alarm and forbidding panic.

Let the rhythm of the lines create the urgency that continues to grow through the words "nation . . . and kingdom . . ." rising against one another and through powerful words like "earthquakes," "plague," and "mighty signs."
These predictions are even more dire and distressing than what went before. Let that be clear.

Reassurance is offered here. Slow your pace and make eye contact with the assembly.

This is perhaps the most distressing news of all. Speak with conviction, but also with confidence and control.

The whole reading pivots on the word "but." Obviously the last line puts all the forgoing in a different light.

He **answered**,
"See that you not be **deceived**,
 for **many** will come in my **name**, saying,
 'I am **he**,' and 'The **time** has **come**.'
Do not **follow** them!
When you hear of **wars** and **insurrections**,
 do not be **terrified**; for such things **must** happen **first**,
 but it will not **immediately** be the **end**."
Then he said to them,
"**Nation** will rise against **nation**, and **kingdom** against **kingdom**.
There will be powerful **earthquakes**, **famines**, and **plagues**
 from place to **place**;
 and awesome **sights** and mighty **signs** will come from the **sky**.

"Before all this **happens**, however,
 they will **seize** and **persecute** you,
 they will hand you **over** to the **synagogues** and to **prisons**,
 and they will have you led before **kings** and **governors**
 because of my **name**.
It will lead to your giving **testimony**.
Remember, you are not to **prepare** your defense **beforehand**,
 for I **myself** shall give you a **wisdom** in speaking
 that all your **adversaries** will be **powerless** to **resist** or **refute**.
You will even be handed over by **parents**, **brothers**,
  relatives and **friends**,
 and they will put **some** of you to **death**.
You will be **hated** by all because of my **name**,
 but not a **hair** on your **head** will be **destroyed**.
By your **perseverance** you will **secure** your **lives**."

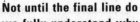 **GOSPEL** Not until the final line do we fully understand why the Church has selected this text for today. If our usual understanding of the tone of apocalyptic writing and of the readings assigned to the end of the year is that it is foreboding and somber, then this Gospel seems to fit the bill. But apocalyptic literature and our liturgy are meant to offer expectant hope as well as warn us of doom and gloom. This Gospel does that well.

In Mark's version of this episode, Jesus addressed only the disciples, but here he also addresses the crowd, giving these teachings a universal quality. In response to questions about the timing of the destruction of the temple, Jesus offers two cautions: do not be "misled" and remember even wars and disasters don't portend an immediate end of the world. But though Jesus endorses restrained response, the calamities he forecasts — natural disasters, persecutions, and even family members turning against other family members — are real and truly distressing.

Jesus describes these coming catastrophes with poetic intensity and a melodic flow. Through the prophecies of persecution and his promises of divine guidance, Jesus ensures that his disciples are ready for the coming trials and confident they'll receive divine support when they come. But Jesus promises neither happiness nor immunity from pain for his followers, only that God will ultimately triumph and that patient strength will bring salvation. That makes the last line the most important in the text, for it speaks to all of us who wait and endure.

OUR LORD JESUS CHRIST THE KING

Lectionary #162

READING I   2 Samuel 5:1–3

A reading from the second Book of Samuel

In those days, all the **tribes** of Israel came to **David**
    in **Hebron** and said:
    "Here we **are**, your **bone** and your **flesh**.
In days **past**, when **Saul** was our king,
    it was **you** who led the Israelites **out** and brought them **back**.
And the LORD said to you,
    'You shall **shepherd** my people Israel
    and shall be **commander** of Israel.'"
When all the **elders** of Israel **came** to David in Hebron,
    King David made an **agreement** with them there
        before the LORD,
    and they **anointed** him **king** of Israel.

The opening line can establish the appropriate solemnity for the declaration of such loyalty and confidence. Slowly elongating the "l," "i," "s," and "m" sounds ("All the tribes of Israel came") will help suggest the sincerity of the gathering tribes.

Hebron = HEB-ruhn

Saul = sawl

During Saul's reign, it was David who led the Israelites into battle and brought them back victorious.

Give each title ("shepherd" and "commander") its due by speaking the lines with great care.

The last sentence is the climax. Stress "elders," "agreement," "before the Lord," and "anointed" to suggest that David, who until now ruled only the southern kingdom, is also worthy to receive the crown of the north and to rule a unified kingdom.

 READING I Israel was always a bit conflicted about the monarchy. Worried that an earthly king usurped God's rightful role as king of Israel, they nonetheless saw the king as a sacrament of God's lordship over the nation, a visible sign of God's constant presence and protection.

Today's solemnity may stir some ambivalence in us. Is Christ the Good Shepherd, the gentle lord who forgives and eagerly dispenses mercy? Or is he the Lord of the universe, the judge before whom we will stand at the end of time? Of course,

neither image alone describes the Lord. Today's liturgy asks us to respect both these realities. By drawing an analogy between King David and Jesus, the liturgy suggests that like his royal ancestor, Jesus is to be viewed as both gentle "shepherd" and firm "commander."

This text expresses the compassionate aspects of kingship. The king's relationship with the people reflects the solidarity between God and nation: "Here we are, your bone and your flesh." "Shepherd" and

"commander" are one in the person of David. Like the God he represents, the king will be a firm yet gentle ruler.

There is another dimension to casting David as a type (foreshadowing) of Christ the King. When we look at David and see that though imperfect and sinful, he was, nonetheless, Israel's greatest king, we realize that God's will can be accomplished even through flawed human beings. By making this point, the liturgy invites us to see in our own lives of failure and success, of mistakes, tragedies and intrigues, the will of God somehow being accomplished.

READING II Colossians 1:12–20

A reading from the Letter of Saint Paul to the Colossians

This reading opens with a prayer. Pray it joyfully!

Brothers and sisters:
Let us give **thanks** to the Father,
    who has made you **fit** to share
    in the **inheritance** of the **holy** ones in **light**.
He **delivered** us from the power of **darkness**

Jesus delivered us from the darkness of sin. That's more good news!

    and **transferred** us to the **kingdom** of his beloved **Son**,
    in whom we have **redemption**, the forgiveness of sins.

Here begins the Christological hymn. For further commentary, see Second Reading for Fifteenth Sunday in Ordinary Time.

He is the **image** of the invisible **God**,
    the **firstborn** of all **creation**.
For in **him** were created **all** things in **heaven** and on **earth**,
    the **visible** and the **invisible**,
    whether **thrones** or **dominions** or **principalities** or **powers**;
    all things were created **through** him and **for** him.

These are categories of angels. Distinguish each from the others. Jesus is greater than them all.

He is **before** all things,
    and **in** him all things hold **together**.
He is the **head** of the body, the **church**.

By being first to die and rise, Jesus makes reconciliation possible for all. Don't let this sound like so much theology; speak these attributes of Christ with conviction and pride. These words were meant to be sung. They point to the Gospel incongruity of a crucified king speaking of "peace" made through the "blood of his cross."

He is the **beginning**, the **firstborn** from the **dead**,
    that in **all** things he **himself** might be **preeminent**.
For in **him** all the **fullness** was pleased to **dwell**,
    and **through** him to **reconcile** all things for him,
    making **peace** by the blood of his **cross**
    through him, whether those on **earth** or those in **heaven**.

The quintuple repetition of "all things" blatantly asserts Christ's lordship. Don't shy from the repetitions, but let them speak of Christ's supremacy.

READING II Of what is Christ lord? This Second Reading, which includes an exultant hymn ("He is the image . . ."), gives the answer five times: All things. All things. All things. All things. All things.

With imagery that recalls the Exodus when God rescued Israel from the "darkness" of slavery and brought the Israelites to the promised land of freedom, the text begins by giving thanks to the Father for bringing us into "the kingdom of his beloved son." But in Jesus, God did not redeem through the use of power, as in the

Exodus, but through weakness and death—the voluntary shedding of Jesus' blood on the cross that brought about "the forgiveness of sins."

The magnificent hymn explains why this passage was chosen for today. It declares the two great works of Jesus that vindicate his lordship: creation and salvation. Jesus not only existed for all eternity, he is the one through whom all things were created. He sustains all things and is greater than all things. While humans are made in God's image, Jesus is the image and likeness of God.

By being first to die and rise, Jesus makes reconciliation possible for all. He has taken his place at the head of his body, the Church, established the kingdom of God, and opened wide its gates so all might enter. And he did this through "the blood of the cross." Christ's supremacy is not like that of earthly kings, for his kingdom is not of this world. His is a far grander kingdom than the human mind can grasp, yet we already are living in it as we await its coming fullness.

GOSPEL   Luke 23:35–43

A reading from the holy Gospel according to Luke

In Luke, the people don't join in; only the leaders sneer.

Give the leaders' and soldiers' dialogue a hostile tone; they mock him even as he dies.

The rulers **sneered** at Jesus and said,
  "He saved **others**, let him save **himself**
  if he is the **chosen** one, the Christ of **God**."
Even the **soldiers** jeered at him.
As they approached to offer him **wine** they called out,
  "If you are **King** of the **Jews**, **save** yourself."
Above him there was an **inscription** that read,
  "**This** is the **King** of the **Jews**."

Reading the inscription can be done in a tone of sad irony.

Now one of the **criminals** hanging there **reviled** Jesus, saying,
  "Are you not the **Christ**?

He speaks out of desperation, but he's too blind to see the hope who hangs beside him.

His anger is justified. He has received and accepted the grace of faith.

Save yourself and **us**."
The **other**, however, **rebuking** him, said in **reply**,
  "Have you no **fear** of **God**,
  for you are **subject** to the same **condemnation**?
And **indeed**, **we** have been condemned **justly**,
  for the **sentence** we received corresponds to our **crimes**,
  but **this** man has done **nothing** criminal."
Then he said,

The Greek verb for "remember" suggests that the phrase may have been repeated several times.

Jesus' confident and compassionate assurance teaches the value of faith and repentance.

  "**Jesus**, **remember** me when you come into your **kingdom**."
He **replied** to him,
  "**Amen**, I say to you,
  today you will **be** with me in **Paradise**."

GOSPEL   This text may seem an odd choice for the solemnity of Christ the King, until you ask what greater proof of lordship there could be than to rule even over death. To the good thief Jesus makes no ambiguous pledge but a sure promise of new life—and he does it while reigning from the throne of the cross. Luke's portrait of Jesus remains consistent with the one he has drawn all along: a compassionate Lord who never shuns the company of sinners and shows solidarity with them in death as he did in life.

The omitted first half of verse 35 says that "the people stood by and watched." Only the leaders and soldiers "sneered" and "jeered" at Jesus. And Luke contrasts the mocking and derisive inscription posted over his head with Jesus' confident promise of salvation to the thief. The first thief echoes the leaders' blasphemies, but might his words hide a secret wish that Jesus could do something to save them all? It's easier to identify with the good thief who, despite his pain, speaks of Jesus' innocence and his own guilt. Under these strangest of circumstances, that thief

becomes the ideal disciple, recognizing his need for conversion and putting all his trust in Jesus. The form of the Greek verb for "remember" that is used here implies that the thief repeated his request many times. Only in one other Gospel context is Jesus addressed by name in as friendly and intimate a manner as here. How ironic that this criminal models for us the unique privilege we all share of having a king we can call by name.